Lions & Eagles & Bulls

Early American Tavern & Inn Signs

FROM THE CONNECTICUT HISTORICAL SOCIETY

Edited by Susan P. Schoelwer

ESSAYS BY

Philip D. Zimmerman

Margaret C. Vincent

Kenneth L. Ames

Alexander M. Carlisle

Nancy Finlay

Catherine Gudis

Sandra L. Webber

Bryan J. Wolf

THE CONNECTICUT HISTORICAL SOCIETY

in association with

PRINCETON UNIVERSITY PRESS

This book is published in conjunction with the exhibition
"Lions & Eagles & Bulls: Early American Tavern and Inn Signs
from The Connecticut Historical Society."

Exhibition dates:
The Connecticut Historical Society, Hartford, Connecticut
October 26, 2000–April 30, 2001

The Hood Museum of Art, Dartmouth College, Hanover, New Hampshire
June 30–September 16, 2001

The Museums at Stony Brook, Stony Brook, Long Island, New York
September 29, 2001–January 13, 2002

The Museum of Our National Heritage, Lexington, Massachusetts
April 13–October 14, 2002

Colonial Williamsburg, Williamsburg, Virginia
November 2003–April 2004

Front Cover: *Sign for Arah Phelps's Inn*, signed by William Rice, circa 1826.
The Connecticut Historical Society, Gift of Nancy Phelps (Mrs. John A.)
Blum, Jonathan Phelps Blum, and Timothy Alexander Blum. Cat. 37.

Back Cover: *Sign for Carter's Inn*, circa 1823. The Connecticut Historical
Society, Collection of Morgan B. Brainard, Gift of Maxwell L. Brainard,
Charles E. Brainard, Mrs. Edward M. Brainard, Mrs. Morgan B. Brainard,
Jr., Mrs. H. S. Robinson, Jr. (Constance Brainard). Cat. 33.

Frontispiece: *Sign for the Vernon Hotel*, signed by William Rice, circa 1834,
The Connecticut Historical Society, Gift of the Sabra Trumbull Chapter,
Daughters of the American Revolution. Cat. 46.

Sign photography by
David Stansbury, Springfield, Massachusetts: cat. 9, 11–12, 16–18, 20,
25–26, 29–32, 34–35, 39, 43, 45–46, 49, 52–53, 56–57, 61–65; figs. 1, 5, 9, 15,
18, 20, 22, 33, 34, 37, 38a,b, 40, 49, 63, 77, 81, 88.
Michael Agee, Williamstown, Massachusetts: cat.1–8, 10, 13–15, 19, 21–24,
27–28, 33, 36–38, 40–42, 44, 47–48, 50–51, 54–55, 58–60; figs. 2, 7, 8, 13, 21,
23, 24a,b, 28, 36, 47, 50, 55, 58–59, 60, 64, 76, 78–79, 93, 102, 109, 111.
Conservation laboratory photography courtesy of Williamstown Art
Conservation Center, Williamstown, Massachusetts: figs. 3, 26a,b, 36, 65,
66a–d, 67–70, 73, 75, 80.
Collections photography by Arthur J. Kiely, Jr., West Hartford, Connecticut: figs. 10, 27, 29–32, 35, 39, 41–46, 48, 52–53, 57, 62, 82–83, 85–87, 90,
96–98, 110.

Designed by Greer Allen. Typeset by John J. Moran.
Color separations by Professional Graphics, Inc., Rockford, Ill.
Printed by CS Graphics, Singapore.

Hardcover edition published in October 2000
in association with Princeton University Press.

Library of Congress Catalogue Card Number: 00-103724
ISBN 1-881264-07-6 (softcover)
ISBN 0-691-07060-1 (hardcover)

Contents

List of Illustrations

PLATES

Foreword

The year 2000 marks the 175th anniversary of The Connecticut Historical Society. Over time succeeding generations of trustees and staff have assembled an unparalleled collection of artifacts, graphics, and research materials that documents the rich history of our state and its diverse people. Among our more spectacular—if little known—holdings is our collection of eighteenth- and nineteenth-century tavern and inn signs. The first of these signs was acquired as early as the 1840s. Subsequent gifts and purchases have enhanced the collection to the point that it is now by far the largest assemblage of early American tavern and inn signs in the nation.

Personally, I have always been particularly drawn to these engaging signs with their lively images and striking shapes. I remember quite clearly the day of my first encounter with both the signs and The Connecticut Historical Society. I had been invited to the institution's headquarters in Hartford to interview for the position of Executive Director, and in the course of my visit I was shown around the building. While deeply impressed with the many treasures I saw in both galleries and storage areas, when the lights were turned on in the room housing a selection of the tavern and inn signs illustrated in this volume it was love at first sight. Being especially fond of vernacular art forms, I was immensely impressed by the signs' simplicity and boldness. So I am

delighted that this important collection will now be shared with a wider public by means of this publication and the associated traveling exhibition.

The exhibition, *Lions & Eagles & Bulls: Early American Tavern & Inn Signs from The Connecticut Historical Society,* and this catalogue have been underwritten with grants provided by: The Henry Luce Foundation, Inc.; Aetna, Inc. and Aetna Foundation; the Connecticut Humanities Council; the Kohn-Joseloff Foundation; the National Endowment for the Arts; the Edward C. and Ann T. Roberts Foundation; and James B. Lyon. Additional support for this catalogue was provided by Furthermore, the publication program of The J. M. Kaplan Fund, and The American Folk Art Society. Our sincere thanks go to all of these extremely generous sponsors.

I would be remiss if, in conclusion, I failed to acknowledge Dr. Susan P. Schoelwer for her diligence in overseeing the editing and production of this catalogue, and Kate Steinway for her creativity in assembling the traveling exhibition.

David M. Kahn
Executive Director
The Connecticut Historical Society, Hartford

Acknowledgments

As Director of the Museum Collections Department at The Connecticut Historical Society, it is my very great pleasure to thank the numerous individuals who have made this publication possible. Executive Director David M. Kahn launched the initiative for a major research, conservation, publication, and exhibition project focusing on the Society's unparalleled collection of early American tavern and inn signs. Philip D. Zimmerman, principal consultant, shaped the project in many important ways. In addition to sharing his extensive knowledge of American decorative arts, connoisseurship, and curatorial practices, Phil painstakingly examined each sign and compiled the individual catalog entries, calling attention to details and relationships no one else had noticed. Project Historian Margaret C. Vincent provided the historical foundation for the project, combing secondary and primary sources to compile a fuller picture of innkeeping in Connecticut than has previously existed. While building a database and untangling the histories of individual signs, Margaret also served as clearing house for inquiries by other project team members. Richard C. Malley, Assistant Director of Museum Collections and Curator of Technology, kept the project steadily moving forward, capably overseeing all handling of the original artifacts—photography, conservation surveys and treatments, loan arrangements—and any research questions involving maritime history. Nancy Finlay, Curator of Graphics, contributed her expertise with visual research and also served as production editor for the catalog, accomplishing remarkable feats in getting essays on time and assembling illustrative materials. Other project assistance was provided by Kristine Cuddy, Intern; Elizabeth Blakelock, Cataloguer; Maranne McDade Clay, formerly Collections Manager; Jennifer Willis, Volunteer. Photographs of signs were taken at The Connecticut Historical Society by David Stansbury and of other collection materials by Arthur J. Kiely, Jr.

We have been most fortunate in our choice of advisors. Kenneth Ames, Bryan Wolf, Catherine Gudis, and Allan Gowans challenged us to think more broadly and critically even as they encouraged us with their enthusiasm and creativity. Each contributed significantly to the formulation and presentation of ideas and information about tavern signs and tavern keeping in early America.

The conservation phase of the project has enjoyed the enthusiastic cooperation of the Williamstown Art Conservation Center, Williamstown, Massachusetts, Thomas J. Branchick. As project leader for the conservation team, Sandra L. Webber, Conservator of Paintings, became deeply engaged in the project, responding promptly to curatorial questions, reviewing catalog entries, and otherwise providing valuable assistance above and beyond the call of duty. Other membrs of the project have also been enthusiastic collaborators: Alexander M. Carlisle, Associate Conservator of Furniture; Katherine Holbrow, Objects Conservator; James Squires, Donald R. Friary Fellow in Paintings Conservation. Sign photography was carried out by Michael Agee with assistance from Merry Armata, Photographic Services. Additional lab assistance came from Katherine Tremblay, Office Manager, and her assistant, Julie Ozolins. William Senseney, Master Blacksmith, crafted reproduction hanging hardware. Analytical testing was conducted at WACC by James Martin, former Director of Analytical Services and his assistant, Nicholas Zammuto, and at the H.F. duPont Winterthur Museum by Janice Carlson, Senior Scientist and Associate Scientist Kate Duffy. Wood analysis was conducted by Dr. R. Bruce Hoadley, Professor of Wood Science and Technology, University of Massachusetts at Amherst. Off-site radiography was conducted at the Fogg Art Museum, Harvard University, and by Frederick U. Conard, Jr., M.D.

The majority of the research for the project was carried out at The Connecticut Historical Society Library, with the invaluable assistance of Judith Ellen Johnson, Genealogist; Martha Smart, Reference Assistant; and Amy Olson, NEH Project Assistant. Extensive research was also conducted at the Connecticut State Library, where the staff of the History and Genealogy Department was especially helpful. Additional investigation took place at The American Antiquarian Society, Worcester, Massachusetts, The Clark Art Institute Library and The Sawyer and Chapin Libraries of Williams College, Williamstown, Massachusetts; The Phillips Library of the Peabody Essex Museum, Salem, Massachusetts; The Shelburne Museum, Shelburne, Vermont; The Wadsworth Atheneum Library, Hartford. Numerous colleagues provided research assistance, including: Ardis Abbot, Vernon Historical Society, Vernon, Connecticut; Lorna Condon, Society for the Preservation of New England Antiquities, Boston; Frances M. Gilman, Clinton Historical Society, Clinton, Connecticut; Lisa Johnson, Stanley-Whitman House Museum, Farmington, Connecticut; Amanda Mahoney, Brandywine River Museum, Chadds Ford, Pennsylvania; William Peterson, Mystic Seaport Museum, Mystic, Connecticut; Anthony Secondo, Enfield Historical Society, Enfield, Connecticut; Mark Tabbert, Museum of Our National Heritage, Lexington, Massachusetts; John Teahan, Wadsworth Atheneum Library, Hartford; Jane Tuttle, Scoville Memorial Library, Salisbury, Connecticut. At The New York Public Library, Department of Art, Prints and Photographs, Roberta Waddell, Margaret Glover, Elizabeth Wyckoff, and Radames Suarez provided assistance with pictorial research, as did Elizabeth Falsey and Cynthia Naylor, at the Houghton Library, Harvard University. Charles Ritchie and the staff of the Department of Modern Prints and Drawings, National Gallery of Art, provided access to drawings of tavern signs in the Index of American Design. The Windsor Historical Society, Windsor, Connecticut; the Wadsworth Atheneum, Hartford, Connecticut; and St. Mark's Lodge No. 36, A.F.&A.M., Simsbury, Connecticut, granted extended access for examination and photography of signs in their collections.

Information on tavern and inn signs in other collections in Connecticut was generously shared by Ms. Barbara Austin, Fairfield Historical Society; Robert E. Ayer III and Dorothy Ayer, Farmington; Dawn H. Bobryk, Simsbury Historical Society; Richard Byrne and Cay Fields, Norfolk Historical Society; Thomas A. Denenberg, Wadsworth Atheneum; Kenneth Duncan, St. Marks Lodge No. 36, A.F.&A.M., Simsbury; Elise Haas, Keeler Tavern Museum, Ridgefield; John Harney, Salisbury; Gail Kruppa, Torrington Historical Society, Inc.; Alyse Kummer, Seymour Historical Society; Dione Longley, Middlesex County Historical Society, Middletown; Mr. and Mrs. W.H. McNeil, Colebrook Historical Society; Rose Marie St. John; Gary Sass; Sherry Sweeney, Robert Silliman, and Elaine Olson, Windsor Historical Society; and Frank J. Whitman, Jr., Silvermine Tavern, Norwalk. Information on tavern and inn signs in collections outside Connecticut came from Lynne Bassett, Old Sturbridge Village, Sturbridge, Massachusetts; Jean Burks and Sharon D. Greene, Shelburne Museum, Shelburne, Vermont; Paul d'Ambrosio, New York State Historical Association, Cooperstown; Judith Elsdon, American Museum in Britain, Bath; Ronald Frazier, Dedham Historical Society, Dedham, Massachusetts; Margaret Hofer, New-York Historical Society; Barbara R. Luck, Abby Aldrich Rockefeller Folk Art Center, Williamsburg, Virginia; Michael Podmanizcky, Henry Francis du Pont Winterthur Museum; Karen Shakelford, The Mariners' Museum, Newport News, Virginia. Carolyn Weekley, Colonial Williamsburg, generously answered questions about Edward Hicks's signpainting. Rob Rizzuto, Alpha Signs, Norwich, Connecticut, shared information about the sign making business today. Barry A. Rosenberg, Chief Curator and Visual Arts Coordinator, Real Art Ways, Hartford, and Robert Cottingham, Newtown, Connecticut, provided a contemporary art perspective on the sign painting tradition. Frank H. Jump, Brooklyn, New York, shared information on outdoor wall murals.

The exhibition was designed by David Lackey, Whirlwind Designs, New York City, and planned and produced by Kate Steinway, Director of Exhibitions and Special Projects at The Connecticut Historical Society, with the assistance of Andrea Rapacz, Exhibitions Coordinator.

Patricia Fidler, Art Editor, Princeton University Press, has had a long-standing interest in the tavern and inn sign collection at The Connecticut Historical Society. The association with Princeton University Press is a strong vote of confidence in the significance of both the collection and the publication, and Patricia's advocacy and advice have been of great value in the production process. Greer Allen's catalog design has given substance to our vision, and I am grateful to him for his enthusiasm, his perseverance, his patience, and his talent. The map of sign locations and the schematic drawings of construction joints were redrawn by John McCrillis. John J. Moran performed the typesetting and Barbara Folsom capably edited essay texts.

Less immediately, but no less importantly, the project has drawn upon the talents and ideas of the entire staff of The Connecticut Historical Society. The Museum Committee, headed by Dr. Thomas P. Kugelman, has continued to commit funds for sign conservation and for the acquisition of important new examples. Our co-workers, the Board of Trustees, donors, foundations, and sponsors are partners in the production of *Lions & Eagles & Bulls*. Behind the scenes, the project benefited from the support of families, parents, spouses, and especially children, who continued to hope that it might really end (even after they had ceased to believe that it would). I am grateful for the contributions of all of those with whom I have been privileged to work on this project. Its successes are to the credit of the entire team.

Susan P. Schoelwer

Contributors

KENNETH L. AMES and his wife, Nancy, live in a late eighteenth-century house in Windham, Connecticut, and are discovering that the town was once far more important than the notorious "Battle of the Frogs" story implies. During the week, Ames serves as chair of Academic Programs at the Bard Graduate Center for Studies in the Decorative Arts, New York City. He is the author of *Beyond Necessity: Art in the Folk Tradition* (1977) and *Death in the Dining Room* (1995).

ALEXANDER M. CARLISLE is the Assistant Conservator of Furniture and Wooden Objects at the Williamstown Art Conservation Center. His experience with wooden objects has ranged from building log cabins to studio furniture. He received his undergraduate degrees in wood furniture design and art history from Boston University and his Master of Science degree in Art Conservation from the University of Delaware/Winterthur Program in Art Conservation.

NANCY FINLAY is Curator of Graphics at The Connecticut Historical Society. She earned her Ph.D. at Princeton University and is the author of *Inventing the American Past: The Art of F.O.C. Darley* (1999) and *Artists of the Book in Boston, 1890–1910* (1985). Her writings are included in *Inspiring Reform: Boston's Arts and Crafts Movement* (1997), *Double Vision: Perspectives on Gender and the Visual Arts* (1994), and *American Art Posters of the 1890s* (1987).

ELLSWORTH S. GRANT is a prolific author on Connecticut history and distinguished former president of The Connecticut Historical Society. Among his most well-known titles are *Yankee Dreamers and Doers: The Story of Connecticut Manufacturing* (1974, 1996) and *The Colt Legacy: The Story of the Colt Armory in Hartford, 1855–1980* (1982).

CATHERINE GUDIS is Assistant Professor of Cultural History at the Honors College of the University of Oklahoma, Norman. She received her Ph.D. in American Studies from Yale University and is currently completing a book entitled, *The Road to Consumption: Outdoor Advertising and the American Cultural Landscape*. Her curatorial projects include the exhibition and publication, *The "Kiss of the Oceans": Culture and Commerce at the San Francisco Panama Pacific International Exposition of 1915*.

SUSAN P. SCHOELWER is Director of Museum Collections at The Connecticut Historical Society. She holds a Ph.D. in American Studies from Yale University and an M.A. from the Winterthur Program in Early American Culture. She has taught at Rutgers, Villanova, and Virginia Commonwealth

Universities and coordinated the exhibition, "Discovered Lands, Invented Pasts: Transforming Visions of the American West," Yale University Art Gallery (1992). She is the principal author of *Alamo Images: Changing Perspectives on a Texas Experience* (1985).

MARGARET C. VINCENT, as Project Historian at The Connecticut Historical Society from November 1998 through May 2000, held principal responsibility for carrying out primary research for the present catalog and its accompanying exhibition. Prior to returning to her home state of Connecticut, she served as Director of Exhibitions at Old Salem, Inc., and as Director of Collections at the Museum of Early Southern Decorative Arts (MESDA), both in Winston-Salem, North Carolina. She is the author of *The Ladies' Work Table: Domestic Needlework in Nineteenth-Century America* (1988). She has moved on from public houses to poor houses, the topic of her current research.

SANDRA L. WEBBER is Conservator of Paintings, Williamstown Art Conservation Center, and adjunct lecturer in the Williams College–Clark Art Institute Graduate Art History Program. Webber completed her graduate work in Art Conservation at the Center for Conservation and Technical Studies, Fogg Art Museum, Harvard University. She is currently writing an article on one of Boston's earliest shipyards.

BRYAN J. WOLF is Professor of American Studies and English at Yale University and the former Chair of the American Studies Program. He is the author of *Romantic Re-Vision: Culture and Consciousness in Nineteenth-Century American Painting and Literature* (1982) and *Vermeer and the Invention of Seeing* (forthcoming, University of Chicago Press). He served as the inaugural Visiting Distinguished Professor of American Art and Material Culture at Stanford University, 1995–96, and is currently co-authoring an art history textbook, *American Encounters, Art and Cultural Identity*, to be published by Abrams in 2002.

PHILIP D. ZIMMERMAN is a decorative arts and museum consultant and antique furniture broker based in Lancaster, Pa. He writes often on early American furniture and related subjects for *The Magazine Antiques* and other publications and is completing a furniture catalogue for the Sewell C. Biggs Museum of American Art in Dover, Delaware. He lectures regularly and holds adjunct faculty appointments at the Bard Graduate Center for Studies in the Decorative Arts and at New York University. Degrees include a doctorate in American and New England Studies from Boston University and a master's degree from the Winterthur Program in Early American Culture.

Introduction:
Rediscovering the Public Art
of Early American Inn Signs

By Susan P. Schoelwer

Long before there were neon lights or golden arches, travelers found their journeys marked by the art work of early American sign painters. Bold and colorful paintings signaled the location of public accommodations: proud lions and patriotic eagles, solemn bulls and prancing horses, rising suns and silvery moons, elegant carriages and festive table settings, ornate scrollwork, and a variety of allegorical figures beckoned weary wayfarers at twilight, or set off one street of town houses from the next. Installed to serve the primary function of outdoor advertising, early American tavern, inn, and hotel signs effectively made an everyman's gallery of streets and roadsides.

Within the colony and state of Connecticut alone, at least 10,000 licensed establishments offered food and lodging to the public, at various times between 1750 and 1850. As Margaret C. Vincent observes in her essay, "'Some suitable Signe,'" each and every one of these establishments was required, by law, to erect an identifying sign. Similar laws existed in other colonies and states.[1] By even the most conservative reckoning, therefore, the number of tavern, inn, and hotel signs produced by American painters between 1750 and 1850 cannot have been fewer than 50,000, and may have numbered many more—a visual vocabulary and cultural tradition linking the earliest settlements of the eastern seaboard with the rawest of western towns. Only a tiny sampling remains of this vast artistic production. The remarkable collection of tavern, inn, and hotel signs preserved at The Connecticut Historical Society—currently sixty-five examples—is by far the largest extant assemblage of this once ubiquitous art form.[2]

The distinctively public art of tavern signs has long gone surprisingly unremarked. Nineteenth- and early twentieth-century antiquarians and local historians recorded the shapes, images, and locations of early signs, as well as traditional lore about owners, establishments, and customs—thus preserving for subsequent generations rich lodes and nuggets of information that would otherwise have been lost. As a starting point for this project, Connecticut historian

Ellsworth S. Grant compiled information on taverns, signs, and services, drawing on local history and antiquarian works, architectural preservation surveys, and other sources.[3] Only a handful of publications focus specifically on the signs themselves, the most ambitious of which is Larwood and Hotten's *History of Signboards*, written pseudonymously by Herman D.J. van Shevichaven and first published in London in 1866. In classic antiquarian tradition, Larwood and Hotten record known English signboards, organized primarily in thematic categories, such as historic and commemorative, heraldic, animals and monsters, flowers, puns and rebuses. As a compendium of English inn sign imagery (and thus, the origins of the American tradition), Larwood and Hotten remain unsurpassed, with later British works focusing primarily on tradesmen's shop signs.[4]

Nothing of comparable scope or focus exists for American sign paintings, although much useful information may be pieced together from historical studies of taverns and travel and from art historical catalogs and studies of folk art and artists. Histories of taverns and travel tend to present tavern and inn signs rather incidentally, as eye-catching asides to the main business of what goes on within doors.[5] Folk art publications, in contrast, feature signs as subjects of interest in their own right, but because signs are only one of many genres presented, coverage is typically cursory, with emphasis on aesthetic appreciation.[6] Epitomizing the aesthetic approach is the monumental Index of American Design, produced by Works Progress Administration artists, circa 1936–40. The Index, preserved in the collections of the National Gallery of Art, contains artists' renderings of numerous eighteenth- and nineteenth-century tavern and inn signs, including fourteen now at The Connecticut Historical Society (see fig. 51).[7] These renderings are notable for their meticulous accuracy, produced by the adaptation of archaeological field documentation techniques; as a widely consulted source of tavern sign imagery, they are not infrequently mistaken for the original signs.[8]

Fig. 2. *Sign for Carter's Inn*, circa 1823, Clinton, Conn. CHS, cat. 33, side 2.

The Morgan Brainard Collection

The most extensive single publication devoted exclusively to American tavern, inn, and hotel signs has long been the 1958 catalog, *Morgan B. Brainard's Tavern Signs,* issued to mark the arrival of the Brainard collection at The Connecticut Historical Society.[9] As Grant notes in his introduction to the catalog section of the present volume, Brainard (1879–1957) began collecting signs in the late 1910s and eventually accumulated a total of fifty-eight examples, including trade shop, toll, and road signs in addition to the predominant category of tavern, inn, and hotel signs. Many of these signs Brainard acquired directly from descendants of original owners, providing unusually strong provenance.[10] The Brainard collection augmented a pre-existing collection of over a dozen tavern, trade, and road signs that had been acquired by The Connecticut Historical Society beginning as early as 1841 (cat. 4). Nearly all of the signs were included in the original collection catalog, with illustrations of both sides (if different) and brief labeling with original location, provenance, and sometimes, notes on underlying layers of imagery or text. An introduction by Thompson R. Harlow, then director of The Connecticut Historical Society, presented information on sign painters, innkeepers and their clientele, and a preliminary typology of sign shapes. Harlow continued to add data to the collection files after the publication of the catalog, and this research greatly aided the present project.

Publication of *Lions & Eagles & Bulls: Early American Tavern and Inn Signs from The Connecticut Historical Society* celebrates the Society's 175th anniversary as part of a major new initiative aimed at sharing its remarkably rich legacy of collecting and research with wider and more diverse audiences, locally, regionally, nationally, and internationally. Since the appearance of the Brainard catalog, The Connecticut Historical Society has acquired nearly two dozen additional tavern, trade, and road signs. Comparable growth has occurred in primary source material and secondary literature in the Society's library collections, richly supporting renewed research. The current catalog focuses exclusively on tavern, inn, and hotel signs, a category that predominates in the collection and may well have dominated period production, especially outside urban areas. Due to the historical legislation regulating public houses, every village or crossroads that had an inn would necessarily have had a sign marking its location for the benefit of travelers. The clientele for most rural trade shops, in contrast, would have been primarily other local residents, who would hardly have needed a sign as either placemarker or endorsement.

Lions & Eagles & Bulls reconsiders American tavern, inn,

and hotel signs from a variety of methodological and theoretical perspectives, using the Connecticut Historical Society collection as a foundation to build upon the efforts of earlier antiquarians, collectors, historians, art historians. A multi-year investigation, funded in part by The Henry Luce Foundation and the Connecticut Humanities Council, combined historical, curatorial, and conservation approaches. Questions raised by curatorial examination suggested new directions for historical research and laboratory analysis; discoveries at the lab confirmed some attributions but contradicted others. Not all questions could be answered within the available time, and some debates remain unresolved, most notably the question of whether the surface relief observed on many signs was deliberately carved, or created as an effect of environmental exposure. Nonetheless, the combination of historical, curatorial, and conservation perspectives serves to both substantiate and to significantly expand the basic information available on early American tavern and inn signs. In the Brainard catalog, Harlow listed sixteen signs "which are a complete mystery to us, showing how broad the subject is and how much research still remains to be done"; owners, locations, and dates for all but four of these "mystery" signs have now been established.[11] Extensive primary source research carried out by project historian Margaret Vincent has provided specific historical contexts for nearly 80% of the tavern, inn, and hotel signs in the Connecticut Historical Society's collection. The strong provenance of these signs is one of the most remarkable and most useful aspects of the collection. While individual signs preserved in local historical societies and historic houses often retain information about original owners and locations, those gathered in leading art and Americana collections bear a high degree of "location unknown" cataloging, as though anonymity provided a certain "folk" cachet.[12]

Historical, Curatorial, and Conservation Findings

Extensive research conducted by Margaret Vincent has provided the historical foundation for reconsidering tavern, inn, and hotel signs from The Connecticut Historical Society. Sources consulted have included newspapers, town records, directories, maps, tavern licenses, tax lists, and account books as well as local histories and other secondary works. Extracting relevant information from these sources, Vincent constructed a database documenting well over 5,000 individual innkeepers active in Connecticut between 1750 and 1850.[13] She also documented the presence of five dozen sign painters active in Connecticut, as summarized in Appendix 1. In addition to identifying and authenticating individual signs in the collection, Vincent's research supplies the essential raw materials for a broader, contextual view of both the production and consumption of tavern and inn signs in early America. Her essay, "'Some suitable Signe,'" traces some of the most significant links between the artifacts and their creators, contents and contexts, purchasers and audiences, designs and functions.

Decorative arts and museum consultant Philip D. Zimmerman contributed curatorial expertise, examining and cataloging each individual sign. In his essay, "Reading the Signs," Zimmerman constructs a multi-faceted "object history," which draws fruitfully on the techniques and scholarship of furniture history, connoisseurship, material culture, and the decorative arts. Going beneath the painted surfaces to examine wood joints, hanging hardware, and other structural features, Zimmerman underlines the complexity of signboards as three-dimensional objects, incorporating both wood and metalworking. His analysis of these features points in turn to the complexity of sign making as the product of multiple crafts or trades, with the possibility of recognizing characteristic shop traditions, comparable to those of furniture makers.

Nancy Finlay, Curator of Graphics at The Connecticut Historical Society, expands the curatorial perspective with an exploration of the sources of inn sign imagery. In "Lions and Eagles," Finlay convincingly situates these images within a larger nexus of "pre-existing visual sources," most notably the mass-produced imagery of prints and book illustrations, and the commercial imagery of coins and paper money. Numerous inn sign images derive from specific, identifiable models, including London mezzotints and illustrated natural histories, and sign painters' informed use of these sources parallels the practice of their studio counterparts. Sign painters' adaptation of images from other media has been sporadically noted in earlier publications; however, Finlay's findings convincingly demonstrate both the extent and the strength of the connections between sign painting and other visual arts.

Conservation work provided yet another perspective on the signs as physical objects. Beginning in the spring and summer of 1998, a team of conservators from the Williamstown Art Conservation Center (WACC) in Williamstown, Massachusetts, conducted an on-site survey of the Connecticut Historical Society sign collection, assessing current physical conditions and establishing priorities for both structural and surface treatments. Subsequent lab work—carried out with partial funding from The Getty Grant Program and the National Endowment for the Arts, Heritage and Preservation Program—included examination under raking, ultraviolet, and infrared light sources; x-radiography; pigment

Fig. 3. *Sign for Stiles's Inn*, circa 1831, Thompson, Conn. CHS, cat. 41. Detail, horses' heads during surface cleaning, Williamstown Art Conservation Center, 1998–99.

and wood analysis. Information gathered from these tests, as well as ongoing observations during treatment, have been incorporated into the object entries, together with notes on the actual work performed. Treatment protocols were generally conservative, primarily addressing structural and surface instabilities by reinforcing failed joints or hardware, removing surface grime, consolidating paint and metal (see Appendix 3). In "'Faithfully and Promptly Executed,'" WACC Conservator of Paintings, Sandra L. Webber, compares and contrasts the practices recommended in nineteenth-century printed literature on sign painting with the physical evidence of the signs in the Connecticut Historical Society collection.[14] In "Weather It Is Or Whether It Isn't," WACC Associate Conservator of Furniture, Alexander M. Carlisle, suggests the concept of "preferential weathering" as an explanation for the intricate surface relief observed on many early signs.

Theoretical and Interpretive Perspectives

Building upon the core investigations described above, three additional scholars were asked to bring their respective specialties to bear on the broader interpretation of sign paintings. In "Signs of the Times: A Brief Cultural History of Sign Painting," Bryan Wolf proposes that we "think about sign painting as the tip of a cultural iceberg." He reads signs as "markers of long-term changes occurring in the everyday lives of ordinary people"—in particular, as evidence of the different values and vocabularies of visual culture and print culture, of the shift from a pre-modern agricultural society to "the entrepreneurial, market-driven and increasingly urban economy of the Early Republic," and of the creation of "imagined communities" that knit America together as a nation.

Catherine Gudis looks backward at eighteenth- and nine-teenth-century tavern and inn signs from the theoretical perspective of cultural landscape studies. In "From Tavern Signs to Golden Arches: A Landscape of Signs," she asks what relevance late twentieth–century interpretations of outdoor signage may have for understanding a more distant era. In *Learning from Las Vegas* (1972), architects Robert Venturi, Denise Scott-Brown, and Steven Izenour identified highway signs as the distinguishing architecture of the auto-mobile age. For many presumably novel features, however, Gudis finds antecedents in, or at least continuities with, the now-displaced signage of earlier roadsides. Moving from the literal landscape to the mental landscape, she probes the symbolic meaning of signs. Experientially, she suggests, tav-ern and inn signs differ from other categories of signage because of the distinctive qualities of the places they mark, places offering a sometimes contradictory blend of "tran-sience and residency, intimacy and anonymity."

In the final essay, "Signs of the Past in the Present," Ken-neth L. Ames continues the intertwined investigation of lit-eral and mental landscapes. Finding the literal landscape abundantly populated by modern signs in old styles, he asks, "Why?" Early twentieth-century interest in old tavern and inn signs, he argues, was paradoxically linked to both the rise of antique collecting—the search for instant her-itage—and the introduction of the automobile—the ulti-mate harbinger of modernization. Countering the oft-repeated saying that the past is a foreign country, he cites evidence to the contrary, concluding that the contemporary "signscape" offers a "powerful de facto alternative to such a narrow and ungenerous vision, for here the past—and the continuing influence of the past—is clearly visible in myriad forms."

Several common themes emerge in these essays, for exam-ple, the shifting balance between visual culture and print culture, easily observed in the content and design of inn signs. As a rule of thumb, the earlier the sign, the more pic-torial it is likely to be. Thus, the earliest sign in the collec-tion, Edward Bull's Black Horse sign, 1749 (cat. 1), commu-nicates visually, via the iconic, traditional figure of the horse—an example of what Wolf calls "organic imagery." The accompanying text—the initials "EB" and the date—contribute little to the sign's communicative function of marking a place to stay. A century later, as Finlay notes, the balance was completely reversed: "lettering on signboards had assumed the major role, and pictorial components were reduced to modest decorations or eliminated entirely." What pictorial elements remained were likely be drawn from mass-produced print sources, book illustrations, inexpensive litho-graphs, even type ornaments. Textual elements were in-

creasingly standardized, with fewer of the charmingly quaint anachronisms found on earlier examples. Even the craft and artisanal aspects of sign making—traditionally passed down orally from masters to apprentices—were increasingly subject to codification in print, as Webber describes, via "how-to" manuals that offered literate crafts-men recipes, helpful hints, and even lettering patterns. Gudis offers yet another perspective on visual and print cul-ture, comparing the messages communicated on outdoor inn signs with those in contemporary newspaper ads: "in lieu of the face-to-face contact one would have by passing over the threshold of an inn after seeing the recognizable sign out-side, the printed ad offers facts and the authority of the signed statement as endorsement." Finally, as Zimmerman calls our attention to an elegantly drawn capital "A" (fig. 20), the reorientation of signs from pictures to lettering is not necessarily a mark of declining artistry.

Questions of Time and Place

Dating the signs has proven a particularly complex process. As Webber notes, visible dates may refer to building con-struction or initial licensing, and must therefore be used with caution to date the signs themselves. In addition, many signs display multiple dates, as a result of refurbishing necessitated by environmental wear or business changes. Unlike an easel painting, which is generally understood to have a single date of production, with any subsequent work regarded as intrusive or subsidiary, a sign painting is more often than not a palimpsest of equally legitimate artistic performances, each enacted as part of the object's func-tional life. Many repaintings are relatively minor, amending a name or a date, or freshening the colors of a faded image; others are more extensive. Updated imagery on an earlier board occasionally produces a jarring disjunction. Humphrey Williams's sign, for example, depicts a stage-coach appropriate to the visible date, 1826; however, the horizontally-oriented image literally does not fit onto the vertically-oriented sign, which in turn conforms to an under-lying date, 1803 (cat. 36). Is this to be cataloged as an 1803 sign with later imagery, or as an 1826 sign on an earlier board? Both classifications are accurate, but relevant to dif-ferent interpretive contexts. Colonial Revival restorations complicate the matter still further, for late nineteenth- and early twentieth-century taste regarded as acceptable, levels of intervention that now seem intrusive. Thus, the General Wolfe sign today acquires added value from its unrestored condition (cat. 4); one hundred years ago, the noted anti-quarian Alice Morse Earle lamented its faded appearance. She preferred the "spruce freshness" of another Wolfe sign-board, repainted in 1887 in a manner similar to the repainted sides of several signs at The Connecticut Historical Society (figs. 49, 93, 111; also cat. 61).[15] The Grosvenor inn sign is another case in point (cat. 60). Curatorial assessment supports the oral tradition that it was originally constructed and painted circa 1765 for Caleb Grosvenor, innkeeper in the village of Pomfret in northeastern Connecticut. More than a century later, it was found behind a partition by Benjamin Grosvenor, who had acquired the property in order to reopen an inn, catering to genteel seekers of the antique. He had both sides of the sign "freshened" in 1894, completely obliterating the original surfaces. Again, the question must be asked: Is this to be regarded as an eighteenth-century sign with a late nineteenth-century image, or as a late nineteenth-century sign painted on an earlier board? Such questions greatly complicate the process of establishing reliable object dates, which in turn provide the foundation necessary for subsequent incorporation of these museum pieces into broader historical vistas, reconnecting them to the economic, artistic, technological, social, and cultural contexts of lived experience.

In order to illuminate the historical development of forms, images, and techniques, the organization of signs in the catalogue section of this volume is chronological, allowing for the inevitable ambiguities. Each sign in the Connecticut Historical Society collection is represented by a full-page color plate of one side, bearing the same number as the catalogue entry, with the other side (if different) represented by a text illustration. The color plate section constitutes a visual timeline that can serve as a guide for dating the large numbers of extant signs that have been separated from their individual histories. In practice, it proved awkward and occasionally misleading to assign dates based exclusively on one criterion (for example, original artifact construction or painting of the uppermost surface). Individual cases required individual, sometimes arbitrary decisions, and one might well argue for slightly different ordering. The Grosvenor sign, for example, is presented as a late example on the basis of its imagery, painted in 1894, with no evidence of an earlier surface; the age of its wooden structure, however, would place it among the earliest signs in the collection. Notes in individual catalogue entries discuss the complexities of multiple production dates.

Reflecting the primary collecting focus of both The Connecticut Historical Society and its benefactor, Morgan Brainard, the majority of signs in the collection were made and used within the boundaries of Connecticut. Several signs derive from towns located just across the borders of New York, Massachusetts, and Rhode Island, outside Connecticut's political jurisdiction but clearly within its cultural orbit. The peculiarities of community formation and place naming in Connecticut not infrequently create situations where strict adherence to period place names would be misleading or incomprehensible to modern readers. One leading source of confusion is the overlapping of town, village, and parish names. Thus, David Loomis's inn (cat. 22) was located within the town of Colchester, but not in Colchester center; its specific location was the village of Westchester, a much more rural setting. The prevailing process of town formation introduces a second complexity, giving new names to old places as outlying villages within established towns repeatedly split off and renamed themselves; this process not infrequently results in inns whose period locations are now part of towns that were then unheard of. Aaron Bissell's inn (cat. 7) is identified in period sources as being in the towns of both Windsor (before 1768) and East Windsor (1768–1846); its site is today part of South Windsor. In cataloguing the signs, primary place names have been assigned with a view toward clarifying the location for the modern reader, with explanatory notes included in the catalogue entries. Thus, the modern designation, Clinton, identifying a town along the Long Island shore, provides a more illuminating geographical context for Jared Carter's 1823 seaview resort (cat. 33), than does the period name, Killingworth, now an inland locale.[16]

There is strong evidence that the collection of tavern, inn, and hotel signs at The Connecticut Historical Society accurately represents production nationally during the period 1750–1850. Significantly, Zimmerman's detailed object analysis finds "few recognizable properties" setting Connecticut signs apart from those produced elsewhere—in sharp contrast to the high degree of regionalism observed in furniture production through the 1820s. Several factors may have made Connecticut something of a center for inn sign production, encouraged by comparatively heavy traffic between urban centers, an extensive road network, and a proliferation of distinct communities, each with its own inn.[17] Connecticut also served as a population source for other areas of the country. Included among the thousands of Yankees who emigrated to new communities, from Vermont to upstate New York and Ohio to Oregon, were both sign painters and innkeepers. According to Vincent's research, Connecticut sign painters can be documented not only in nearby Rhode Island, Massachusetts, Long Island, and New York City but in such far-flung locales as Savannah, Charleston, St. Louis, Tennessee, and California. Given the widespread dispersal of both painters and patrons from Connecticut, it is hardly surprising to find the forms, images, and positioning of Connecticut tavern and inn signs repeated across the country. George Caleb Bingham (1811–79), the "Missouri Artist," included tavern and hotel signs in three of his well known election paintings, widely disseminated as prints. *Canvassing for a Vote*, 1852 (fig. 4), depicts an intent

Fig. 4. George Caleb Bingham, *Canvassing for a Vote*, oil on canvas, 1852. The Nelson-Atkins Museum of Art, Kansas City, Missouri (Purchase: Nelson Trust).

political discussion taking place in front of a rural inn, reputed to have been based on the Compass and Square tavern operated by Bingham's father in the family home in Franklin, Missouri, in the early 1820s. This frontier inn, a five-bay brick dwelling, is marked by a sign ornamented with a familiar eagle and suspended overhead from a free-standing, two-story post, an arrangement entirely consistent with Connecticut country inns of the early nineteenth century. *The County Election (2)*, 1852, depicts a more populous community, which, just as in Connecticut, boasts more up-to-date travel facilities: a "hotel," larger than a private residence, built explicitly for public accommodation, and marked by new-fashioned, text-only signs (see fig. 104).[18] Views by other artists corroborate the typicality of patterns documented in Connecticut, as does the remarkably detailed description in James Fenimore Cooper's *The Pioneers* (1826), vividly contrasting old-fashioned tavern and new-fangled hotel (see Afterword).[19] The collection of tavern, inn, and hotel signs at The Connecticut Historical Society thus possesses broad and exemplary interpretive potential.

Reconnecting the Art of Sign Painting

Both pictorially and graphically, tavern and inn signs display a broad range of artistic skills, talent, and training. At one end of the spectrum, the "immensely charming" silhouetted decanter and goblets on David Loomis's inn sign of 1811 (cat. 22) was probably painted by a relatively

unschooled painter, perhaps, as Zimmerman suggests, by the same craftsman who made the wooden board. At the other end of the spectrum, as Finlay observes, "the artist who painted the General Wolfe signboard (cat. 4) was among the most sophisticated painters in eighteenth-century Connecticut." Unfortunately, the artists whose work appears in *Lions & Eagles & Bulls* remain, for the moment, largely anonymous. From a selective survey of Connecticut newspapers between 1760 and 1850, Vincent has compiled a list of over sixty painters advertising signs among their wares (see Appendix 1). Only a few of these painters can be convincingly linked to specific signs. The exception to this rule is William Rice (1777–1847), who so dominated the northwestern and northcentral Connecticut market in the 1820s and 1830s that at least eighteen of his signs have currently been identified, recognizable as much by his distinctive style as by his signature. Only two non-Rice signs in the collection bear pre-1850 signatures (cat. 23, 52): Horace Rose's "bird-in-hand" sign of 1813, painted by Harlan Page (1791–1834) of Coventry, Connecticut, and the Lake Gowanus Hotel sign from South Salem, New York, signed by New York City sign painter George Crossingham, probably in the 1830s.[20] External documentation supports an attribution of the Liberty head on Joseph Phelps's inn sign, 1801, to East Windsor artist Abner Reed, more commonly known as an engraver (see fig. 63).[21]

Any further attempts at attribution are presently speculative, but they may inspire a search for related documents, signs, or even studio compositions. Vincent's list of sign painters known to have been active in specific locations at specific times can be used to consider who might have been in position to create certain extant signs. Middletown sign painters Solomon Jones and Thomas K. Bush, for example, established their partnership in 1823, the year in which a quite novel image was painted on Carter's sign, in nearby Killingworth (now Clinton), Connecticut (fig. 2). In addition, the partners' shop stock, liquidated in 1825, included a "drawing machine," possibly a pantograph, which may have been the source of transfer marks observed around the outlines of the imagery (see fig. 70). Nathaniel Wales, who advertised as a portrait and sign painter in Hartford and Litchfield, Connecticut, between 1803 and 1815, is a plausible attribution for the unusual double portrait sign from the Sill inn in Windsor, Connecticut (fig. 5). The sign's imagery joins two celebrated War of 1812 heroes—the dashing Captain James Lawrence, made immortal by his dying words, "Don't give up the ship," and the victorious Commodore Oliver Hazard Perry, who named his flagship the *Lawrence* and sailed into battle under a flag bearing Lawrence's words, capturing the entire British fleet on Lake Erie ("We have met the enemy and they are ours"). Although both portraits were based closely on print sources, the style of execution closely resembles Wales's known male portraits.[22] While a great many signs will doubtless remain anonymous, the possibility of additional attributions offers a tantalizing opportunity for further investigation.

A large number of artists are known to have practiced sign or, more generally, ornamental painting, at one point or another in their careers. Far from being limited to second- or third-tier painters whose oeuvre remains deservedly obscure, this group includes not a few of art history's luminous stars. Benjamin West (1738–1820), America's first noted painter, appointed official painter to King George III in England in 1772, acquired his early training in art from William Williams (1721–91), a British portraitist, scenery, ornamental, and sign painter who emigrated to America in the 1740s. According to Williams, signs in eighteenth-century Britain served as "the nursery and reward of painters, for great sums were expended on those ornaments, and the best artists of the age employed in executing them."[23] West himself is credited with painting at least two known signs before leaving America in 1759.[24] Thomas Cole (1801–48), founder of the Hudson River School, painted signs and stage scenery in the early 1820s in Steubenville, Ohio, where his father manufactured wallpaper and window shades. John Neagle (1796–1865) apprenticed to Boston sign and coach painter Thomas Wilson and subsequently plied this trade, as an itinerant in Cincinnati, circa 1819, before

Fig. 5. *Sign for Sill's Inn and Bissell's Inn*, circa 1814, Windsor, Conn. The Windsor Historical Society. Portrait of War of 1812 naval hero, Captain James Lawrence.

establishing himself as a successful portraitist. Genre painter David Gilmour Blythe (1815–65) also painted signs in Ohio and western Pennsylvania.[25] John Quidor (1801–81), now recognized as an important Romantic painter, earned his living as a sign and ornamental painter in New York City and Illinois.[26] Noted mid-nineteenth century genre painter William Sydney Mount (1807–68) began his career as an apprentice in the New York City sign and ornamental painting business run by his older brother, Henry.[27] In Missouri, George Caleb Bingham painted parade banners, traditionally the province of ornamental and sign painters.[28]

Newspaper advertisements and other documents attest to the large numbers of artists who offered sign and other forms of ornamental painting in addition to the studio genres more commonly represented in modern museum collections—especially portraiture in oil, watercolors, pastels, or in miniature. Yet Edward Hicks, the Pennsylvania Quaker artist-preacher best known for his "Peaceable Kingdom" paintings, is perhaps the only notable artist for whom we can presently identify bodies of work in both the sign painting and studio painting categories.[29] Even here a significant imbalance exists between Hicks's historically documented production and his currently recognized oeuvre. As Carolyn Weekley observes in her recent monograph, *The Kingdoms of Edward Hicks*, the artist trained, made his living, and established his contemporary reputation as an ornamental painter, primarily painting coaches for several large coach and carriage making enterprises in the Bucks County, Pennsylvania, area. His account books record the creation of nearly three dozen tavern and trade signs between 1806 and1835; of these, only six have been identified, together with a handful of household items attributed on the basis of family history. No examples of his primary work—coach painting—have been identified. In contrast to these originally public and commercial manifestations of Hicks's art, the easel paintings on which his modern reputation rests were created largely as a private and non-commercial sideline, "often rendered as presentation pieces for friends and family." Today, sixty-two versions survive of Hicks's favorite scene—the Biblical prophecy of the Peaceable Kingdom—together with several farmscapes, pastoral landscapes, and history paintings.[30]

The passage of time, environmental exposure, and changing aesthetic tastes have effected a notable reevaluation. Sign paintings, explicitly intended for public display, were arguably the most widely shared manifestation of the visual arts in early America, visible—indeed, inescapably so—to audiences of all social classes and categories. Easel paintings, in contrast, were typically intended for viewing in more private, restricted contexts—inside patrons' homes, artists' studios, in galleries or portfolios—by audiences who effectively represented a cultural elite. Today, the once-private images of easel paintings are accessible to vastly expanded audiences, the originals enshrined publicly in museums while their replicas are all but universally disseminated via photographic and digital reproductions. The once-common imagery of sign paintings, in contrast, has become uncommon, known to and appreciated by relatively select audiences of antique or folk art collectors, but virtually invisible to the general public for whom they were created.

The close integration of sign painting with other visual and decorative arts is vividly exemplifed by the Johnston family in eighteenth-century Boston. John Johnston (1752–1818) is perhaps the earliest American artist who can be firmly documented as the creator of an extant sign painting, commissioned in 1797 by the Boston Dispensary, depicting the Biblical story of the Good Samaritan. Johnston served his apprenticeship with John Gore, Boston's leading house, sign, and ornamental painter, and in 1777 he joined his brother-in-law Daniel Rea in running the ornamental painting business originally established by his father—painter, japanner, and engraver Thomas Johnston (ca. 1708–67). Thomas Johnston's family and business connections placed his sons and apprentices in the midst of pictorial and decorative arts production in colonial Boston. His work for the prolific silversmith Jacob Hurd, for example, might have provided ready access to British prints, which were sold by Hurd's son, Nathaniel, and which figure prominently as compositional sources for artists associated with the Johnston shop, including John Johnston, his older brother William Johnston (1732–72), and John Greenwood (1727–92). Like John Johnston, Greenwood is credited with at least one sign. Given the documented coincidence of sign and easel painting in the works of his counterparts, there is no reason to suppose that William Johnston, the first professional artist active in Connecticut, may not have painted signs as well as portraits on his visits to New London, New Haven, and Hartford in the early 1760s. In any case, the Johnston shop/studio tradition underlines the extent to which sign painting and sign paintings were integral components of the visual culture of early America, produced frequently by the same artists and drawing upon the same, commonly circulated visual vocabulary.[31]

Several explanations might be advanced for the relegation of sign paintings to the dusty corners of art history. The most obvious is physical survival, which disproportionately favors easel paintings, displayed in comparatively protected indoor settings. Of the once prodigious public art of sign painting, only a tiny sampling persists, and these survivals are rarely more than shadows of their original selves. Given the severe weathering suffered by many signs, a significant act of imagination is often necessary to envision their original artistry. A second factor is certainly the status traditionally assigned various genres of painting, with history painting at the pinnacle and the more prosaic genres of landscape, portraiture, and still life occupying the lower ranks. Sign painting, offering little scope for moral uplift, logically ranked lower still. As a result, although numerous highly esteemed artists are known to have practiced sign painting, they generally did so only early in their careers, either in training or in pursuit of economic livelihood (particularly in non-cosmopolitan areas that did not support resident studio artists). It may be no coincidence that William Rice, the only signpainter known to have regularly signed his work, ceased to advertise portrait painting after moving to Hartford circa1817; he made his reputation henceforth on the basis of signs and ornamental painting. Finally, laboratory analysis of the Connecticut Historical Society signs suggests a technical factor that may have exacerbated the loss of signs painted by artists trained in the studio tradition. As noted by Webber, the preferred order of surface layers reverses between sign and easel paintings, with oil-rich layers applied first in sign paintings and last in easel paintings. If financially-strapped studio artists took up sign painting as a sideline, they might well have continued to work in their usual manner, producing signs less likely to endure under outdoor conditions.

The communicative function of signs inherently placed limits on the free play of artistic creativity, particularly as it came to be understood in the nineteenth century, as the outpouring of individual genius. What was wanted in a successful sign was not a unique, and thus disassociated, vision, but rather distinctive rendering of a familiar theme, a recognizable image selected, from a repertoire of familiar motifs, for its capacity to mark a particular place in both the physical and mental landscape of viewers. The peculiar cultural positioning of signs effectively shifts the creative balance between artist and audience, as Wolf observes: "The sign-maker creates images that circulate within an already established field of cultural meanings. His signs must answer to the needs and perceptions of his public." The artist thus becomes "really only a collaborator," whose creation is dependent "in large part on the viewing expectations of his audiences." Long before the emergence of modernism as an artistic movement, the forms and imagery of tavern and inn signs made a virtue of "simplicity and standardization," as Gudis suggests: "They employed structures and an iconography that were easily repeated, repeatable, and thus readable by many different kinds of audiences, coming from different regions and locales." The importance of replicability is readily apparent in surviving signs. Out of sixty-five signs, each with two sides, in the Connecticut Historical Society collection, laboratory examination has thus far located traces of free-hand drawing on only one image: the charioteer on the Temperance Hotel sign from 1826–42 (see fig. 68). Numerous signs display evidence of various reproductive aids, either templates or mechanical drawing devices such as pantographs.

Cultural historians have recently made the tension between visual and verbal culture a central focus of critical analysis and interpretation. In *American Iconology*, David Miller argues that "the close but contradictory relation between visual and verbal culture in this country takes us to the heart of what is distinctively American about both."[32] Noting that the late nineteenth-century Philadelphia painter, Thomas Eakins, began his career as a writing instructor (his father's profession), Michael Fried calls attention to the "crucial role that writing and writinglike activities" assume in his compositions. Eakins's passage from writing master to artist, moreover, calls into question the relationship between artisanship and high art, a relationship central to the reconsideration of sign painting. One of Eakins's most famous paintings explores this tension, depicting *William Rush Carving His Allegorical Figure of the Schuylkill River*, 1876–77 (Philadelphia Museum of Art). A ship carver by profession, Rush earned his livelihood by the three-dimensional counterpart of sign painting; yet he ranked, in Eakins's estimation, as "one of the earliest and one of the best American sculptors." By juxtaposing a classical nude and a ship's figurehead—both unfinished—Eakins calls attention "precisely to the *continuity* between vocations that modern scholars are inclined to regard as essentially distinct."[33]

If "the complex, often elusive interplay between image and text, the visual and the verbal, in nineteenth-century American culture has yet to be fully appreciated," surely this is a task with which tavern and inn signs, the public art of everyday life, can be of significant assistance.[34] Consideration of these historic artifacts can also enhance both understanding and appreciation of signs in our own everyday lives. Such attentiveness might take the form of noting the physical evidence of continuities between past and present. Surveying the physical landscape of Connecticut today, Ames observes that tavern and inn signs predominate as models for revival and reproduction. Turning to the cultural landscape, Gudis calls attention to powerful symbolic associations that go far in illuminating why historic inn signs—placemarkers for "home away from home"—might prove particularly effective in marking and marketing modern enterprises that provide goods and services that were once among the comforts of home, not only restaurants and motels, but also boarding schools, insurance and real estate agencies, convalescent homes and funeral parlors. Contemporary Connecticut artist Robert Cottingham (b. 1935) offers yet another vision, having made historic signage a major theme of his work. Cottingham's *Facades* series celebrates the artistry of American signs in what might be described as a gallery of close-up, monumental portraits, exemplified by the rebus-like *Champagne* (fig. 6). Cropping, enlargement, oblique angles, and other compositional manipulations release Cottingham's signs from the invisibility of the workaday world, prompting new awareness of their striking visual qualities as well as their emotive power: they are "emblems of America."[35] The process of reexamining early American tavern and inn signs has had a comparable, eye-opening effect on those involved in the production and presentation of *Lions & Eagles & Bulls*, and we hope it will prove similarly illuminating for those who read it, now and in years to come.

NOTES

1 Kym S. Rice, *Early American Taverns: For the Entertainment of Friends and Strangers* (Chicago: Regnery Gateway, in association with Fraunces Tavern Museum, New York, 1983), p. 74; Donna-Belle Garvin and James L. Garvin, *On the Road North of Boston: New Hampshire Taverns and Turnpikes, 1700–1900* (Concord: New Hampshire Historical Society, 1988), p. 32; Jean Lipman, et al, *Five Star Folk Art: One Hundred American Masterpieces* (New York: Abrams, in association with The Museum of American Folk Art, New York, 1990), p. 82.

2 According to Helene Smith, *Tavern Signs of America: Catalog* (Greensburg, Pa: McDonald/Swärd Publishing Co., 1988), the next largest collections are as follows: Old Sturbridge Village, 22; Pennsylvania Farm Museum, Landis Valley, 20; Shelburne Museum, 12; Bucks County Historical Society, Doylestown, Pa., 9; Pocumtuck Valley Memorial Association, Deerfield, Mass., 8; National Museum of American History, The Smithsonian Institution, 7; New York State Historical Association, 7; H.F. duPont Winterthur Museum, 6.

3 Ellsworth S. Grant, "The Tavern Signs of Morgan B. Brainard: Connecticut Historical Society, Hartford, Connecticut" (unpublished report, The Connecticut Historical Society, 1997).

4 Herman Diederik Johan van Schevichaven [Jacob Larwood] and John Camden Hotten, *The History of Signboards, from the Earliest Times to the Present Day* (London: John Camden Hotten [1866]). Numerous editions followed, including a special, large-format edition with added plates, 4th ed. (London: John Camden Hotten, 1868). For an assessment of Shevichaven's importance, see Ambrose Heal, *The Signboards of Old London Shops* (London: Batsford, 1947), pp. 13–15.

5 Tavern and travel histories include Alice Morse Earle, *Stage-Coach and Tavern Days* (New York: MacMillan Co., 1900); Elise Lathrop, *Early American Inns and Taverns* (New York: Robert M. McBride, 1926); Marian Dickinson Terry, ed., *Old Inns of Connecticut* (Hartford: The Prospect Press, 1937); Rice, *Early American Taverns*; and Garvin and Garvin, *North of Boston*. For additional references, see Ames, "Signs of the Past in the Present," Chapter 9, n. 5.

6 For example, see Lipman, et al., *Five Star Folk Art*, pp. 82–84; Jean Lipman and Alice Winchester, *The Flowering of American Folk Art, 1776–1876* (New York: Viking Press, in cooperation with the Whitney Museum of American Art, 1974), pp. 220–25; Nina Fletcher Little, *Little by Little: Six Decades of Collecting American Decorative Arts* (Hanover, N.H., and London: University Press of New England for the Society for the Preservation of New England Antiquities, 1998), pp. 107–12; James S. Ayres, *Two Hundred Years of English Naïve Art, 1700–1900* (Alexandria, Va.: Art Services International, 1996), pp. 112–41.

7 Renderings of the following Connecticut Historical Society signs are preserved in the Index of American Design, National Gallery of Art, Washington, D.C.: cat. 5, 6, 7, 12, 15, 20, 21, 23, 27, 33 (both sides), 37 (both sides), 40, 54 (both sides), and 55 (both sides). Published compilations of Index renderings are Erwin O. Christensen, *The Index of American Design* (New York: Macmillan, and Washington, D.C: National Gallery of Art, 1950); and Clarence P. Hornung, *Treasury of American Design: A Pictorial Survey of Popular Folk Arts Based upon Watercolor Renderings in the Index of American Design, at the National Gallery of Art*, 2 vols. in 1 (New York: Abrams, 1976).

8 Subsequent publications of Index renderings have been less careful to distinguish these two-dimensional, twentieth-century watercolors from the three-dimensional signs from which they were copied; see, for example, J. Morgan Sincock, *America's Early Taverns* (Lebanon, Pa: Applied Arts Publishers, 1992), p. 16 and inside front cover.

9 The Connecticut Historical Society, *Morgan B. Brainard's Tavern Signs* (Hartford: The Conecticut Historical Society, 1958), pp. 4–13. Hereafter cited as *MBTS*.

10 Morgan Brainard Papers, The Connecticut Historical Society Library.

11 *MBTS*, p. 5.

12 Smith, *Tavern Signs*, pp. 18–19, 25, 33–39 (listings for Henry Ford Museum, Metropolitan Museum of Art, Old Sturbridge Village, Shelburne Museum).

13 Just under five hundred inns had previously been identified; see Grant, "Tavern Signs of Morgan B. Brainard," pp. 29–43.

14 For additional information on the techniques of sign painting, see Scott W. Nolley and Carolyn J. Weekley, "The Nature of Edward Hicks's Painting," *Magazine Antiques*, February 1999, pp. 281–90.

15 Earle, *Tavern Days*, p. 145.

16 The essential reference on this topic is Arthur H. Hughes and Morse S. Allen, *Connecticut Place Names* (Hartford: The Connecticut Historical Society, 1976).

17 A comparison of turnpike routes in New England states convincingly illustrates the density of the road network in Connecticut; see Frederic J. Wood, *The Turnpikes of New England*, abridged ed., with introduction by Ronald Dale Karr, New England Transportation Series (Pepperell, Massachusetts: Branch Line Press, 1997), maps on pp. 24–25, 190, 228, 266, 312–13.

18 Michael Edward Shapiro, et al., *George Caleb Bingham* (Saint Louis: The Saint Louis Art Museum, in association with Harry N. Abrams, New York, 1990), pp. 18–20. Notably, the French artist responsible for redrawing *Canvassing for a Vote* for lithography moved the eagle upward, nearly out of the picture frame, and inserted the word, "HOTEL"; see Ron Tyler, et al., *American Frontier Life: Early Western Painting and Prints* (Fort Worth: Amon Carter Museum and Abbeville Press, New York, 1987), p. 179.

19 Other notable depictions of tavern, inn, and hotel signs include John Quidor's illustrations of Washington Irving's tale of Rip Van Winkle, set in the Hudson River Valley but possibly painted during the artist's residence in Quincy, Illinois, between 1834 and 1851: *Rip Van Winkle: At Nicholas Vedder's Tavern*, 1839 (M. and M. Karolik Collection, Museum of Fine Arts, Boston) and *The Return of Rip Van Winkle*, 1849 (see fig. 105); Bryan Jay Wolf, *Romantic Re-Vision: Culture and Consciousness in Nineteenth-Century American Painting and Literature* (Chicago and London: University of Chicago Press, 1982), pp. 152–67; Betty I. Madden, *Arts, Crafts, and Architecture in Early Illinois* (Urbana, Chicago, and London: University of Illinois Press, published in cooperation with the Illinois State Museum, Springfield, 1974), p. 162. Basil Hall's 1828 drawing of the *Village of Shawneetown on the right bank of the Ohio, in the State of Illinois* (Lilly Library, Indiana University) depicts a horizontally-oriented, rectangular sign suspended at roof-peak level from a crossbar between two posts; while the architecture of the inn itself reveals a French influence, the configuration of sign and posts is indistinguishable from Connecticut installations; Madden, *Arts, Crafts, and Architecture*, p. 77.

20 Three other signs bear signatures corresponding to post-1850 over- or repaintings: *Sign of the Duke of Cumberland*, Louis James Donlon, 1914 (cat. 2); *Sign for Abbe's Inn and the Lion Hotel*, Luther Knight, 1866 (cat. 31); *Sign for the Grosvenor Inn*, "A.H." [Augustus Hoppin], 1894 (cat. 60).

21 Abner Reed's manuscript day book records work done by himself and an apprentice on a sign for "J. Phelps" in February 1801, at a cost of 42s; The Connecticut Historical Society Library, cited in *MBTS*, p. 11.

22 See Nina Fletcher Little, "Little Known Connecticut Artists, 1790–1810," *Connecticut Historical Society Bulletin*, vol. 22, no. 4 (October 1957): 98–100, 111–2. Margaret Vincent noted Wales's presence at an appropriate time and place; Richard C. Malley, Connecticut Historical Society Curator of Technology, identified the portrait subjects; and Elizabeth Wyckoff, Prints and Photographs, New York Public Library, located print sources.

23 William Williams, *An Essay on the Mechanic of Oil Colour* (Bath, 1787),

Fig. 6. Robert Cottingham, *Champagne*, oil on canvas, 1992. Courtesy of artist.

pp. 10–11; quoted in Ayres, *English Naïve Art*, pp. 116–19; Dorinda Evans, "William Williams," in *Philadelphia: Three Centuries of American Art* (Philadelphia: Philadelphia Museum of Art, 1976), p. 89.

24 Earle, *Tavern Days*, credits West with two signs, *Sign of the Hat*, Leacock Township, near Compass, Pa., probably early 1760s; *Sign of the Three Crowns*, Salisbury Township, Pa., dated 1771. According to Smith, *Tavern Signs* (p. 44), both are in the collection of the Sheraton-Lancaster Resort, Lancaster, Pa., together with a third sign that has been attributed to West or Jacob Eicholtz. Unless there is evidence of earlier work, the dates associated with all three signs contradict any attribution to West.

25 Rhea Mansfield Knittle, "Early Ohio Taverns: Tavern-sign, Barge, Banner, Chair and Settee Painters," The Ohio Frontier Series, 1767–1847, no. 1 (Ashland, Ohio: By the author, 1937), pp. 34–35, 38.

26 Wolf, *Romantic Re-Vision*, p. 119.

27 Deborah J. Johnson, *William Sidney Mount: Painter of American Life* (New York: American Federation of Arts, 1998), p. 17.

28 Nancy Rash, *The Painting and Politics of George Caleb Bingham* (New Haven and London: Yale University Press, 1991), pp. 15–17.

29 An unidentified oil portrait signed by documented Connecticut sign painter Luther Allen recently surfaced; *Magazine Antiques*, May 2000, p. 680.

30 Carolyn Weekley, with the assistance of Laura Pass Barry, *The King-doms of Edward Hicks* (Williamsburg, Virginia: Abby Aldrich Rockefeller Folk Art Center, The Colonial Williamsburg Foundation, in association with Abrams, New York, 1999), esp. pp. 4–5.

31 Nina Fletcher Little, *Paintings by New England Provincial Artists, 1775–1800* (Boston: Museum of Fine Arts, 1976), pp. 138–42; Patricia E. Kane, et al., *Colonial Massachusetts Silversmiths and Jewelers* (New Haven: Yale University Art Gallery, distributed by University Press of New England, Hanover, N.H., and London, 1998), pp. 80–83, 90–92, 617, 1016, 1020–21; Earle, *Tavern Days* (p. 165) illustrates a drawing for an inn sign ordered from Greenwood in 1749 by Nathaniel Ames of Dedham, Mass.

32 David Miller, ed., *American Iconology: New Approaches to Nineteenth-Century Art and Literature* (New Haven and London: Yale University Press, 1993), pp. 279, 289. For further articulation of the conceptual approach underlying this volume of essays, see W.J.T. Mitchell, *Iconology: Image, Text, Ideology* (Chicago and London: University of Chicago Press, 1986).

33 Michael Fried, *Realism, Writing, Disfiguration: On Thomas Eakins and Stephen Crane* (Chicago and London: University of Chicago Press, 1987), pp. 19–21.

34 Miller, ed., *American Iconology*, p. 278.

35 Jacquelyn Serwer, "Heroic Relics: The Art of Robert Cottingham," *American Art* 12 (Summer 1998): 7–25.

Signs of the Times:
A Brief Cultural History of Sign Painting

By Bryan J. Wolf

In early summer of 1776, Thomas Jefferson was not a happy man. His draft of the Declaration of Independence, submitted to the Continental Congress for approval, had been subjected to a series of revisions—Jefferson called them "depradations" and "mutilations"—that the author felt helpless to control. He turned to Ben Franklin for advice. Franklin, in turn, attempted to comfort Jefferson by way of an anecdote. He related the tale of a young hat maker who had recently finished his apprenticeship and was eager to set up a shop of his own.

His first concern was to have a handsome signboard, with a proper inscription. He composed it with these words, "JOHN THOMPSON, HATTER, MAKES AND SELLS HATS FOR READY MONEY," *with a figure of a hat subjoined; but he thought he would submit it to his friends for their amendments. The first he showed it to thought the word* "HATTER" *tautologous, because followed by the words "makes hats," which show he was a hatter. It was struck out. The next observed that the word* "MAKES" *might as well be omitted, because his customers would not care who makes the hats. . . . He struck it out. A third said he thought the words* "FOR READY MONEY" *were useless, as it was not the custom of the place to sell on credit . . . the inscription now stood,* "John Thompson sells hats." "SELLS HATS!" *says his next friend. "Why nobody will expect you to give them away, what then is the use of that word?" It was stricken out, and* "HATS" *followed it, the rather as there was one painted on the board. So the inscription was reduced ultimately to* "John Thompson" *with the figure of a hat subjoined.*[1]

Franklin's wry anecdote may not have done much to reassure Jefferson, but it helps us. The tale of the hatter is one of the earliest accounts we have of sign making in colonial America. We need to ask what relevance it has for an exhibition of inn and tavern signs in the early Republic. The answer, I suspect, is threefold. Franklin relies implicitly on the old adage that "A picture is worth a thousand words." His tale cues the listener to the differences between print culture and visual culture. Franklin's story suggests how

important it is for sign painters to let the picture do the talking: don't repeat with words what you have already said visually. The first lesson we learn from Franklin, then, is about visual economy: the more iconic the image, the more powerful its message.

The second lesson is a bit more complicated. Franklin's story is really a comment on *audiences*. The hatter's sign, like Jefferson's draft of the Declaration of Independence, is ultimately a public document—its meaning derives from the way its viewers interpret it. The author in this way is really only a collaborator—what he creates depends in large part on the viewing expectations of his audience. From this perspective, sign painting is an elaborate version of taking the public's pulse. The sign maker creates images that circulate within an already established field of cultural meanings. His signs must answer to the needs and perceptions of his public.

The third lesson is the revolutionary one. Franklin's story treats the young hatter as a model for the young nation. Newly independent, both need to establish themselves within the larger commercial world. And the way to accomplish this task is by self-advertisement: signs, images, and, in the case of the Declaration, documents that announce the presence of a new arrival within the community of citizens or nations, respectively. Like Franklin's hatter, Jefferson's nation must be ready for business.

And our business, in turn, is to read back from those signs to the historical moment that produced them. We need to think about sign painting as the tip of a cultural iceberg. Tavern signs, in their own quiet way, document the long-term changes occurring in the everyday lives of ordinary people. From inn and tavern signs we learn a great deal about the values, aspirations, and assumptions, of our early national culture.

In the hundred years from 1750 to 1850, tavern and inn signs underwent small but significant changes. These changes reflect the larger transformations that were taking place in

Fig. 7. *Sign for the Temperance Hotel*, circa 1826–42, Plainfield and Colchester, Conn. CHS, cat. 54, side 2.

Fig. 8. *Sign of the Black Horse*, circa 1771, Saybrook Point, Conn. CHS, cat. 6, side 2.

the world around them. They reveal, in particular, the radical shift from a premodern agricultural society in what was then British North America to the entrepreneurial, market-driven, and increasingly urban economy of the early Republic.

There are three narratives to be told here. The first concerns what we might term issues of "nationalization." Historians have defined the first seventy-five years after the American Revolution as a period of intense nation building. The United States in the early national period was less a unified federal republic than a motley assortment of people divided by class, economic, racial, and regional differences, with little to unite them but an untested document called the "Constitution" and a collective will to succeed. Planters from Tidewater Virginia thought of themselves primarily as Virginians and modeled their behavior on the culture of an Anglican, high-church gentry across the ocean. Small farmers in the Connecticut River Valley saw themselves as independent yeomen and bristled at the prosperity of their mercantile neighbors in Boston and New Haven. And

shipbuilders in Philadelphia allied themselves with an urban, artisanal mid-Atlantic working-class culture. What brought people together from these different regions and economic strata was less a shared history than a shared visual and public culture: festivals, holidays, celebrations, and signs that collectively brought the idea of the "nation" to life.[2]

America, in other words, was an invented concept. The nation did not spring to life full-blown, like Pallas Athena from Zeus's head. Rather, like all inventions, the new nation required a great deal of tinkering at the start. People needed instructions in how to think beyond the local frames of reference they were accustomed to—how to imagine themselves primarily as "Americans" rather than as Virginians, New Englanders, or Philadelphians. They needed ways to marry the local to the national, to understand their everyday lives as defined by a different sort of space and a different measure of time: the newly mapped, newly modern world of the nation-state. Just as commerce was slowly weaving together the disparate parts of the nation into a single—though com-

Fig. 9. *Sign for Hammon's Inn*, dated 17?? and 1818, Foster, Rhode Island. CHS, cat. 25, side 2.

plicated—economic unit, so too a new visual culture had begun to transform local places and events into integral moments within a unified national history. Towns like Concord and Lexington, for example, shed their provincial New England identities to become part of an incipient revolutionary tradition: the place where the sounds of liberty "were first heard round the world." Fourth of July celebrations subsumed what had once been local trade festivities and working-class social rituals into newly national events: parades and picnics that celebrated the shared history of a single people.

Tavern signs participate in this trend. They help to create what anthropologist Benedict Anderson calls "imagined communities."[3] They are part of a process of "nationalization," a way of directing the built environment and the visual culture that surrounds it to the ends of patriotism. One of the conspicuous changes that defines tavern and inn signs of the nineteenth century is their immersion in a language of nationalism. The organic imagery and heraldic inscriptions that dominated signage of the eighteenth cen-

tury became increasingly politicized in the nineteenth. Look, for example, at the stately black horse on the vertical tavern sign marked "Entertainment" from the third quarter of the eighteenth century (fig. 8). Like many other commercial signs from the prerevolutionary era, the horse on this board probably alludes to a slogan repeated on many signboards of the period: "Entertainment for Man and Horse." American signboards from the eighteenth century include a wide variety of organic images: bulls, beehives, swans, grapes, fish, rising suns, sheaves of barley or wheat, and even an occasional mermaid. All go back to English and Continental antecedents, and all participate in a preindustrial worldview defined by agricultural values, social hierarchies, and emblematic ways of seeing (the beehives, for example, signify "industriousness," while the sheaves of wheat allude to the successful completion of an agricultural cycle).

In the closing decades of the eighteenth century, the imagery on tavern signboards slowly began to change. In 1782, the new nation adopted the eagle as its official symbol, incorporating it into the Great Seal of the United States. In

Fig.10. S.V. Hunt after Frederic Edwin Church, *West Rock, New Haven*. Engraving from *A Landscape Book by American Artists and American Authors* (New York: G.P. Putnam & Son, 1868). CHS, Graphics Collection. In the text accompanying the engraving of Church's 1849 painting, Mary E. Field emphasized West Rock's history: "The artist here gives us not only a beautiful and well-known scene, but illustrates a passage in colonial history. That rugged pile recalls a story of trial and fortitude, courage and magnanimity, the noblest friendship, and a fearless adherence to political principles from religious motives."

the years that followed, American eagles spread their wings in sign after sign. Signboards with eagles have been dated as early as 1800; over a dozen tavern signs displaying American eagles have been documented in New England before 1825 (fig. 9). In a similar vein, emblems and coats of arms from individual states began to replace the traditional beehives and bulls. The Connecticut state coat of arms, for example, appeared with a tree that may represent the Charter Oak in a tavern sign for Joseph Porter dating to the early nineteenth century (cat. 27). This juxtaposition of the state coat of arms with the Charter Oak linked Porter's inn not only to local traditions but to a discourse of freedom and resistance that bound the history of Connecticut to the larger history of the nation.

In a parallel fashion, Hartford artist Frederic Edwin Church, a leading figure among second-generation Hudson River School painters, produced an image of *West Rock, New Haven*, 1849 (fig. 10), that invokes, as its nineteenth-century

audience would have recognized instantly, a revolutionary moment from the seventeenth century. The caves of West Rock sheltered the three regicides who fled from Britain to New Haven following the collapse of the Puritan Revolution. Church's historically minded canvas, like the less accomplished efforts of Porter's sign painter, draws a parallel between a local Connecticut site and a larger, national history, defining each through their shared associations with images of political resistance. What was happening with tavern signs, as elsewhere in the visual culture of the nineteenth century, was an effort to identify local places and peoples with a national vision. And this effort took the form, not only of paintings, parades, and Fourth of July celebrations, but of inn signs decked out in their patriotic best.

Perhaps the most arresting example of the role tavern signs played in an emerging national culture is Richard Caton Woodville's painting of 1848, *War News from Mexico*, an image composed at the conclusion of the war waged by the

Fig. 11. Richard Caton Woodville,
War News From Mexico, oil on canvas, 1848.
The Manoogian Collection, on loan to the
National Gallery of Art, Washington.
Photograph © Board of Trustees,
National Gallery of Art, Washinton, D.C.
Woodville painted signs for patrons
in Ohio and western Pennsylvania.

United States against Mexico from 1846 to 1848 (fig. 11).
Woodville not only situated his folksy figures on the porch of
a local inn, but suspended from the pediment of the portico
a sign that reads "American Hotel." An eagle lifted directly
from the seal of the United States divides the word "American" into two parts.

Two aspects of Woodville's painting demand our attention.
The first is the clustering of figures between the porch's
Doric columns. All of these figures are white males, a micro-
cosm of the voting public of the time. In the right foreground, on the steps of the porch, sits a black slave in well-
worn garments. A young child in tattered clothing stands
next to him. To the right of the painting, at the level of the
white males but on the other side of a column separating her
from them, a matronly figure leans out of a tavern window.
Our interest is drawn to the spatial relations among these
figures. All exist under the aegis—that signboard—of the
"American Hotel," and all occupy a social space commensu-

rate with their political status: the white males at the center, the black slaves on the peripheries, and the white
woman at the level of the males but debarred visually and
symbolically from political participation. Woodville has
transformed a diverse and divided population into an intimate family gathering. Under the sign of the "American
Hotel," he has created a vision of American society as an
extended family, hierarchically arranged and *unified*. Simple
as Woodville's inn sign may be, then, it functions to important political and ideological ends. It works to unify a population divided by gender, race, and war (most New Englanders adamantly opposed the Mexican War), rendering the
nation in idealized fashion as an *imaginary* community.

The second aspect of the painting worth noting is the relation between the paper reader in the center and the old man
in knee breeches to the viewer's right. Each is linked to the
other by the top hats they both wear. The knee breeches of
the elderly gentleman recall an earlier era, linking the older

Fig. 12. John Neagle, *Pat Lyon at the Forge*, oil on canvas, 1829.
Courtesy of the Pennsylvania Academy of the Fine Arts,
Philadelphia. Gift of the Lyon Family. Neagle served his
apprenticeship at a Boston ornamental and coach painting shop.

man with the generation of Founding Fathers (note that no
other figure wears knee breeches). His presence in the painting, and his placement within close earshot of the center
reader, are Woodville's way of linking *his* war—the Revolutionary War of 1776—with the Mexican War of 1846. The
artist created a genealogy of "freedom" in the painting, a
narrative that links an eighteenth-century war fought for
independence to a contemporary war, as if the latter—the
war with Mexico—were simply another battle to extend the
frontiers of freedom. In this way the painting serves as a
justification for the doctrines of Manifest Destiny, hinting as
it does that the expansion of the United States westward
must be understood as an extension of freedoms won along
the eastern seaboard almost a century earlier. Woodville is
thus linked to our Connecticut signboard makers by an insistence—shared by all—that local history be read within the
context of national history. Both local and national histories

tell the same story: the birth of the nation as a struggle for
freedom.

Not all tavern signs shared in this effort to convert the
nation into a unified community. To the contrary, a second,
but related, set of tavern signs tended to appeal to distinct
subcommunities within the nation. Numeous extant inn
signs include esoteric Masonic imagery (cat. 11, 19, 23).
They appeal to a particular segment of the public, and they
ask their viewers to understand the inn or tavern as a conge-
nial place for members of the Masonic brotherhood. Other
signs make a similar appeal to Temperance Movement sup-
porters (cat. 54). Such images provide tantalizing glimpses
into the often fractious world of antebellum politics. Jack-
sonian society was riddled with what historian David B.
Davis has described as "paranoid" fears of groups and organizations perceived as secret and conspiratorial: Masons,
Catholics, and Mormons, for example.[4] The reasons are not
hard to find. Such organizations appeared to cut against the
grain of an egalitarian culture. Nativists feared that
demands for unconditional loyalty would lead to brainwash-
ing and subversion. They felt that any organization or sect
that held "secret" proceedings—or practiced exclusionary
rituals—threatened the unity and well-being of the nation
as a whole. Such feelings were in part the result of ethnic
tensions: Protestants mistrustful of Irish Catholic immigra-
tion; Westerners hostile to the collective power and competition of Mormon settlers.

But the problem was also political. There was no better way
to promote national unity than by ferreting out "subversion" wherever it might be found. Anti-Masonry allowed
working-class populations fearful of their status in a rapidly
industrializing society to assert—once again—their patriotism and their control over their environment. Conspiracy
theories allowed those who espoused them to articulate common values and, as Davis notes, to join in "a dedicated
union against evil." Though we may never know what moti-
vated Ariel Lawrence or Horace Rose to include Masonic
imagery in their tavern signs, we can be certain that such
imagery was neither accidental nor neutral. It represented
one shot in an ongoing struggle among different sects,
classes, and organizations over who possessed the right to
speak for the nation.

Nor are these Masonic signboards an exception to some rule.
John Neagle's 1829 painting of the blacksmith, inventor, and
entrepreneur Pat Lyon shows a robust working man surrounded by the tools of his trade (fig. 12). Notice, however,
the board and graph in the painting's lower right corner, neither of which is directly related to the craft of blacksmithing. The diagram on the paper is a proof of the

Pythagorean theorem from the first book of Euclid. As Bruce Chambers has shown, the Pythagorean diagram was a central symbol in Masonic rituals.[5] Neagle's inclusion of the diagram, together with his prominent placement of another "concealed" Masonic emblem, the lambskin apron that features prominently in Masonic costume, suggests that he designed his portrait of Lyon for two audiences. Those who knew nothing of Masonic forms would find nothing "unusual" in the painting, while those who were initiated into the rites of freemasonry would recognize in Lyon a fellow traveler. The tavern signs that display Masonic images seem, like Neagle's painting, to participate in a cognitive game of hide-and-seek with similar gusto.

Yet other signs include clever rebuses or visual puns without any apparent reference to a sect, religion, or organization. George E. Crofut's inn sign, a late example, displays on its panel a large black crow sitting on a tall but defoliated tree (cat. 59). Next to the crow, as if suspended from heaven, a bare foot emerges from what is either the hem of a woman's skirt or some form of curtain. Dangling in the sky like an unclaimed prop, the foot points in the direction of an apostrophe and the letter "s" to form the words—which do not otherwise appear in the image—Crow Foot's Inn. Directly below the foot stands the inn.

What links both Masonic signs and the Crow Foot's Inn sign together is the way in which each invites the viewer to decode its displays, thus to affirm the viewer's powers of mastery not only over the images themselves but, ultimately, over an ambiguous social environment. Nineteenth-century culture often relied on such activities: visual puzzles and paradoxes that challenged the viewer to arrive at a solution. The stories of Edgar Allan Poe are filled with secret codes and cryptographic riddles. What matters is not the solution that the reader might arrive at but the *process* of coding and decoding. These cognitive games empowered the spectator by creating, if only momentarily, the impression—or the illusion—that the viewer was master or mistress of the surrounding environment. The perils of the city or the threats of an undecipherable political or social world could be overcome by simple acts of informed perception. The point is not that inn signs of the nineteenth century were created for the same reasons (or audiences) as Poe's short stories, but that they both adopted the same strategies: hidden messages, secret codes.

A coda, or endpoint, to our story. There is a final narrative that we need to consider when we look at nineteenth-century signboards. This narrative centers on visual culture itself. Inn signs of the eighteenth century, as we noted,

reflect an artisanal culture tied to organic forms and shapes. The use of familiar furniture forms (chair backs, split pediments) in vertical formats to frame and hang tavern signs links them to the spaces of the parlor and hearth (see figs. 21–22). The tavern sign, in effect, brings the outdoors *inside*. It provides the weary traveler with an image of sociability: a surrogate family within a semipublic space

By the mid-nineteenth century the typical inn sign had become a horizontal and imageless text, proclaiming simply "Hotel" or "Inn" (cat. 42, 44). This change in format reveals a larger shift in visual culture itself away from an "organic" notion of society and a shared vocabulary of emblematic forms (bulls, horses, grapevines) toward increasingly neutral, uncommented, "informational" forms of exchange. In the former, signs are read at leisure by those who expect an inn to provide them, as the sign promises, with a surrogate home. In the latter, signs offer the same sort of information that newspapers of the period offered: facts, dates, and places all reduced to print form and designed to assist in the rapid exchange of goods and services.

The viewer in the earlier mode participated in the social world the sign conjured up; he was (or was assumed to be) part of a traditional agrarian society with a fixed social hierarchy. By the second decade of the nineteenth century, however, the viewer took on the role of visual *consumer*, someone who manipulated what he saw and read for the purposes of profit. The point, again, is not that the typical viewer of a mid-nineteenth-century printed sign was willy-nilly a merchant capitalist, but that, regardless of his or her occupation, the viewer tended to see the world within the terms of a market culture—as so much printed information to be read and digested at once. Tavern signs at mid-century simply reflect this penetration of the market into virtually all facets of social experience.

NOTES

1 Quoted in Robert A. Ferguson, *The American Enlightenment, 1750–1820* (Cambridge, Mass., and London: Harvard University Press, 1997), p. 14.
2 For a discussion of the role of festivals in the making of a national culture, see David Waldstreicher, *In the Midst of Perpetual Fetes. The Making of American Nationalism, 1776–1820.* (Chapel Hill, N.C., and London: University of North Carolina Press; published for the Omohundro Institute of Early American Culture, Williamsburg, Va., 1997).
3 Benedict Anderson, *Imagined Communities. Reflections on the Origin and Spread of Nationalism* (London and New York: Verso, 1983; rev. ed., 1991).
4 David Brion Davis, "Some Themes of Counter-Subversion: An Analysis of Anti-Masonic, Anti-Catholic, and Anti-Mormon Literature," *Mississippi Valley Historical Review* 47, no. 2. (September 1960).
5 Bruce W. Chambers, "The Pythagorean Puzzle of Patrick Lyon," *Art Bulletin* 58 (June 1976): 225–33.

Reading the Signs:
An Object History of Tavern Signs from Connecticut, 1750–1850

By Philip D. Zimmerman

Every sign tells a story. On one level, signs exist to communicate information, typically simple facts. Tavern and inn signs, for example, were made and used to identify places of business. The exteriors of eighteenth-century tavern buildings, whether in urban or rural settings, were often indistinguishable from sizable domestic dwellings. Signs suspended from large posts, either freestanding or attached at right angles to the building facade, labeled the establishment from afar for anyone approaching from either direction. But a quick glance at the variety of signs, each representing a different way of saying "this is an inn," affirms that signs do much more than merely mark certain buildings. On another level, signs embody artistic and symbolic traditions that in turn build upon cultural references, assumptions, and values.

Myriad choices and decisions faced the maker and buyer (or user) as they determined the form and decoration of each sign. Some decisions, creative or otherwise, were deeply rooted in consistent attitudes and habitual practices, hence barely conscious on the part of the individuals involved. Because each party approached the problem of designing a sign with many shared ideas about what it should be, further discussion about those characteristics was unnecessary. In contrast, what name to use, whether to include a date, what images might appear, and how colorful and ornate everything should be were just some of the decisions that had to be made before a sign maker could create something that served the needs of the tavern or inn keeper. Whether intentional or subconscious, these many choices and influences allow present-day students to "read" signs for deeper meanings in addition to appreciating purely visual properties.

Signs made for use in another time and conditioned by particular human experiences are meaningful sources of history. Similarly, bold shapes, colors, lettering, and images combine with more subtle details of materials, texture, and patina to create distinctive and engaging visual qualities for aesthetic inquiry and enjoyment. In general, historians and art historians favor those fine and decorative artworks and objects that have survived the ravages of time and use without significant changes or alterations, for such differences can alter or obscure original messages or intentions. Indeed, the destructive effects of excessive weathering—what one London publication of 1734 called "the Violence of Rain, or the Injury of Weather"—can strip a sign of much of its original artistic and historical content.[1] Degradation and erosion of surfaces—natural consequences of the passage of time and of outdoor use in particular—may invite renewal, through repainting or other means, of decorative surfaces by a subsequent owner. Change in ownership or related circumstances may occasion complete or partial redecoration, resulting in a sign that has lost its integrity as a product of its original maker to become instead a more complex, dynamic blend of times and intentions.

Some old signs do survive "untouched" or in "pristine" condition and readily communicate the visual messages of their makers. But complete as they may seem, they provide only part of the story: they lack context. Like any modern example of commercial art, tavern signs were a component within a larger landscape in which people played out different aspects of their lives. Factors of the physical setting affected how people experienced signs. For example, how high were signs hung? How did bright sun or darkness affect their appearance? Did dust and dirt obscure some visual qualities? Interestingly, many signs have survived with one side noticeably more weathered than the other, attesting to the impact of prevailing air currents, exposure to moisture, and other local circumstances. Beyond these physical matters, did signs influence people's lives—or did people simply ignore them? Were people enchanted by colors and images? Did they respond to patriotic symbols or historical references? Did they even notice the pictorial qualities of individual signs?

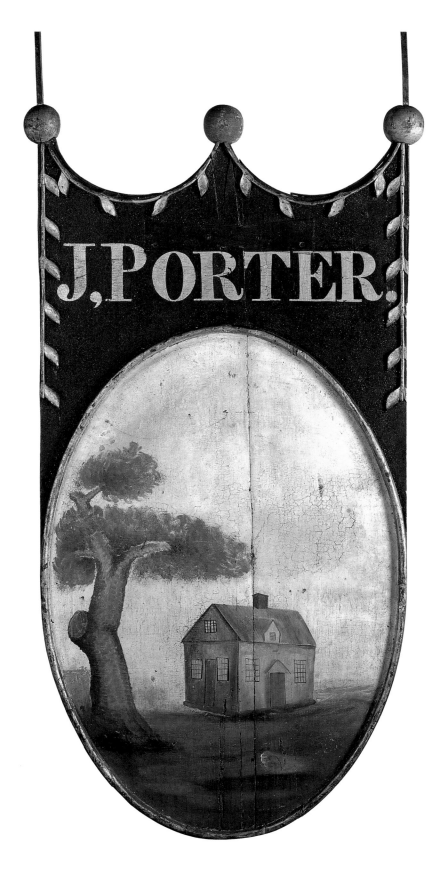

Fig. 13. *Sign for Porter's Inn*, circa 1820–25, Farmington, Conn. CHS, cat. 27, side 2.

The broader roles and issues of signs studied in context and in the world they represented introduce a range of interpretive possibilities limited only by the imagination of the investigator. In comparison, the window into a specific time and place that the pristine sign affords can seem narrow, perhaps even insignificant. But pursuit of taverns, tavern life, entertainment, temperance, travel and transportation, urban landscape, sign makers and related artisans, and so on can overwhelm the signs themselves, undermining their inherent appeal as large, colorful objects that communicate directly and serve as eye-witness documents of everyday life and artistic vision. Perhaps a richer understanding as well as enjoyment of tavern signs lies somewhere between the extremes of context- and content-based approaches.

Marking Time

Signs express their time of manufacture in several ways. The size, shape, and orientation of signboards changed through the decades, as did smaller decorative elements and motifs. The turnings of posts and finials, profiles of moldings, and shapes of pediments and skirts all correspond to broader style patterns. Painted images also reflect the subject matter, style of presentation, color patterns, graphic style, and word choice in fashion at a particular time.

Until the end of the eighteenth century, signs were relatively small—small enough for one person to heft—and had vertically oriented, rectangular picture fields.[2] Almost all of these signs had decorative pediments, and most had shaped skirts, also called aprons, as well. An unusual sign laden with Masonic imagery, made for Ariel Lawrence about 1797 (cat. 11), was composed horizontally. Although horizontal signs did not become common for another twenty-five years, the date accurately signals the first of several changes in form. Introduction of ovals and shields constituted the first popular alternative to the vertical rectangle. Surviving signs suggest that the earliest representations of these neoclassical design elements were painted onto rectangular signboards, as the Connecticut arms on E. Marsh's sign, circa 1798 (cat. 12). But sign makers soon began to cut the signboards themselves to these shapes, fixing them into the rectangular outlines of frames or allowing them to swing freely (cat. 18, 21). The maker of the Joseph Porter sign, circa 1820–25, pursued this design impulse to near excess, setting an oval picture field within a shield-shaped signboard (fig. 13).

Although traditional designs continued to be made in significant numbers, tavern signs of the 1820s increasingly shifted orientation from vertical to horizontal. An oval shape, also turned ninety degrees, typified the 1830s. Sev-

Fig. 15. *Sign for Hemingway's Tavern and Churchill's Inn*, circa 1836 and 1838, Harwinton, Conn. CHS, cat. 49, side 2. An early attempt to remove the upper layer of paint partially revealed "HEMINGWAY STORE and TAVERN".

eral of these signs survive with their original iron scrolls applied to the perimeter, lending an airy delicacy to these otherwise solid masses (fig. 15). In a similar vein, the large Harrington inn sign of 1833 and the Thompson Hotel sign are shaped with languid curves and scrolls in such a way as to liberate their profiles from the blocky rectangle (cat. 41, 43).

From the late 1820s on, most signs were rectangles, larger in overall dimensions than before (often requiring two people to lift them) and were made more substantial by bold, deeply coved moldings around the edges. The massiveness of these signs provided a suitable background for large, block lettering that announced clearly and prominently the name of the establishment. The change in scale, both in overall size and decoration, likely responded more to changing circumstances in cities and towns than to any sense of fashion or taste. Taller and more numerous buildings, better roads and transportation, and more business establishments translated into increasing competition for the traveler's attention. The larger signs were easier to see, and their visual messages to read. Unlike earlier signs that often had detailed, sometimes narrative, pictures, the later signs tended to rely more heavily on words set off by color, texture, and painted ornamental devices. In short, these signs measured a change in the speed of life.

Sign Making

Fabrication of tavern signs drew upon a range of traditional trades. Foremost among these were woodworking and sign painting. The latter was a specialty of painting on wood for outdoor use, typically encompassing house and ship painting, and occasionally ornamental painting in rooms and on fire buckets and the like. Sign decoration sometimes involved wood carving, and application of smalt, metal foil, ornamental ironwork, and other specialized treatments in addition to painting. It differed from—and occasionally served as training for—portraiture and miniature painting executed by artists who worked for members of polite society. Several published manuals addressed aspects of sign painting and decoration (see Chapter 6); however, the written record offers limited information on the actual fabrication of wooden signs. At best, woodworkers' accounts merely verify that a particular artisan made a sign for someone at a certain time. On 16 June 1800, sign painter Abner Reed of East Windsor recorded in his account book that he "bro[ugh]t L. Terry's sign from Birges. / P.M. painted it. 11s."[3] Although the identity of Reed's employee "P.M." is unknown, Jonathan Birge (1765–1820), a cabinetmaker, also in East Windsor, is probably the individual noted. A Boston, Massachusetts, bill of 1797 records "making a sign the molding worked out of solid, [hanging] irons and screws, putting up ditto at your shop for the Dispensatory $7.00." An accompanying receipt reveals that the painting of this sign cost thirty dollars.[4] Thomas Janvier, a skilled cabinetmaker of Cantwell's Bridge (Odessa), Delaware, recorded making two signs in May 1796, for £1.06.03 each, about the cost of making a side chair.[5] Given the paucity of documentary references, the best evidence about the making of these signs lies in their physical properties.

The range of designs and construction techniques in use at any one time suggests that signs were made by woodworkers of various skill levels and specialties, from house carpenters and joiners at one end of the spectrum to more accomplished furniture makers at the other. Because the demand for sign making was low, it was itself not a recognized specialty—as opposed to sign painting. The mix of woodworking skills represented by a single sign included shaping and finishing boards, cutting moldings into rails and other components, turning large framing elements, and assembling parts with mortise and tenon joints. Despite the variety of tasks, in most cases the complexity or refinement required to execute each one did not exceed the capabilities of a single worker. However, some signs are sufficiently heavy or large that they may have required more than one maker at different stages of their manufacture, a role readily filled by less skilled day laborers, piece workers, or apprentices.

Signs were made of boards either set into structural frames or decorated with moldings applied to the edges.[6] The signboards themselves were either made from a single board or created by joining two or more narrower boards at their edges. Over time, some signboard seams have opened up to reveal the kinds of joints used. The simplest were edge-to-edge glue joints, many of which have held up remarkably well. Tongue-and-groove joints required more work but produced a stronger joint. Sometimes the boards were held together by a narrow spline or batten that fitted into grooves cut into each board edge. Yet another technique employed tabs of wood, or "floating tenons," that were glued into mortises cut into each board edge.

The majority of eighteenth-century signs and many early-nineteenth-century examples were boards set within a structural frame. The simplest frames were rails and stiles, assembled with mortise-and-tenon joints. Channels in the inner edges of the rectangular frame held the sign panel in place. Additional pieces of wood, cut to shape, were often added to the top and bottom rails to become ornamental pediments and skirts. More elaborate frames incorporated decoratively turned posts joined by rails that in turn supported the signboard (fig. 16a). These objects required a higher level of woodworking skills, especially to engineer the

joints properly. Two signs offer a case in point. In Edward Bull's Sign of the Black Horse, the signboard slides into long, rectangular holes (i.e., mortises) cut through each of the rails (fig. 17a). Each rail joins the upright post with side-by-side tenons that fit into side-by-side mortises, a time-consuming and exacting joint to cut. In contrast, the nineteenth-century sign for Baker's inn also has long mortises in the rails to hold the signboard, but uses single, rather than double, tenons (fig. 17b). Over time, one of the tenons sheared along the grain of the wood and failed. The double tenon joint held properly, but it was not efficient to make. Other signs attributed to the same maker as the Edward Bull sign suggest that he resolved the conflict between durability and economy. In these examples, two side-by-side rails enclose the signboard (instead of the single, solid rail). Using the end of each narrow rail as a tenon produced paired tenons far more easily than cutting that vexing double tenon in a solid rail (fig. 17c).

The eighteenth-century sign for Aaron Bissell's tavern exhibits a simple, but noteworthy, variation of turned-post frame construction (cat. 7). Here, the columns are doweled through rails that lie flat rather than on end (fig. 16b). Finials and drops cap the dowels, much like the construction of flat stretchers and turned legs in William and Mary style case furniture. Unlike the more substantial mortise-and-tenoned frames that support the weight of the signboard, this lighter-constructed frame is purely ornamental. The iron hanging straps must be attached to the signboard itself instead of the top rail, or the frame would be pulled apart by the weight of the sign.

In some signs, the signboard swings freely from metal hinges attached to the top rail of the frame (cat. 18, 19, 21, 26). Style considerations alone, namely the introduction of oval and shield-shaped signboards, caused this change in construction. Some makers fixed the shaped boards to the top and bottom rails, and sometimes the side posts as well, but those compositions did not seem to float within the frame (cat. 13, 30). The use of swinging signboards passed out of favor as styles changed.

Signs with applied moldings were made throughout the eighteenth and nineteenth centuries. Moldings helped to stabilize and protect signboards while setting off the picture plane. Sign makers achieved similar visual effects in one of three ways. One, molding strips were applied to the faces of the signboard. Two, they were nailed into the edges. In either case, additional strips of shaped wood might be added along the inside edges of the molding and signboard to increase the complexity of the molding profile. Or, three, the signboard edges slipped into a channel cut into the molding,

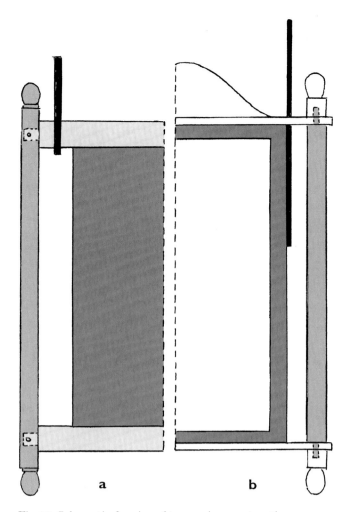

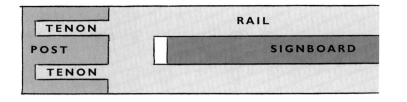

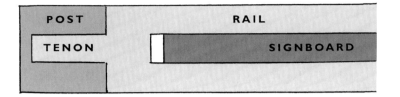

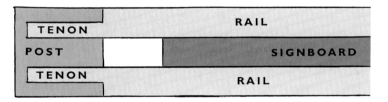

Fig. 16. Schematic drawing of tavern sign construction, contrasting horizontally- and vertically- oriented joints. The most common manner of joining the frame is horizontally-oriented (a): the horizontal rails are tenoned into the vertical posts, with wooden pins preventing the joint from pulling apart. In the alternative, vertically-oriented method (b), the vertical posts are doweled up and down into the horizontal rails (based on cat. 7). In this vertically-oriented construction, hanging hardware must be attached directly to the signboard itself, as the framing does not provide structural support. Numerous internal variations occur in the cutting of the joints themselves, as detailed in fig. 17. Drawing by author.

Fig. 17. Cross-section view of signboard in frame, contrasting construction with single (a,b) and double rails (c). Using a single rail requires that the craftsman cut a long mortise hole for the signboard to fit through, as well as tenons at each end. Double tenons (a) are stronger but more time-consuming to cut; single tenons (b) are quicker to cut but vulnerable to sheering or splitting along the grain of the wood between mortise and tenon. Using double rails greatly simplifies construction (c). The signboard fits between the two rails, eliminating the need to cut a mortise; and each rail-end serves as a tenon, reducing the amount of cutting required. Drawing by the author, based on cat. 1 (a); cats. 3, 6 (b); cat. 29 (c).

Fig. 18. *Sign for Daniel Loomis's Inn*, signed by William Rice, circa 1820, Coventry, Conn. CHS, cat. 27. Detail, upper corner of sign, depicting original iron hardware attachment and the characteristic coped molding found on signs from the Rice shop in Hartford. The end of the framing member that is parallel to the horizontal grain of the signboard is cut to slide over the molded profile of the vertical framing member. This movement is intended to accommodate expansion and contraction of the large signboard due to changes in humidity.

a technique used most often in the larger signs of the 1820s and later, notably those by William Rice. Rice signs often exhibit another refinement. Rather than being cut to a miter in the corners, the ends of the moldings applied to the long sides (i.e., horizontally oriented and parallel to the grain of the wood) were shaped to fit the curved inside contour of the short-side moldings (fig. 18). In theory, this construction allowed the one set of moldings to slide over the other without splitting or warping as the large wood panel expanded and contracted with moisture changes. In practice, the bottom moldings were free to move and exhibit the effectiveness of this design today. However, the upper moldings were held in place by the L-shaped hanging straps that Rice used, and consequently several of these moldings have pulled away from the signboard as it has shrunk over time.

The complex design vocabularies rendered in turnings, pediment and sign shapes, ornamental devices, decorative borders, and lettering and numbers all marked the passing of time. Several, but not all, of these changes can be linked to broader style periods of shared characteristics. Most notably, such neoclassical motifs as shield and oval shapes, urn turnings, and stylized vines came into and fell from use coincidentally with changes in decorative arts and architecture. Other changes can be arranged chronologically but without any evident association with a particular style period. Decorative turnings, which factor significantly into the overall ornament of signs, are a case in point. In general, the bolder and more fully articulated examples are earlier, becoming simpler, more uniform, and less robust through time. Certain compositions, notably the bisymmetrical arrangement of ring-and-baluster (or vase) turnings, recall decoratively turned stretchers on chairs, whereas elongated balusters suggest similarly turned rear posts (see figs. 21–22). However, neither type of turning fits neatly into a particular style period. Instead, turning profiles seem to depend more upon local practices than formal styles.

Sign Decorating

Like construction, sign painting exhibits a broad range of skill levels. Some signs, such as the 1808 Angell tavern sign and the David Loomis inn sign of 1811, appear to have been painted by the craftsmen who constructed them, craftsmen who were evidently more experienced at woodworking than at painting (cat. 20, 22). Palettes are limited to readily available pigments, namely black, white, and earth tones; pictorial and graphic designs are rudimentary; and composition relies upon simple conventions and often shows inadequate planning. The overall effect can be immensely charming to modern eyes and must also have appealed to viewers at the time of manufacture. Elijah Fitch (1778–1841), innkeeper in

Bolton, Connecticut (fig. 19), for example, patronized the same unschooled and anonymous maker of the David Loomis sign.

Trained painters executed signs that are readily recognized by their elegant and sometimes complex images rendered in a broad range of colors, often enhanced by such specialized materials as gold leaf and crushed colored glass, called smalt.[7] Precision, clarity, balance, and creativity are but some of the properties that distinguish these works. Certainly, the large body of signs by William Rice represents the high end of the trade, but other sign painters, equally well-trained and accomplished—yet anonymous—created such bold statements as the Temperance Hotel sign (cat. 54) and Jared Carter's "Stranger's Resort" (cat. 33), which may represent the work of Solomon Jones and Thomas K. Bush, sign painters of Middletown, Connecticut, who advertised in the *Middlesex Gazette* in 1823, the year the sign was probably made.

Some sign painters evidently incorporated carving as a decorative technique. Written sources describing this technique are essentially nonexistent, and the physical evidence can be ambiguous at times. It is clear that lettering was typically laid out by scratching, or "scribing," guidelines into the signboard with an awl or similarly pointed instrument. On some signs, the image as well as the lettering reveals the presence of incised lines that outline or define major elements.[8] Close inspection of these lines indicates that they were cut with a knife rather than scribed. Knife blades separated, rather than crushed, the grain of the wood, leaving a neater cut (fig. 20). The lines may have followed direct drawing on the signboard as well as transferral of the image from a pattern or other source. Some sign decorators then carved away a thin layer of the entire background, leaving the central image or lettering raised about one-sixteenth of an inch or less, as on such signs as Edward Bull's Black Horse, 1749; Zenas Dyer's Beehive and Plow, painted around 1823 by leading Hartford sign painter William Rice; Aaron Fox's inn sign, circa 1834; and the Chafee House, made after the Civil War (cat. 1, 34, 45, 58). Surface relief enhanced the clarity of the signs, which must have been coated with dust and dirt from time to time. The delicacy of work can be surprising, especially for an outdoor sign intended to be seen from a distance.

Styles of lettering and numbering also mark time. Although many variations existed at any one period, as perusal of typeface pattern books attests, certain practices are revealing. Eighteenth-century numbering commonly allowed certain numbers, notably 7s and 9s, to drop below the bottom level of 1s, 4s, and 6s. The use of a modified *f* for the letter *s*

Fig. 20. *Sign for Fox's Inn*, circa 1834, probably Norwich, Conn. CHS, cat. 45. Detail of capital letter, "A" in raking light, showing surface relief. The cleanness of cuts across the wood grain suggests that this lettering was cut with a knife rather than scribed.

Fig. 19. *Sign for Fitch's Inn*, circa 1810, Bolton, Conn. © Collection of The New-York Historical Society. Probably made for Elijah Fitch (1778-1841), who operated a tavern in Bolton from 1810 until his death. The idiosyncratic lettering helps link this simple sign to the 1811 David Loomis inn sign, from the village of Westchester, located about 15 miles south of Bolton (cat. 22).

in the Grosvenor Inn sign (cat. 60), as well as the raised pellet separating the initial and name, were common printing and engraving practices that fell out of favor by about 1790 and 1810, respectively. Block lettering with shading to make it appear three-dimensional did not occur before the 1820s. Punctuation also changed. Into the 1830s, commas were regularly used to separate initials from surnames, and just about anything served as apostrophes. Periods commonly followed names and the word "inn" or "hotel" throughout the period of study.

Place

The many idiosyncrasies in sign construction and ornamentation raise questions of whether patterns of geographical manufacture and use can be discerned and, if so, how they can be interpreted. Was there anything special about tavern signs made in Connecticut or in particular regions within the state? Such regional identification rests on recognition of common practices in the use of certain materials, construction techniques, and/or decorative features. Moreover, to be significant, these common denominators must be unlike those used in other regions. To a limited degree, some signs do embody local characteristics that allow them to be placed within defined areas or places. In contrast to regional or

local features observed in furniture and some other decorative objects, however, there are few recognizable properties that distinguish Connecticut signs from others made elsewhere in the Northeast.

Construction of signs varied enormously, but wood types did not. Throughout Connecticut and the rest of New England signs were made predominantly of white pine, a wood that was plentiful, responded easily to being worked, and weathered well. Some signs include other woods, notably maple or birch, ash or chestnut, and other native hardwoods. Of the other materials found on signs—pigments, smalt, gold leaf, iron—none is limited to any definable region or locale in Connecticut or the rest of New England and New York. European signs, in contrast, were not made of white pine and differed in their design vocabulary (cat. 65).

Construction practices are too diverse to form recognizable patterns of regional scale. Further study of surviving signs may eventually identify shop-level practices such as the peculiar contoured-corner join of many William Rice signs. But it seems unlikely that such shop traditions will aggregate into recognizable differences on a regional basis. The nature of sign making may simply have been too episodic—limited demand being supplied by many kinds of woodworkers—to conform to predictable construction patterns of the type observed in furniture studies. As the study of signs proceeds, however, choices of decorative details and images may provide useful clues for sorting signs by geographical origin.

Another aspect of change across the land that is visible in architecture, furniture, and certain other artifact types occurred between urban and rural areas. Urban areas generally provided greater specialization and better quality in the various trades as well as more demanding and discerning buyers. These factors produced objects that show better materials and more sophisticated techniques and express more clearly and exactly the prevailing principles of style and taste. But here, too, tavern signs do not exhibit significant or predictable patterns. Thus, a relatively urbane sign such as the General Wolfe portrait (cat. 4) was used in the small, rural town of Brooklyn. One likely explanation for the absence of urban/rural patterns recognizes that many taverns and inns were sited along travel routes that not only conveyed people but served as information highways. Consequently, a tavern located many miles away from urban centers might still be closely linked to the cultural ideas and values of those centers by the stream of travelers.

Reading Shapes and Images

Signs were made to communicate practical information required for daily living, which they did through both words and the visual language of shapes and images. Selection of certain words, shapes, and images inherently responded to specific wants and needs, but they were also influenced by traditions and conventions that were most probably not subject to much discussion or negotiation between sign maker and buyer. Although inclusion of a date signaled a particular event, the phrase "Entertainment by" was in common use and could apply to almost any circumstance. Likewise, placement of names and words along the bottom of the rectangular sign plane, sometimes segregated in a band, was standard practice, paralleling the composition of widely distributed engraved portraits on paper. Shaped by the beliefs and practices of the culture in which they were made, signs also communicated deeper cultural meanings and values through less direct or obvious signals. Evidence for these deeper messages exists primarily in the form of inferences that the modern historian can read into the objects to help elucidate how they functioned in their time.

Numerous parallels can be observed between signs and other contemporary artifacts, at least some of which must have been evident to makers, buyers, and those who saw tavern signs. The arrangement of signboard, turned posts, and pediment in eighteenth-century signs echoes that of the back,

posts, and crest rails of early-eighteenth-century "great chairs" (figs. 21–22). Pediment designs of several eighteenth-century tavern signs resemble the scroll pediments of grandly conceived exterior doors on houses and important buildings as well as imposing secretaries or high chests of drawers in the homes of prosperous and influential members of the community. Certain signs, especially some made around 1800, are unambiguous adaptations of contemporary looking glasses. For example, except for the simplified double-ogee skirt, the Marsh's inn signboard and pediment imitate the shape of looking glasses often associated with New York City (cat. 12).[9] Two other signs at the Shelburne Museum and Winterthur are literal translations of looking glasses with ornate foliated and scrolled silhouettes.[10] Although no precise reasons for these linkages can be suggested, the connections indicate that, like the objects they imitate, signs required a sense of design. Well into the nineteenth century, unadorned, purely utilitarian signboards were not appropriate road signs.

Sign design was not accidental. Even before a traveler or stranger in town could read the words or make out an image, the outlines of tavern signs and their placement in front of the appropriate buildings communicated the essential information, much as does a modern stop sign. Yet more than merely marking which domestic structure took in boarders, a tavern sign must have conveyed to travelers a sense of genteel domesticity, an awaiting haven from the apprehensions and discomfort of the stranger's world. Because strangers had no recognized place or status in unfamiliar communities of colonial times, signs that directed them to sources of "provisions and lodging in some comfortable manner" enforced social order and codes of conduct that surpassed mere physical comfort. Laws passed in the early years of New England settlement required that each town provide at least "one sufficient inhabitant to keep an Ordinary [i.e., tavern or inn] . . . that such passengers and strangers may know where to resort." Duly regulated establishments accommodated the needs of those who did not belong and who were perceived by community leaders to be potentially disruptive to the careful ranking and position of each resident.[11] Perhaps coincidentally, increasing variety in size, form, and placement of signs occurred after the relaxation of local-government price controls on the serving of liquor after the Revolution and the restructuring of some tavern businesses to cater to specific segments of the population or to certain types of travelers.

As more decorative details on the sign came into focus or grew familiar through repeated visits, the tavern-goer acquired impressions of the character of the establishment (a character that was not necessarily realized). Choice of a

Fig. 21. *Sign for Bull's Inn*, 1749, Center-brook, Conn. CHS, cat. 1, side 2. The text of this sign, the earliest in the CHS collection, displays idiosyncratic spelling and orthography typical of eighteenth-century signs: a reversed "7" and the word "hors". The overall organization of the sign echoes that of contemporary chair backs. Its turnings, more complex and ornate than those on later signs, resemble those on chair stiles and stretchers (see fig. 22). Not shown to scale: the sign is actually taller (48-1/2") than the chair (46-1/2").

Fig. 22. *Armchair*, probably Wethersfield area, Conn., 1760-90. CHS, Bequest of George Dudley Seymour. The banister back bears a close resemblance to the form of early Connecticut inn signs.

name usually referred to the owner or to a generic emblem such as Black Horse or Red Lion, but the General Wolfe and Duke of Cumberland taverns (cat. 2, 4) appropriated the likenesses of those notable figures for whatever benefit might accrue to the owners. Inclusion of the word "inn," and later "hotel," also communicated a desire to be perceived in a more particular way.

Some signs communicated by direct representations of everyday things. Pictures of wine bowls, grape clusters, decanters, and wine glasses unambiguously signaled avail-ability of wine and spirits within. Whereas horses, bulls, and suns were relatively imprecise, eagles, state and national coats of arms, personifications of Liberty, and related sym-bols were explicitly patriotic and national. Sign painter William Rice seems to have built on these sympathies by juxtaposing a powerful eagle with a lion in chains on oppo-site sides of his signs, notably the Arah Phelps inn sign of around 1826 (cat. 37). A. N. Mason's inn sign, from the 1840s, appealed to more local sentiments and lore in its depiction of a man hiding the Connecticut charter in a hol-low tree, presumably the celebrated "Charter Oak" (cat. 51). Incorporation of Masonic symbols, whose specific meanings

were not publicly known, into the painted design radiated prestige in addition to signaling membership in this interna-tional network of like-minded men.

One particularly playful use of images entailed substituting a picture for a word or syllable. Called a rebus, it challenged the viewer to decode or solve the picture puzzle.[12] One such puzzle is the Read sign, which features a tree prominently displayed on each side (cat. 5). That alone is not perplexing, but a single yellow circle centered in the pediment is con-founding—unless this sign is "read" (coincidentally, note the play on this word) as a rebus: son (sun) of liberty (tree), a very timely allusion in 1768, when the sign was made. Another word picture of note, not technically a rebus but an image intended to be read, is the 1786 Woodward tavern sign, which carries a "bird-in-hand" picture on each side (cat. 8). More than merely a representation of a popular aphorism, it is a fitting reminder to both innkeeper and cus-tomers that future promises—the two birds in the bush, or debts payable at some future time—do not compare to what is in hand.

And Time Again . . .

Signs that remained in use for decades—even generations—show the topography of wear. Lead-white painted backgrounds are worn away, exposing the bare, somewhat silvery pine boards beneath. Colors of the lettering and image are muted, sometimes mere ghosts of what they once were. Undulating ridges of hard and soft growth rings in turned posts and rails of the frames substitute texture for color. In repainted signs, earlier names, dates, or pictorial images sometimes show through superimposed decoration as subtle raised outlines visible only when light catches them. On other signs, later images may have worn away to expose earlier images, also worn, creating a kind of double exposure.

The effects of weathering often erode and obscure fine details of workmanship, but they can also produce aesthetically pleasing results. Weathering can create new color patterns that enhance visual qualities of massing, notably on decorative turnings; it mellows and softens color palettes; and, most remarkably, it sometimes sculpts surfaces of painted detail in ways that are simply amazing to behold. The painted backgrounds of signboards typically received fewer coats of paint than did images and letters, which were usually painted over the background color. The additional protection from the elements afforded these multilayered areas on the signboard reduced erosion and wear, thus leaving them standing above weathered backgrounds. In some

instances, notably the ratlines of the ship pictured in the Hayden inn sign, the soft relief profiles exhibit all the lavish detail and intricacy of a sixteenth-century cabinet panel carved for European nobility (figs. 24a–24b).

The visual properties of such heavily weathered or reused signs can be confusing or difficult to read. Painted images of later date superimposed on wooden signboards and frames of an earlier style are not "pure" statements but express mixed messages. One of the basic challenges of signs is that they seem to lie outside the usual models of object appreciation and investigation. Inherent in the design and intention of these paintings and woodworkings is outdoor use, including all of the effects of exposure, like patina on a medieval bronze. Longevity, usually marked by reuse, enriches certain qualities of signs. Superimposed decorative layers fascinate us as a kind of stop-action picture of change over time, not unlike the captivating image of Marcel Duchamp's Cubist painting of *Nude Descending a Staircase, No. 2*, 1912, inspired by the stop-motion photography of the 1880s by Eadweard Muybridge, Thomas Eakins, and others (fig. 25). Blended images, freed from the constraints of representing a single time or reality, can also assume qualities that evoke other currents in twentieth-century art.

To the degree that historical references contribute to the appeal of tavern signs, multiple images and names transform

24A

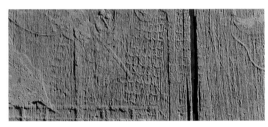

24B

Fig. 25. Marcel Duchamp, *Nude Descending a Staircase, No. 2*, oil on canvas, 1912. Philadelphia Museum of Art: The Louise and Walter Arensberg Collection. © 2000 Artist Rights Society (ARS), New York/ADAGP, Paris/Estate of Marcel Duchamp. Duchamp, like certain photographers of the 1880s, captured movement and changes over time in a single work through super-imposing images, not unlike some tavern signs with multiple images.

certain signs into compelling and memorable objects that outshine single-image counterparts. Additional names associated with a sign typically enable historians to link it to specific owners and a specific time and place, whereas single names may not. A search in the historical record for "A. Hinman's" identity, for example, yielded the names of several appropriate innkeepers at work in Connecticut when the sign was probably made (cat. 13). Sequential images on the same signboard stand as incontrovertible evidence of changing values and modes of expression. Some signs document the vitality of national iconography and symbolism in the early years of the nation: the Blatchly sign, with dates of 1788 and 1794, displays an allegorical figure of Justice, an American flag, and two maritime compositions (fig. 26). In other signs, notably for the Abbe Inn and Tea Room and the Village Hotel, simple letters on a black field covered gloriously rendered American eagles (cat. 19, 24). Thus, a single object may not only be double-sided, such as signs that pair state and national symbols, but may supply four sources of history and fascination.

That many signs exhibit repainted and altered names and images testifies to the dynamic qualities of the history and creative processes associated with them. Integral to the value owners ascribed to them was an expectation that they be updated or revitalized when necessary. Signs were not to be discarded—or preserved. Preservation efforts began only when signs began to acquire a sense of belonging to a glorified past. Thus, it is not unreasonable to consider those pristine examples as essentially unused and nonrepresentative, although not without significance. A case in point is Carter's "Strangers' Resort" sign (cat. 33). The sign differs from most others in its name, subject, and painting style. Carter had it painted around 1823 to help advertise his pioneering efforts to create a "resort," a place of refreshment beyond mere thirst. His idea failed. Within a few years the business fell into arrears, the property was sold, and the sign came down and was preserved by the family through several generations.

As inn and tavern signs marked places of business in their

26B

26A

Fig. 26. *Sign for Blatchly's Inn*, 1788 and 1794, Madison, Conn. CHS, cat. 10, side 1. This sign, shown during treatment at Williamstown Art Conservation Center, presented one of the most complex surface histories in the collection. On this side, an allegorical figure holding the scales of justice had been painted, circa 1794, over an earlier image of a fully-rigged sailing vessel; the allegorical figure itself was repainted and "improved" by an early twentieth-century restorer. View (a) shows the sign with twentieth-century overpaint removed from the right half. View (b) illustrates the outline of the underlying sailing vessel, traced onto mylar under raking light; the mylar is superimposed over the sign in (a) to indicate the relationship between the two image layers.

day, so they now mark specific historical moments and aesthetic visions. They render in physical form the circumstances, talents, and visions of makers and users. They also preserve layers of meaning that enriched community life. In contrast to original users, who likely thought of tavern signs as simple bearers of simple messages, these signs invite multiple inquiries into their complex historical and cultural properties and structure.

The Connecticut Historical Society tavern sign collection is particularly well suited for inquiry. The objects considered here form the largest, most comprehensive collection of American signs in the world. Although primarily of Connecticut origin, these signs are not regional. That the collection is geographically focused is one of its great strengths: it provides depth, rich comparisons, and intimate portrayals. What these signs say about local people and conditions and about artistic accomplishment is broadly applicable to the American experience.

NOTES

1 *Builder's Dictionary*, 2 vols. (1734; reprint, Washington, D.C.: Association for Preservation Technology, 1981), s.v. "painting."

2 The notable exception to the shape is a square Rhode Island example, dated 1725, which may be the earliest surviving American tavern sign. This sign was not examined by the author; it is described as having been repainted. See Howard M. Chapin, "Rhode Island Signboards," *Rhode Island Historical Society Collections* 19, no. 1 (January 1926): 22; 19, no. 2 (April 1926): 54. The earliest surviving sign of any kind with an American history is that of Boston painter Thomas Child and his wife, Katherine. It was made in London before 1697, the first date on an addition made in Boston that squared the dimensions of the sign. See Jonathan L. Fairbanks and Robert F. Trent, eds., *New England Begins: The Seventeenth Century*, 3 vols. (Boston: Museum of Fine Arts, 1982), no. 451, vol. 3, pp. 477–78. Also square is another early trade sign, dated 1718 and reportedly from Providence, Rhode Island; Chapin, "Rhode Island Signboards," 19, no. 1 (January 1926): 21; 19, no. 2 (April 1926): 58.

3 The Connecticut Historical Society, *Morgan B. Brainard's Tavern Signs* (Hartford: Connecticut Historical Society, 1958), p. 11; "Connecticut Cabinetmakers, Part I," *Connecticut Historical Society Bulletin* 32, no. 4 (October 1967): 108. Additional information about Birge appears in Penrose R. Hoopes, *Shop Records of Daniel Burnap, Clockmaker* (Hartford: The Connecticut Historical Society, 1958).

4 Bill from woodworker Thomas Clements to the Boston Dispensary and receipt from painter John Johnston, quoted in Nina Fletcher Little, *Paintings by New England Provincial Artists, 1775–1800* (Boston: Museum of Fine Arts, 1976), p. 140.

5 Charles G. Dorman, *Delaware Cabinetmakers and Allied Artisans, 1655–1855* (Wilmington: Historical Society of Delaware, 1960), p. 98.

6 Of the sixty-five tavern and inn signs in the Connecticut Historical Society collection, only one sign was originally made without decorative moldings or a frame: the curved-silhouetted Harrington inn sign, 1833 (cat. 43).

7 An early discussion of smalt and its application appears in *Builder's Dictionary*, s.v. "smalt."

8 This practice is difficult to quantify because paint and erosion readily obscure these guidelines.

9 Charles F. Montgomery, *American Furniture: The Federal Period* (New York: Viking Press, 1966), nos. 214–15, pp. 262–63.

10 Charles Banner sign, dated 1806, illustrated in Helene Smith, *Tavern Signs of America: Catalog* (Greensburg, Pa.: McDonald/Swärd Pub. Co., 1988), p. 34; unpublished S. Bean sign dated 1824 at Winterthur (acc. no. 60.218).

11 The first Connecticut law was passed 3 June 1644; quoted in Chapter 4.

12 Two engraved rebuses printed in London in 1778 and presented as letters exchanged between England and America are reproduced in E. McSherry Fowble, *Two Centuries of Prints in America, 1680–1880; A Selective Catalogue of the Winterthur Museum Collection* (Charlottesville: University Press of Virginia for the Henry Francis du Pont Winterthur Museum, 1987), pp. 164–65.

Fig. 27. Photograph of *Sign for Wadsworth's Inn* (cat. 55), as found in barn by collector Morgan Brainard, circa 1916. CHS Library.

"Some suitable Signe . . . for the direction of Strangers": *Signboards and the Enterprise of Innkeeping in Connecticut*

By Margaret C. Vincent

Between 1750 and 1850, more than five thousand signs hung at different times in front of taverns, inns, and hotels in Connecticut. Thus, the extensive collection in the Connecticut Historical Society—some fifty signs from identifiable local establishments—represents barely 1 percent of those which were made during this era. To put this collection in context, ongoing research has identified nearly three hundred additional American inn signs, including at least forty-five from Connecticut, in both public and private collections. Documentary references to dozens of signs that have not survived have also been collected. Furthermore, extensive documentation on the business of innkeeping in Connecticut makes possible certain conclusions about all five thousand signs, plus those that were made in the years prior to 1750.[1]

The Earliest Signs

Although the earliest extant Connecticut inn sign bears the date 1749, the history of Connecticut inns began a century earlier. In 1644, a few years after the first English settlers arrived in Connecticut, leaders enacted a law that read, in part:

Whereas many strayngers & passengers that vppon occasion haue recourse to these Townes, and are streightened for waint of entertainment, It is now Ordered, that these seuerall Townes shall pruide amongst theselues in ech Town one sufficient inhabitant to keepe an Ordinary, for pruisio and lodgeing in some comfortable manner, that such passengers or strayngers may know where to resorte; and such inhabitants as by the seuerall Townes shall be chosen for the said searuice shall be prsented to two Magistrats, that they may be judged meet for that imployment, and this to be effected by the severall Townes wthin one month, under the penalty of 40s. a month, ech month ether Towne shall neglect yt.[2]

While it might seem that this law would immediately produce several new inns (or ordinaries, as they were commonly called until the early eighteenth century), only a few 1640s establishments are documented. In the year the law was passed, or perhaps a few years before, Thomas and Ann Ford opened what is believed to have been the first inn in Hartford. The separate New Haven Colony named William Andrews as its first tavern keeper in 1645. Windsor and Wethersfield, the only other Connecticut Colony towns in the 1640s, appointed innkeepers as early as 1648. Before 1650, these four establishments (and perhaps a few that cannot be documented), served the fifteen hundred or so residents of Connecticut and the handful of travelers who passed through the area.[3]

By the 1670s, some fifteen thousand Europeans were living in twenty-five towns scattered along the Connecticut River and the coast. A traveler on the main roads could usually find an inn in each town center and at a few other locations. For example, riding eastward along the coast, a traveler could stop at Christopher Comstock's in Norwalk, Henry Rowland's in Fairfield, Richard Beach's in Stratford, and Richard Bryan's in Milford, before reaching John Harriman's in New Haven.[4] Hartford was large enough to support more than one inn; in addition to the Fords, Joseph Mygatt, on the south side, near the present capitol, was licensed in 1656.[5] A few other ordinaries opened at places where travelers needed refreshment. John Bissell (1648) at Windsor, Richard Smith, Jr. (1675) at Wethersfield, and John Whittlesey (1662) at Saybrook, all ran ordinaries at their ferry stations along the Connecticut River, as did their several successors.[6] Further, in 1662 Jonathan Gilbert, an innkeeper and fur trader in Hartford, was granted a license to keep an ordinary in Cold Spring (present day Meriden), a convenient stopping place halfway between Hartford and New Haven.[7]

Whether signs hung in front of these early inns is unknown. It is possible that at first signs were unnecessary, given the

Fig. 28. *Sign for Arah Phelps's Inn*, signed by William Rice, circa 1826, North Colebrook, Conn. CHS, cat. 37, side 2.

Fig. 29. Page from *Timothy Root's Account Book*, 1743, Farmington, Conn., with *copper engraving plate for Root's hat labels*, circa 1740. Courtesy, Stanley-Whitman House, Farmington. Root's account book records charges to Thomas Croswel of Hartford for entertainment, dinner, punch, wine, and wheat. Root's house was located near the intersection of Main Street and Meadow Road (on what is now Hatter's Lane).

small number of residents and travelers. But, clearly, without a sign an inn was visually unremarkable, looking identical to the surrounding dwellings. As the number of homes grew, travelers had increasing difficulty in finding the place to stay. Finally, a 1672 Connecticut Colony law ordered

that every person licensed for Common Entertainment shall have some suitable Signe set up in the view of all Passengers for the direction of Strangers where to go, where they may have entertainment; and such as shall have no such Sign by the first of SEPTEMBER 1673. *shall pay a fine of* TWENTY SHILLINGS *to the Public Treasury, and so* TWENTY SHILLINGS *every quarter of a year till they have effected the same.*[8]

Sadly, not one of the three dozen or so signs required by the 1672 law survives today. Nor do any of the two hundred or so additional signs presumably erected between 1672 and 1749. Note that the law itself did not specify the nature of the signs, only that they had to be "suitable." Nothing is known of their shape, and little is known of their decoration. Indeed, the form the new Connecticut Colony signs took may not have mattered; just having a signboard might have been all that was necessary to identify the building as the public house.

Only a few surviving references—mostly from the cities

where multiple taverns required some form of distinction— shed light on the appearance of these early signs. For example, Alexander Hamilton's 1744 travel diary records a "Half-moon" in New Haven and an "Anchor" in New London.[9] Information from other colonies suggests additional designs, for example, the Sun, Cross, Swan, and Salutation taverns in Boston in 1731.[10] Given these few available references, it seems likely that the very earliest Connecticut signs were copies of those already known in Great Britain. Larwood and Hotten's *History of Signboards* cites a list of London tavern signs, from a pamphlet by "Taylor, the water-poet," written during the reign of Charles I (1625–49). Two hundred signs bore only forty-three different images. Among these were angels, anchors, bells, bulls, bears, crowns, green dragons, white horses, lions, half moons, suns, and more.[11]

Interestingly, the black horse was not on this list, suggesting a possible American addition to the imported iconography. Even by the 1730s the black horse seems to have been used extensively in the colonies. The *Vade Mecum* of 1731 mentions two Black Horse taverns on the road from Boston to Londonderry, New Hampshire.[12] In addition, early accounts of Samuel and Sarah Flagg's Hartford inn suggest that it had a sign with a horse as early as 1732.[13] Thus, Edward Bull's sign, the only surviving pre-1750 Connecticut example, bearing the image of a horse in silhouette, can be

Fig. 30. *Rising Sun Tavern*, North Haven, Conn., photographed circa 1935. CHS Library. Traditionally called the "Rising Sun Tavern," this North Haven structure served as a tavern as early as 1771. Without its signboard, it looks like many other dwellings of its era. The photograph is one of a series taken by WPA photographers in the 1930s.

assumed to have been fairly typical of the mid-eighteenth-century inn sign (cat. 1).

Except for these few examples, we can only speculate about the images on the signs for even the most well-documented pre-1750 Connecticut inns. Consider, for example, Timothy Root on the western side of Farmington. Root was a hatter prior to obtaining his tavern license in about 1742, after which he ran both operations simultaneously for a few years. His extant account book records numerous Farmington neighbors buying hats and rum.[14] Scattered throughout is evidence that he also catered to strangers, and therefore by law he must have had an inn sign. Thirty-four men from other towns stopped at his tavern between 1742 and 1747 for rum, food, grain for animals, or occasionally a bed for the night. Only twelve of these thirty-four were regular customers. Did Root mark his house with one of the traditional British images? Or did he have a tavern sign with an image of a hat? Even he himself sheds no light, for on the paper insert he left in his hats, he merely identified himself as "Timothy Root/ Hatt-Maker/ Near the Litchfield Gate/ in/ Farmington" (fig. 29).[15]

Information about imagery on Connecticut inn signs improves for the third quarter of the eighteenth century, particularly with the establishment of various local newspa-

pers beginning in the 1760s. By this time, the seventeenth-century term, "ordinary" had almost disappeared from references. In the latter half of the eighteenth century, only "inn" and "tavern" were in widespread use, with the word "inn" statistically far more common in documentary references than the word "tavern." Although there may have been subtle differences in meaning, these two terms were sometimes used interchangeably. Neither "inn" nor "tavern" appeared on the signs themselves; rather, the word "entertainment" served to communicate the services provided, in conformity with the legislation requiring signage for "the direction of Strangers where to go, where they may have entertainment."

Existing data suggest that inn signage changed little between 1750 and 1775. For example, early issues of the *Connecticut Gazette* in New London featured several advertisements for named inns. In October 1766, Captain Coit advertised his New London tavern at "the Sign of the Red Lyon," and a month later there is a notice for "At the Sign of the SUN near [the] Ferry Wharf, . . . kept by Amos Hallam, A good House of Entertainment for Gentlemen Travellers."[16] A year and a half later, Charles Jeffery opened the "Sign of the Anchor" on the beach.[17] According to tradition, David Bull's Hartford tavern sign featured a bunch of grapes.[18] Along the road from Hartford to New York, the sign for the Hitchcock/Todd tavern in North Haven (fig. 30) pictured a "Rising Sun," and Samuel Penfield's Fairfield inn was known as the "Sun."[19] Rural inn signs included Isaac Lawrence's Brazen Bull in Canaan and William Bingham's "at the sign of Man and Horse" in Canterbury.[20]

At the end of the colonial period, we can document two types of imagery not found on earlier signs: coats of arms and portraits of famous heroes. According to tradition, John Peck's 1767 tavern in Lyme featured a sign with his family coat of arms (three anchors, a lion, and the words "hope and courage"). Both the British Royal Arms and the Scottish Royal Arms are found on extant Connecticut signs from this era (cat. 3, 62). Of heroes, we know that both British General James Wolfe and His Royal Highness, William Augustus, Duke of Cumberland, graced signs in other colonies as well as Connecticut (cat. 2,4).[21]

There may be a connection between new imagery and the Masons' use of taverns. Freemasonry in Connecticut had begun officially in 1750 with the founding of the New Haven Lodge, and it is well documented that the early lodges met in local taverns. New Haven innkeeper John Lothrop had a conspicuously Masonic sign, described in his 1769 *Connecticut Journal* ad as the "Sign of the Mason's Arms."[22] The Duke of Cumberland, featured on a Rocky Hill, Connecticut, inn sign, was not only a Mason but also a royal patron of

the fraternity; his death in 1766 prompted a special memorial observance at St. John's Lodge No. 4, Hartford (see cat. entry 2). However, not all taverns that hosted Masonic meetings had related signs. In 1763, the year of its founding, the St. John's Lodge No. 4 met at the Widow Sarah Flagg's inn in Hartford. Her tavern already had a black horse on its sign, and there is no indication that she changed her signage to acknowledge the Masonic presence.[23]

The hero signs also call attention to an evident correlation between tavern keeping and local militia rank, giving credence to the oral tradition that to be successfully voted captain, a candidate had to provide drinks for the company. Edward Bull is a typical example of a militia captain who kept a tavern (cat. 1). Militia records show his rise in the ranks of the North Saybrook trainband. He was elected ensign and sergeant in 1751, and was promoted to captain in 1753, holding that post until 1760. His tavern predated his rise to ensign by only two years. The argument becomes stronger when we look at the subsequent tavern keeper in North Saybrook, Benjamin Williams, who became—not coincidentally—the next ensign and captain of the militia.[24]

Similarities among inn signs in prerevolutionary Connecticut were partly a function of the similarities among the innkeepers themselves. Militia leadership was not the only characteristic Edward Bull had in common with his fellow

Fig. 31. *Tavern License of Mrs. Grace Grant*, Windsor, Conn., 1735. CHS Library. Grace Miner Grant was licensed to serve liquor annually beginning in 1715, five years after the death of her husband Samuel, who is not recorded as being a tavernkeeper. Not long after this license was issued, Grace passed the business on to her son, Ebenezer, a prosperous merchant, whose 1737 license also survives.

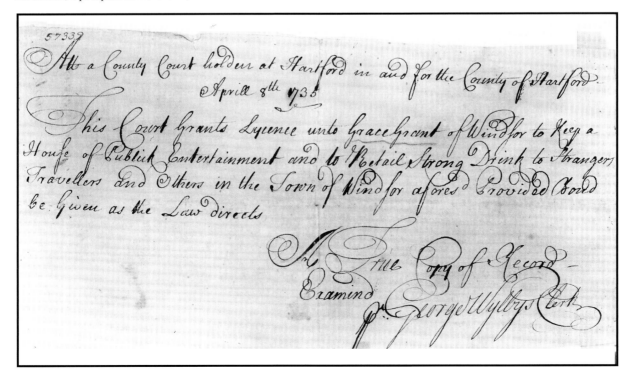

innkeepers. First, he was financially comfortable: when still an infant he had inherited a large amount of land from his father. In 1739 Edward married Temperance Clark and moved from Saybrook Point to the relatively young community called variously "Patapaug" or "Second Society," later called Centerbrook, five or six miles north. Town records indicate that, like his fellow innkeepers in other towns, Edward Bull was active in local government, serving variously in 1748 and later years as tithingman, lister, constable, and surveyor of highways. In several years he also served as a selectman from the Second Society, traveling to Saybrook Point for regular meetings. He was presumably literate, owning a number of religious books, and was also a member of the newly formed Second Society Congregational church, though he does not appear to have performed any particular duties there.

Not all colonial tavern keepers were men. Women had played a major role in running taverns even in the early years of the colony. The first licenses were sometimes issued jointly to husband and wife. Traveler's diaries relate just as many stories about landladies as their husbands. And some women were even nominally represented on colonial signs by the inclusion of their initial along with their husband's (cat. 2, 3). But what of the two or three dozen Connecticut women—all widows—who ran taverns by themselves prior to 1780?[25] What images and inscriptions were on their signs?

Approximately half of these independent women innkeepers inherited inns previously run by their deceased husbands, while the rest opened new establishments in their widowhood. Many are well documented, including Mrs. Grace Miner Grant (1670–1753), innholder in East Windsor from as early as 1715 until at least 1733 (fig. 31); Mrs. Dorothy Burnham of East Hartford (first licensed 1753); and Mrs. Abigail Stow Shaylor, innholder in Middletown from 1759 to 1781. In each case, the reputation accorded these women indicates that they knew their business and did it well.

Abigail Stow Shaylor, for example, took up innkeeping after having supported her children by running a shop—probably spinning and weaving—for nine years after her husband, ship captain Reuben Shalor, had been lost at sea. For the next two decades she ran one of the most active taverns in Connecticut. One could find a traveling doctor ("medicine salesman") at her house, arrange for boat passage, or meet boat travelers. The *Middlesex Gazette* records a large number of probate meetings held at her house, and she was regularly listed in the almanacs as the place to stay in Middletown. She even managed to please the rather fussy John Adams, who found her menu ("the finest and sweetest of Wheat Bread, and Butter, as yellow as Gold, and fine Radishes,

very good Tea and sugar") more to his liking than the Indian pudding and pork and greens served him the following day at Aaron Bissell's, in East Windsor.[26] Mrs. Shaylor's inn sign has not survived, but contemporary descriptions indicate no significant differences between her inn and those of her male neighbors. By extension, there is little reason to doubt that her sign and those of the other women tavern keepers were also essentially similar to those purchased by men.

Whatever its image, Mrs. Shaylor's sign had to compete in the landscape with a growing number of signs. The number of licensed inns located in Middletown center rose from just one in 1758 to six in 1760, and by 1762 a total of twenty-one innkeepers served in the ten villages and communities contained within Middletown's borders. In Connecticut, a "town" was and still is, legally, a large geographical area, sometimes several square miles, with at least one main settlement. As the colony's population grew, some towns split to form new towns. Others simply created multiple villages within their existing borders, each usually served by a single tavern. As in Middletown, the seventeen inns licensed by the town of Farmington in 1761 were dispersed among numerous villages, including what are today Farmington, Plainville, Southington, Bristol, Burlington, and Avon. Thus, although a traveler still rarely had a choice of taverns in any one location (outside the major cities), he could travel a few miles farther on and find another place to stay.[27]

The quantity of signs in the landscape increased dramatically throughout Connecticut in the third quarter of the eighteenth century. In 1750 there were probably only a hundred inns throughout Connecticut. By the beginning of the Revolution there may have been as many as five hundred Connecticut inns—more than seventy have been documented in 1776 in Windham County alone. It is easy to assume that the proliferation of inns was a result of the political upheavals, as lore about the Revolution identifies taverns as places in which patriots congregated. While it is true that revolutionary activities and militia activities were often found in or near taverns, the increase probably had as much to do with the settlement patterns of a fast-growing population.[28]

Revolutionary Changes

Following the Revolution, the number of taverns continued to grow, but at a less feverish rate: by 1800 there were over six hundred fifty licensed Connecticut innkeepers operating simultaneously. Increases were seen most notably in the cities. Hartford had fifteen taverns in 1798, most within a few blocks of the State House. Competition among the nearby taverns increased, so advertising in the local newspa-

Fig. 32. *Newspaper advertisement for William Richards's Coffee House, Middlesex Gazette*, Midddletown, Conn., 17 September 1791. CHS Library. The term, "coffee house," appeared most frequently in Connecticut port cities, and may have had a connotation of serving mariners.

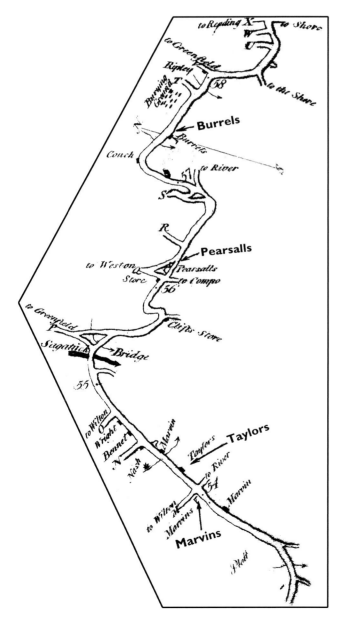

per became more common, as did references to an establishment as "at the sign of —," instead of "at the house of Mr. —." These references provide important information about signs no longer extant.[29]

No immediate changes can be discerned in the iconography of inn signs following the Revolution. Many colonial taverns continued to operate, and though some landlords repainted their signs to eliminate royal imagery, many did not. New establishments frequently adopted traditional imagery. For example, in 1792 Timothy Canfield "opened a House of ENTERTAINMENT, at the Sign of the HORSES, a few Rods North of the Printing-Office, in Middletown." New London was home to the "Fox and Grapes," while Hartford had both the "Beehive" and the "Lamb."[30]

Only in the 1790s did new images appear in significant numbers—most notably Masonic and patriotic symbols. Freemasonry in Connecticut experienced a resurgence in the 1790s, with the chartering of twenty new lodges. Western Star Lodge No. 37 in Norfolk, chartered in 1796, illustrates the strong connection between innkeeping and freemasonry—six of the thirteen charter members ran nearby inns. Benjamin Welch, Giles Pettibone, Jr., Joel Walter, and Ariel Lawrence all were (or later became) innkeepers in Norfolk, while Ovid Burrall and Arah Phelps ran inns in Canaan to the west and Colebrook to the east. Lawrence's sign, filled with Masonic symbols, suggests how prominent these images were becoming (cat. 11).[31]

The preeminent new tavern sign image of the 1790s was, of course, the eagle—clearly inspired by the great seal of the United States, which had been adopted in 1782. In 1791, William Richards opened in Middletown a new "Coffee-House . . . at the Sign of the spread Eagle, where he hopes the Attention to Customers, may be honored with their Approbation." Included in his advertisement is an engraving of a two-headed eagle, perhaps identical or similar to his sign (fig. 32).[32] Surprisingly few other eagles can be reliably asso-

Fig. 33. "From New York to Stratford [Conn.]" (detail), from Christopher Colles, *A Survey of the Roads of the United States of America* (New York, 1789). CHS Library. This segment of Colles's map records four taverns along a four-mile section of the post road between Norwalk and Fairfield, Connecticut: Marvin's, at the corner of the road to Wilton, mile 54; Taylor's, just east of Marvin's, along the main road; Pearsall's, at the crossroads to Weston, mile 56; and Burrel's, about one-half mile west of the Greenfield road. Colles's *Survey*, considered the earliest American road guide, promised travelers a wealth of useful information, including cross roads, intersecting watercourses (with and without bridges), the names of "the most noted inhabitants," churches (specified as Episcopal or Presbyterian), town houses, gaols, bridges, mills, blacksmiths' shops, and taverns (each marked with a tiny signpost).

Fig. 34. *Sign for Holcomb's Inn*, 1802, East Granby, Conn. Courtesy, St. Mark's Lodge No. 36, A.F.&A.M., Simsbury, Conn.

ciated with Connecticut tavern signs dated prior to 1800, in sharp contrast to the proliferation of political imagery in Philadelphia, the nation's capital during the 1790s. There, one could find the "Spread Eagle," the "Old Spread Eagle," and the "Sign [of the] Black Eagle," as well as the "Pennsylvania Arms" and the "Washington," among the seventy-one operating inns and taverns.[33]

If William Richard's inn sign paralleled surviving examples, it bore a new type of inscription, "W. Richards" rather than simply "W.R." The shift from initials to surnames may have corresponded to increased reliance by travelers on printed sources of information—maps and almanacs—that gave mileage and places to stay, identified by the innkeepers' last names, along major routes. These sources indicate increasing numbers of establishments, and presumably increasing competition. In 1744, Alexander Hamilton had passed only one inn on the eleven-mile, "exceeding rough and stonny" stretch between Norwalk and Fairfield, along the Long Island Sound shore in southwestern Connecticut. This was

"Mr. Taylor's . . . a man of 70."[34] Taylor's remained the only inn mentioned in almanacs like Bickerstaff's and Low's in the 1760s and 1770s. By 1789, however, Christopher Colles's road map records six establishments along the same road (fig. 33).[35] Major Ozias Marvin's is remembered today as a spot where George Washington stopped, but Samuel Pearsall's (sometimes spelled Passell's) was the only one of the six recommended to travelers in Bickerstaff's 1801 almanac, or the 1808 *Connecticut Register* list of "best innkeepers." It is logical to assume that Mr. Pearsall would have put his name on the sign, encouraging guide-reading travelers to stop at his place rather than at those of any of his competitors.[36]

A new shape also appeared in inn signs of the first decade of the nineteenth century. The orientation was still vertical, but the rectangular board was replaced by a free-hanging oval or shield-shaped board. Many of the extant examples bear Masonic motifs—at the simplest, the single emblem of square and compasses, symbolizing reason and faith (cat.

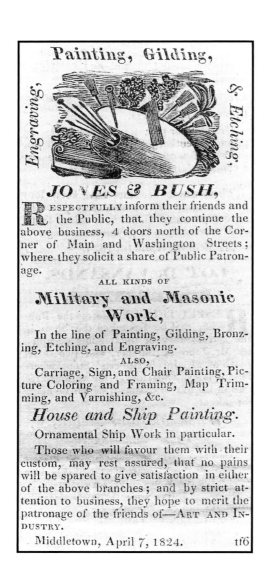

Fig. 35. *Newspaper advertisement for Jones & Bush, Middlesex Gazette,* Middletown, Conn., 7 April 1824. CHS Library. Like most ornamental painters, Solomon Jones and his partner Thomas K. Bush advertised a wide range of services in addition to signpainting.

33). A few elaborate signs are covered with Masonic imagery, as on Luther Holcomb's sign, from the Turkey Hills section of East Granby (fig. 34).[37] This particularly fine sign includes the pillars of King Solomon's Temple, the arch of heaven, the all-seeing eye of the Supreme Being, the anchor of hope, crossed keys of secrecy, radiant sun, crescent moon, seven stars, gavel, altar, and Bible, in addition to the square and compasses. The opposite side features a rendition of great seal of the United States.[38]

William Rice and His Contemporaries

Several features of the Holcomb sign decoration—its expanded palette, gilding, and vine-covered columns—heralded the emergence of a new generation of ornamental painters. Advertisements from the late 1790s and early 1800s indicate that these artists offered a variety of work—in their

words, "painting in all its various branches." Not only did they paint signs, but also houses, ships, carriages, boats, and an assortment of finer work such as painting on glass, military regalia, and Masonic ceremonial objects. For many of these diverse products, their clients were the same, as there was still a strong correlation between Masons, the militia, and tavern keeping. Further, the painters themselves traveled in the same circles. Solomon Jones, an ornamental painter in Middletown, belonged to St. John's Lodge No. 2, and was also sergeant of the Ninth Company, Second Regiment Light Artillery (fig. 35).[39]

Preeminent mong the ornamental painters of the first quarter of the nineteenth century was William Rice (1777–1847).[40] When he first came to Hartford in 1816, Rice's work was much like that of his fellow painters, if the sign he painted for Thomas Tarbox of East Windsor is an indication (fig. 36). By 1818, Rice was working "At the sign of the Lion; opposite PORTER's Tavern, State Street." Rice was not just a good painter, he was a shrewd businessman. Though it may not have been his invention, he adopted a new sign shape—a horizontal rectangle—and covered it with designs, particularly lions and eagles, that became effectively his own brand (fig. 37). Soon his signs were featured on virtually every country inn west of Hartford. His style is so recognizable that even a fragment of a sign, missing the corner with his ubiquitous signature, can be firmly attributed to him, as can a few signs seen in engravings picturing them in situ (see fig. 39).[41]

Rice's success was based in part on a phenomenon not of his own making: the improvement of the road system and the consequent increase in travel (fig. 38). Beginning in the 1790s, many existing Connecticut roadways were systematically improved, including the Upper, Middle, and Lower post roads from New York to Boston. New roads were laid out, such as the Straits Turnpike, incorporated in 1797, connecting Litchfield and New Haven. Since the location of a road was critical to existing and would-be tavern keepers, it is not surprising to find that the turnpike investors and innkeepers were often the same men. Meetings to establish or maintain turnpikes were scheduled at various taverns along the route. Thus, there grew a network of tavern keepers who knew each other well, and who worked together to sponsor traffic along the entire route.[42]

Although stages had been running prior to the Revolution, departures had often been irregular. Beginning in the 1780s, routes and timetables became more reliable, and innkeepers in major cities began vying for the patronage of stage drivers like Jacob Brown, who advertised in 1783:

Fig. 36. *Sign for Tarbox's Inn*, signed by William Rice, dated 1807 and 1824, East Windsor, Conn. CHS, cat. 19, side 1. This is the earliest known William Rice sign, probably painted on an itinerant visit to the Hartford area, before he established his home and business in the city. The sign had been repainted, probably in the 1830s, for the "Village Hotel," with gold lettering on a black background. An earlier restoration attempt had partially removed this over-paint, exposing traces of an eagle underneath. The remaining overpaint was removed from side 1 at Williamstown Art Conservation Center in 1999, revealing the previously undetected Rice signature. Sign shown with 1830's paint removed from right side.

Fig. 37. *Sign for Abbe's Inn and Lion Hotel*, signed by William Rice, circa 1822, and by Luther Terry Knight, 1866, Enfield, Conn. CHS, cat. 31, side 2.

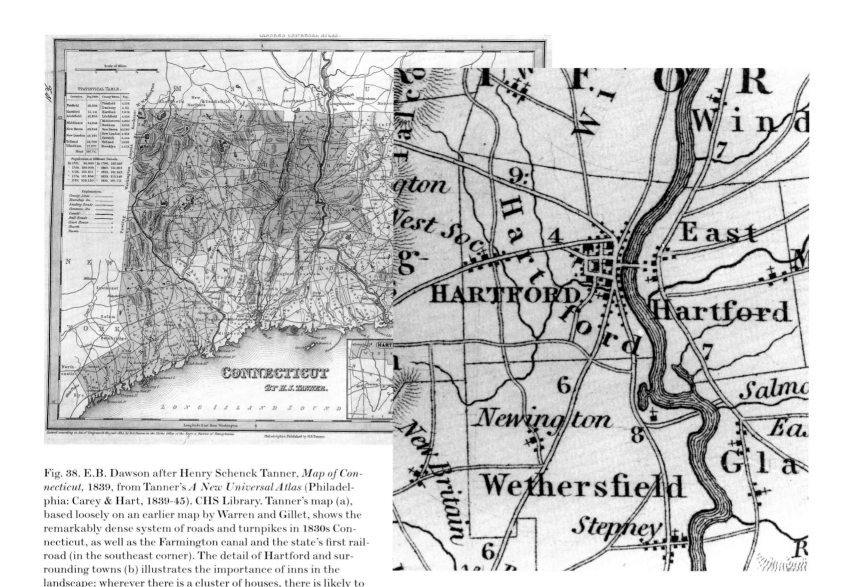

Fig. 38. E.B. Dawson after Henry Schenck Tanner, *Map of Connecticut, 1839,* from Tanner's *A New Universal Atlas* (Philadelphia: Carey & Hart, 1839-45). CHS Library. Tanner's map (a), based loosely on an earlier map by Warren and Gillet, shows the remarkably dense system of roads and turnpikes in 1830s Connecticut, as well as the Farmington canal and the state's first railroad (in the southeast corner). The detail of Hartford and surrounding towns (b) illustrates the importance of inns in the landscape: wherever there is a cluster of houses, there is likely to be both a church and an inn.

Key to symbols on map above: ⚑ inn   ⚓ church

The Hartford Stage Waggon, WILL *leave David Bull's Inn, on every Monday morning at four o'clock, and go to New-Haven the same day, Wednesday morning at the same hour leave New-Haven and return to Hartford, and on Friday morning proceed to Springfield and return to Hartford the next day . . .* JACOB BROWN. N.B. *The stage will leave Smith's Coffee-House New Haven and Parson's Tavern Springfield.*[43]

Connecticut's small size meant that much of the state could be traversed in a day or less: the stage from Litchfield to New Haven took only eight or nine hours, and that from New Haven to New York took only ten hours.[44] Consequently, stage travel between these cities did not usually increase the demand for overnight accommodations. Connecticut inns competed to serve as meal stops, though, for such contracts on a regular stage run would mean a steady income. Thus, Mr. Cowles of New Hartford could boast, in a

for-sale ad, that his

stand is situated on the Great Western Turnpike leading from Hartford to Albany, near the junction of the New-Hartford and Pittsfield Turnpike with the former, twenty miles from Hartford, in a flourishing Manufacturing Village, and is the best country stand in the State. Said stand commands a good run of custom, three Lines of Stages passing through the Village daily, which breakfast and dine at this House.[45]

It was to this group of strategically positioned innkeepers, specifically in Litchfield, Hartford, and Tolland counties, that Hartford sign painter William Rice marketed his talents in the 1820s and 1830s (fig. 39). As an indication of Rice's dominance of the market, only one non-Rice sign from these years has been found to date in all of northern Litchfield and Hartford Counties (fig. 40) His signs were probably not inexpensive, as his customers tended to be pro-

Fig. 39. *Litchfield House,* Litchfield, Conn., circa 1853, lithograph. CHS, Graphics Collection. The sign for the Litchfield House, run by Stiles D. Wheeler beginning in 1846, could have been painted by William Rice, although Litchfield was a large enough town to support several local craftsmen. This was not the largest nor the most prestigious of the four hotels in Litchfield. Those honors fell to the much larger Mansion House, on the other side of the Court House, where professionals such as Samuel Church, Judge of the Court, chose to stay.

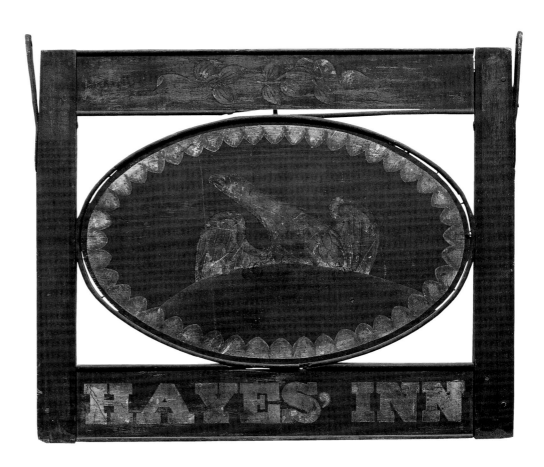

Fig. 40. *Sign for Hayes's Inn,* circa 1828, Granby, Conn. CHS, cat 39, side 2. This is the only known inn sign surviving from northern Litchfield and Hartford Counties in the 1820s and 1830s that was *not* painted by William Rice.

prietors of well-established inns. Arah Phelps's inn in Cole-brook had been operating for at least three decades when Rice sold him a new sign (cat. 37). It is likely that Rice's patrons derived a certain status from their new and improved signs.[46]

Rice's works are strikingly devoid of Masonic iconography, a change probably attributable to an overall decline in Masonic activity after about 1825. More surprising is the absence of travel imagery, especially in contrast to signs decorated by other contemporary sign painters. In areas of Connecticut where Rice was not active, a large number of signs dating from around 1815 to 1840 feature a variety of horse-drawn vehicles: from public conveyances like the stagecoach on Humphrey Williams's sign, Centerbrook, 1826, to the elegant private carriages on the 1823 sign for Carter's inn, Killingworth, and the 1831 sign from Vernon Stiles's Hotel, Thompson (cat. 33, 36, 41).[47]

The horizontal signs introduced by Rice and his contemporaries quickly replaced the vertical signboards of earlier times, even in hotels in continuous operation. The early antiquarian John Warner Barber documented a few vertical signs in his 1830s drawings, but by 1850 all of the eighteenth-century Connecticut inns still operating (about fifty establishments) had replaced their earlier signs.[48] In rural areas the replacement of an early sign often accompanied an expansion or remodeling of an older building or its complete replacement by a new, larger structure. New Greek revival ells or simple extensions were added to eighteenth-century, gable-end buildings. Larger, brick buildings, some with a gable facing the street, appeared in a few towns. For this reason if no other, signs of the second quarter of the nineteenth century are frequently larger than the signs they replaced.

Changing Trade Practices

Demand for new signs was fueled not just by aesthetic innovations but also by a need to signal functional changes in the hostelry industry. Three trends are noteworthy for their impact on signage. First, certain inns developed as destination sites, encouraging visits by families. Second, the entire industry came under fire from temperance reformers interested in curbing the overuse of spirits. And finally, the modern hotel replaced the earlier tavern or inn.

Beginning in the first decade of the nineteenth century, a few Connecticut inns began identifying themselves as destination sites, for recreation or health purposes. The most famous of these was probably Stafford Springs, already popular in the eighteenth century. John Adams had visited

there in 1771 for rest and relaxation, but found the nearest inn a half-mile from the springs. This changed in 1803, when Dr. Samuel Willard opened a new inn at the springs. Throughout the next half-century, despite occasional business lags, visitors came from many places to partake of the waters. By the 1820s special stagecoaches were running from Hartford, and the proprietors sought business from New Yorkers by boasting that their establishment could be reached by steamboat to Hartford.[49]

In the 1820s, a series of resorts sprung up along the coast of Connecticut, offering salt air and seafood as alternatives to mineral waters. In 1823, Jared Carter of Killingworth (cat. 33) announced his opening of "a pleasant and healthful resort for valetudinarians who may wish the benefits of the sea air," promising patrons "an extensive view of the sound" and "a constant supply of sea food." Not to be outdone, the proprietors of Sachem's Head in Guilford, less than ten miles away, assured potential visitors that

No place on the Sound is better situated for persons labouring under any indisposition to enjoy the benefit of salt-water bathing, or of sea-food of all kinds—and no attention shall be wanting, on the part of the proprietor, to render his house a pleasant resort./ An elegant and convenient SAIL-BOAT *is attached to the establishment. The road from Guilford to S. Head has been put in a good state of repair, and is now very safe and pleasant./ Those who are in the habit of regaling themselves in the hot season, with a visit to the salt water, are assured that D. P. will endeavour to make his House as pleasant as any on L. I. Sound.*[50]

In the northeast corner of Connecticut, Captain Vernon Stiles developed a destination site of a different sort (cat. 41). Situated in Thompson, near the Massachusetts and Rhode Island borders, his inn catered to young couples too eager to wait for the requisite second announcement, required by those states, of their intentions to marry. Stiles became a justice of the peace and performed a number of weddings himself.[51]

Stiles was also one of several tavern keepers who fell under the scrutiny of a growing anti-alcohol movement; in 1838 the Windham County Temperance Society chastised him for selling 920 gallons of wine.[52] Laws that attempted to curb the overconsumption of alcohol had been enacted regularly, starting during the first years of the colonies. The cause gathered more popular support in the nineteenth century, when it was taken up by religious leaders, most notably the Reverend Lyman Beecher, who had moved to Litchfield in 1811. In 1834 there were over a million temperance advocates nationally, and in 1836 eleven weekly or monthly publications catered to the "American Society for the Promotion of Temperance." In 1846 Connecticut had approximately 330 local temperance societies, with about 110,000 pledges to total abstinence made since 1841. Some towns were so anti-alcohol that they refused to approve any tavern licenses. Some innkeepers responded by developing a non- or moderate-alcohol establishment, with the curious name of "Temperance Tavern." In 1846, there were fifty-seven temperance taverns in Connecticut.[53]

The effect of the temperance movement on tavern signage is less clear. Nationally, a number of signs contained the word "temperance," but no particular iconographic motifs have yet been identified.[54] One Connecticut sign has the word "Temperance" painted over an earlier owner's name (cat. 54). But it is probable that for many preexisting establishments, the main sign remained the same, with smaller new signs using the word "Temperance" being added to indicate to the traveling public the reformed nature of the place. In 1841, C. A. Colton announced his acquisition of the Exchange Hotel in Hartford with a declaration of temperance principles: being "convinced from sad experience that intoxicating liquors are injurious to persons in health, and wishing to benefit rather than injure even indirectly his fellow men, [he] has excluded such liquors from the house" (fig. 41). Since Colton did not change the name of his hotel, presumably the signage did not change either.[55]

Colton's reference to his establishment as a "hotel" suggests additional innovations in the business of entertaining strangers. The first Connecticut use of this word appears to be in a 1779 advertisement for Ephraim Minor's Hotel in New London, but this is unusually early. It would be another twenty years before the construction of the Chelsea Hotel in Norwich, one of the next establishments designated by the new name. The word seems to have implied a new concept in hostelry, originating primarily in cities, generally denoting larger, nondomestic structures built specifically for the purpose, and encompassing such amenities as individual rooms, private parlors, separate dining and drinking areas, and meeting spaces.[56]

In the first half of the nineteenth century, a number of hotels were erected or greatly expanded in Hartford, including Bennet's City Hotel (1819), Ripley's United States Hotel (1827), and Carter's American Hotel (1845). Ripley's is particularly instructive for the topic of signage. Major John Ripley had come to Hartford from Windham in 1797 to run a tavern on the north side of State Street, opposite the State House. There is no image of the building dating from this year, but it was presumably a modest, residential building—five bays with gable ends—and its sign must have been a

Fig. 41. *Broadside for Colton's Exchange Hotel* (Hartford, Conn.: Elihu Geer, 1841). CHS Library. Charles A. Colton served as proprietor of the Exchange Hotel in the year 1841 only. More well-known landlords were Joseph P. Morgan and Selah Treat. Perhaps Colton's insistence on following temperance principles (adopted by Treat in 1837) did not sit well with the largely business-oriented clientele of the hotel.

typical, vertical board. It is possible that Ripley brought a sign with him, since he had been running a tavern in Windham since 1775. When his son, Jabez Ripley, took over in 1823, he immediately remodeled his father's tavern, bringing it into the nineteenth century. He named it a "coffee-house," added a full third story with an oval window, and hung up a horizontal sign similar to those painted by William Rice in the same year (fig. 42). (Rice was working in the same block as Ripley's, so it is quite conceivable that he provided the sign.) These alterations would seem to have brought the building sufficiently up to date, but only four years later Ripley expanded it even more and renamed it the "United States Hotel." Pictured on a billhead of 1827 is a very large, four-story building. Gone is the oval window, the recently added William Rice sign, and the pole from which it had hung. Instead we see a long, narrow board with the words "UNITED STATES. HOTEL." mounted flush against the facade above the second story (fig. 43).[57]

Ripley's United States Hotel sign foreshadowed future trends in outdoor signage throughout Connecticut and the

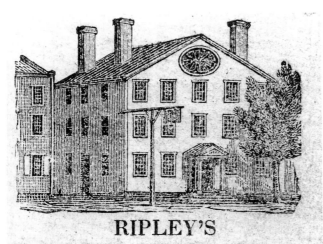

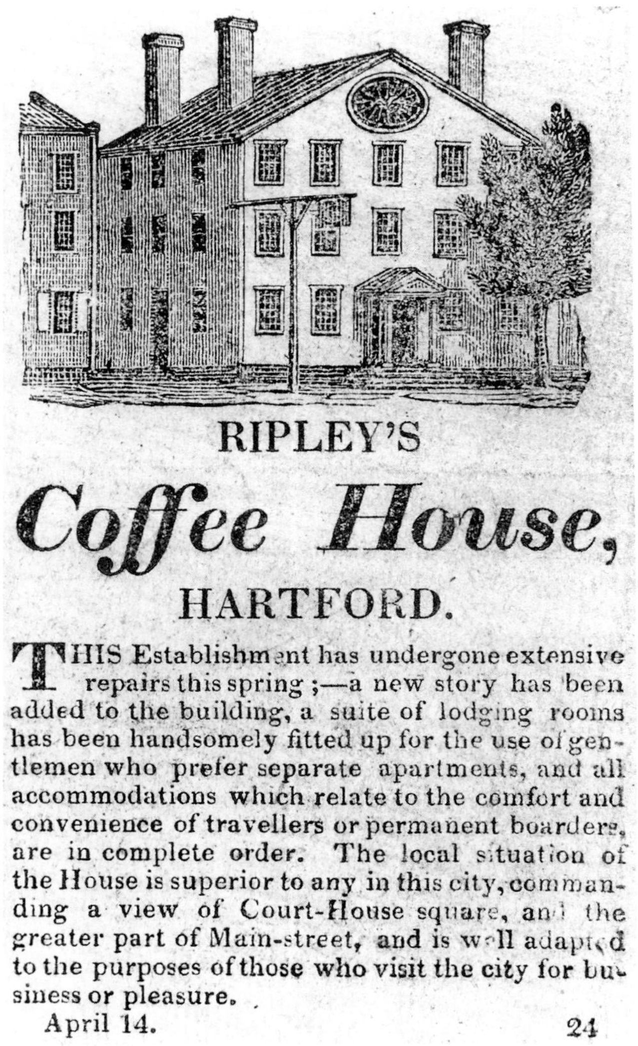

RIPLEY'S UNITED STATES HOTEL.

DIRECTLY NORTH OF THE STATE HOUSE AND FRONTING SOUTH ON THE PUBLIC SQUARE
HARTFORD, CON.

Fig. 43. *Bill from Ripley's United States Hotel*, Hartford, Conn., 1827. CHS Library. The same building that appears in fig. 42 was enlarged again in 1827 to become Ripley's United States Hotel. With the expansion, the hotel dwarfed the building to the left, which appears in both images. More suitable to the new size is the modern sign attached directly to the building front.

Fig. 42. *Newspaper advertisement for Ripley's Coffee House, American Mercury,* Hartford, Conn., 22 April 1823. CHS Library. Ripley's ad features a three-story, gable-fronted building, probably enlarged from a two story, gable-end structure. The new oval sign and the oval window, both adorned with an eagle, could have been supplied by nearby sign painter and fanlight maker William Rice.

nation. However, the shift to flush-mounted, imageless bands of text was generally preceded by a transitional type of signage in Connecticut villages, and even in the smaller cities. In these transitional examples, a horizontally oriented rectangle or oval framed two or three lines of text, set off by small amount of nonfigural decoration. A geographical pocket of such signs survives from western Connecticut—Woodbury and environs—as well as from the port city of New London in southeastern Connecticut (cat. 44, 53, 56). This group of signs may have advertised establishments catering to a more utilitarian crowd, such as drovers or itinerant traders, but it may be that they were simply produced by painters not skilled enough to create more realistic imagery. Their graphic emphasis may also have been perceived of as stylish by rural innkeepers who undertook expansions and modernizations similar to their urban counterparts, albeit on a smaller scale. Rice himself produced

a series of less elaborate signs that relate to this group (cat. 50).

Industry and Railroads

As early as the 1830s, country inns were being challenged by newer establishments in industrial towns. In Enfield, along the Connecticut River north of Hartford, the village center moved a few miles to the north when Orrin Thompson and others established carpet-weaving enterprises. These factories, in what came to be called Thompsonville, and the gunpowder factories in nearby Hazardville, attracted workers from all over New England and Europe, almost tripling Enfield's population between 1810 and 1850. The arrival of the first weavers from Scotland in 1828 produced a housing shortage, and it became customary for arriving workers to

Fig. 44. *Thompsonville Hotel*, Thompsonville, Conn., postcard (photolithograph), circa 1900. CHS, Graphics Collection. The name "Thompsonville Hotel" can be traced as early as 1849, and the establishment may have operated under different names prior to that. This turn-of-the-century postcard pictures a largely unchanged structure, complete with an 1840s-style sign out front and a late-nineteenth-century sign above the second story.

live in inns or hotels. While Robert M. Abbe's hotel in the old center of Enfield remained in operation as a wayfarers' stop in 1850 (cat. 31), two new hotels had opened in Thompsonville to cater to the recently arrived immigrant workers (fig. 44). Ezra Harris, who ran the Thompsonville Hotel, had twenty-seven guests in 1850, hailing from Ireland, England, France, and Germany as well as Connecticut and Massachusetts. Mostly men in their twenties and early thirties, these guests were effectively boarders—twenty were already gainfully employed in the factories or ancillary businesses. Unlike the Abbe Hotel, which relied on its sign to attract passersby, the Thompsonville Hotel needed only the most utilitarian identification.[58]

Concurrently, stage travel and the rural inns met with significant competition after the construction of railroads. The first Connecticut railroad was in operation in 1837, but it went only from the Rhode Island border to Stonington, a few miles away. The principal effect of railroads would be felt from 1838 to 1844, during which time four major routes began operating: Hartford to New Haven; Bridgeport to New Milford, Canaan, and northward into Massachusetts; Norwich to Worcester via Plainfield and Putnam; and Hartford north to Springfield.[59]

The inpact the railroads had on inns can be clearly traced in Meriden. Long known as the halfway point on the old road from Hartford to New Haven, Meriden had boasted a tavern since the mid-seventeenth century. When the turnpike came through in the 1790s, the principal tavern was Dr. Ensign

Hough's, a large gambrel-roofed building in the northwest corner of the town center, just to the north of the Congregational Church (fig. 45). In the 1830s, the railroad line was laid quite to the west of the town, a deliberate decision made by residents who did not want it bordering their properties. New, business-minded investors soon erected a building close by the tracks, offering convenient meal service to hurried travelers. A broadside for Nelson Merriam and Henry M. Foster's new hotel indicates just how modern were both the establishment and its sign—a simple text strip reading, "Meriden Hotel" (fig. 46).[60]

Significantly, Merriam and Foster's hotel did not bear the proprietors' names. Like Ezra Harris's Thompsonville Hotel and many others, the Meriden Hotel was clearly an investment property, which would change hands frequently. Increasingly, even in nonindustrial and nonurban settings, establishments were being run by professional first-generation hotelmen who merely rented their hotels from absentee owners. The rise in professional proprietors left little room for female innkeepers. In the 1830s, Sarah Atwood Crane of Bethlehem ran the inn left her by her husband, Gideon, for only two years, handing over the reins to her second husband, Edwin Hannah; when he died in 1859 the hotel closed. Both husbands' names appear on the tavern sign, but hers does not (fig. 47). As the duration of an innkeeper's tenancy shortened, hotels began taking on generic names, often reflecting their locations or their clients. Names no longer referred to an image on a sign, because fewer signs in fact had images. By mid-century, gone were the "Red Lion" and

Fig. 45. John Warner Barber, *Meriden*, circa 1830s, ink, wash and graphite drawing on paper. CHS, Graphics Collection. In Barber's bucolic portrayal of Meriden, a stage filled with passengers rides north from New Haven toward the building in the distance, just to the right of the two churches. Known as Hough's Stage House and later as the Central Hotel, this inn was well situated, just seventeen miles from both New Haven and Hartford. According to tradition eight stages a day stopped there in the 1820s.

Fig. 46. *Broadside for Meriden Hotel*, Meriden, Conn. (detail), lithograph (Hartford: E.B. and E.C Kellogg, 1842). CHS, Graphics Collection. A few years after Barber depicted Meriden (fig. 45), the railroad opened, decreasing the stage business and diverting traffic through the new town center west of the old green. New structures were erected at this location, including the very modern 1842 Meriden Hotel.

"Anchor" of the previous century, replaced by the "Village Hotel," the "Mansion House," and the "American House."

The death of William Rice in 1847 is significant to the history of inn signs in Connecticut, for after his demise fifty years would pass with few, if any, new figural signs. The latest known Rice sign is from the Sidney Wadsworth's Hartford inn, dated 1844 (cat. 55). Rice's son Frederick continued the business until his own death in 1876, but he does not appear to have produced any elaborate, two-sided rectangular signs after his father's death. As time passed, the signs that the elder Rice and his contemporaries had painted began to disappear as well.

The second half of the nineteenth century saw the growth of more industrial towns and more railroads. More of the rural inns, bypassed or outmoded, shut their doors. Of the approximately 500 hotels in operation in 1850, fewer than 150 were still in operation ten years later. Those which remained replaced their fading signs with the new, stark styles; boards with black grounds and gold letters, hung flat on the sides of buildings, now identified nearly every hotel in the state. Only a few holdouts are noteworthy, particularly in towns whose center greens remained intact. Cheshire, for example, still evoked a bucolic setting in the mid-nineteenth century, and Levi Munson retained an old-style sign with a horse-drawn vehicle when he took over the local hotel in 1850.[61]

In the last decade of the nineteenth century, a yearning for simpler times brought about a revival of earlier signs. In sharp contrast to the ever-growing modern hotels, several old taverns were reopened or, if in continuous operation,

were significantly "improved." In Enfield, William A. Abbe reopened the old building that had earlier housed Peter Field's inn (1814–23) and William Abbe's Hotel (ca. 1853–69, perhaps later). For the new clientele he added a tearoom (cat. 24). In Windham, George Challenger purchased the old hotel on the north end of the green. He added a porch, dormer windows, and new furniture, and opened up for summer boarders.

The new landlords marked these colonial revival inns with an assortment of signs. Some had little to do with the historical past (fig. 48). Others were eighteenth- and nineteenth-century boards modernized with new layers of black and gold paint, like that of the revived Abbe Inn and Tea Room (cat. 24). A few were eighteenth-century signs repainted in an attempt to re-create the original designs, as on the 1892 Windham Inn sign (cat. 62), while other old, weathered images were "freshened" or improved in accord with early-twentieth-century tastes (cat. 2, 7, 10, 23). As curious as some Colonial Revival signs may appear today (fig. 49), their importance can hardly be overstated. Tributes to the "colonial" inn, particularly as recorded and popularized by Alice Morse Earle and other antiquarian writers, undoubtedly helped save many old signs from destruction.[62] Although some examples were heavily overpainted by collectors or later owners, others were preserved intact, providing rare glimpses of what were once familiar signs of welcome.

NOTES

1   During the course of a one-year research project, information on Connecticut taverns was collected and compiled in a database. Tavern licenses, newspapers, town records, directories, maps, tax lists, and secondary local histories provided well over 5,000 innkeepers' names. We estimate the total number of men and women who served in that

Fig. 47. *Sign for the Hannah Hotel,* circa 1836, Bethlehem, Conn. CHS, cat. 47, side 2.

capacity between 1750 and 1850 at approximately 10,000, of whom probably half purchased new signs.

2   J. Hammond Trumbull, *The Public Records of the Colony of Connecticut, Prior to the Union with New Haven Colony,* 15 vols. (Hartford: Brown & Parsons, 1850), vol. 1, pp. 103–4.

3   William DeLoss Love, *The Colonial History of Hartford. U.S. Bicentennial Edition* (Chester, Ct.: Centinel Hill Press, 1974; reproduced from the 1935 ed.), pp. 216, 236, 283; Charles J. Hoadly, ed., *Records of the Colony and Plantation of New Haven, From 1638 to 1649* (Hartford: Case, Tiffany and Company, 1857), p. 166.

4   Norwalk Town Records in D. Hamilton Hurd, comp., *History of Fairfield County, Connecticut* (Philadelphia: J. W. Lewis & Co., 1881), p. 521; Mrs. Elizabeth Hubbell Schenck, *The History of Fairfield, Fairfield County, Connecticut,* 2 vols. (New York: by the author, 1889), vol. 1, p. 403; Lewis G. Knapp, *In Pursuit of Paradise: History of the Town of Stratford, Connecticut* (West Kennebunk, Maine: Phoenix Publishing, for the Stratford Historical Society, 1989), p. 64; Hoadly, *Records of New Haven,* vol. 2, pp. 230, 425.

5   Trumbull, *Records of Connecticut,* vol. 1, p. 283.

6   Ibid., vol. 1, pp. 174–5; Sherman W. Adams and Henry R. Stiles, *The History of Ancient Wethersfield* (Henry R. Stiles, 1904; facsimile ed. Somersworth, N. H.: New Hampshire Publishing Co., 1974), p. 132; Harriet Chapman Chesebrough, *Glimpses of Saybrook in Colonial Days* (Celebration 3 1/2, 1984), pp. 40–41.

7   Love, *Colonial History of Hartford,* p. 236.

8   *The Book of the General Laws for the People within the Jurisdiction of Connecticut: Collected out of the Records of General Court, Lately Revised, and with some Emendations and Additions Established and published by the Authority of the General Court of Connecticut holden at Hartford in October, 1672.* (Cambridge, Mass.: Printed by Samuel Green, 1673), pp. 34–36.

9   In Richard Buel, Jr., and J. Bard McNulty, eds., *Connecticut Observed: Three Centuries of Visitors' Impressions, 1676–1940* (Hartford: The Acorn Club, 1999), pp. 19, 23.

10   [Thomas Prince], *The Vade Mecum for America* (Boston: Kneeland and Green for Henchman and Hancock, 1731), 206–14.

11   Herman Diederik Johan van Schevichaven [Jacob Larwood] and John Camden Hotten, *The History of Signboards, From the Earliest Times to the Present Day,* 4th ed. (London: John Camden Hotten, 1868), p. 9.

12   [Prince], *The Vade Mecum for America,* p. 196.

13   George S. Dunkelberger, comp., *An Early History of St. John's Lodge, No. 4 A. F. & A. M., Hartford Conn. 1762–1937* (Hartford: The Case, Lockwood & Brainard Co., 1937), pp. 45–46.

14   Discussions of inn patronage by local residents is beyond the scope of this essay, since neighbors needed little direction in finding the inn. The author acknowledges that most inns catered to both local and transient guests. For in-depth studies of experiences in taverns, see Kym S. Rice, *Early American Taverns: For the Entertainment of Friends and Strangers* (Chicago: Regnery Gateway, in association with Fraunces Tavern Museum, New York, 1983); Donna-Belle Garvin and James L. Garvin, *On the Road North of Boston: New Hampshire Tav-*

Fig. 48. *Farnum Tavern*, Lakeville, Conn., depicted circa 1935. CHS Library. The Farnam tavern, built by Peter Farnam in the 1790s, still stands in Lakeville. It went through several names during the nineteenth century—A. J. Wardwell's Hotel; Tupper, Wood & Co. Hotel; and the Hotel of C. L. Robinson—to name a few. Proprietors during the Colonial Revival era reinvoked the name of the first tavernkeeper. They also manufactured or repainted a sign with a design that has no historical relevance.

erns and Turnpikes, 1700–1900 (Concord: New Hampshire Historical Society, 1988); Peter Thompson, *Rum Punch and Revolution: Tavern-going and Public Life in Eighteenth-Century Philadelphia* (Philadelphia: University of Pennsylvania Press, 1999); David W. Conroy, *In Public Houses: Drink and the Revolution of Authority in Colonial Massachusetts* (Chapel Hill and London: University of North Carolina Press; published for the Institute of Early American History and Culture, 1995).

15 Timothy Root Account Book, Stanley-Whitman House Museum, Farmington, Connecticut. Although the majority of Root's customers were white males, a few women and African Americans do appear in his accounts.

16 *Connecticut Gazette* 3 October 1766: p. 3, col. 3; 7 November 1766: p. 3, col. 3.

17 *Connecticut Gazette* 29 April 1768: p. 3, col. 3.

18 According to Dunkelberger, *St. John's Lodge* (p. 47): "David Bull's was the most noted tavern in Hartford, and was called the 'Bunch of Grapes' Tavern, from the carving of a bunch of grapes as a sign. It stood at or near the point of intersection of Asylum street with the west side of Main, Asylum street not being opened. A Frenchman who visited the house during the Revolutionary War is quoted as saying, 'A very good inn, kept by Mr. Bull, who is accused of being rather *on the other side of the question;* a polite method of designating a tory.' Mr. Bull was not a member of St. John's Lodge."

19 Marion Dickinson Terry, ed., *Old Inns of Connecticut* (Hartford: The Prospect Press, 1937), pp. 117, 185.

20 *Connecticut Gazette*, 8 April 1768: p. 3, col. 3.

21 On the Peck sign, see Terry, *Old Inns*, pp. 153–59.

22 *Connecticut Journal*, 17 November 1769: p. 3, col. 3.

23 Dunkleberger, *St. John's Lodge*, pp. 45–46.

24 Militia records are found in the Connecticut Archives, Connecticut State Library, Hartford. This Benjamin Williams was the grandfather of Humphrey Williams who owned cat. 36.

25 This number is an estimate. Eighteen female innkeepers working before 1780 have been documented to date.

26 In Buel and McNulty, eds., *Connecticut Observed*, pp. 35–39.

27 On Connecticut town structure, see Bruce Colin Daniels, *The Con-

necticut Town: Growth and Development, 1635–1790 (Middletown, Conn.: Wesleyan University Press, 1979).

28 Connecticut's population jumped from about 38,000 in 1730 to 130,600 in 1756 and nearly 200,000 in 1774, largely due to a high birthrate.

29 The practice of referring to inns by their sign imagery seems to have been an urban phenomenon, observed in Hartford, New London, and New Haven, but only rarely in the countryside.

30 *Middlesex Gazette,* 19 May 1792: p. 3, col. 3; Frank D. Andrews, comp., *Directory for the City of Hartford for the year 1799* (Vineland, N.J.: privately printed, 1910).

31 An Arah Phelps sign also survives, but it appears to be from the second quarter of the nineteenth century (cat. 37).

32 *Middlesex Gazette,* 17 September 1791: p. 3, col. 3. Joseph Teel's tavern in Norwich was known as, at the sign of General Washington, in the 1790s; *Norwich Packet,* 5 September 1793: p. 3, col. 3.

33 Edmund Hogan, *Prospect of Philadelphia, Part 1* (Philadelphia: Francis & Robert Bailey, 1795).

34 In Buel and McNulty, eds., *Connecticut Observed*, p. 24.

35 The six inns were identified as Major Ozias Marvin's, Mr. Taylor's (probably a son or grandson of the earlier man), Samuel Pearsall's, Burrets's, Jenning's, and Osborn's; Christopher Colles, *A Survey of the Roads of the United States of America* (New York: C. Colles, 1789).

36 Isaac Bickerstaff, *Almanack* (Boston: E. & S. Larkin, S. Hall, et al., 1801); *The Connecticut Register, for the Year of our Lord, 1808* (New London: Ebenezer P. Cady), pp. 138–41. Several non-Connecticut signs are known that display surnames in conjunction with colonial dates. Since none of these signs has been examined firsthand, it is impossible to eliminate the possibility of postcolonial repaintings, which may have substituted names for initials on earlier signs.

37 Little is known about Holcomb, a third-generation tavern keeper, who was licensed from 1802 until his death in 1809 at the age of thirty-five. His sign is now preserved by Saint Mark's Lodge No. 36, A.F.&A.M., in Simsbury.

38 Kenneth E. Duncan, "Historic Sign," *Connecticut S & C* (Summer 1986), p. 6; on Masonic symbolism, see John D. Hamilton, *Material Culture of the American Freemasons* (Lexington, Mass.: Museum of Our

National Heritage, 1994); and *Bespangled, Painted, and Embroidered: Decorated Masonic Aprons in America, 1790–1850* (Lexington, Mass.: Museum of Our National Heritage, 1980).

39 E. G. Storer, *The Records of Freemasonry in the State of Connecticut* (New Haven: E. G. Storer, 1859), p. 359; *Middlesex Gazette,* 12 April 1826: p. 3, col. 3.

40 For full references on William Rice, see Appendix 1, q.v.

41 *American Mercury,* 12 May 1818, p. 25. The sign for the Seymour Inn in Colebrook was long ago cut down to make a table top, but it contains all the characteristic features of a Rice sign; now in the collection of the Colebrook Historical Society.

42 The clearest overview of the Connecticut turnpike system is Frederic J. Wood, *The Turnpikes of New England* (Boston: Marshall Jones Co., 1919).

43 *Connecticut Courant,* 8 July 1783: p. 2, col. 3.

44 *Connecticut Courant,* 16 January 1811: p. 3, col. 4; *Litchfield Enquirer,* 1 October 1829: p. 1, col. 1.

45 *Connecticut Courant,* 22 February 1836: p. 3, col. 5.

46 Other long-established inns known to have acquired new Rice signs include Jeffrey O. Phelps's inn, Simsbury (Simsbury Historical Society); Thaddeus Griswold's inn in Torrington (Torrington Historical Society); Luke Viets's in Granby (no longer extant); and J. H. Pettibone's in Norfolk (Norfolk Historical Society). One exception to this pattern was Reuben Pinney's purchase of a Rice sign in 1836, to announce his inn in Riverton, newly opened to compete with the older Ives inn (now the Riverton Inn); John Warner Barber had depicted Pinney's house a few years earlier; see original watercolor drawing, The Connecticut Historical Society.

47 Vehicles also ornamented signs from William Keeler's Hotel, Ridgefield (Keeler Tavern Museum, Ridgefield); Minor Bradley's, Guilford (Shelburne Museum); Abel Jacobs's, a competitor of Vernon Stiles's in Thompson (Silvermine Tavern, Norwalk); and David B. Clark's in Seymour (present location uncertain). For a description of Clark's sign, see Rev. Hollis A. Campbell, William C. Sharpe, and Frank G. Bassett, *Seymour Past and Present* (Seymour: W. C. Sharpe, 1902), p. 43.

48 Barber's drawings, in Christopher P. Bickford and J. Bard McNulty, *John Warner Barber's Views of Connecticut Towns, 1834–36* (Hartford: The Acorn Club, The Connecticut Historical Society, 1990); engravings of Barber's views, in John Warner Barber, *The Connecticut Historical Collections* (By the author, 1836).

49 *Middlesex Gazette,* 26 July 1826: p. 3, col. 5.

50 *Middlesex Gazette,* 24 April 1823: p. 3, col. 5; *Connecticut Courant,* 1 June 1824: p. 3, col. 6.

51 This is an often-repeated story; see, e.g., Richard M. Bayles, ed., *History of Windham County, Connecticut* (New York: W. W. Preston, 1889), pp. 705–6.

52 [Windham County Temperance Society], *Temperance Report, 1838* (Brooklyn, Conn.: Carter & Foster, 1838), p. 19.

53 "Temperance Movement," *Dictionary of American History* (New York: Charles Scribner's Sons, 1976), vol. 7, pp. 22–23; T[otal] A[bstinence] Society, *Second Annual Report* (New Haven, 1846).

54 See also Arthur Kern and Sybil Kern, "Alcoholism and the Temperance Movement in Early American Folk Art," *Magazine Antiques,* February 1998, pp. 292–99.

55 *Connecticut Courant,* 17 July 1841: p. 3, col. 5.

56 *Connecticut Gazette,* 3 June 1779: p. 2, col. 3; *Chelsea Courier* [Norwich] 1 March 1797: p. 3, col. 3.

57 Major John Ripley licensed in town of Windham, 1775–96, Windham

County Court Records; *Connecticut Courant,* 11 September 1797: p. 2, col. 5; 15 April 1823: p. 3, col. 5; 9 April 1827: p. 3, col. 6. The earliest known use of the term "coffee house" in Connecticut appeared in Thomas Allen's advertisement for the London Coffee House, in New London; *Connecticut Gazette,* 10 April 1770: p.3, col. 3. The term became more popular from about 1790 to 1820, roughly contemporary with the term "hotel," with coffee houses known in New London, Hartford, New Haven, and Middletown.

58 U.S. Census for 1850. The number of long-term lodgers at the Thompsonville Hotel suggests a blurring of definition between hotel and boardinghouse, though a glimpse at Chancy Haxon's boardinghouse nearby suggests a slightly older resident, and several no longer single. See also Ruth Bridge, ed., *The Challenge of Change: Three Centuries of Enfield, Connecticut, History* (Canaan, N.H.: Phoenix Publishing for the Enfield Historical Society, 1977).

59 See also Gregg M. Turner and Melancthon W. Jacobus, eds., *Connecticut Railroads; An Illustrated History* (Hartford: The Connecticut Historical Society, 1989).

60 C. Bancroft Gillespie, comp., *An Historic Record and Pictorial Description of the Town of Meriden* (Meriden: Journal Publishing Co., 1906), p. 363.

61 The sign is clearly depicted in a contemporary print in the Connecticut Historical Society Graphics Collection.

62 Alice Morse Earle, *Stage–Coach and Tavern Days* (New York: Macmillan Co., 1900).

Fig. 49. *Sign of the Bull's Head,* dated 1760, East Windsor, Conn.; overpainted circa 1910-20. CHS, cat. 7, side 2.

Lions and Eagles
and Other Images on Early Inn Signs

By Nancy Finlay

Throughout most of the eighteenth and early nineteenth centuries, a limited number of subjects were depicted on the hanging signboards in front of taverns, inns, and hotels. Although the repertory increased somewhat in the early nineteenth century, most imagery continued to conform to a few clearly defined types: animals, drinking symbols, famous men, and coats of arms. This limited group of types probably helped travelers to quickly identify an establishment as an inn or tavern and perhaps provided additional information about the owner's political affiliation, possible Masonic connections, or stance on temperance. By the middle of the nineteenth century, the lettering on signboards had assumed the major role, and pictorial components were reduced to modest decorations or eliminated entirely. Pictorial signboards reappeared at the end of the nineteenth century in the context of the Colonial Revival movement. At this time, many old signboards were taken out and repainted, and new signs were created in imitation of early originals.

Most of the images on early inn signs were derived from preexisting visual sources and directly reflect the kinds of visual sources available. Mass-produced images such as prints, book illustrations, coins, and paper money provided inspiration for Colonial artists and craftsmen in all fields, including sign painters. The most common engraved designs in the seventeenth and early eighteenth centuries were the images that were stamped on coins and printed on paper currency. Such images would have been widely disseminated and familiar to everyone.[1] In some cases, in the very early days, they may have been virtually the only printed images available to ordinary farmers and small tradesmen. A remarkable correspondence exists between the motifs on Colonial and early American money and the designs on inn signs. For example, the images on Colonial and Continental currency in use in Connecticut during the eighteenth century included the rising sun, ships, pine trees, the allegorical

figure of Liberty, and the Connecticut state seal.[2] All of these images are also to be found—often in strikingly similar form—on inn signs, generally of a roughly contemporary date. One of the most striking visual relationships, however, is between the image on the Massachusetts Pine-Tree shilling, cut by Joseph Jenckes at the Lynn Iron Works in 1652 (fig. 52)[3] and the design on the signboard of the Read inn in Lisbon, Connecticut, dated 1768 (cat. 5)—despite the fact that the two are separated by almost one hundred miles and more than one hundred years. Nevertheless, some connection obviously exists: the Pine-Tree shilling, though it did not circulate much beyond New England, was in use as common currency in Connecticut in the seventeenth century,[4] and a virtually identical design (fig. 53) reappeared on coins and paper money issued by the Colony of Massachusetts in the 1770s.[5] Clearly an ongoing tradition existed, and the Lisbon sign painter was aware of it. Philip Zimmerman has linked this imagery with the revolutionary Sons of Liberty, founded in 1765. Presumably this association was clear to potential patrons of the inn during the tumultuous years immediately preceding the Revolution.

By the third decade of the eighteenth century, European prints were quite widely available in America. Printsellers' shops existed in Boston, New York, and Philadelphia, and itinerant peddlers catered to the smaller towns and rural areas. Maps and engravings were also sold by Colonial booksellers and sometimes by cabinetmakers and other tradesmen.[6] A few wealthy individuals formed substantial collections of such works, and even middle-class colonists might own an engraving or two. Contemporary accounts suggest that innkeepers were especially likely to decorate with maps, broadsides, and engravings, either framed and glazed or pasted directly on the walls themselves. In addition, engravings were widely used in the teaching of art. Both amateurs and aspiring professionals learned to draw by copying foreign engravings, and most artists owned at least a few prints

Fig. 50. *Sign for Wadsworth's Inn*, signed by William Rice, 1844, Hartford, Conn. CHS, cat. 55, side 2.

Fig. 52. *Shilling*, Lynn, Mass., 1652. CHS. One of the earliest American coins, this shilling features a stylized pine tree. This motif reappears in a similar form on Massachusetts coins and currency in the eighteenth century, and on the 1768 sign for Read's inn (cat. 5).

Fig. 51. Alfred Parys, *Tavern Sign*, watercolor and graphite on paper, circa 1940. Index of American Design, © Board of Trustees, National Gallery of Art, Washington. Artist's rendering of Read's inn sign, 1768 (cat. 5), one of fourteen inn signs now at The Connecticut Historical Society that were recorded in the Depression-era Index of American Design. Artists employed by the Works Progress Administration used archaeological fieldwork techniques to produce a meticulously accurate visual archive; for two-dimensional works like tavern signs, the accuracy of these renderings is so high that photographic reproductions of the drawings can be difficult to distinguish from those of the original signs.

Fig. 53. *Note for 15 Pounds*, State of Massachusetts Bay, 1779. CHS. Like the sign of the Read tavern (cat. 5), this banknote incorporates a rising sun as well as a pine tree. In both cases, this may be a rebus referring to the Revolutionary Sons (suns) of Liberty (tree).

Fig. 54. Richard Houston after Hervey Smith, *Major General James Wolfe, Commander in Chief of His Majesty's Forces on the Expedition against Quebec*, mezzotint, London, circa 1760. Print Collection, The New York Public Library. Astor, Lenox and Tilden Foundations. Following Wolfe's death on the Plains of Abraham before Quebec in 1759, printmakers rushed to produce portraits of the hero for the popular market. Many of these reproduce the same sketch by Wolfe's fellow officer, Capt. Hervey Smith.

Fig. 55. *Sign of General Wolfe*, circa 1768, Brooklyn, Conn. CHS, cat. 4, detail. One of the best known signs in the Connecticut Historical Society collection, the General Wolfe sign was cited and reproduced in publications at least as early as 1880, when it appeared in F.W. Salem, *Beer: Its History and Its Economic Value as a National Beverage* (Hartford: F.W. Salem, 1880).

from which they derived compositions and motifs.

The sign that hung in front of Israel Putnam's tavern in Brooklyn, Connecticut, was directly based on a contemporary mezzotint portrait of the British general James Wolfe, hero of the Battle of Quebec during the French and Indian Wars (figs. 54, 55). Wolfe was extremely popular with Americans of Putnam's generation. A similar engraving of him hung on the wall of George Washington's Mount Vernon,[7] and the model for Putnam's sign may have belonged to Putnam himself. Although the immediate source was almost certainly Richard Houston's full-length profile portrait, based on a contemporary sketch by Captain Hervey Smith, Houston's mezzotint itself was widely copied.[8] As early as 1762, Nathaniel Hurd of Boston copied the head and shoulders from this portrait in a group of three medallion portraits of Wolfe, William Pitt, and George III, entitled "Britons, Behold the Best of Kings."[9] Hurd's bust-length profile portrait may have served as the source for the image that

appeared on the sign of the Wolfe Tavern in Newburyport, Massachusetts.[10] Putnam operated his tavern from 1768, shortly after his return from service in the French and Indian Wars, until 1775, when he rushed off to Cambridge, Massachusetts, to join the Patriot cause, immediately upon receiving news of the battles of Lexington and Concord. During this time, General Wolfe served as an effective signboard; his hand, outstretched in a gesture of command, was easily interpreted as an invitation to the passing traveler to enter and be served.

After the Revolution, typically American imagery began to appear on contemporary inn signs, most notably, after 1782, eagles more or less closely based on the Great Seal of the United States, which was adopted at that date. As during the earlier Colonial period, coins and currency may have played a role in the dissemination of such imagery, but by the early nineteenth century, eagles—usually clutching olive branches and clusters of arrows—were virtually everywhere.

No. 12. 87 cts.   No. 13. 50 cts

No. 14. 75 cts.   No. 15. 87 cts.

No. 16. $1.   No. 17. 50 cts.

No. 18. 75 cts.   No. 19. 25 cts.

No. 20. 50 cts.   No. 21. 50 cts.   No. 22. 37 cts.

BOSTON TYPE AND STEREOTYPE FOUNDRY.

Fig. 56. "Type Ornaments, Nos. 12-22," *Specimen of Printing Types from the Boston Type and Stereotype Foundry* (Boston: Dutton and Wentworth, printers, 1828). By permission of The Houghton Library, Harvard University. Type ornaments nos. 17 and 18 are closely based on the Great Seal of the United States; nos. 12 and 14 are loosely derived from the same source. Nos. 13, 19 and 20 are more naturalistic adaptations. These and similar ornaments were widely used by printers of the period and helped to popularize the eagle as a symbol of the United States.

They were featured on military insignia, in architectural ornaments, in over-mantle paintings, on stoneware jugs, and on the stern boards of sailing vessels and the wheelboxes of steamships.[11] Type ornaments (fig. 56) and crude woodcuts of eagles were used, not only on official documents, but also on a broadside issued in Windham, Connecticut in 1807 advertising Thompson Lee's Genuine Bilious Pills or Family Physic,[12] and—complete with arrows and olive branch—as an illustration for the letter *E* in a children's alphabet book published in the late 1820s by the New York publisher Mahlon Day. Eagles also proved popular with American printmakers. J. T. Porter of Middletown depicted a feisty American eagle seizing John Bull by the horn on his engraved title page for *Americans Triumphant, or John Bull in Distress* (1823), a poem celebrating American naval victories during the War of 1812 (fig. 57). Since many sign painters of this period were simultaneously active in other fields—as engravers, coach painters, house painters, miniature painters, and painters of designs on drums, chairs, clock faces, and so on—it is not surprising that virtually identical imagery appears in so many different areas of the decorative arts. William Rice, who featured eagles on many of his inn signs, at least as early as the 1810s, also painted military and political standards and banners, many of which would have featured eagles as well. The poses of the eagles that appear on nineteenth-century inn signs evolved over time in a way that exactly parallels developments in other arts. The earliest eagles, from shortly before 1800 to about 1825, are stiff, upright birds, closely based on those which appear on seals and coinage. Their wings are outstretched symmetrically; their bodies are often all but obscured by the shield of the United States. Later eagles stretch out to assume a more horizontal format, with their bodies as well as their heads and necks twisted to one side. They are often shown perched on their shields rather than hidden behind them. Many of them are quite naturalistic when compared to the earlier, more heraldic and stylized birds. Rice's sign of circa 1820 for Daniel Loomis's Coventry inn (fig. 58) conforms to the earlier type; his sign for the Wadsworth inn on Albany Avenue in Hartford (probably 1844) conforms to the later (fig. 60). A lithograph by D. W. Kellogg depicting a log cabin erected in Hartford during William Henry Harrison's 1840 presidential campaign (fig. 59) includes an eagle signboard that combines aspects of both types. While the eagle is stretched out to fill the horizontal format of the sign, it is still half-hidden behind the shield, and the cannons and piles of cannon balls closely resemble those in the Loomis inn sign. Almost certainly the signboard in the lithograph is an example of the political work of William Rice.

Not surprisingly in a period during which there was considerable tension between the individual states and the federal

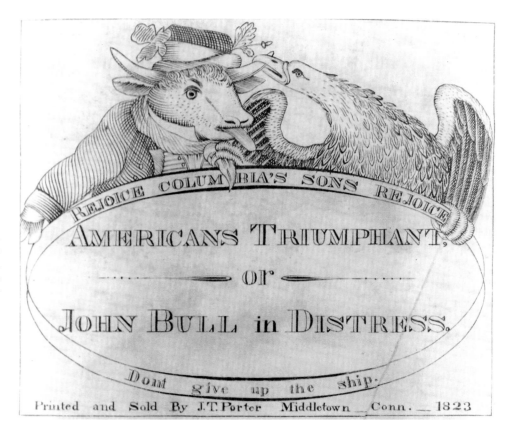

Fig. 57. *Americans Triumphant, or John Bull in Distress.* (Middletown, Conn.: Printed and sold by J.T. Porter, 1823). CHS Library. John Bull is personified on this pamphlet as an actual bull, being attacked by an American eagle. The bulls and eagles on at least some inn signs probably held similar political meaning for contemporary patrons.

government, specific Connecticut imagery also appears frequently on early nineteenth-century inn signs. Feelings over the Jefferson embargo and the War of 1812 ran so high that Connecticut actually proposed seceding from the Union in 1814. Most signs bearing the Connecticut coat of arms are substantially later than this, however, and it is equally true that the Connecticut arms, which features three grapevines, was an appropriate symbol for an establishment that served alcoholic beverages. The grapevines on inn signs could be rather loosely interpreted. The vines on the sign of E. Marsh (cat. 12) loop to the left rather than to the right, as they do on the state seal. This may indicate that artist was tracing or directly copying a printed source and failed to reverse the design when transferring it to the board. But two of the vines in Rice's Loomis sign (cat. 28) loop to the left and one to the right, suggesting that he, at least, was simply indifferent to their orientation. The rather naturalistic grapevine on the J. Williams sign (cat. 32) may also be an indirect allusion to the state seal.

The early nineteenth century saw a virtual explosion of visual imagery. While images of any kind remained relatively scarce in the eighteenth century, new inexpensive printmaking techniques brought a wide array of pictures into every corner of American life in the years just after 1800. Wood engraving was refined by the British artist Thomas Bewick in the last years of the eighteenth century. Because wood engravings combine easily with movable type, the technique

was ideally suited for book and magazine illustrations. Wood engravings—some of them directly based on Bewick's own compositions—were incorporated into all kinds of American books, magazines, and broadsides. Lithography, which was invented in Bavaria by Alois Senefelder in 1796 or 1798, also offered an inexpensive way to produce large numbers of popular prints. Because Senefelder attempted to retain control of his patent, lithography did not spread to the United States until the late 1810s, but by the mid-1820s many American artists were experimenting with the new process. Both wood engravings and lithographs were far easier and cheaper to produce than copperplate engravings and etchings, and they quickly became far more plentiful. Whereas an eighteenth-century artist had had a relatively restricted range of imported copperplate engravings to choose from, nineteenth-century artists had access to a virtually limitless selection of wood-engraved book illustrations and lithographs. By the 1840s, photographs began to be available as well, though there is no evidence that sign painters ever employed photographic sources for their motifs, at least until the Colonial Revival at the end of the nineteenth century. By that time, photographs and photographically illustrated books would have been among the most convenient visual resources for artists seeking to reproduce early signs or motifs.

Unlike the eagles, which are all more or less loosely based on the Great Seal of the United States, the lions that appear on

Fig. 58. *Sign for Daniel Loomis's Inn*, signed by William Rice, ca. 1820, Coventry, Conn. CHS, cat. 28, side 2. The eagle on this relatively early Rice sign compares closely with the bird in the Boston Type Foundry's type ornament no. 12 (fig. 56). Some such design undoubtedly served as Rice's prototype.

Fig. 59. *Log Cabin, Hartford, Conn.* (detail), hand-colored lithograph. (Hartford: D.W. Kellogg & Co., 1840). CHS, Graphics Collection. This log cabin, erected to promote the 1840 Presidential candidacy of William Henry Harrison, displays a painted eagle closely resembling eagles on inn signs by William Rice.

nineteenth-century inn signs ultimately are derived from illustrations in European natural history books. These illustrations were remarkably conservative. Almost invariably they reproduced standard poses that originated in the late eighteenth and early nineteenth centuries—despite frequent claims by the authors that the pictures illustrating their texts were drawn from life at the local menagerie.[13] Copies began to appear in American natural histories at an early date, and the more exotic and popular animals were soon appropriated for use in children's storybooks and alphabets, and on broadsides and advertisements for traveling wild animal acts and exhibitions. One such menagerie, featuring "The Mammoth Lion, much superior in size and beauty to any ever exhibited in this country," was on view at Bishop's Hotel in New Haven early in November 1826.[14] This association between actual lions and inns and hotels in Connecticut may have prompted the proprietors to feature these animals on their signs. On the other hand, lions, like eagles, were clearly a specialty of the Hartford sign painter William Rice, and may simply have been offered to customers as part of his standard stock-in-trade.

Rice's early lions appear to derive ultimately from French illustrations to the works of the Comte de Buffon, the great

Fig. 60. *Sign for Wadsworth's Inn*, signed by William Rice, 1844, Hartford, Conn. CHS, cat. 55, side 1. This eagle, representative of Rice's later work, appears on the opposite side of same sign as the lion in fig. 50. Rice very often paired lions with eagles, suggesting that this combination of emblems may have held particular meaning for customers. The eagle surely symbolized the United States; it is possible that the lion represented Great Britain.

eighteenth-century naturalist, perhaps filtered through other as yet unidentified sources. In contrast, the lion on the sign Rice executed for Sidney Wadsworth in 1844 (see fig. 50) is clearly based on a format popularized by Thomas Bewick in his *Natural History of Foreign Quadrupeds*, printed and published in Alnwick in the north of England in 1809. Bewick's lion was copied by the pioneer American wood engraver Alexander Anderson at an early date (fig. 61) and was reproduced in various contexts throughout the nineteenth century. A crude copy in Henry Althans's *Scripture Natural History of Quadrupeds with Reflections Designed for the Young*, published in Hartford in 1828 (fig. 62) may have been based either on the Bewick original or on Anderson's copy.[15] A similar lion also appears in a lithograph published by the Hartford lithographers Kelloggs & Comstock between 1848 and 1850. The lion on the Wadsworth sign resembles the Anderson and Bewick lions in its sophistication and detail more than it does these later cruder copies, suggesting that Rice had direct access to one of the early natural history texts.

Sign painters had much closer ties to the artistic mainstream than has often been recognized. Although the extensive use of preexisting visual sources for virtually all sign-board imagery might appear to reflect the sign painters' lack of formal training and need for models that could be copied, even academically trained artists frequently employed such sources in their paintings. This was especially true for representations of exotic animals such as lions, difficult or contorted poses such as those typical of American eagles, or conventional subjects, such as coats of arms, which needed to rendered accurately. The American painter Benjamin West, during his prodigiously successful career in Great Britain, frequently incorporated figures based on well-known ancient statues into his historical compositions. Far from denoting a lack of imagination or creativity, such quotations deliberately evoked classical parallels and served to situate the paintings in which they occurred in the ongoing artistic tradition.

The images on the vast majority of eighteenth- and early nineteenth-century inn signs were very familiar images indeed and therefore must have been readily identifiable to many contemporary viewers. Probably, the fact that at least some viewers could recognize the visual sources of the images on inn signs helped to confirm the status of these signs as works of art. For other, less sophisticated viewers, the brightly painted signs must have been among the most

Fig. 61. Alexander Anderson, *Lion*, wood engraving, circa 1830. Print Collection, The New York Public Library. Astor, Lenox and Tilden Foundations. Alexander Anderson was one of the most important and prolific American wood engravers of the early nineteenth century. This lion, which probably appeared in a natural history book, was directly copied from a wood engraving by the British artist Thomas Bewick. The Bewick/Anderson lion was copied over and over again by other artists and engravers. It served as the direct source for Rice's sign for Wadsworth's inn (fig. 50).

Fig. 62. Henry Althans, *Scripture Natural History*. (Hartford, Conn.: D.F. Robinson & Co., 1827-28. CHS Library. This rather crudely executed beast is also based on the Bewick/Anderson lion.

impressive artworks seen in their experience. A young farm boy growing up in the early nineteenth century related how he decided to become an "ornamental or sign painter" because, based on his experience in rural Connecticut, he considered sign painting "the highest branch of painting in the world."[16] Although this view was clearly somewhat extreme, many American sign painters were artists of remarkable talent. Abner Reed of East Windsor is remembered today primarily as an engraver of coins and currency, and as one of the most gifted American printmakers of his period, but he also decorated sleighs, carriages, military standards and signs—especially inn signs (fig. 63).[17] Luther Allen of Enfield is well known as a portrait painter, but also advertised his willingness to undertake copperplate engraving, hairwork, coach and carriage painting—and sign painting and gilding.[18] Other sign painters, whose work is thus far anonymous and whose training and other achievements are therefore unknown, were equally talented, regularly produced works of great charm, and occasionally created masterpieces of singular power and originality. The artist who

Fig. 63. *Sign for Joseph Phelps's Inn*, attributed to Abner Reed, 1801, East Windsor, Conn. The Wadsworth Atheneum. Reed was one of the most prominent Connecticut artists known to have painted tavern signs. He enjoyed a substantial reputation as a printmaker and as a teacher. Attributed to Reed on the basis of entries in his account book, this sign features a capped female head, representing Liberty, and on the other side, an eagle. Both emblems are drawn directly from the design of a United States coin, ca. 1795. Barely visible beneath this image is another, with the legend "The 13 United States," above a circle of interlacing rings; this design was painted circa 1777 by an unknown artist for East Windsor innkeeper David Bissell.

painted the General Wolfe signboard was among the most sophisticated painters in eighteenth-century Connecticut. The study of these men and their work can tell us much about what it meant to be an artist in early America.

NOTES

1   David McNeely Stauffer, *American Engravers upon Copper and Steel* (New York: The Grolier Club, 1907), p. xxi.
2   Wyman W. Parker, *Connecticut's Colonial and Continental Money* (Hartford: The American Revolution Bicentennial Commission of Connecticut, 1975).
3   Stauffer, *American Engravers*, pp. xxi–xxii.
4   Parker, *Connecticut's Colonial and Continental Money*, p. 10.
5   A one-cent Pine-Tree coin issued by Massachusetts in 1776 is illustrated in *The Standard Catalogue of United States Coins from 1652 to Present Day* (New York: Wayne Raymond, 1950), p. 12. The design has been attributed to Paul Revere.
6   E. McSherry Fowble, *Two Centuries of Prints in America, 1680–1880. A Selective Catalogue of the Winterthur Museum Collection* (Charlottesville: University of Virginia Press for the Henry Francis du Pont Winterthur Museum, 1987, p. 10.
7   Ibid., p. 20.
8   For a discussion of Wolfe portraits, see *Wolfe: Portraiture and Genealogy* (Quebec House: Permanent Advisory Committee, 1959).
9   Fowble, *Two Centuries of Prints*, pp. 295–96.
10 Mary Caroline Crawford, *Little Pilgrimages among Old New England Inns* (Boston: L. C. Page, 1907).
11 Philip M. Isaacson, *The American Eagle* (Boston: New York Graphic Society, 1975).
12 CHS Library Broadside Collection 1807 L481t.
13 My research on natural history illustrations involving the great cats was originally conducted for my dissertation, "Animal Themes in the Painting of Eugene Delacroix" (Princeton University, 1984). It is striking that the same images appear in both European and American contexts.
14 *Connecticut Herald* , 7 November 1826, p. 35.
15 Drawing on Buffon, Althans associated the lion with the virtues of strength, courage, generosity, and gratitude. It is possible, though by no means certain, that the lions on Rice's inn signs may have suggested similar associations to contemporary viewers.
16 Quoted in William Dunlap, *A History of the Rise and Progress of the Arts of Design in the United States*, 3 vols. (Boston: Frank W. Bayley and E. Goodspeed, 1834), vol. 3, p. 234. Francis Alexander (1800–1880) was born in Killingly, Connecticut, and began his career there. In 1827 he moved to Boston where he became a well-known portrait painter.
17 *Connecticut Courant,* 23 July 1798, p. 25; 23 November 1803, p. 25; 9 January 1805, p. 34; 18 December 1805, p. 35. See Appendix 1, q.v.
18 *Connecticut Courant,* 19 January 1801, p. 35. See Appendix 1, q.v.

6 "Faithfully and Promptly Executed": *A Conservator's View of Sign Painting*

By Sandra L. Webber

The Painters, the Advice, and the Analysis

Connecticut's eighteenth- and nineteenth-century sign painters were typical of their period in both their degree of talent and the number of services they offered. Very few, if any, found sufficient work painting signs to exclude other employment. Indeed, the difficult business of earning a living as a painter is apparent from the scope of their advertisements.[1] Almost one-third of the sign-painting firms identified in Connecticut between 1780 and 1850 were known to have sold painting supplies, and for several this was a primary source of income. While 60 percent of those studied provided "coarse" paint work for houses and ships, 80 percent also offered some form of decorative painting in addition to signs. Over 40 percent of the businesses offered wallpapering or glazing, although 72 percent of that group were companies that also painted houses. Some 30 percent advertised only decorative (non-house) work, with signs perhaps being the least delicate of their ornamental painting repertoire. Military banners, Masonic pieces, heraldry, and even portraiture were among their more accomplished work. Many fine artists both here and abroad, including a few from Connecticut, were known to have painted signs during their training or for friends, board, or cash. Other painters were principally employed in related fields such as coach making, chair making, printmaking, or drafting, all of which may have contributed skills or source material to their sign production. Earlier signs reveal everything from poor spelling, awkward lettering, and simplistic images to very sophisticated design and lettering. Disparity between image and word execution on a single board might even reflect more than one hand at work. About half of the Connecticut artists had partners or coworkers, and larger firms had shop assistants and apprentices. Although a few painters were known to have survived as itinerants, some artists remained in one locale for many years. Of the forty-three painters studied, 25 percent stayed in one town for ten or more years, and nearly half lived in Hartford for at least part of their careers. Only eight painters who advertised between 1780 and 1850 promoted sign painting as their desired principal activity. By the 1830s, demand may have been sufficient for a few shops to specialize, which corresponds with the publication of the first manuals featuring decorative painting. That the field was competitive by mid-century is borne out by the painters' own advertisements. While several gifted self-promoters labeled their sign work "the best in New England," others publicly lamented the treatment they received from rival firms and eventually quit the arena.[2] The technical demands of sign painting clearly fell midway between house and easel painting, and the more successful artisans were those who combined the practical recommendations of the first with the design sensibilities of the second.

The varied backgrounds and expertise demonstrated by sign painters in Connecticut to some extent paralleled the available painters' instruction books. Although earlier painters had fewer published guides, during the nineteenth century painting manuals offered ever-increasing levels of technical advice. The primary goal of these recipe books was to assist the painter in producing an artistic, and at the same time durable, exterior design. As one manual cautioned, "An artistic sign is attractive in more ways than one, but an unattractive sign is agreeable to no one."[3] Artisans, who traditionally learned by apprenticeship, collected paint recipes such as those found in an anonymous cabinetmaker's workshop journal of 1801. Early house painting manuals, such as Hezekiah Reynolds's 1812 *Directions for Ship or House Painting,* primarily listed paint recipes for commonly used exterior colors. Published in New Haven, this pamphlet might easily have found its way into Connecticut sign painters' shops, whose techniques may have stemmed from a working knowledge of house and ship painting. In contrast, studio painting manuals, such as Robert Dossie's 1764

Fig. 64. *Sign for Warner's Hotel*, signed by William Rice, dated 1836, location undetermined. CHS, cat. 50, side 2.

Handmaid to the Arts, gave sign painting no assistance at all. But by 1838, *The Painter's, Gilder's and Varnisher's Manual*, published in London and New York, offered many valuable pages of direction for exterior painting.[4]

More specific trade manuals were written by practicing decorative painters in the mid-nineteenth century, and like most such publications, they presented long-used, traditional techniques along with the newest in pigment selections. Orson Campbell offered his *Treatise on Carriage, Sign and Ornamental Painting* in 1841 for the benefit of "American citizens whose circumstances [would] not permit them to go through a regular course of Apprenticeship," but who, having started such businesses, needed "a knowledge of theory as well as practice." Instruction at this time covered surface preparation, lettering, and proper color selection, but the greater part dealt with paint recipes and applications. In much the same vein, Jesse Haney published "valuable recipes and professional secrets he'd been offering to his apprentices for [forty] years," in his 1870 *Sign, Carriage and Decorative Painting*. Coach work, if executed properly, was considerably more demanding than sign painting, requiring more careful consideration of fancy detailing, finishing, and aging issues. According to Haney, "there was no class of painter so unwilling to share knowledge as coach painters, and that coach work was so different from the rest, that having great knowledge of the other branches of painting was to no avail."[5]

The study of painters' advertisements and instruction manuals provides a valuable counterpoint to laboratory inspection and technical analysis of the surviving signs. Surprisingly, the effects of weathering on the signs substantially aided the collection of historical information; when viewed in raking light, outlines and letters became visible from beneath overlying paint layers. For example, the Perkins inn sign was found to have two earlier names, which in turn helped pinpoint the geographic location of the inn (cat. 15). Mylar overlay drawings were used to separate earlier proprietors' names and underlying designs, and to determine whether templates had been used to duplicate images. For example, although the Thompson Hotel sign has variations from one side to the other, it appears that a single drawing or template was used for the main image (fig. 65). The fact that neither side has the correct number of legs for a pair of horses was perhaps a common error, as "horses' legs proved beyond the powers of most artists, [even when] the lettering attained a high degree of excellence." Cross-sections and pigment identification helped to determine the likely dates of paint surfaces, although the condition of paint and wood surfaces made analysis difficult on some signs (fig. 66). Questions about the unusual choice of a hard-wood support for A.

Fig. 65. *Sign for Stiles's Inn*, circa 1831, Thompson, Conn. CHS, cat. 41. During treatment by Conservator of Paintings Sandra L. Webber, at Williamstown Art Conservation Center, 1998-99.

Hinman's inn sign led to the investigation of the yellow paint used for the sun (cat. 13). An early date was supported by the discovery of a pale Litharge-based color, probably Patent or Montpellier's Yellow, used by house painters until the introduction of Chrome Yellow around 1815. In a reverse case, the early board of the Grosvenor inn sign was discovered to have zinc white as its lowest paint scheme, a pigment not extensively used in oil until around 1850 (cat. 60). Wood identification was done by eye in the majority of cases, with expert analysis of samples when necessary to answer specific questions.[6]

Style and Design

The fashion for large, double-sided, swinging signboards in America was a direct import from European and English designs of the seventeenth and eighteenth centuries. In some London streets, large signboards, projecting out from buildings, were so numerous they blocked light and air movement, and when they fell down in the wind, buildings were torn apart and people were killed. In the early 1760s Paris and London ordered all projecting signs to be removed and affixed flat to walls, and in 1770 Philadelphia restricted the use of signboards to tavern keepers alone.[7] Despite occasional accidents in Connecticut, neither the population nor the signs were congested enough to pose a general hazard. By 1650 Connecticut colonial law stipulated that each town had to provide "entertainment" for travelers and their horses, and by 1673 it became mandatory to exhibit a sign at each establishment. This law and the many stage routes from Boston to New York may be responsible for a proliferation of signboards in Connecticut. Several early tavern signs resemble London trade signs of the same period, having only the initials of the proprietor over a pictorial image or

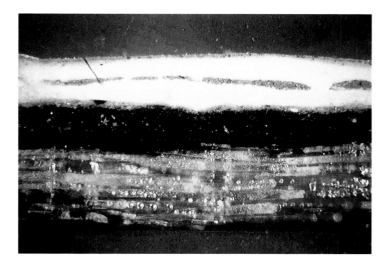

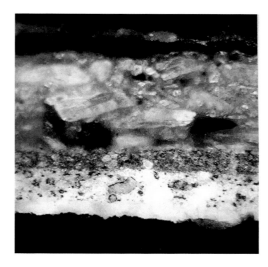

Fig. 66. Cross-sections of paint samples during microscopic examination, Williamstown Art Conservation Center, 1999. For this analytical procedure, tiny samples of paint layers (about the diameter of a pencil lead) are cut to reveal cross sections for examination with both optical and scanning electron microscopes. Optical characteristics, reproduced in the accompanying figures at magnifications of 100x–400x, are viewed under visible and ultraviolet light to distinguish between paint layers. This evidence helps in interpreting the complex histories of many signs.

(a) Sample from Porter's inn sign, grassy area below house (cat. 27, side 2), with at least nine layers of paint; the presence of two distinct layers of lead white suggests two repaintings over the original treatment.

(b) Sample from "R" in Porter's inn sign (cat. 27, side 1), also shows at least nine layers. The last layer shows the presence of gold leaf; a layer of green in the middle includes blue, white, coarse yellow, and black particles. Other intermediary layers probably related only to changes in background color, not relettering.

(c,d) Sample from "T" in Stiles's Inn and Thompson Hotel sign (cat. 41, side 1), viewed in normal light (c) and ultraviolet light (d). There are at least twelve layers of paint, coatings, and grime. The sample exhibits severe fracturing, displacement, and embedded grime, possibly due to the sign having been in or near a major fire.

emblem (cat. 1–3). Although several signs have no written identification, most have either the name of the inn or the proprietor (often interchangeable) or both. Thirty-six percent of the signs had different images on each side, while the majority repeated the same image, with both formats surviving throughout the entire period studied (1750–1890). Dates on signs must be used with caution to date the sign itself: most refer to the date of the building, or one or more taverner's first licensing dates.[8]

Tavern and inn signs created in Connecticut during these two centuries reflect prevailing trends in sign painting, evolving with changes in style and taste to fit new demands. Although wood was the support for all the signs in this study, the form, framing, construction, scale, and weight of signboards varied considerably over time. Several sign-painting firms apparently had joiners' tools and skills; however, it is likely that many painters were not particularly gifted at construction and relied on local joiners for their boards. The fact that at least three sign painters advertised ready-made tavern signs may indicate a steady business, and also that boards may have been constructed in groups ahead of time. This could point to an outside artificer who perhaps offered the painter a better price if he ordered more than one sign at a time. Several signs made by Hartford-based painter William Rice (active circa 1800–47) exhibit similar construction techniques, and it is tempting to ascribe this workmanship to his joiner son-in-law, whose property adjoined the painter's.[9] Eighteenth- and early-nineteenth-century signs would also have required the services of a turner, as the framed or trimmed board was often supported by turned posts. Of fifty-seven signs examined, fifteen have surviving posts with vertical image boards, most dating between 1749 and 1815. As signboards increased in size, and the orientation became horizontal, posts disappeared in favor of various styles of frame molding.[10]

All signs swung from wood or wrought-iron arms projecting from one or two tall posts, large trees, or the building itself. Early town views indicate that signposts were up to twenty feet in height or that signs projected from the eaves of second or higher stories of inns. By 1870, one instruction book set the normal viewing distance of signs at between fourteen and fifty feet. Most people traveled only by day for safety reasons, however, dusk or night coach arrivals were not unusual, and perhaps the taller signs were able to catch the falling evening light. Lanterns, whose use was considered a nuisance even by coach drivers, were only infrequently used to illuminate country signboards. The overhead beam still attached to the medium-weight Hinman sign gives some idea of the size of the support arm needed for secure display (cat. 13). The fact that only one end is shaped probably indi-

cates that the beam extended from one post or from the building. A blacksmith would have been needed to forge the iron hangers, fasteners, and in some cases the supporting arms. Early New England support brackets usually resembled a common fire crane, rarely approaching the elaborateness or expense of their London counterparts—although several nineteenth-century signs have attached ornamental ironwork (cat. 48, 49). There is scattered evidence that innkeepers contracted directly with blacksmiths for these fittings, or that the ironwork was billed separately. Acquiring hardware would have been relatively easy, as nearly every town had a blacksmith, and some larger inns with commodious stabling had a smith in residence. A resinous black oil paint was sometimes used to protect the ironwork from corrosion and quite a few Connecticut signs have remnants of such coatings.[11]

Supports and Grounds

Many early New England signs were constructed using a single white pine board for the primary support (cat. 2, 10, 14) or a single fielded panel (cat. 4–5). The dimensional ratio for the earlier vertical boards was roughly a square and a half high. The earlier signs may have been oriented vertically for structural reasons, "to minimize the supporting arm necessary for display."[12] White pine was the traditional wood for a number of reasons: the species was plentiful and grew to large size, boards were readily available and easy to cut and work; and, important, for sign painters, pine was quite durable in exterior situations.[13] Haney offered a rare bit of advice on the best cut of wood for signboards; while admitting that others promoted a center-cut board as being less liable to warp and shake, he preferred boards cut from the outside of the log, arguing that they were more seasoned and the grain angle more stable. Cracks would also be better hidden, as a split's opening would be on the diagonal, allowing less light to pass through. Such diagonal cracks were observed in several signs, including Blatchly's "Scales of Justice" (cat. 10), but many boards had square-sided cracks, typical of center-cut boards.[14] Knots were supposed to be removed and plugged with oil-based putty, but little evidence of this practice was observed, with the exception of fills on the Humphrey Williams sign, possibly inserted prior to repainting in 1826 (cat. 36). The small size of knots that were seen on the signboards suggests that clear pine was deliberately selected (see Edward Bull's Black Horse sign, cat. 1). Clear pine boards were only slightly more expensive and would have guaranteed one less worry during years of outdoor exposure. Contrary to the assertion of early-twentieth-century furniture historian Russell Kettell, that early signboards were typically 1-1/4" thick, many examples in the Connecticut Historical Society collection measured

Fig. 67. Sandra L. Webber, *Hayden's "Old Ship,"* watercolor on paper, 2000. Courtesy of artist. Conservator's conjectural rendering of original color scheme of Hayden's inn sign, 1762 and 1766 (cat. 3, side 1), based on laboratory examination of the weathered shapes, incised lines, and visible paint traces.

between 5/8" and 1" thick, with 3/4" being fairly common. Only a few signs reached Kettell's standard of 1-1/4", as on the single 32"-wide pine board used for Field's inn sign, circa 1814 (cat. 24). Only rarely does the thickness exceed Kettell's figure, as in the 1830s signs (cat. 44, 48) for Fitch's inn (1-3/8") and Mechanic's Hotel (1-1/2"). Many nineteenth-century boards were quite light, belying their size and the illusion of weight created by deep frame moldings.[15]

The weathering problems associated with exterior display were factored into all aspects of the techniques prescribed and used to create signs. Both linseed oil and shellac were recommended as sealants for resinous woods, often mixed with calcium carbonate (a.k.a. whiting or chalk). However, some authors advised against using shellac outdoors due to its vulnerability to water. Combinations of colors were given for light fastness as well as for artistic and eye-catching effects. Vehicle-to-pigment ratios for various layers or special uses were calculated for greatest longevity. The rule of thumb for the progression of layers on an easel painting calls

for "fat over lean," in other words, oil-rich layers applied last to avoid cracking of the paint film. For exterior work the reverse is true; the oil-rich layer is applied directly to the wood to penetrate it and protect it from deterioration. This was especially true when using new wood. Both raw linseed oil and various metallic pigment driers were recommended as additives to hasten the drying of the boiled linseed oil in common use. All manuals warned against using turpentine for sign painting, as it weakened the paint film's strength, thereby accelerating deterioration by weather.[16]

In discussions of sign painting, the term "grounds" signifies, not only the initial priming layer, but also the final body color of the signboard. For a white sign, three to five layers of oil paint were advised, with sanding or pumicing between applications. A cost-cutting measure of using Spanish white (two parts chalk, one part alum) for the first layer was sometimes advocated. Subsequent layers had decreasing amounts of oil and increasing amounts of the more expensive, superior, and heavy-bodied White Lead pigment. For darker-bodied signs or well-aged wood no more than three layers were needed, the lowest layer often pigmented for quicker covering, much like today's toned primers. William Rice appears to have used a gray first ground for a number of his signs, and several late productions from the Rice shop used an unusual black priming. These preparation layers were supposed to be laid "straight and true, corresponding with the grain of the wood," but there is ample evidence in the worn paint of many signs that speed or laziness sometimes broke this rule, as well as the one regarding the number of ground layers recommended.[17]

The oil generally used to make paint during this period was much thicker and the pigment particles coarser than paint made today, so the stiffer consistency left more pronounced brush marks across the surface. By at least the mid-eighteenth century, paints could be supplied in either a pre-mixed or powdered form. Although common or popular colors were among those pre-made for house and ship use, painters' manuals recommended making one's own boiled linseed oil paint. Nut (walnut) oil, long known to cause less yellowing than linseed oil, was recommended for sign painting, as it was reputed to be more durable outside. Nut oil was advertised in Boston as early as 1736, although it was not listed by Connecticut painters who carried paint supplies. *The Painter's, Gilder's and Varnisher's Manual* of 1838 suggested that nut oil was expensive, and in 1841 Campbell felt it was difficult to obtain and likely adulterated. By 1850 George Field discounted its use, along with poppy oil. These and other complaints may explain the seemingly ubiquitous appearance of boiled linseed oil recipes. The latter reportedly had a greater tendency to whiten or chalk as it weathered, which can be seen in the unsaturated colors of the aged signs. Weathering has altered the paint on many signs to such an extent that they appear matte, like milk-based or emulsion type paints. Although occasionally mentioned for use by house painters who became ill from paint fumes, the exterior durability of water-based paints was not known, so they were probably not often used for sign work. Insufficient media remained to enable drawing of conclusions on many signs; however, those that were analyzed revealed an oil-based vehicle.[18]

Brushes and other studio tools were discussed in several manuals, most favoring camel hair or sable "pencils" for fine work. Old brushes were recommended for final paint layers, perhaps in the hope they would not shed hairs into the paint. Large brushes would have been used to apply the ground color, as is evidenced by the sweeping skeletal brush strokes exposed on many weathered surfaces.[19]

Words and Pictures

Once a board was primed or grounded with a body color, images and lettering would have to be laid out on the surface. Depending on the final color of the sign, various methods might be employed to locate designs. To avoid leaving visible marks on a white or light-colored sign, guidelines were incised into the surface using a rule and the point of dividers or a compass, penknife, engraving needle, or carpenter's scribe. Dark signs (often smalted or sanded) had grit substrate layers applied after the lettering was completed, so graphite or snapped chalk lines could be used as guides. At least 25 percent of the Connecticut Historical Society signs have visible scribe lines for the placement and height of lettering. On several signs with arched lettering layouts, centering holes and scribed arcs indicate that curved guidelines were swung with compass or dividers (cat. 13, 19, 34, 48). Some signs also bear lines for the width of serifs, especially where the lettering is large and constitutes the entire design. Occasionally, the letters themselves were even scribed into the surface prior to painting (cat. 16, 23, 24). Several authors describe making a rule the same width as the broad stroke of the letters, with one end cut in the oblique angle of the capital A, the letter considered most subject to errors.

White practice boards were used to learn the correct lettering form, width, and spacing, and soft 1" sable or camel brushes with at least 8" handles were recommended for painting the strokes in a proper manner. It is very clear from the instruction books that all lettering was applied freehand with brushes, no matter what form or extent of layout may have been used beforehand. Great pride was taken in this ability, and some master painters needed very little preparation before applying the letter strokes. Supporting this conclusion are the surviving brush marks in the bodies of letters and the sharp paint deposits along their edges. While some late artists may have used stencils to draw letters in place, a brush would have been used to control the neatness of the paint or gold size layer. Overgilding, an unwanted transfer of metal leaf beyond the oil size layer, can be seen on many signs, especially where the once-covering smalt has been lost.[20]

Similarly, an artist needed to lay out the motifs or pictures on the board before he began painting, whether he was drawing his own designs or using images from another source. Of the Connecticut Historical Society signs examined to date in the laboratory, evidence of free–hand drawing directly on the signboard has been observed only once, around the charioteer on the Temperance Hotel sign (fig. 68). Layout was generally accomplished by a variety of transfer techniques,

Fig. 68. *Sign for the Temperance Hotel*, circa 1826–42, Plainfield and Colchester, Conn. CHS, cat. 54, side 1. Detail, showing unusual evidence of free-hand drawing directly on signboard.

Fig. 69. *Sign of the Bird–in–Hand*, 1786, location undetermined. CHS, cat. 8. Detail of bird-in-hand, with mylar overlay of tracing taken from opposite side of this sign. The tracing can be aligned with the hand, as shown, or with the bird, but not with both simultaneously, indicating that the pattern used to lay out the design must have slipped during the process.

Fig. 70. *Sign for Carter's Inn*, circa 1823, Clinton, Conn. CHS, cat. 33, side 2. Detail of whip during cleaning, showing faint outlines around painted forms, which may indicate that a pantograph was used to lay out the image.

used as much to save time as to produce a neater effect. An accomplished painter might need only the simplest of guides, such as outlines or center marks drawn directly on the surface. Both sides of the Hinman sign display centering holes and compass arcs for the sun's disk, and divider holes marking the spacing of rays (cat. 13). Many signs revealed light scribe lines around the forms, used to locate them in correct position. Images that were large, complex, or needed repeating, might employ the age-old technique of a paper cartoon with a dark drawing media on the reverse or a template with punched holes or lines for pouncing the design on to the surface using charcoal dust. Many Connecticut signs with duplicate images display evidence of some transfer method, even on examples that are very worn, poorly executed, or "painterly" in treatment. While most repeated images were laid out facing the same direction on each side, some mirror-images also occur, whether intentionally or accidentally (cat. 1, 7). The use of templates did not guaran-

tee accomplished results; the bird-in-hand on Woodward's tavern sign (1786), was distorted when a template became misaligned during transfer (fig. 69). The artist of the large Thompson Hotel sign used a template to replicate Lafayette's coach, reproducing its peculiar ironwork trimmings and other details so faithfully as to suggest that he had seen either the original or an illustration of it (cat. 41). Yet he neglected to use compass and dividers, and it is doubtful if even a drunken wheelwright's apprentice could have produced wheel spokes so askew! Somewhat surprisingly, the very painterly bird-in-hand vignette on Horace Rose's inn sign was replicated exactly from side to side, including the entire lettering scheme (cat. 23).[21]

Painters' manuals rarely mentioned sources and methods of producing imagery for signs. A newspaper notice of 1825 documents that Middletown, Connecticut, signpainters Solomon Jones and Thomas K. Bush had among their possessions both a twenty-eight volume illustrated Encyclope-dia and a "drawing machine," which was probably either a camera obscura or a pantagraph. An inexpensive and hand-made camera obscura could have been used to project and copy objects from life or from existing prints, as recom-mended in Campbell's 1841 *Treatise*, especially for represent-ing "certain objects such as carriages, boots, saddles, shoes, etc." A pantograph is an joint-armed parallelogram for reproducing images to scale in different sizes. A "tracing point" at one end draws a new image mechanically as the artist traces the outlines of the original. This device would have been especially useful for capturing more complex or fancy images, such as the dining and coaching scenes for Jared Carter's inn, circa 1823 (fig. 70). The outlines drawn around the sign's details are slight compared to the heavier and deeper scribe lines seen on other signs and were perhaps caused by a device exerting very little pressure on the sur-face. In contrast to the Thompson Hotel sign, use of a com-pass ensured that the Carter carriage wheels were perfectly round and the spokes properly aligned.[22]

As Bryan Wolf suggests in his commentary on Benjamin Franklin's parable of the hatter's sign (see Chapter Two), words remained a relatively inconsequential element of signs even late in the eighteenth century. Even on well-executed signs textual errors were not uncommon, including reversed or malformed letters, like the "7" on Bull's Black Horse sign; misspellings, as in "hors"; and arbitrary word breaks, like "Enterta / inment," on the Duke of Cumberland sign (cat. nos. 1, 2, 5). Nearly all of the lettered Connecticut Hisorical Society signs used the Roman alphabet, which had been prevalent in English-speaking countries since the early six-teenth century and was favored for public and private mon-uments because of its "elegance and distinctness of lineation [*sic*]." New England sign painters, like contemporary grave-stone cutters, used both the capital and lowercase forms. Nearly 70 percent of the signs examined used only Roman capitals, although sometimes two heights were combined. The remaining 24 percent of written signs used both capital and lowercase letters, and several also included italicized capitals or script. The struggle to fit the word "Entertain-ment" on the limited space of a vertical board may have accounted for the early use of lowercase forms. The gigantic size of the preposition "BY" on Van der Hayden's sign (cat. 61) would never have passed muster with Henry Carey Baird, whose fifth rule of sign painting was "always make the most important words the largest, most distinct and easily read."[23]

In the nineteenth century, increasing emphasis on lettering in signs paralleled generally rising levels of literacy. The painter's education, as well as his dexterity, was exposed by

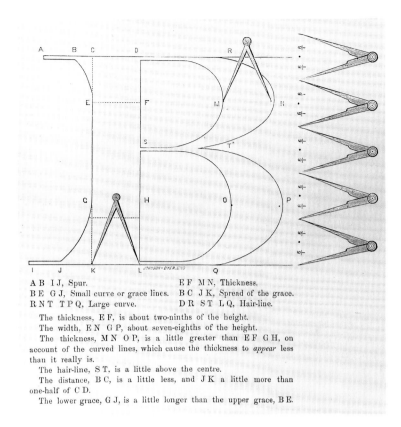

Fig. 71. Page from Lyford and Boyce, *The Art of Lettering and Sign Painter's Manual* (Boston: A. Williams & Co., 1871.) Courtesy, American Antiquarian Society. Roman capital letter proportions, listing the names and dimensions for various parts of a letter.

his lettering skill, and as time progressed his commissions might be affected by poorly executed words. The charming idiosyncrasies of earlier signs became less common, with the reversed *N*s on Wightman's circa 1824 sign a striking excep-tion (cat. 26). Published manuals, by definition addressed to literate craftsmen, provided detailed edification of the cor-rect manner of drawing and painting letters, especially capi-tals (fig. 71). During the Victorian era, specialized alphabet books emerged, introducing block and decorative designs that found their way on to some Connecticut signs (cat. 42, 56). The developing trend of using only lettering on signs was much lamented by technical authors, who disparagingly termed the new trade "Sign-writing." English author James Callingham observed in 1871 that the class of workmen known as sign painters had become almost unknown in Lon-don. His practical advice accordingly focused on lettering, with instructions on how to condense, shade, double shade, and even stretch individual forms. The same year, Lyford and Boyce of Boston published *The Art of Lettering and Sign*

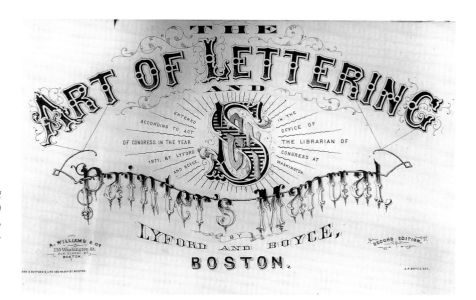

Fig. 72. Title page from Lyford and Boyce, *The Art of Lettering and Sign Painter's Manual* (Boston, A. Williams & Co., 1871.) Courtesy, American Antiquarian Society. The central word, "SIGN," is so interlaced as to be almost unintelligible.

Painter's Manual, which was comprised of forty pages of practical and fanciful lettering samples followed by a mere five pages of painting instruction (fig. 72). Some books had no text at all, being only collections of useful alphabets to copy, such as Delamotte's 1864 *Modern Alphabets* (fig. 74). In 1861 Henry Carey Baird remarked, "there is nothing left for the exercise of [artistic] genius or taste, but the arrangement or setting out [of letters] and the choice of colours."[24] Connecticut artists must have paid heed to the prevailing advice, for the execution of lettering is as accomplished as the image on signs such as Deodat Bement's and Jared Carter's inns and almost all of the Rice signs (cat. 9, 19, 28, 33, 34, 37, 46). In contrast, Aaron Fox's 1834 sign displays beautifully rendered lettering and intricate flourishes framing an extremely awkwardly drawn animal head (cat. 45).[25]

Paint, Gold, Smalt, and other Special Effects

A sign painter needed to use his knowledge of color and design to produce effects that would represent the establishment mentioned, grab the attention of travelers, and hopefully leave a lasting impression on viewers. It is quite possible that tavern and inn signs offered greater scope for sign painters to show off their talents, due to the scale and boldness of design required. Although few exmples are signed, tavern signs probably functioned as ads for artists, with information passing orally from owner to audiences. In general, America's early signboard imagery was probably less flashy, bawdy, or comic than London's. Perhaps under the influence of a more subdued Puritan aesthetic, New England's early signs displayed inoffensive and "simple motifs easily recognized even by the illiterate traveller." One author dismissed these early signs as "commonplace and lacking [in] originality," claiming that American signs became "unique" only after the Revolutionary War, when distinctly

national themes replaced European emblems. However, the earlier signs, typically painted with a limited palette, on either a white or colored ground, are among the strongest in design. The silhouetted tree on the Read tavern sign, now blackened with oxidation, was initially a bright copper-green, probably thickly-applied verdigris (cat. 5). Artists found the pigment verdigris difficult to grind and apply due to its large particle size; however, there were few greens available except as mixtures of blues and yellows. Later manuals warned against using verdigris outdoors because of its chemical instability.[26]

Full color imagery using bolder graphic design and/or more painterly techniques evolved quickly after the Revolution. The Woodward sign's background color originally contained Prussian blue, which has mostly faded and weathered away, leaving the ground the same off-white color as the letters (cat. 8). Detailed imagery such as that on the Porter and Carter signs was beautiful and fancy (cat. 27, 33), but not as readable from afar as the old silhouette designs. However, the gilded lettering, set against a dark background, would have been quite legible. Although extensively gilded signs had been prevalent in early London, Connecticut examples suggest that gold was less commonly used in America, perhaps beginning around 1810. In the 1820s and 1830s the inn name often appeared in pale, often gilded, letters against a dark band set below the images on the main board. Twenty-one signs had at least one paint job with gold lettering, and at least fourteen had gold leaf in their imagery. Squares of leaf can be seen in the eagle's wings of the Daniel Loomis sign, where wear has revealed the edges of the gold sheets (cat. 28). Exterior gold leaf, laid with an oil-based size, was never varnished because coatings dulled its reflectance. The experienced Jesse Haney claimed a single gold layer might endure for up to forty years outdoors. Although signs were generally not varnished, Haney recommended coating the

Fig. 73. *Sign for Collins's Hotel*, circa 1825–35, Straitsville, Conn. CHS, cat. 42, side 2, with mylar overlay showing design of original lettering, covered by the present surface which was probably painted in the 1840s. The smalted background sets off the boldly gilded and shaded block lettering.

Fig. 74. Page from F. Delamotte, *Examples of Modern Alphabets, Plain and Ornamental* . . . (London: Lockwood, 1864). Courtesy of Williams College Library. The "Shaded Roman" alphabet, used in painting the Collins Hotel sign (fig. 73).

"more decorative or ornamental style" signs. It is likely that several signs in the collection were originally varnished, especially the more painterly and detailed compositions: Israel Putnam's General Wolfe, Rose's Bird-in-Hand, Carter's "Strangers' Resort" (cat. 4, 23, 33).[27]

To set off gold letters visually, manuals recommended the use of a dark ground, usually smalt or sand. This treatment gave the ground the appearance of stone, much as sand in paint was used to accentuate rusticated effects on wooden buildings. Smalt is a coarse, cobalt-blue glass pigment that had been superseded in easel painting by pigments with better coloring and working properties. By the end of the seventeenth century, few fine artists would have chosen to use this gritty, hard-to-brush-out paint. Although smalt had been used for exterior surfaces such as sundials, it is unknown just when strewn smalt made its appearance for sign work. William Rice, ever the consummate promoter and fierce competitor, in 1818 advertised a "new superior style . . . with mineral Smalt, which will never tarnish, but grow brighter

with age." During the first half of the nineteenth century, smalt became so popular that manuals even coined the verb "Smalting" to describe the process of strewing textured materials into a thick matrix of paint. Colored sands were used in the same manner on the Village Hotel sign, although true blue smalt was considered by some to hold its color better and be more "lively" in effect (see fig. 102). To color match and embed the sparkly smalt, Prussian blue and white were combined to form a thick layer, carefully applied around previously completed gold letters. With the sign held flat, smalt was strewn into the wet paint and the board tapped hard against the table to "set" the smalt, then turned over so loose smalt could be collected for reuse. Seventeen Connecticut signs had either smalt or sand surfaces, with an amazing array of particle sizes or grades. The larger the particle, the deeper the color and the more expensive the smalt. Although all smalt is larger in grain size than ordinary pigments, the smalt on Carter's inn sign reached the highest magnitude—approximately 1/16" to 1/8" across (cat. 33).[28]

Fig. 75. *Sign for Wadsworth's Inn*, signed by Rice, 1844, Hartford, Conn. CHS, cat. 55, side 1. Detail of eagle's wing, showing copper-colored leaf, a decorative treatment advertised by William Rice's son, Frederick.

As New England expanded and competition grew, larger and more elaborate signs were required to set apart individual establishments. Sign painters adopted new and flashier techniques as commissions demanded more punch from their signs. The sign for the large and busy Collins Hotel, located along Strait's Turnpike from New Haven to Albany, would have been very expensive because of its size, the amount of smalt used, the design selected, and the fact that it was double-sided (fig. 73). Smalt was more expensive than either paint or sand, and lettering costs were factored either by the linear foot or the individual letter. Gilded letters, more expensive than painted ones, increased in cost with each 3" increment in height, and shading was also extra. The Collins sign, possibly first painted in the 1830s, was repainted some years prior to 1846 when the hotel closed. Apparently the hotel was prosperous for an extended period of time, as the second paint job would have been as expensive as the first. The Collins' Hotel sign is said to have hung "across the street supported from long poles by chains." While cleaning this sign, it was discovered that the gilded letters were extremely bright in low ambient light, making them as visible as in full daylight, a phenomenon that may explain the increased popularity of gold lettering in the 1820s and 1830s.[29]

Some additional flashy surface effects were more successful than others. The use of tin leaf on the Temperance sign was a poor choice, as many design elements on the eagle side are now irrevocably altered by deep tarnishing (see fig. 7). Many Rice signs show unusual techniques, including the ill-advised use of "flocks" on the Dyer beehive and plow sign (cat. 34). Flocked surfaces, commonly used on wallpaper, were made by applying dry pigment into a mordant layer. Less durable than smalt or sand, flocks tended to wash away when used outdoors. The Rice shop had a number of other singular techniques in its repertoire. In the 1850s Frederick Rice advertised his use of copper-colored leaf, a material still brightly reflecting its distinctive color on Sydney Wadsworth's eagle wings (fig. 75). The most spectacular paint job in the collection, both for condition and technical tour de force, is Rice's enormous sign for the Vernon Hotel (cat. 46). Elaborate in design, detail, and lettering, the surface decoration displays every trick from realistic paint techniques to the rare use of low-relief carving. This possible demonstration piece reads like a portfolio of sign-painting genius. Besides the strong draughtsmanship and design, we see gilding with glazes, flocks, blue and green smalts, and a glittery red application featuring tiny clear glass flakes.[30]

New England Weather and the Yankee Mentality

Both weathering and frugality contributed to the reuse of many Connecticut tavern signs. Left outside, sometimes for decades, in the harsh New England climate, paint and wood surfaces slowly etched away. More than half the signs studied were either partially or completely repainted during their useful outdoor years, often redated or spruced up by second- or third-generation family proprietors. The renewal or exchange of old signs for new ones was even built in to several painters' ad campaigns. When establishments changed hands, signs might receive new names, or even all-new images. The removal of heavy twentieth-century over-paint from one side of Blatchly's sign revealed what is left of a female figure of Justice, which in turn overlays an earlier sailing brig (see fig. 26). Haney's *Manual* gave three drastic methods of eradicating old paint in preparation for reusing a board, including the use of alcohol and a chisel, caustic lye baths, and setting fire to the paint. Among the Connecticut Historical Society signs, only J. Williams's Sign of the Grapes has evidence of what looked like charring below the paint (cat. 32). Luckily, as far as we can tell, most repaints were executed directly over old paint schemes, often with an obscuring white ground between old and new paint. This effectively protected what remained of the earlier decoration.[31]

Whether descendants preserved their own family sign-boards, or collectors rescued or bought them, we owe our thanks to these perspicacious individuals for saving the efforts of New England's less-well-known artisans. The use of such charming signs dwindled toward the end of the nineteenth century, nearly putting traditional sign painters out of work. However, various colonial revivals and folk art audiences have helped to fuel interest in early American design, creating a resurgence in the craft of painted wooden signs. In today's fast-paced industrial and electronic age, there is something comforting and inviting about a well-executed signboard that nostalgically evokes the honest pleasures of friendly hospitality. With that in mind, perhaps the Connecticut Historical Society's collection will be an inspiration for those artists who wish to pursue this time-honored and public art form.

NOTES

1   The title of this essay is taken from the wording of several nineteenth-century Connecticut sign painters' ads; Connecticut painter statistics were factored by the author for this essay using 43 of the painters identified by Margaret Vincent, "Connecticut Sign Painters 1780–1850" (unpublished research report, Connecticut Historical Society, 1999; findings summarized in Appendix 1). Hereafter, research cited as Vincent, "Sign Painters"; statistical chart, as Webber, "Painter Statistics."

2   William Rice and William Laughton of Hartford both bragged about their abilities; *American Mercury*, 12 May 1818, p. 2, col. 5; *Connecticut Courant*, 20 June 1820, p. 3, col. 5; cited in Vincent, "Sign Painters," pp. 43, 61.

3   Jesse Haney, *Haney's Manual of Sign, Carriage and Decorative Painting* (New York: Haney's Journal Office, 1870), p. 7.

4   Apprentice journal in "Paints and Recipes for Wooden Work—ca. 1801," *Connecticut Historical Society Bulletin* 9 (April 1943): 9–16; Hezekiah Reynolds, *Directions for Ship or House Painting* (New Haven: Eli Hudson, 1812), or facsimile with introduction by Richard

Candee (Worcester, Mass.: American Antiquarian Society, 1978), or Candee, "Preparing and Mixing Colors in 1812," *Magazine Antiques*, April 1978, pp. 849–53; Robert Dossie, *Handmaid to the Arts*, 2 vols. (London: J. Nourse, 1764); *Painter's, Gilder's and Varnisher's Manual* (London: M. Taylor, and New York: W. Jackson, 1838), pp. 191–205; hereafter cited as (1838) *Manual*.

5   Orson Campbell, *Treatise on Carriage, Sign and Ornamental Painting* (New York: Russell Lewis, 1841), preface; Haney, *Manual*, pp. i–ii, 74.

6   On drawing horses' legs, see Russell Hawes Kettell, *Pine Furniture of Early New England* (New York: Dover, 1929), p. 150. Mylar drawings of many signs were done by the author and James Squires, Donald R. Friary Fellow in Paintings at Williamstown Art Conservation Center. Pigment analyses were performed at WACC by James Martin, formerly Director of Analytical Services, and Nicholas Zammuto, formerly research assistant; and at the Winterthur Museum by Janice Carlson, Senior Scientist, and Kate Duffy, Associate Scientist; and interpreted in conjunction with the author. Patent Yellow was a combination of sea salt with the Massicot type of Litharge and was much lower in tinting strength than Chrome Yellow; see Campbell, *Treatise*, p. 3; Rutherford Gettens and George Stout, *Painting Materials: A Short Encyclopedia* (New York: Dover reprint of 1942 von Nostrand volume, 1966), pp. 106, 129; Rosamund D. Harley, *Artists' Pigments c. 1600–1835*, 2d ed. (London: Butterworths, 1982), pp. 99–102. On Zinc White, see Gettens and Stout, *Encyclopedia*, p. 177. Wood identification: "The Williamstown Art Conservation Center's 1998 CHS Sign Survey, covering approximately 70 Signs," written by Alex Carlisle (furniture), Katie Holbrow (objects), and Sandy Webber (paintings), hereafter cited as WACC, "Sign Survey"; wood analysis: R. Bruce Hoadley, University of Massachusetts, Amherst.

7   English signs: Sir Ambrose Heal, *The Signboards of Old London Shops* (London: B. T. Batsford, 1947), pp. 2, 12; Jacob Henry Burns, *A Descriptive Catalogue of the London Traders, Tavern and Coffee House Tokens Current in the Seventeenth Century* (London: Henry Benjamin Hanbury Beaufoy, 1855) pp. xciv–xcv; Charles Hindley, *Tavern Anecdotes and Reminiscences of the Origin of Signs, Coffee Houses, Etc.* (New York: S.& D. A. Forbes, 1830), p. 173; Herman D. J. van Schevichaven [Jacob Larwood] and John Camden Hotten, *The History of Signboards, From the Earliest Times to the Present Day*, 6th ed. (London: John Camden Hotten, [1866]), pp. 26–31. Full wording of the 1762 London law: Cecil Austen Meadows, *Trade Signs and Their Origins* (London: Routledge & Kegan Paul, 1957), pp. 7–8, or Larwood and Hotten, *The History of Signboards*, p. 29; Philadelphia signs: Kettell, *Pine Furniture*, p. 147.

8   Hartford sign painter Chauncey Case was seriously injured by a falling sign; cited in Vincent, "Sign Painters," p. 18; J. Hammond Trumbull, *The Public Records of the Colony of Connecticut, Prior to the Union with New Haven Colony* (Hartford: Brown & Parsons, 1850), p. 534, and *The Book of the General Laws for the People within the Jurisdiction of Connecticut . . .* (Cambridge, Mass.: Samuel Green, 1673), pp. 34–36, cited in Margaret Vincent, "Connecticut Inns and Hotels and Their Signboards 1750–1850" (unpublished research report, (Connecticut Historical Society, 1999), pp. 4–5. Sign statistics were factored by the author, for this essay, based on 59 Connecticut Historical Society tavern signs examined and recorded in WACC, "Sign Survey," and the subsequent examination and treatment reports of signs. The statistical chart is hereafter referred to as Webber, "Signboard Statistics."

9   Vincent, "Sign Painters"; verbal information on Rice's son-in-law came from Margaret Vincent, 30 November, 1999.

10   Webber, "Signboard Statistics."

11   On the hanging of signs, see Alice Morse Earle, *Stage–Coach and Tavern Days* (New York: MacMillan, 1900), p. 167; Kym Rice, *Early American Taverns: For the Entertainment of Friends and Strangers* (New York: Fraunces Tavern Museum, and Chicago: Regnery Gateway, 1983), pp. 51, 68, 74; Donna-Belle Garvin and James L. Garvin, *On the Road North of Boston: New Hampshire Taverns and Turnpikes 1700–1900*

(Concord: New Hampshire Historical Society, 1988), pp. 30, 32, 68; Edward Field, *The Colonial Tavern: A Glimpse of New England Life in the Seventeenth and Eighteenth Centuries* (Providence: Preston & Rounds, 1897), pp. 73, 76; Larwood and Hotten, *History of Signboards*, p. 7; on viewing distances, see Haney, *Manual*, p. 14; Webber, "Signboard Statistics"; WACC, "Sign Survey." Paint recipe for iron: (1838) *Manual*, p. 181: the ingredients required were bitumen, resin, umber, and boiled linseed oil.

12 Kettell, *Pine Furniture*, p. 150.

13 Lyford and Boyce, *The Art of Lettering and Sign Painter's Manual*, 2d ed. (Boston: A. Williams & Co., 1871), p. 42; R. Bruce Hoadley, *Understanding Wood: A Craftsman's Guide to Wood Technology* (Newtown, Conn.: Taunton Press, 1980), pp. 36, 186; Kettell, *Pine Furniture*, pp. 150–51. Two apparent exceptions are the hardwood of the Hinman sign and the yellow pine found on William Gordon's sign (cat. 13, 40). The fact that the latter was constructed from two boards, despite the sign's size, may reflect the generally smaller diameter of this species. The Hinman sign, created from a single board, developed commonly seen splits near the restraining frame attachments as it dried and aged.

14 Haney, *Manual*, p. 13.

15 Kettell, *Pine Furniture*, p. 151. In 1833, 10' to 12' long, 1" to 1–1/4" thick, 10" wide "best clear pine boards" cost only pennies more per length than pine plank; see James Gallier, *The American Builder's General Price Book and Estimator . . .* (New York: Stanley & Co., 1833), p. 60. Thickness measurements were taken by the author and by Richard Malley, Connecticut Historical Society Curator of Technology, using calipers.

16 On sealing wood, see Henry Carey Baird, *The Painter, Gilder and Varnisher's Companion* (Philadelphia: Henry Carey Baird & Co., 1861), p. 310; Lyford and Boyce, *Manual*, p. 42; Haney, *Manual*, p. 13; on paint layering, see Campbell, *Treatise*, p. 41; Haney, *Manual*, p. 13–14.

17 On Spanish White, see Reynolds, *Directions*, p. 9 (original pamphlet pagination); Spanish White composition, see Harley, *Artists' Pigments*, p. 163. A cross-section through a letter on the Loomis inn decanter sign (cat. 22) showed the appropriate number of white layers below the more medium-rich black used for the lettering. Extra medium was added for the black, probably to make it flow off the brush more smoothly. We also noted that many signs retained black as their last remaining color after severe weathering. Whether this was a function of a higher media content or merely its placement as the final layer was not determined.

18 Richard Candee, introduction to facsimile of Reynolds, *Directions for Ship or House Painting*, p. vi; "John Merritt (paint) advertisement," *Boston News-Letter,* 23 September 1736; Vincent, "Sign Painters"; (1838) *Manual*, pp. 55, 112, 118; Campbell, *Treatise*, pp. 15–16, 41–42; George Field, *Rudiments of the Painter's Art or Grammar of Colouring* (London: John Weale, 1850), pp. 135–37, 139–40; Haney, *Manual*, pp. 11, 13–14.

19 Reynolds, *Directions*, p. 8; Haney, *Manual*, pp. 11–12. Haney recommended an easel, bench, slab and marble muller, a set of palettes (hardwood or ivory) and, for brushes: Number 2-300, sash tools from Number 4-8, flat French tools of various sizes, a few rounds bound in tin and a stock of sable tools, short, medium and long to suit all subjects. He states that camel-hair brushes lay in color better than sable.

20 Campbell, *Treatise*, pp. 42–43, 109; Haney, *Manual*, pp. 18; James Callingham, *Sign Writing and Glass Embossing—A Complete Practical Illustrated Manual of the Art* (Philadelphia: H. C. Baird, 1871), p. 45; and James M. Gaynor and Nancy L. Hagedorn, *Working Wood in the Eighteenth Century* (Williamsburg, Va.: Colonial Williamsburg, 1993), pp. 65–68; Baird, *Companion*, p. 212; WACC, "Sign Survey." There may be a few signs with stencil-painted "restorations," such as the bronze paint letters on the Spencer sign (cat. 21).

21 A surviving pattern paper with cut-out lines, used by John Bellamy of Maine to replicate carved gangway boards for the navy, represents this intermediate process; Philip M. Isaacson, *The American Eagle* (Boston: New York Graphic Society, 1975), p. 119. A photograph of Lafayette's coach is reproduced in Stephen Jenkins, *The Old Boston Post Road* (New York: G. P. Putnam, 1913), p. 25. The Thompson Hotel sign may also have been in a fire and was used outside, during the summers, until sometime in the twentieth century.

22 *Middlesex Gazette,* 4 January 1826; cited in Vincent, "Sign Painters," p. 39. On the pantograph and camera obscura: Campbell, *Treatise*, p. 107; Gettens and Stout, *Encyclopedia*, pp. 284, 304–5, 284. Pantographs had been in existence since at least 1635, and probably earlier. Camera obscuras and lucidas had also been used since the seventeenth century and were replaced by the camera.

23 On Campbell, *Treatise*, pp. 42–43, 99; WACC, "Sign Survey"; Webber, "Signboard Statistics"; Callingham, *Sign Writing*, pp. 26–27, 30, 56, 150; 211

24 Callingham, *Sign Writing*, p. 9; Lyford and Boyce, *Manual;* F. Delamotte, *Examples of Modern Alphabets Plain and Ornamental* (London: Lockwood, 1864).

25 Baird, *Companion*, p. 211.

26 Garvin and Garvin, *New Hampshire Taverns*, p. 32; Field, *Colonial Tavern*, pp. 83–84. On London signs, see Burns, *Descriptive Catalogue*, pp. lxxxviii–xciii; Larwood and Hotten, *History of Signboards*, pp. 28, 512–26. On verdigris, see Campbell, *Treatise*, p. 9.

27 On Prussian Blue, see Barbara H. Berrie, "Prussian Blue," in *Artists Pigments: A Handbook of Their History and Characteristics: Volume 3*, ed. Elizabeth W. Fitzhugh (Washington, D.C.: National Gallery of Art, 1997), p. 199. The color was stated to fade, especially when mixed with white; Callingham, *Sign Writing*, pp. 157, 160. Gold sheets could also be cut to fit smaller dimensions than the full 3 3/8" squares sold. Double-gilding for extra longevity had been recommended in early English signs, but was scarce here due to expense. Varnishing all leaf metals except gold is recommended to prevent or delay tarnishing; (1838) *Manual*, p. 71, and Haney, *Manual*, p. 31; most exterior varnish recipes called for the use of copal resin dissolved in hot boiled linseed oil.

28 Rice ad: *American Mercury*, 3 November 1818, p. 3, col. 3," cited in Vincent, "Sign Painters," p. 51; WACC, "Treatment Records" and "Sign Survey"; Webber, "Signboard Statistics." On smalt, Dossie, *Handmaid to the Arts*, vol. 1, p. 94; Lyford and Boyce, *Manual*, p. 43; Campbell, *Treatise*, p. 109; Haney, *Manual*, pp. 24, 33; on rusticated paints, Albert Lowell Cummings and Richard M. Candee, "Colonial and Federal America: Accounts of Early Painting Practices," and Ian C. Bristow, "House Painting in Britain: Sources for American Paints, 1615 to 1830,"in *Paint in America: The Colors of Historic Buildings*, ed. Roger W. Moss (Washington, D.C.: National Trust for Historic Preservation, 1994), pp. 25, 52.

29 Elise Lathrop, *Early American Inns and Taverns* (New York: Tudor, 1936), pp. 49, 56–57; on lettering costs: Gallier, *American Builder's Price Book*, p. 119; Haney, *Manual*, p. 36.

30 On silver/Dutch metal leaf, Campbell, *Treatise*, p. 10, and Baird, *Manual*, p. 76. On flocks, see Haney, p. 34; Frederick Rice ad: *Geer's Hartford City Directory for 1854–5* (Hartford: Elihu Geer, 1854); WACC, "Sign Survey." Of the 59 signs reviewed by the author, very few can be said to be carved. These include details on the Porter, Vernon Hotel, and Chafee signs, and possibly much of the Hayden sign (cat. 3, 27, 46, 58). Most "relieving" effects were caused by long-term weathering exposure. Signs that had received disfiguring twentieth-century coatings of oil or shellac were cleaned and left uncoated (cat. 3, 8, 13, 15, 38, 40, 51).

31 WACC, "Sign Survey" and "Treatment Records"; Webber, "Signboard Statistics"; on paint removal: Haney, *Manual*, p. 32, and Lyford and Boyce, *Manual*, p. 47. For signs with completely different second surfaces, see cat. 10, 19, 24, 30, 36, 38. For examples of single images with repainted names, see cat. 2, 15, 40, 47, 54.

Weather It Is or Whether It Isn't

By Alexander M. Carlisle

The continued examination of the signboards in the collection of The Connecticut Historical Society has raised any number of questions concerning the variety of tradesmen involved in creating the signs, their methods of work, and the resulting products. Many of these questions have already been answered in Sandra Webber's thorough essay, " 'Faithfully and Promptly Executed.' " One question that continues to inspire lively discussion is whether certain signs were carved with chisels and gouges, or somehow treated by other means, to result in the outstanding shallow relief so plainly visible today.

Particularly intriguing are the inn signs of Deodat Bement, Uriah and Ann Hayden, Aaron Fox, and that depicting the Duke of Cumberland (fig. 77; cat. 2, 3, 9, 45). The most striking qualities of these signs are the fine detail and crisp edges of the surface relief, which would challenge even a highly skilled carver working in the softwood surface of an Eastern white pine panel. In the fully rigged warship of the Haydens' "Old Ship" tavern sign, for example, each sweep of rigging is neatly set out in lines as fine as one-sixteenth of an inch wide and raised a mere three sixty-fourths of an inch above the background surface (see fig. 24).[1]

A bright raking light set nearly parallel to the signboard surface shows these slightly raised areas to best advantage. This technique has proved a useful tool in uncovering images, dates, and tavern owners' names on signs that had been painted over as the tavern changed hands or the image was updated to appear more contemporary. A good example of this is the discovery, on the Abbe Inn and Tea Room signboard, of a large eagle image that had been thoroughly obscured by a later layer of black paint (fig. 78).

As yet, little evidence has been uncovered to support the theory that the shallow relief images on the signboards in question were actually carved with edge tools. There are no visible signs of traditional carving techniques such as "set-in" marks on the image perimeter,[2] or supporting evidence such as surface chipping or gouge marks uncovered in raking light. Clear evidence of such tool marks does remain visible elsewhere, as in the lettering and in the scroll-shaped motif, derived from a ship's "billethead," on the George Chafee signboard (fig. 79), as well as in the shallow relief carved volutes and decorative scrollwork on the red drapery side of the Vernon Hotel signboard (cat. 46, side 2). Significantly, the complex but heavily weathered Hayden signboard does appear to retain signs of edge-tool relief around the lettering, although no comparable marks are visible around the image. This contrasting evidence on a single signboard undermines the possibility that the traces of carving have been obscured by weathering.[3] What this evidence suggests, in fact, is quite the opposite: that the remarkable detail in these shallow reliefs is the direct product of weathering, and that long years of climatic abuse and irregular histories of repainting have actually formed—not obscured—the raised images.

This concept of "preferential weathering" is supported by other signboards in the collection that may be considered as intermediates in the weathering process. An excellent example occurs in the Daniel Loomis signboard (fig. 76). In contrast to the signboards in question, which have lost almost all of their decorative paint coating, the Loomis sign retains a largely continuous paint and gold leaf layer on the decorative images, set against a bare, weathered, and worn background. Close examination of these weathered surfaces shows a preferential reduction of the areas now without paint and a preservation of the areas that have retained a paint coating. The preferential reduction of the unprotected surfaces by weathering is highlighted by the lines of harder latewood growth rings that extend, with some frequency, nearly to the tops of the painted passages.[4] These traces of the former surface plane of the signboard would have been lost had they been relieved by edge tools.

Fig. 76. *Sign for Daniel Loomis's Inn*, signed by William Rice, ca. 1820, Coventry, Conn. CHS, cat. 28, side 2.

Fig. 78. *Sign for Fields's Inn and Abbe Inn*, circa 1814–20 and circa 1914, Enfield, Conn. CHS, cat. 24, side 1, before treatment. In raking light, the shallow relief of an eagle is visible beneath the gold on black layer, updating the sign for the Colonial Revival Abbe Inn and Tea Room. This overpainting was subsequently removed from one side of this sign at Williamstown Art Conservation Center, 1999.

Fig. 77. *Sign for Bement's Inn*, circa 1786–1810, Wallingford, Conn. CHS, cat. 9, side 2. Although little of the original colored paint remains, raking light makes visible the skillful lettering and well-designed layout, featuring a man's saddle and saddle blanket.

The painted image that remains has been worn thin enough to reveal distinct brush marks, visible throughout the sign images, but especially clear in the painted cannonballs along the lower edge (fig. 80). The thinnest, or feathered, portions of the brush strokes have been worn away completely, uncovering the wood substrate, which has already begun to wear away and recede. The cause of this uneven wear would seem to be the varying thicknesses of the paint strokes as laid down by a stiff brush.[5] As the thin paint streaks wore away first, the wood surfaces in those areas became more deeply eroded, leaving the thicker, raised, and quite painterly brush strokes to describe the round shape of the cannonballs.

The mechanism that causes this remarkable and complex surface is an environmentally precipitated erosion brought about by the combined effects of sunlight, wind, wind-borne debris, moisture, fungus, freezing, and thawing. These environmental attacks are far more devastating to a bare white pine surface than a painted one, which is why we paint wooden houses. Sunlight, and in particular ultraviolet rays, promote chemical reactions that break down molecules into smaller components. Since a paint coating relies on a contin-

uous film of larger interlocked molecules, this process slowly degrades the surface. Wind and moisture in the form of rain leach away these degraded components, wind-borne debris acts like a sandblaster to scour away what it can, and freeze/thaw cycles take advantage of the moisture content of the surface to break it apart. Once the paint is gone, the wood is broken down in much the same way, only faster.[6]

The preferential part of the mechanism takes advantage of the relative toughness of the protective paint film. The most astute manufacturers today will not really guarantee their products without the application of a specific, measurable, film thickness. Protection is not just a matter of applying a coat of paint, but also of the thickness of that coat of paint. Imagine the process of building up a decorative signboard image. First comes the application of the background color with one, two, or more coats of paint. Then the decorative image and lettering are added, with additional colors built up to articulate the individual backgrounds and the details, then shading and flourishes are added at the end. A signboard is not just one even thickness of paint, but a range of thicknesses as broad as the image is complex. It makes perfect sense that the details remain raised in a weathered signboard while the background recedes step by step as the relative thicknesses of the paint films are worn away. The Daniel Loomis signboard provides a perfect example of this phenomenon, with the thin background paint worn completely away while the detail of the image retains the full color and variety of its surface.

The relative depth of relief in the surfaces of such signboards as Uriah and Ann Hayden's may be indicative of more years of weathering, or a history of repainting. Repainting a weathered signboard suggests an additional set of factors. If, like the Daniel Loomis sign, the background had worn away to bare wood before repainting, a new layer of paint would have been applied over the eroded wood surfaces as well as

Fig. 79. *Sign for the Chafee House*, circa 1865-89, Middletown, Conn. CHS, cat. 58. Detail of relief-carved surface, showing visible gouge marks and punchwork decoration.

Fig. 80. *Sign for Daniel Loomis's Inn*, signed by William Rice, ca. 1820, Coventry, Conn. CHS, cat. 28, side 2. Detail of cannonballs, showing weathered surface.

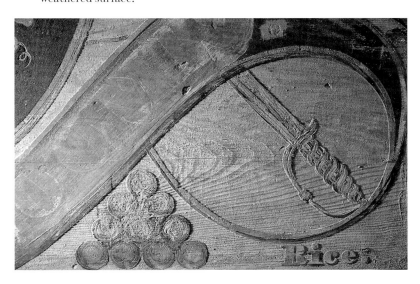

over the paint-protected surfaces. Although the remaining coated surfaces would provide a suitable base for additional coats of paint, the weathered wood might not be so hospitable due to changes in its surface chemistry. A weathered wood surface becomes a less cohesive and more acidic surface than a fresh surface, and is less supportive of good paint adhesion. Additional factors include surface dirt, mold, and fungal spores driven into the surface by wind and rain. These also degrade a paint bond and would likely cause early failure of the repainted background, further promoting the discrepancy between the raised detail and the erosion of the background.

In conclusion, there are strong indications that weather is the mystery carver responsible for the finely raised detail visible in the Hayden frigate, the Duke of Cumberland figure, and signs belonging to innkeepers Deodat Bement and Aaron Fox. However, examples of shallow-relief wood carving exist, in such signs as those of the Vernon Hotel, George Chafee and Joseph Porter (cat. 27). Together with other signs at The Connecticut Historical Society, these works stand as exemplary testimony to the variety and skill brought to bear in creating early American outdoor advertising art.

NOTES

1   Eastern white pine or *Pinus strobus,* the most common substrate of the signboards in the collection of The Connecticut Historical Society. The Hayden signboard has been identified as yellow poplar, *Linodendron tulipifera.*

2   The "set-in" marks are cuts made with edge tools perpendicular to the wood surface to establish the outline of a carved image detail.

3   Irregular passages in the heraldic crest, where the surface relief is particularly deep, do appear to have been reduced with edge tools. This work, evidently intended to clarify portions of the image, is likely to have occurred at the time other alterations were made, including the addition of the word, "Entertainment," and new owners' initials and dates, "UHA/1766." Although these instances might be interpreted as remaining evidence that the crest was originally relief-carved, substantial evidence remains to support the probability that preferential weathering is the primary factor in the current raised image. This evidence includes late wood growth rings that bridge the image outline across passages which would certainly have been relieved with edge tools had the image been orginally carved, and the clear lack of "set-in" marks around the jewels of the central crown, where traditional wood carving techniques would certainly have left traces.

4   The concentric growth rings of a tree generally alternate between light and dark, with the broader light-colored, and less dense, ring characterizing the earlywood or fast spring growth, and the darker, and more dense, ring characterizing the slower late summer and fall growth.

5   As described in Sandra Webber's essay, the quality of paint was often thicker and less refined than modern paints, leaving visible brush strokes and an uneven thickness of paint film.

6   Sunlight breaks down lignan, the "adhesive" that binds the wood structure, leaving the remaining cellulose to simply fall away. Studies have shown that an unprotected softwood surface will lose one-fourth of an inch per hundred years through erosion and weathering.

From Tavern Signs to Golden Arches:
A Landscape of Signs

By Catherine Gudis

Past the orange roof and turquoise tower, past the immense sunburst of the green and yellow sign, past the golden arches beyond the low buff building, . . . beneath the red and white longitudes of the enormous bucket, coming up to the thick shaft of the yellow arrow piercing the royal-blue field, he feels he is home. Is it Nashville? Elmira, New York? St. Louis County? . . . Where?

Somewhere in the packed masonry of states.

—Stanley Elkins, *The Franchiser*[1]

Thus begins Stanley Elkin's 1976 novel, a story of the highway travels and travails of Ben Flesh. A self-made businessman, Flesh buys and sells, leases and loans, the commercial spaces bearing other men's names—Howard Johnson, Ronald McDonald, Colonel Sanders. They are the links in the chains that line and sign the strips of twentieth-century America. Ironically enough, however, Flesh is lost in a landscape of his own franchised creation. The highway environs offer little to moisten his parched memory.

The amnesia that Flesh experiences while driving along the highway strip is one to which many of us can relate. Yet Elkin's novel also helps to elucidate a longer historical span of the built environment. It begs the question of how this landscape of signs came to be and how earlier wayfarers may have understood the signs that marked their urban and rural journeys. Did the signs that advertised the inns, taverns, and hotels of early America mark, not only a respite from the rough road, but a sense of excitement at the possibility of new experiences? Were the signs a form of publicity that really was public-minded—serving public interest and marking public space? Or were they merely signs of advancing commercial markets, which would grow along the roadsides just as surely as travelers would grow in numbers along the thoroughfares in years to come?

In light of such considerations, we might also wish to examine our own feelings of déjà vu in reading the passage above. Are today's urban and rural journeys really a traipsing through homogenous, placeless landscapes where there is no there, there, as Gertrude Stein put it? Or is there a mental landscape that accompanies the physical landscape of signs, a landscape where golden arches are not the only thing on the horizon? From tavern signs to golden arches, the advertisements at the side of the road have long been dominant features of the built and natural environment, as expressive of commercial growth as they are indicative of social, cultural, and technological change. Seen in this light, perhaps the historical landscape of signs is one that can inform us in our travels and travails in the "packed masonry of states" we call home.

Beginning in the eighteenth and nineteenth centuries, the signs that marked the American roadside environment served to foster and promote travel and tourism while they expanded notions of the marketplace and public culture. Especially as turnpikes and stagecoach travel between New York and Boston increased in the late eighteenth century, the tavern and inn signs dotting the New England countryside were constituent elements of a transforming commercial and cultural arena. The signs helped to articulate new sites for social and commercial exchange. They spoke to an audience in motion, broadcasting the availability of goods and services to travelers, who would otherwise be left to the elements or to the whims of whichever local residents were willing to open their homes to passing strangers. Promising social and commercial exchange, these site-specific outdoor advertisements indicated the spaces and places where public discourse and opportunities for personal and pecuniary gains might be had. Importantly, the signs that marked the way to the inns, taverns, and hotels of Connecticut's eighteenth- and nineteenth-century towns and rural villages also helped to disperse and mobilize the market, creating corri-

Fig. 81. *Sign for Dyer's Inn*, signed by William Rice, circa 1823, Canton, Conn. CHS, cat. 34, side 2.

Fig. 82. John Warner Barber, *South Western View of Ashford, Conn.*, ink, wash, and graphite drawing on paper, circa 1830s. CHS, Graphics Collection. Two tavern signs tower over the road, much like modern billboards.

dors of consumption through which individuals could realize themselves as anonymous participants in a rapidly nationalizing mass culture.

The audience for these tavern signs was a mass audience, comprised of an anonymous mix of visitors whose passage through towns and along turnpikes and highways was facilitated by signs. As Margaret Vincent notes, the laws of the Connecticut Colony as early as 1644 suggest that inns and taverns were aimed toward a traveling public of strangers and passengers for whom food and lodging was not just a desire but a necessity. By 1673, laws required that such facilities be made known to strangers and that signs be erected to indicate the presence of such places for "entertainment of man and horse" (see Chapter 4). In newspaper advertisements for taverns and coffeehouses and in drawings of townscapes, we see freestanding signposts and boards looming high, above at least the height of horsemen and carriages, and higher even than the height of taverns themselves.[2] Ink drawings of Connecticut in the 1830s by John W. Barber (fig. 82) reveal that the freestanding signpost not only distinguished one building from the next but served as a portal or gateway to the town or community, welcoming strangers to what would otherwise have been a silent and anonymous depot. Like a firmly planted tree, such signposts helped to naturalize the advertisement and served as a totemic embodiment of the rooted community of townspeople and innkeeper.

Even more important, in an age when buildings' functions were not necessarily expressed in their appearance, the signs were essential place markers. The signposts, and the hanging signs affixed to the facades of some buildings, distinguished structures whose purposes might otherwise be difficult to discern (except for churches). The tavern becomes recognizable by the mere presence of the signpost or hanging bracket, regardless of what imagery or text might be featured on the sign displayed. Without these signposts and hanging signs as place markers, we today (and, presumably, travelers of long ago) could scarcely begin to guess which structures are private and which will accommodate passing strangers, an anonymous public. How else could we discern a private home from a public lodging house?

Tavern and inn signs in the Connecticut Historical Society collection provide good examples of the emergence of commercial architecture aimed toward mobile, mass audiences. These examples significantly predate the findings reported by architects Robert Venturi, Denise Scott-Brown, and Steven Izenour in their much acclaimed *Learning from Las Vegas* (1972), which identified signs as the distinguishing architecture of the automobile age. Their study took note of the dominant features of the roadside environment and demonstrated how buildings targeted to moving audiences communicated via tall signs set along the road. Architecturally, the structures to which the signs directed viewers were hardly notable by comparison. Far from it; towering

Fig. 83. United Advertising Company, *Texaco Station and McDonald's Hamburgers*, probably southwestern Connecticut, circa 1965, silver gelatin print. CHS, Graphics Collection.

and often illuminated or oscillating signs, such as those along the Las Vegas Strip, helped to decorate buildings that were otherwise nothing more than utilitarian sheds (figs. 83, 84). The commercial sign, *not* the monolithic architecture of a singular building, was the most significant architectural expression of the automobile age. It would seem to have been a characteristic of the stagecoach age as well (see fig. 82).

Although the horse and carriage riders of the distant past and motorists of more recent times certainly traveled under different conditions, the signs marking the roadside environment in each age bear comparison. Indeed, at least since the late 1600s, signs have become an increasingly important element of architecture and the built environment. They served as formal embellishments that clarified the function of different buildings and the lines between increasingly separate public and private spaces. For instance, displayed from hanging brackets or atop the tall signposts for inns and taverns of the 1700s are boards framed by broken pediments and turned spindles that borrow elements from such domestic items of furniture as bookcases, cabinets, chair backs, headboards, and looking glasses (see figs. 21, 22). Use of these elements in this exterior and public context extended a private invitation to wayfaring travelers and bridged the distance between the cold outside world and the warmth of home and hearth. Although the outdoor and public setting of these icons of private life and interior spaces may have struck a discordant note, the contrast was a useful advertise-

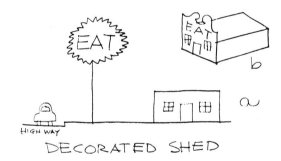

Fig. 84. "Decorated shed," from Robert Venturi, Denise Scott Brown, and Steven Izenour, *Learning from Las Vegas* (Cambridge: The MIT Press, 1972). Courtesy The MIT Press.

ment for the somewhat contradictory blend of transience and residency, intimacy and anonymity that the tavern promised.

Because the frames of the signboards were utilitarian and constructed with familiar furniture technology, they were easily reproduced. Their widespread use thus ensured a recognition that comes with repetition and an identifiable set of features that allows its form to be called a typology. What was held within the frame could hardly matter. In fact, the signboard supported within this frame generally included scant text and imagery. Words were limited to

Fig. 85. Nelson A. Moore, *Main Street between Pearl and Gold Streets, Hartford*, circa 1850, salt print. CHS, Graphics Collection. These mid-nineteenth-century buildings display typical commercial signs—narrow, horizontal bands of lettering mounted flush on the walls. As buildings grew larger, occupants multiplied, and each floor acquired its own sign.

Fig. 86. Frederick J. Moore, *Main and State Streets, Hartford*, ca. 1885-87, albumen print. CHS, Graphics Collection. As sign text proliferated, building facades increasing functioned as architectural notice boards.

"entertainment" or "entertainment for man and horse," and proprietors' names were rarely included. Perhaps this was to attain the right balance of domestic offerings to an anonymous public of passersby, for whom the name or details of accommodation might mean little. The mere presence of the signpost or bracket and the standardized frame there displayed could communicate the main purpose of the building (even if it was set back a bit from the road), regardless of the reading or visual literacy skills of the travelers.

In contrast to the signs themselves, newspaper advertisements for newly opened inns and taverns in the *New London Gazette* in the 1760s and 1770s offered far more personal assurances by their owners of the quality and civility of the accommodations provided. Ostensibly, these ads were written and paid for by the innkeepers or tavern owners, and employed a standardized language of polite society as it might have been in that time and place. Nevertheless, the ads in these printed sources send a message different than what one might glean from the roadside sign. In the printed ads an authorial (and authoritative) presence—key to the power of print—is made evident by the inclusion of the proprietors' names and assurances that they are "humble servants," reasonable, obedient, and able to provide reliable service to "genteel" "gentlemen and ladies," "travellers and

Others."[3] In lieu of the face-to-face contact one would have by passing over the threshold of an inn after seeing the recognizable sign outside, the printed ad offers facts and the authority of the signed statement as endorsement. It attempts to provide a personal context for the public offerings of the tavern, the owner's voice is transcribed in print as a counterpart to the domestic references of the signboard.

The differences between outdoor tavern signs and printed advertisements for taverns in the eighteenth century aptly correspond to those observed in mid- to late nineteenth-century advertising history. Printed ads in the nineteenth century used narrative testimonials and "reasons why" the goods and services advertised were the best available. Well into the 1900s, after halftone photos were easily produced and affordable, such text-based copy was still in use. In contrast, outdoor advertising never employed such extensive use of text. Though individual words might comprise the image area of some nineteenth-century outdoor advertisements, text-heavy testimonials and other such "signed" narratives were quickly abandoned in favor of silhouetted images, singular massed forms, and other iconic representations.

It is also of note that almost all of the tavern signs of the eighteenth century in the collection of The Connecticut His-

Fig. 87. United Advertising Company, *Outdoor advertising signs for Kellogg's, Packard, Hellman's, Sunkist,* probably southwestern Connecticut, ca. 1938–40, silver gelatin print. CHS, Graphics Collection.

torical Society are vertical in orientation. By around 1815, however, the orientation of many signs changed from vertical to horizontal. Perhaps this shift echoed the increased speed with which people were able to travel as turnpikes and roads were better maintained and the way better marked. This was surely the case in rural areas. A different type of horizontal advertising also appears in more densely populated towns and cities, where hanging and freestanding signs were pushed farther and farther off the streets and sidewalks until they were no longer three-dimensional advertisements at all. Rather, by the last third of the nineteenth century, the sign became part of the architectural facade (fig. 85). Not surprisingly, this happened at the same time as buildings became more distinct in terms of their purposes: shops had bigger windows, private residences were relegated to back rooms, upper floors, or other areas entirely. The freestanding sign was no longer the distinguishing architectural feature of the commercial establishment, and at this time sign-laden facades and walls of buildings became more and more dominant in images of the city. These surfaces became two-dimensional spaces for rent or lease, transforming the exteriors of buildings into yet another site of commerce.

The signs on the buildings helped to intensify the density and commercial congestion of the city and its streets. Even as buildings rose vertically toward the end of the nineteenth century, the ads on their sides often extended horizontally, as if to articulate the multiple tiers or floors that comprised the vertical expanse. They served as two-dimensional architectural markers as well, indicating the commercial function of the buildings—with shops on ground floors, offices above, and leased space for painted and posted signs on the sides—and the increasingly concentrated commercial function of the city center. With their sides coated with advertising signs for both on-site businesses and off-site goods and services, downtown buildings expressed their dedication to commerce; the multitude of closely located buildings adorned with advertisements served to express the same purpose for the central city (fig. 86).

In the signs of the first part of the 1800s, the horizontal orientation of the boards and imagery of, for instance, moving horse and carriage or winged eagle, had visualized the movement of increased traffic along country roads. It was a premonition of signs to come. By the late 1800s, even as buildings grew taller in dense urban areas, streetcar and railroad lines were extending outward horizontally from and between growing numbers of towns and cities. Signs for all sorts of goods and services—not to mention new kinds of roadside accommodations for man and mechanical beast—announced the way. Their horizontal orientation and location alongside railways and auto thoroughfares were perhaps

Fig. 88. *Sign for Bement's Inn*, circa 1786–1810, Wallingford, Conn. CHS, cat. 9, side 1, detail. The curved secondary horn on this saddle reveals it to be a lady's sidesaddle, in contrast to the man's saddle shown on the other side (fig. 77). This is a rare eighteenth-century example of gender-specific marketing.

strategically aimed toward embodying movement and keeping pace with faster-moving, twentieth–century audiences (fig. 87).

As tavern and inn signs shifted orientation from vertical to horizontal in the 1810s, many also began to feature more text than had signs of the previous century. As mentioned earlier, outdoor signs never used as much text as print advertisements; however, the trend toward including words as, or alongside, images might be related to a rise in literacy. Or perhaps it reflected increased competition and thus a greater desire to distinguish one establishment from another. At the same time as text becomes notable in tavern signboards, sign painters such as William Rice began to employ increasingly sophisticated imagery, with complicated compositions carefully rendered. Rice's ornate painting of a beehive and plow, with the phrase "hold or drive," is a case in point (cat. 34). Rice almost always signed his works, as if to offer a personal testimonial or endorsement, similar to the printed ads of innkeepers of the earlier period. Signing his work was a way of announcing his artistry and exemplifying the care his patron might also offer to his customers.

Signs by other, unnamed artists, such as that which employs a rebus for "Crow Foot's Inn," suggest a playfulness and thoughtfulness on the part of the painter (cat. 59). No doubt this artist also imagined that his viewers would be similarly playful and thoughtful, and grateful enough to frequent George E. Crofut's establishment as a result. By expressing the qualities of wit and individuality, these signs and the taverns they marked might be distinguished from otherwise generic and anonymous imagery and architecture. Such delightful individualism in the face of an increasingly standardized typology of signs suggests that some sign painters and proprietors along the roadside marketplace were already engaging in advertising strategies usually associated with the development of mass culture in the twentieth century. Once an architectural typology of signs had been established, the range of imagery or text could enhance or further endow the tavern with other qualities beyond pure functionalism.

The pictures, texts, and architectural structures of the roadside tavern markers, even those so skillfully rendered by William Rice, required little knowledge in order to be understood. They aimed to capture the attention of passersby and to convey information to literate and illiterate alike. To do so they frequently employed fairly singular images, akin to what we today call the logo. Thus, in the Connecticut Historical Society collection we find prototypes for the familiar signs found along today's roads—the golden arches and the Taco Bell.

This is not to say that within this "logo-istic" imagery there remained no room for interpretation, however literally the signs served as markers for services available. For though a tavern advertised the availability of food, drink, and accommodations, the quality of these provisions—and whatever else might be exchanged—remained uncertain. The sign could never capture or signify all that was actually to be provided at its site, and thus became an interpretative exercise for the imagination of the traveler.

Perhaps some signs even provoked travelers to self-interpretation, asking themselves who they were and what they thought they were doing on the road. Although advertising signs served as a form of mass message, they had to speak to individuals, on an individual basis. Tavern signs operated within a fairly limited range of narrative and formal structures; nevertheless, they can be said to express psychological or other subjective associations. The signs marked a place of anticipated opportunities for social and commercial exchange. In their setting and function they symbolized passages of different sorts—passage to and through town and tavern, passage to an unknown future. In this landscape of mobility, travelers experienced a sense of possibility, independence, self-sufficiency, and, perhaps, self-creation. Stopping at an inn allowed a traveler to be or become something or someone other than what he or she might have been known as at home. Thus, the road and its way stations offered, not just fluidity of movement, but a fluid sense of identity as well.[4]

Such an expansive vista of the eighteenth- and nineteenth-century cultural landscape is difficult to imagine when one is faced today with the scanty material remains of travel in the period. The assortment of tavern signs in the Connecticut Historical Society collection, however, offers good evidence from which to construct a portrait of the past that may also help us see the contemporary landscape more clearly. For instance, the forms, images, and placements of the early tavern signs in the collection suggest their relative simplicity and standardization. They employed structures and an iconography that was easily repeated, repeatable, and thus readable, by many different kinds of audiences, coming from different regions and locales. Though some of these messages required an insider's familiarity with the symbolic vocabulary used (such as Masonic symbols, which identified a more exclusive club, cat. 11), even these obtuse messages communicated to wayward and welcomed travelers (fig. 88). In fact, the way in which outdoor signs work as place makers is as much through the knowledge that they speak to those other than oneself as through the recognizability of their messages. For instance, a female traveler and her female companion might quip to one another that a tavern sign advertising refreshment for "men and horses" clearly did not speak to them.[5] They might choose to defy that message and seek some kind of accommodation anyway; or they might continue on their way. In any case, they recognized a message and interpreted their own relationship to that message and the place it represented. In that private exchange, their understanding of the road and their relationship to it was also defined. Perhaps this exchange occurred only to those two women, perhaps to hundreds of women like them.

By the turn of the twentieth century, roadside signs were more and more conspicuous elements of the landscape of mobility, but they were also being contested. The success of earlier sign advertising had helped to mobilize markets out of cities and into rural areas. Prospects began to change, however, with the increasingly horizontal diffusion of towns, suburbs, and automobile-oriented travelers and tourists. The rural landscape whose signs had once beckoned welcomingly now blared dissonantly to an urban population seeking escape and salvation in the nearby countryside and more distant wilderness. These visitors had little desire to look at advertisements slathered on trees or buildings, much less on the barns that so romantically symbolized an agrarian past. The painted signs for Mail Pouch tobacco and other products (put up in exchange for a new coat of paint on all the other walls of the barn) offended road-traveling nature

Fig. 89. Standard Oil Company, *Results: "Sign-ic or Scenic?" Contests*, 1929. Collection of author. "Why Sign Away Beauty?" asks the first-prize winning slogan.

lovers, who sternly criticized this interruption of the pastoral scene by signs of the market. (These critics conveniently ignored the paradox of their criticism: they deplored the pollution of ads as they traveled through the woods and fields in oil-belching cars, along paths paved in concrete and asphalt.) Their criticism may have been the result of a different conception of public space and its boundaries. The complaint directed toward outdoor advertising in the 1920s, for instance, targeted the broadcasting of the commercial message as much as the location of ads along the roadside, where they might disrupt the view (fig. 89). The road itself had become the public space, not the taverns or other establishments being advertised or bearing the advertisements.

By the turn of the twentieth century, and more firmly by the 1920s and 1930s, most travelers saw the rural environment as a place separate from the market. They held this view without realizing that they themselves were embodiments of a mobile market (how else were they traveling if not by their consumption and purchase of gasoline, food, etc.?), and that farmers and other landowners had private interests staked to the land and landscape. Needless to say, this city-bred nostalgia for a rural pastoral free of commerce and commercial boundaries was sheer silliness to rural landowners. For

these country folk, farmland was a site of commodity production (whether they articulated it as such or not), and the advertising sign was a service and source of income. The problem posed by the ad-painted barn, as well as other site-specific advertising signs, was that they interrupted the scenic vista, historically valued as part of nature. Such signs commodified the landscape and removed it from the purely "natural."

As the distance, frequency, and speed of travel continued to increase over the course of the twentieth century, so did demand increase for a new aesthetic whose goal was to communicate quickly, easily, and memorably to the masses of mobile audiences who comprised the rapidly expanding commercial culture. Perhaps taking cues from the earlier legacy of sign design, by the twentieth century advertisers and sign painters who had previously been known for their text-based ads and signs were again embracing the singular image, the icon, the massed image as an ideal form for their crafted signs. By the 1910s through 1930s, they developed what I call an *aesthetics of speed*, which relied on the logo, on pictures rather than text, and which stretched horizontally to follow the implied direction of movement of their passing audience (fig. 90). The horizontal strip, the logo, and the sprawling landscape of mobility define both today's urban environment and the electronic frontier (figs. 91, 92). Commercial signs have marked the way toward a culture more oriented to individual movement (whether by car or by computer) than to a public culture rooted in a physically defined place and market.

Throughout their history, roadside signs have served paradoxical ends: in the process of establishing place identity and marking public space, they also created a sense of placelessness that may be said to come from fostering a standardized appearance and impulses toward movement, rootlessness, and commodification. Yet, at the same time, subjectivity, individualism, and mobility of all kinds are characteristic elements of this landscape as well. If we consider the realm of imaginative possibilities that movement and mobility may promise—that of being or becoming something or someone else, somewhere else—then the seemingly deadening effect of repetition may be tempered.

But what of the quotation with which we began, that apt summary of the experience of traveling the highway strip and the interstate? Ironically enough, by the end of Elkin's novel, we learn that the placelessness experienced by Ben Flesh is not a product of the landscape of corporate capitalism or the repetition of mansard roofs and golden arches, in the development of which Flesh has played a part. Rather, his amnesia is the result of a failure of the flesh: he has a hastening physical condition that has made of his memory—his interior, mental landscape—a kind of placeless repetition of meaningless signs. The signs that should inspire reflection and imaginative possibilities are, for him, without dimension, the effect of his own dementia. Flesh is thus a doubly ironic character. He is not only geographically lost in a world he has helped to build, he is mentally lost in a constantly deconstructing world where the signs lack significance and have no reference. They have left no mark; there is no there,

Fig. 91. *Outdoor advertising sign, Camel cigarettes logo,* Route 1, New Haven, Conn., circa 1997. Photograph by author.

there. Yet, if Flesh had his mental faculties, he might indeed be able to see the signs and read them, too, making sense of the familiar landscape of signs.

NOTES

1 Stanley Elkin, *The Franchiser* (New York: Farrar, Strauss & Giroux, 1976), pp. 1–2.

2 See, for instance, *Hartford Courant,* 22 May 1806: p. 8, col. 6, and ink drawings by John W. Barber from the 1830s in the collection of The Connecticut Historical Society.

3 Margaret Vincent, "Connecticut Inns and Hotels and Their Signboards" (unpublished research report, Connecticut Historical Society, 1999), p. 7.

4 The transformative experience of travel and tourism is addressed in John Sears, *Sacred Spaces* (New York: Oxford University Press, 1989); Dona Brown, *Inventing New England* (Washington, D.C.: Smithsonian Institution Press, 1996); and Marguerite S. Shaffer, "Negotiating National Identity," in Hal K. Rothman, ed., *Reopening the American West* (Tempe: University of Arizona Press, 1998), pp. 122–51. On the mix of travelers and local residents in one eighteenth-century Connecticut tavern, see Vincent's discussion of Timothy Root's tavern, Farmington, in Chapter 4.

5 "Caution to Tavern Keepers," *Connecticut Courant,* 5 June 1797, p. 3, col. 4, cited in Vincent, "Connecticut Inns and Hotels," p. 7.

Fig. 92. *Bus with advertisement,* New York City, circa 1999. Photograph by author.

Signs of the Past in the Present

By Kenneth L. Ames

Signs are familiar features of everyday life. It is difficult to travel very far in Connecticut or any other settled part of America these days without encountering them, sometimes in nearly overwhelming numbers. Like other categories of material culture, signs vary widely in purpose, quality, references, and associations. Most highway signs, for example, are intended to be strictly informational and are therefore rigidly codified. Not surprisingly, they are neither visually interesting nor intellectually engaging. On the other hand, signs marking businesses, institutions, and various other sites and functions can be quite remarkable examples of design and cultural performance.

Among the most satisfying modern signs are those created in the manner of tavern and inn signs of the eighteenth and early nineteenth centuries. Anyone traveling around Connecticut today will find the state's abundant historical remains sympathetically augmented by hundreds of modern signs in these old styles. At their best, these signs are sensitive dialogues with the state's historic landscape and sources of considerable aesthetic delight. As far as I can tell, they have received little commentary or praise. They deserve more of both.

A full account of the reintroduction of old styles of signage has not yet been written. A literary passage and a photograph created a half-century apart, however, document two phases of the process. The literary passage is from Robert Louis Stevenson's juvenile classic *Treasure Island*. Some readers may recall that in an early, pivotal scene in that book, a meeting of two old shipmates at the Admiral Benbow inn takes a violent turn. Conversation between Black Dog and the old captain suddenly gives way to an explosion of oaths, followed by the sound of furniture being knocked about, a clash of steel and a howl of pain, then the sight of Black Dog, blood streaming from his shoulder, in hasty retreat. "Just at the door," states our narrator, "the captain

aimed at the fugitive one last tremendous cut, which would certainly have split him to the chine had it not been intercepted by our big signboard of Admiral Benbow."[1]

"Our big signboard" plays an important role here. First, it lends historical credibility to the setting, for it was a signboard more than any other exterior feature that distinguished a tavern or inn from a private residence in the eighteenth century. Second, it shapes the plot. Because the captain's cutlass strikes the signboard instead of Black Dog, the pirate escapes and the now familiar story of treasure, intrigue, and mayhem unfolds. When the tale first appeared as "The Sea Cook" in *Young Folks* magazine in 1881–82, the scene was considered significant enough to illustrate.[2] Thirty years later, N. C. Wyeth revisited the scene, creating the melodramatic image, complete with its swinging signboard, familiar to generations of readers since (fig. 94).

At first glance, Marion Post Wolcott's elegantly serene 1940 Farm Services Administration photograph of Woodstock, Vermont, on a snowy night (fig. 95) might seem to have little in common with Wyeth's scene of raucous violence. But here too a signboard figures in the story. Signs, some only partially legible in the falling snow, identify businesses along the street. On the right, the word "DRUGS" appears. On the left, "LUNCH" is visible just across the intersection, while, closer in, the familiar bold AAA logo of the American Automobile Association, established in 1902, stands out clearly. This thoroughly twentieth-century logo is suspended from a vertically oriented signboard in the style of the eighteenth century. The awning over the door obscures part of the sign but the words "Cupboard Inn" are clearly visible. Physically joined, these two signs fuse past and present. The AAA sign and the automobiles, temporarily stationary and slowly turning white under the lightly falling snow, document an age of unprecedented individual spatial mobility. The old-style sign for the inn, however, introduces the idea of time

Fig. 93. *Sign for the Grosvenor Inn*, signed by Augustus Hoppin, 1894, Pomfret, Conn.; painted on eighteenth-century signboard. CHS, cat. 60, side 2. An advertising brochure issued by the Ben-Grosvenor Inn in the 1930s described the inn as "a continuation of a long line of coaching inns conducted by the Grosvenor family since 1765." The Colonial Revival image of George Washington evokes equestrian figures on eighteenth-century signs but uses a more dramatic palette.

Fig. 94. N.C. Wyeth, *Captain Bones Routs Black Dog*, illustration for Robert Louis Stevenson, *Treasure Island* (New York: Charles Scribner's Sons, 1911). Private Collection. Photograph Courtesy of the Brandywine River Museum. Wyeth was not the first to illustrate Stevenson's classic *Treasure Island*, but his illustrations are among the most memorable. Quaint old inns and taverns served as the settings for increasing numbers of poems and novels, beginning in the late nineteenth century. In the United States, this phenomenon was closely linked with the renewed interest in early Americana known as the Colonial Revival.

travel. Through the modern miracle of the automobile it is possible to leave the present and drive off into the past, which still survives in the countryside and out-of-the-way places like Woodstock, Vermont.[3]

Stevenson's story and Wolcott's photograph nicely bracket changing attitudes toward historical signs. In the late nineteenth century, ancient signs, along with countless other forms of aging material culture, were being discovered and reappraised by antiquarians, collectors, and historians. By 1940, as a facet of what is commonly called the Colonial Revival in this country, replications, paraphrases, and creative variations on historical signs had become common parts of the landscape, particularly in the older parts of the country.

When Stevenson was writing, the literature on historical signboards was scanty. The only major publication was Larwood and Hotten's *History of Signboards,* first published in London in 1866 and repeatedly reissued.[4] By the time of Wolcott's photograph, more than twenty publications dealing variously with signboards, taverns and inns, and travel in search of the old had appeared. Several concentrated on London, but well over half examined American material, usually in New England.[5] The association of signboards, taverns, and inns with travel seems logical enough, considering their close connection in the eighteenth century. By the early twentieth century, they were connected once again, but within a changed cultural context. In the eighteenth century, tavern and inn signs had been communicative markers, often of aesthetic merit; by the twentieth century they had become antiques as well. The buildings they once identified had also been transformed into historic structures, possibly, one hoped, filled to the brim with ancient and desirable objects. The history of renewed interest in old inn and tavern signs, then, is intimately linked to the rise of antique collecting in America. And antique collecting, in turn, owes much to the introduction of the automobile.

Americans were actively collecting antiques by the 1870s.[6] They searched the houses of friends and neighbors, attended auctions, snooped through secondhand shops in cities, and drove into the countryside with horse and buggy. With the introduction of the automobile, the countryside and its treasures really opened up. Automobile trips in search of antiques had become so commonplace by the second decade of the twentieth century that the satirical *Collector's Whatnot* of 1923 gleefully spoofed them, providing city collectors with foolproof strategies for duping simple country folk out of their heirlooms.[7]

Travel in search of antiques was often also a search for America's past, for an earlier way of life thought to be still preserved in the small towns and villages bypassed by the railroads and industry. As it turns out, New England, and Connecticut in particular, was rich in such places, and within easy driving distance from anywhere in the Northeast. These quietly decaying backwaters were discovered by moneyed people from the city looking for pleasant drives or summer homes in places they found picturesque and quaint, to use two common terms of the period (fig. 96). Wallace Nutting's 1923 *Connecticut Beautiful* ignored Connecticut's cities and mill towns to portray a state of bucolic countryside, liberally adorned with old pastures, apple trees, country lanes, and charming old houses.[8] The image was true, as far as it went.

To identify themselves to carloads of antiquers looking for bargains in the country, shops dealing in antiques needed signs. What better sign to mark a shop selling venerable goods than one in the venerable style of the eighteenth century? Evidence, scanty though it is, indicates that antique dealers joined inn and tavern keepers as the first to reintro-

Fig. 95. Marion Post Wolcott, *Snowy Night*, silver gelatin print, 1940. Reproduced from the Collections of the Library of Congress. Although Farm Security Administration photographs typically document the hardships of rural life during the Depression, Wolcott's photograph of Woodstock, Vermont, depicts a typical New England small town in winter. The hanging signs for the Cupboard Inn and the American Automobile Association provide a perhaps unconscious link to the Colonial past.

Fig. 96. Morton C. Hansen, *Ye Signe of Ye White Swan*, wood engraving, 1921. CHS, Graphics Collection. This quaint scene may have been an illustration for an automobile advertisement.

Open After May 20

THE OLDE HOUSE at Sandwich, New Hampshire, stands beside the highway in one of the most picturesque and unspoiled of the early mountain communities of New England.

Old in fact, as in name, the house and shop afford fitting background for a collection of antique glass, china, pottery, and furniture, gathered from homes of the countryside and from once-thriving rural towns.

KATHARINE F. BRYER
SANDWICH
NEW HAMPSHIRE

Fig. 98. *Advertisement for "The Magazine Antiques,"* from *Magazine Antiques*, June 1928. CHS Library.

Fig. 97. *Advertisement for "The Olde House at Sandwich,"* from *Magazine Antiques*, May 1928. CHS Library.

duce signs in the old manner. The pages of *Antiques* magazine, established in Boston in 1922, provide useful documentation. Advertising began rather tentatively in *Antiques* but swiftly picked up steam. By July 1922, small advertisements, mostly without images, were numerous. Among them was a notice for Jaquith Mansion, a 1778 structure in Washington, New Hampshire, that sold "Oriental and Colonial Antiques."[9] Distinguishing this notice from others around it was a small but unmistakable evocation of a tavern sign. The accompanying text, "Sip and Sup at Jaquith Mansion," indicates that this operation sold food as well as antiques, thereby providing visitors with a multisensory time-travel experience.

By 1924 the average advertisement in *Antiques* had become larger and usually involved more text, an image, or both. A notice for a business identifying itself as "The Place" in Longmeadow, Massachusetts, illustrated a sign announcing that it served as both a teahouse and an antique shop.[10] A more historically referential two-sided sign appeared in the half-page advertisement Katherine Loring of Wayland, Massachusetts, placed in the June issue of 1925.[11] The side facing Worcester depicted a cock weathervane; that facing Boston, a plump male in eighteenth-century garb. Both sides bore the date 1815, presumably when the structure housing the shop was built.

From 1925 on, shop signs in the old manner figured regularly in advertisements in *Antiques*. Frances Nichols, Charles Street, Boston, displayed a sign with a primitive eagle and shield. Bernstein Antiques of Sound Beach, Connecticut, used a shape more likely derived from a mirror, adorned with the profile silhouette of George Washington. In 1927, Flayderman & Kaufman, another Charles Street, Boston, shop, displayed a scroll-top signboard, replete with Victorian lettering.[12] In May 1928, Katharine Bryer of Sandwich, New Hampshire, took out a one-page advertisement which, in word and image, documented succinctly the ideological and cultural conditions propelling the antiques trade in the 1920s (fig. 97). Half of the advertisement was given over to a photograph of the shop and its old-style, swinging sign suspended from a metal bracket. The brief text announced that the shop opened after May 20, implicitly confirming the seasonal activity of the business. It went on to note:

THE OLDE HOUSE at Sandwich, New Hampshire, stands beside the highway in one of the most picturesque and unspoiled early mountain communities of New England.

Old in fact, as in name, the house and shop afford fitting background for a collection of antique glass, china, pottery, and furniture, gathered from homes of the countryside and from once-thriving rural towns.[13]

Fig. 99. Ipswich Mills Teahouse, Ipswich, Mass., 1923, modern silver gelatin print from original negative. Courtesy, The Society for the Preservation of New England Antiquities.

Similar advertisements appeared throughout the rest of the decade. The most remarkable–and possibly the most influential–use of a sign in the style of the eighteenth century to promote the sale of antiques, however, was created by the magazine itself. In its June 1928 issue, *Antiques* ran a full-page notice promoting itself as the ideal advertising medium for those in the trade (fig. 98).[14] The text, appropriately enough, was placed within the silhouetted form of an eighteenth-century tavern sign. The association of the antique trade with this form of historical sign could not have been more explicit.

Although the business of selling antiques has changed dramatically since the 1920s, a few shops around the state still use signs in the old manner. One example hangs in front of the shop of Nathan Liverant & Son in Colchester, a business established in 1920. The wording of the sign is modern, but its form replicates the late-eighteenth-century Aaron Bissell sign in the Connecticut Historical Society's Brainard Collection (cat. 7).[15]

The advertisements for Jaquith Mansion and "The Place," noted above, documented the occasional combination of food and antiques. With or without antiques as a sideline, tearooms and teahouses were common eating establish-

ments in the early years of the twentieth century, usually catering to a female clientele. Tearooms joined inns in identifying themselves with hanging signs in the old tradition. Examples documented in the photographic archives of the Society for the Preservation of New England Antiquities in Boston include the Puritan Tea Room, the Ipswich Mills Tea House (fig. 99), The Ipswich Tea House and Inn, the Brown Owl Tea Room, and The Teakettle and Tabby Cat.[16]

Another early advertisement in *Antiques* identifies a different cultural obsession that kept old-fashioned signage in public view. A shop in Amherst, Massachusetts, illustrated its advertisement with a sign bearing the simple legend "Antiques" attached to a (presumably) metal frame with a silhouette of coach drawn by four-in-hand. The shop identified itself as "At the Sign of the Coach."[17] By the 1920s, coach travel had become obsolete as an efficient form of transportation. The railroad had taken over its long-distance runs in the nineteenth century; the trolley, then the automobile and bus, eliminated the rest of its routes in the twentieth. The demise of coaching was already being noted in the 1870s;[18] by 1925 coaching was only a vanishing, usually romanticized, memory.

Mythologizing scenes of coaching were part of popular

JUST AN OLD-FASHIONED CHRISTMAS WITH OLD-FASHIONED CHEER AND OLD JOYS AND NEW JOYS TO MINGLE ALL YEAR

Fig. 101. Modern signs inspired by historic tavern and inn signs, eastern Connecticut, 1999. Photographs by author.

Fig. 100. Christmas card, circa 1920-50. Collection of author.

visual culture from the 1920s through 1950s and were frequently represented in Christmas cards of the era. These images typically showed a coach, overflowing with passengers and baggage, making its way through a snowy landscape toward an old inn or tavern. Signs were worked into these designs in various ways, as the example illustrated here indicates (fig. 100). Sometimes the signs plausibly evoked historical reality, as in "Ye Red Lion" and "Ye Bell & Hand Inne." In other instances, they conveyed more seasonal greetings, such as "Ye Inn Of Gude Cheer" or, simply, "Merry Christmas." On one card from about 1940, the coaching scene itself is framed within a hanging signboard.[19]

Today, signs based to varying degrees on historical prototypes abound throughout Connecticut. A small sample included here from east of "The Great River" (fig. 101) indicates something of the richness to be found many times over in other regions and communities statewide. Not surprisingly, the most historically accurate signs identify old inns and taverns, or other buildings and institutions (churches, schools, historical agencies) conscious of the value of historical associations. Other signs are only loosely based on historical precedent but preserve some of the quality of the old in design, lettering, contour, or structure. Many are made of wood, as they were in the eighteenth century, but others today are made from a synthetic "sign foam" that looks like wood when painted but does not warp, split, or shrink.[20]

Contemporary signs in old styles have value on at least four counts. First, they provide linkage to past design, and by extension to past culture and society. In this way, they help to stabilize and ground the present. Second, because these signs are created on request for individual businesses and organizations, they are not generic, not produced in tedious multiples. Most are what artisans call "one-offs," meaning

that only one model is created. Each, then, has a high degree of individuality, even its own personality. Third, many of these signs are dignified, even elegant, graphic statements, informative in a restrained and stately way. It is not surprising that they appear in areas of higher-than-average wealth and education. Fourth, as material objects, works of art, and examples of human creativity and manufacture, some of these signs are simply wonderful. There is no other way to put it. They represent the apogee of the genre. Signs just don't get any better. The reason for this is fairly straightforward. Many of the people who make the best signs in Connecticut have extensive artistic training.[21]

It is a too common tendency in historical writing to emphasize change and to ignore or even disparage continuity. The disciplines of art history and design history have typically focused on novelty and innovation but paid little attention to the continuing vitality of older modes and conservative design impulses. The current cultural landscape of Connecticut, however, offers a powerful de facto alternative to such a narrow and ungenerous vision, for here the past—and the continuing influence of the past—is clearly visible in myriad forms. Despite the fact that new construction continually transforms the Connecticut landscape, the state is richly furnished with evidence of previous ways of life. Old roads, based on still older Indian trails; town greens and commons; churches and meetinghouses; and literally hundreds of pre-1800 houses still adorn the state. Just as important, in Connecticut, thousands of people care deeply about these material remnants of the past. Appropriately, a significant proportion of new material culture makes conscious and deliberate reference to historical precedent, linking present with past and honoring historical continuity. Signs are among the most obvious and abundant examples of this practice.

This essay extends an invitation to look more closely—and more appreciatively—at the signscape, both in Connecticut and beyond its borders. A remarkably high percentage of contemporary signs are based on colonial and nineteenth-century prototypes, on tavern, inn, and hotel signs like those in the collections of The Connecticut Historical Society. These historically referential signs are a significant art form of our time, an art form that anyone can enjoy, at no cost, just by moving through the landscape.

NOTES

1 Robert Louis Stevenson, *Treasure Island* (New York: Charles Scribner's Sons, 1911), p.15.

2 See Jenni Calder, *Robert Louis Stevenson: A Life Study* (New York: Oxford University Press, 1980), p. 168. Students of sign use may object to Stevenson's artistic license in this scene. Most signs depicted in eighteenth-century prints and paintings hang well above the reach of an outstretched arm, even with cutlass attached.

3 Wolcott's photograph has been reproduced several times. It appears, for example, in Charles Edward Crane, *Winter in Vermont* (New York: Alfred A. Knopf, 1941), opposite p. 162, and in Bernard Mergen, *Snow in America* (Washington, D.C.: Smithsonian Institution Press, 1997), on p. 221, and again on the back of jacket. It has also been published as a Christmas card.

4 Herman D. J. van Schevichaven [Jacob Larwood] and John Camden Hotten, *The History of Signboards, From the Earliest Times to the Present Day,* 9th ed. (London: Chatto and Windus, 1884).

5 Representative American titles include: Alice Morse Earle, *Stage-Coach and Tavern Days* (New York: Macmillan Co., 1900); Mary Caroline Crawford, *Little Pilgrimages among Old New England Inns* (Boston: L. C. Page, 1907); Stephen Jenkins, *The Old Boston Post Road* (New York: G. P. Putnam's Sons, 1913); L. H. Baker, *The Favorite Motor Ways of New England* (New York: Henry MacNair, 1915); Clifton Johnson, *Highways and Byways of New England* (New York: Macmillan, 1915); Fritz A. G. Endell, *Old Tavern Signs* (Boston: Houghton Mifflin, 1916); Samuel Adams Drake, *Old Boston Taverns and Tavern Clubs* (Boston: W. A. Butterfield, 1917); Mary Harrod Northend, *We Visit Old Inns* (Boston: Small, Maynard, 1925); Howard M. Chapin, *Early American Signboards* (Providence: Rhode Island Historical Society, 1926); Elise Lathrop, *Early American Inns and*

Taverns (New York: Robert M. McBride, 1926); Clara Walker Whiteside, *Touring New England* (Philadelphia: Penn Publishing Co., 1926); and Marian Dickinson Terry, ed., *Old Inns of Connecticut* (Hartford: Prospect Press, 1937). The last is a particularly lavish publication.

6 See, for example, Annie Trumbull Slosson, *The China Hunters Club* (New York: Harper & Brothers, 1878).

7 Cornelius Obenchain Van Loot et al. [Kenneth Roberts, Booth Tarkington, and Hugh Kahler], *The Collector's Whatnot* (Boston: Houghton Mifflin, 1923). Robert and Elizabeth Shackleton, *The Quest of the Colonial* (New York: The Century Co., 1907), entitle one chaper, "On Rambling Driving Trips" (p. 118).

8 Wallace Nutting, *Connecticut Beautiful* (Garden City, N.Y.: Garden City Publishing Co., 1923). For what it is worth, Nutting dedicated this book to The Connecticut Historical Society. Early automobile travelers encountered not only the surviving (or revived) past in their journeys but also the new in the guise of the past. See William B. Rhoads, "Roadside Colonial: Early American Design for the Automobile Age, 1900-1940," *Winterthur Portfolio* 21 (Summer/Autumn 1986): 133–52.

9 *Magazine Antiques,* July 1922, p. 46.

10 Ibid., December 1924, p. 328.

11 Ibid., June 1925, p. 355.

12 Ibid., September 1925, p. 181; May 1926, p. 347; April 1927, p. 257.

13 Ibid., May 1928, p. 355.

14 Ibid, June 1928, p. 456.

15 Conversaton with Nathan Liverant, December 1999.

16 For a discussion of early-twentieth-century tearooms, see Cynthia A. Brandimarte, "'To Make the Whole World Homelike': Gender, Space, and America's Tea Room Movement," *Winterthur Portfolio* 30, no. 1 (Spring 1995): 1–19.

17 *Magazine Antiques,* November 1927, p. 426.

18 See, for example, Eastman Johnson's 1871 painting "The Old Stage Coach," Layton Art Gallery Collection, Milwaukee Art Museum.

19 An undated A. M. Davis card in the Connecticut Historical Society collections is illustrated with a stylized tavern sign bearing the archaicized inscription "At ye Signe of Goode Will." On another Davis card, mailed in 1926, a sign bearing the words "Merry Christmas," is accompanied by a punning text ("I'm sending this as a little sign/Of the joy I'm wishing a friend of mine").

20 Conversation with Rob Rizzuto, Alpha Signs, Norwich, Conn., December 1999.

21 Ibid.

10

Afterword: Signs in American Art and Cultural History

By Susan P. Schoelwer

The bull, the lion &c. are fled,
and left only their names behind.

The painter William Williams penned these words in 1787, lamenting the passing of an era. For nearly one hundred years after the Great Fire of London in 1666, the extended process of rebuilding the city had combined with rising consumerism to foster a "golden age" of sign making. As shop and innkeepers jockeyed for patronage in an increasingly impersonal urban setting, competition inspired more and more elaborate signs, projecting farther and farther out into the streets. By the mid-eighteenth century, the proliferation of these pendant signs had become something of a nuisance, with casualties occasionally reported due to falling signs. Subsequent municipal regulations required trade signs to be mounted flush against building walls, although tavern and inn signs continued to be allowed to project out into the public space.[1]

Although Williams was speaking explicitly of signs in eighteenth-century English arts and culture, his comment applies with equal relevance to early American tavern and inn signs. Although American signs rarely matched the elaboration of the most lavish English examples, they were similarly composite art forms, uniting the distinct crafts or trades of painting, woodworking, carving, and metalsmithing. Sign making in America also had its "golden age," corresponding roughly to the era of nation building, from the last quarter of the eighteenth century to the mid-nineteenth century. By the time the nation turned to rebuilding after the Civil War, the bull, the lion—and the eagle, the major American addition to the iconography of inn signs—were fast disappearing from the streets and roadsides. Major changes in sign making and design occurred, not in response to legal fiat, but as a result of changing patterns in architecture and urban design, demographics, literacy, transportation, production technology. Within decades,

what few examples remained of the old, hand-crafted, wood-framed, pictorial signs were rediscovered and given new meaning as relics of bygone days and an idealized past. This apotheosis, transforming tavern and inn signs from functional, commercial art into emblems of antimodernism, can be traced in both the artifacts themselves and in the meanings assigned them in the broader cultural discourse of nineteenth-century America.

James Fenimore Cooper, for example, understood well the multiple levels on which inn signs functioned. He opens *The Pioneers*—the first novel in the Leatherstocking series to be published, in 1826—with scenes of Elizabeth Templeton returning, after several years at school, to her home in a small village in upstate New York. The rapid pace of development had transformed the frontier town almost beyond her recognition; not until she rounded a corner and glimpsed the village inn and its sign did she begin to feel at home. Cooper carefully catalogues the characteristic features of a village inn, already old in the early nineteenth century—its prominent corner location, its undistinguished domestic structure, and its sign, which was "suspended from a common ale-house post, and represented a figure of a horseman, armed with sabre and pistols, and surmounted by a bearskin cap, with a fiery animal that he bestrode 'rampant.' All these particulars were easily to be seen by the aid of the moon, together with a row of somewhat illegible writing in black paint, but in which Elizabeth, to whom the whole was familiar, read with facility, 'The Bold Dragoon.'" Although still "one of the most frequented inns of the place," the old inn faced competition from a new hotel, a balustraded "edifice" marked by a new-style sign: "Before the door stood two lofty posts, connected at the top by a beam, from which was suspended an enormous sign, ornamented around its edges with certain curious carvings in pine boards, and on its faces loaded with masonic emblems. Over these mysterious figures was written, in large letters, 'The Templeton Coffee-

Fig. 102. *Sign for Tarbox's Inn and the Village Hotel*, dated 1807 and 1824, as repainted circa 1831, Enfield, Conn. CHS, cat 19, side 2.

Fig. 103. Ralph Earl, *Landscape View of the Canfield House*, oil on canvas, circa 1796.
Photograph by Robert F. Houser, courtesy of The Litchfield Historical Society, Litchfield, Conn.

House, and Travellers' Hotel,' and beneath them, 'By Habakkuk Foot and Joshua Knapp.'" In contrast to the familiar, homely comforts of the old public house, the new hotel betokens progress, ambition, modernization, and a growing market economy (its proprietors are also the owners of the village store, hatter's shop, and tan-yard). Cooper's attention to detail in describing both inn and hotel testifies vividly to their symbolic significance, even as it corroborates the broader geographic applicability of the conclusions presented in this volume on the basis of documented inns in Connecticut.[2]

The degree to which tavern and inn signs function as symbolic as well as literal placemarkers finds extensive testimony in representations of inn signs in American art as well as literature. As placemarkers in imagined landscapes, inn signs may embody a variety of meanings. In Ralph Earl's idealized *Landscape View of the Canfield House*, circa 1796, a tiny, inconspicuous but unmistakable inn sign in the lower right corner betokens progress and urbanity (fig. 103). Near the sign, along the road that runs before the Canfield estate, stands a rather mundane house with livestock shed nearby, details that at first seem not only compositionally distracting but at odds with the architectural pretensions of the main house. These inclusions mark the road as an improved turnpike, carrying commerce and culture to the rural hinterlands of Sharon, in Litchfield County, Connecticut. The splendid isolation of the Canfield country seat is thus visibly connected to the larger world.[3]

During the first half of the nineteenth century, tavern and inn signs proliferated not only as art, but in American art. Sign painting existed as part of an artistic continuum, emerging oft-times from the same painting shops and partaking of a shared vocabulary of visual forms and images. Artists who at some point in their careers engaged in sign or, more generally, ornamental painting seem to have been especially inclined to grant these commercial arts compositional and symbolic significance within more self-consciously artistic productions. Bryan Wolf points to Richard Caton Woodville's narrative painting, *War News from Mexico* (see fig. 11) as testimony to the role inn signs played in the creation of a national, democratic culture. Woodville's contemporary, George Caleb Bingham, offers even more vivid evidence of the pivotal position of inn signs at the convergence of visual and political culture. Bingham's father, Henry Vest Bingham, operated a tavern, "The Square and Compass," in the family homestead in Franklin, Missouri. Following a pattern documented by Vincent for eighteenth-century Connecticut, Henry Bingham moved from innkeeping into local politics. The family inn also provided young George's first encounters with a professional artist, as Chester Harding lodged at the Square and Compass while completing his portrait of frontier hero Daniel Boone. Bingham's apprenticeship with a local cabinetmaker may have included sign making; his later production of painted political banners indicates that he did at some point acquire experience as an ornamental painter. Three of his major compositions depicting political scenes feature meticulously rendered inn signs.

Fig. 104. George Caleb Bingham, *County Election 2*, oil on canvas, 1852 (detail).
From the Art Collection of Bank of America, Saint Louis.

Because Bingham expressly intended these political scenes for widespread dissemination as prints, he consciously composed them to be "as *national* as possible—applicable alike to every Section of the Union, and illustrative of the manners of a free people and free institutions." *Canvassing for a Vote*, 1851–52, portrays a scene that must be similar to many he had witnessed at his father's tavern: a group of men, seated before a house, marked as an inn by the eagle sign hanging overhead (see fig. 4). *County Election 2*, 1852, depicts a much larger crowd gathered in an obviously more populous community (fig.104). At the center of the composition is the inn, a new and impressive brick structure designated by its sign, the "Union Hotel." The austere design of this sign— with its simple letters on a plain background, the upper word arcing over the lower, and the absence of any pictorial motif—recalls that of the Village Hotel in Enfield, Connecticut (fig. 102). Bingham's *Verdict of the People*, 1854–55, also centers on an inn sign, this one displaying the federal eagle over the word, "Hotel."[4]

From the vantage point of the Missouri frontier in the 1850s, Bingham envisioned inn signs as vibrant elements of current political culture, even as he recognized that the world he portrayed was already passing. Other artists, especially in longer settled regions, had already begun to reenvision inn signs as markers of a nostalgically idealized past, relics of the civic virtues of the early Republic, now irrevocably tarnished by party politics and sectionalism. In New York City, sign and ornamental painter John Quidor painted darkly

romantic narrative scenes based on the tales of Washington Irving. Quidor's *The Return of Rip Van Winkle*, 1849, portrays the pathos of the old man's reentry into a village he no longer recognizes (fig. 105). Quidor's rendering of the scene communicates not only the passage of time separating Van Winkle from his past, but also the time distancing the viewer from the moment depicted, which itself belongs to a bygone era. The dramatic scene occurs in front of the village inn, with changes in signage marking the passage of time. George Washington's portrait graces the tavern sign, hanging prominently from a bracket arm extending out from the gable end of the building, dating the scene to the years immediately after the Revolution. Shadowy traces of an earlier image of King George III communicate not only the revolutionary transformation of the political and social community, but the perceptible ancient-ness of this place. Over the door leading into the inn is a newer-style sign—a long, narrow horizontal board, mounted flush against the wall, bearing simply the words, "The Union Hotel / by Jonathan Doolittle." While this type of sign is historically inaccurate for the time period that the painting purports to depict, it would have been in use long enough for the anachronism to escape notice by Quidor's viewers.

In the second half of the nineteenth century, imagery virtually disappeared from signs in the everyday landscape, replaced by all-text panels like Quidor's "Union Hotel" name band. The new signs, proliferating in urban areas, bespoke not only increasing literacy, but also dramatic and

Fig. 105. John Quidor, *The Return of Rip Van Winkle*, oil on canvas, 1849. Andrew W. Mellon Collection. Photograph © Board of Trustees, National Gallery of Art, Washington, D.C.

disruptive changes in the social and economic fabric of everyday life—urbanization, industrialization, standardization, in short, modernization. As Zimmerman observes, the new-style signs "measured a change in the speed of life." Not surprisingly, the old-style signs, preserved largely in non-urban areas, began to acquire new symbolic associations, evoking idealized memories of a pre-industrial world. In a bucolic view of *West Springfield [Massachusetts]* in the 1860s or 1870s, by Hartford painter Nelson A. Moore, an old inn sign dangles blankly from a tree limb over a dusty road through an almost deserted village green (fig. 106). Gone are the lively crowds that surrounded Quidor's inn, likewise the intent political discussion engaging Bingham's taverngoers. The human figures in Moore's village are tiny, isolated, desultory, with evidently nowhere to go and little to do. Both Bingham and Quidor's inn signs marked the locations of vibrant public spaces—Bingham's set in the present, Quidor's in a passed time. Moore's inn sign, in contrast, exists in a timeless space, its blank surface inviting viewers to escape, at least imaginatively, the discomforts of modernity. New England's country inns presumably offered just such a respite for the artist himself, whose numerous sketching trips through the New England countryside provided a dramatic change of pace from the workaday environs of the photography studio he operated on Hartford's congested Main Street in the 1850s (see fig. 85).[5] By the end of the cen-

tury, countless other city dwellers were following Moore's example, touring the New England countryside in search of antiques and authenticity, stopping to rest and sup at old-fashioned but newly fashionable taverns, inns, and tea rooms.

Signs also captured the attention of artists intrigued by the visual qualities of text itself. Late nineteenth-century still life painters like William Harnett, John Peto, and John Haberle made a speciality of trompe l'oeil compositions featuring bits of text (tickets, broadsides, newspaper, currency), rendered so meticulously that Harnett was once arrested as a suspected counterfeiter. In *Chinese Firecrackers*, circa 1890, New Haven artist John Haberle presents the consummate visual irony of a facsimile signboard painted on studio canvas (fig. 107). The faded lettering and worn white ground convincingly replicate the surface of actual signs that once hung outside the inns of David Loomis of Westchester and Elijah Fitch of Bolton, Connecticut (cat. 22, fig. 19).[6]

One need not travel far in search of twentieth-century artists whose work explores the formal and symbolic dimensions of text. Elements of outdoor signs—replicated verbatim or quoted piecemeal—appear in compositions as disparate as John Sloan's poignant street vignette, *Hairdresser's Window*, 1907 (Wadsworth Atheneum), Joseph

Fig. 106. Nelson Augustus Moore, *West Springfield [Massachusetts]*,
oil on canvas, ca. 1860-80. New Britain Museum of American Art.

Fig. 107. John Haberle, *Chinese Firecrackers*,
oil on canvas, circa 1890. Wadsworth Atheneum.

Fig. 108. Charles Demuth, *The Figure 5 in Gold*, oil on composition board, 1928. The Metropolitan Museum of Art, The Alfred Stieglitz Collection, 1949 (49.59.1). Photograph © 1996 The Metropolitan Museum of Art.

Stella's monumental *The Voice of the City of New York Interpreted*, 1920–22 (Newark Museum), Reginald Marsh's intimate etching of the Bowery, *Tatoo, Shave, Haircut*, 1932, or Edward Hopper's haunting roadside nightscape, *Gas*, 1940 (The Museum of Modern Art). Continuing through the second half of the twentieth century, from Pop Art to Photorealism to Postmodernism, Andy Warhol, Stuart Davis, Jasper Johns, Robert Indiana, Robert Cottingham (see fig. 6), Edward Ruscha, Jenny Holzer are but a few of the better-known figures who have continued to draw upon the words and imagery of the sign making tradition as both artistic theme and formal vocabulary.

Examining the roots of modernism, art historian Wanda Corn argues that early twentieth-century painters consciously struggled to invent "Americanness," replacing the expansive landscapes of their nineteenth-century predecessors with the iconography of "skyscrapers, billboards, brand-name products, factories, and plumbing fixtures." The reemergence of the sign painting tradition in modernist aesthetics is epitomized in Charles Demuth's "poster portraits," highly abstract compositions that employ objects and text to indirectly symbolize, rather than literally represent, the portraits' subjects. *The Figure 5 in Gold*, 1928, a symbolic portrait of poet William Carlos Williams, exemplifies the modernist embrace of the sign as art (fig. 108). Its dominant

feature, as Corn describes, is "a single number—not a hand-written number, but the kind of five that appears on commercial signs . . . big, gilded, and unmistakable." Many of Demuth's symbolic references to Williams are expressed by painted letters, using the typefaces and graphic style of commercial signage; like the Masonic imagery on early inn signs, these references are deeply coded, decipherable only to an exclusive group of viewers. Demuth's "billboard cubism," Corn argues, "self-consciously fused the high principles of modernism with the lowbrow practices of street signage."[7]

In the 1920s and 1930s, the quest for an authentic American aesthetic linked modernism with a burgeoning enthusiasm for collecting American folk art. Demuth and other leading modernist painters and patrons became enthusiastic collectors of "primitive" portraits and landscapes, carved shop figures and ship's figureheads, weathervanes and whirligigs, trade and tavern signs. The design imperative, more than any conceptual principles or historical commonalities in the materials themselves, set the standard for determining what would—and would not—be classified as folk art. Nearly eighty years after New York modernists contributed to the first folk art exhibition, at the Whitney Studio Club, in 1924, the term, "folk art," remains a conceptual and historical conundrum. Any attempt to formulate a verbal definition must come quickly to terms with the realization that the adjectives most commonly associated with folk art are imprecise, frequently contradictory, and often inaccurate in describing historical circumstances of production and use: non-academic, out of the mainstream, naïve, unschooled, non-derivative, hand-crafted, middle-class, popular, art of the "common man." The attempt to define folk art intellectually or historically inevitably fails because folk art is inherently a visual construct, more easily recognized than described. Visual paradigms, not verbal definitions, provide the working vocabulary for identifying and classifying broad categories of folk art, reaffirmed in each successive generation of folk art exhibitions and publications.[8]

Tavern and inn signs have long been celebrated among the standard categories of folk art, with examples represented in all of the major folk art collections, exhibitions, and catalogs. Focused on an aesthetic category that is fundamentally modernist in origin and orientation, however, folk art has remained a largely separate strand within the fields of American art and cultural history. By shifting the focus to one specific category of folk art, the present study offers an opportunity to reconnect tavern and inn signs to the broader study of American culture, art, and history. Essays in this volume raise numerous questions that point the way, both explicitly and implicitly, toward future directions in investigation, interpretation, and analysis. Some point back toward the artifacts themselves, asking how we can expand or clarify the body of data available on the signs, their production, and use, individually or in the aggregate. Others point outward, asking how what we know about the signs intersects with past, present, or even possible future discourses in a variety of fields. Tacking between the concrete and the conceptual enhances both perspectives. As one example of many that might be cited from the evolution of this project, Finlay's iconographic research pointed to the importance of coins and currency as design sources for specific inn sign images. This concrete finding informed subsequent research on individual signs, prompting the discovery of further links between inn signs and other forms of commercial imagery (see cat. 27). The prevalence of these connections leads to the suggestion that inn signs are themselves forms of commercial imagery. Located at one particular intersection of art and commerce, they negotiate, in theoretical terms, between systems of visual representation and capitalism. From this theoretical perspective, we can consider, generally, whether what we have learned about inn signs corroborates, challenges, or modifies the general interpretive paradigms that frame our understanding of the exchange of images, ideas, cash, and capital in the early Republic. Alternatively, we can return to individual signs, in search of additional concrete evidence of connections between art and enterprise, within specific communities at specific points in time.

In the interests of encouraging further discovery, the present volume is deliberately open ended, its findings suggestive rather than definitive. Its primary purpose is to call attention to a fascinating group of artifacts, to make those artifacts accessible not only for appreciation and investigation as artistic and cultural productions in their own right, and also to make them available to those who might use them as material evidence in formulating more pointed, theoretical arguments or interpretive analyses. It seems clear, for example, that tavern signs are richly relevant to a number of fields of inquiry, including American history and art, American studies, material and visual culture, cultural studies. They also blur, and thus call into question, conventional distinctions separating the visual arts into subcategories of fine, popular, decorative, vernacular, commercial, public, advertising, graphic. These broader connections and theoretical or methodological implications remain for others to explore more fully, building upon the findings of the present reconsideration of early American tavern and inn signs from The Connecticut Historical Society.

NOTES

1   William Williams, *An Essay on the Mechanic of Oil Colour* (Bath, 1787), pp. 10–11, quoted in James Ayres, *Two Hundred Years of English Naïve Art, 1700–1900* (Alexandria, Va.: Art Services International, 1990), pp. 113–17.

2   James Fenimore Cooper, *The Pioneers,* Great Illustrated Classics (New York: Dodd, Mead, 1958), pp. 109–11, 141–42.

3   The balance between literal depiction and idealization in this landscape has long been a subject of debate. Because Canfield owned numerous properties, the exact location of this house has not been identified. Turnpike building was already well underway in Connecticut by 1796, but would not reach Sharon until the next decade. It seems likely that this particular detail testified, therefore, to Canfield's confidence in the future prospects of his situation, more than to his present surroundings; Elizabeth Mankin Kornhauser, et al., *Ralph Earl: The Face of the Young Republic* (New Haven and London: Yale University Press, and Wadsworth Atheneum, 1991), pp. 208–10; Frederic J. Wood, *The Turnpikes of New England* (Boston: Marshall Jones, 1919), pp. 371–72, 379, 383–84.

4   Michael Edward Shapiro, et al., *George Caleb Bingham* (Saint Louis: The Saint Louis Art Museum in association with Abrams, New York, 1990), pp. 19–20; Nancy Rash, *The Painting and Politics of George Caleb Bingham* (New Haven and London, Yale University Press, 1991), p. 120.

5   Moore Picture Trust with Ellen Fletcher, *Nelson Augustus Moore (1824–1902)* ([New Britain, Conn.]: Moore Picture Trust, 1994). Between 1855–65, Moore operated one of Hartford's leading photography businesses; William F. Robinson, "The Connecticut Yankee & The Camera: 1839–1889," *Connecticut Historical Society Bulletin* 47 (Winter 1982): 101–2, 130.

6   Elizabeth Mankin Kornhauser, *American Paintings Before 1945 in the Wadsworth Atheneum*, 2 vols. (Hartford: Wadsworth Atheneum and Yale University Press, New Haven and London, 1996) vol. 2, pp. 428–29.

7   Wanda Corn, *The Great American Thing: Modern Art and National Identity, 1915–1935* (Berkeley, Los Angeles, and London: University of

California Press, 1999), pp. xv, 201–13. See also Robin Jaffe Frank, *Charles Demuth: Poster Portraits, 1923–1929* (New Haven: Yale University Art Gallery, 1994).

8   For brief histories of American folk art collecting, see Beatrix T. Rumford, "Uncommon Art of the Common People: A Review of Trends in the Collecting and Exhibiting of American Folk Art," in Ian

M.G. Quimby and Scott T. Swank, *Perspectives on American Folk Art* (New York: Norton for the Winterthur Museum, Winterthur, Del., 1980), pp. 13–53; Jean Lipman and Alice Winchester, *The Flowering of American Folk Art, 1976–1876* (New York: Viking, in association with the Whitney Museum of American Art, 1974), pp. 8–14.

Fig. 109. *Sign for Mason's Inn*, circa 1830-60, probably New London County, Conn. CHS, cat. 51, side 2. The shadowy vignette to the viewer's right appears to depict the 1687 hiding of the Connecticut Charter in a hollow oak tree, later known as "The Charter Oak."

Catalogue:
The Connecticut
Historical Society
Collection
of Early American
Tavern *&* Inn Signs

Plates

Cat. 1. Sign for Bull's Inn, dated 1749

Cat. 2. Sign of The Duke of Cumberland, dated 1753(?) and 1773

Cat. 3. Sign for Hayden's Inn, dated 1762 and 1766

Cat. 4. Sign of General Wolfe, circa 1768

Cat. 5. Sign of the Pine Tree, dated 1768

Cat. 6. Sign of the Black Horse, circa 1771

Cat. 7. Sign of the Bull's Head, dated 1760 and 1797

Cat. 8. Sign of the Bird-in-Hand, dated 1786

Cat. 9. Sign for Bement's Inn, circa 1786–1810

Cat. 10. Sign for Blatchly's Inn, dated 1788 and 1794

Cat. 11. Sign for Lawrence's Inn, circa 1797

Cat. 12. Sign for Marsh's Inn, circa 1785–1810

Cat. 13. Sign for Hinman's Inn, circa 1795–1815

Cat. 14. Sign for Caulkins's Inn, dated 1769, 1798, and 1839, probably made circa 1790s

Cat. 15. Sign for Perkins's Inn, dated 1830, probably made circa 1800–20

Cat. 16. Sign for the Griswold Inn, circa 1800–25

Cat. 17. Sign of the Punchbowl, dated 1803

Cat. 18. Sign for Lewis's Inn, circa 1805–20

Cat. 19. Sign for Tarbox's Inn, signed by William Rice, dated 1807 and 1824

Cat. 20. Sign for Angell's Inn, dated 1808

Cat. 21. Sign for Spencer's Inn, dated 1810

Cat. 22. Sign for David Loomis's Inn, dated 1811

Cat. 23. Sign for Rose's Inn, signed by Harlan Page, circa 1813

Cat. 24. Sign for Field's Inn, circa 1814–20

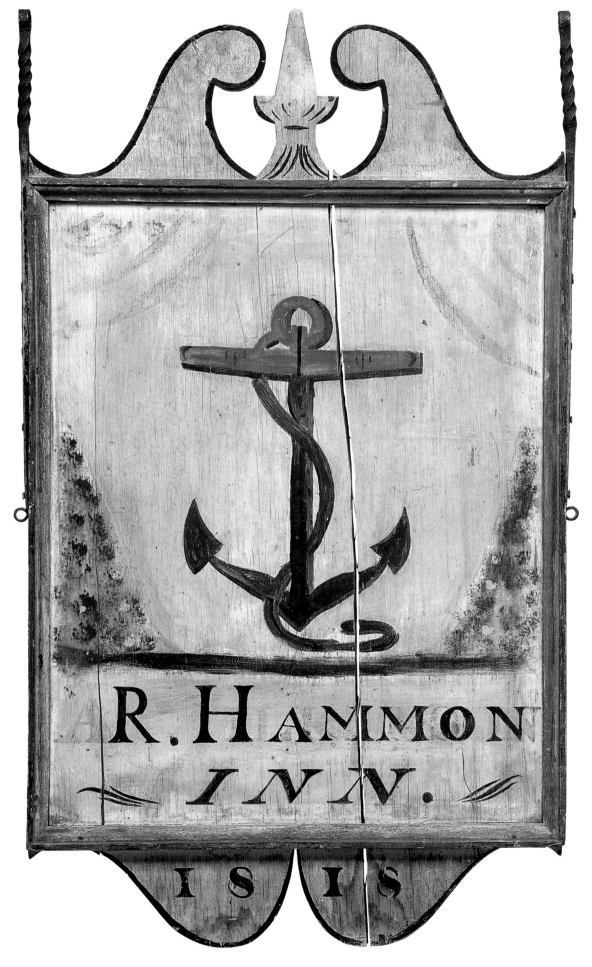

Cat. 25. Sign for Hammon's Inn, dated 17?? and 1818, probably made circa 1790–1800

Cat. 26. Sign for Wightman's Inn, circa 1815–24

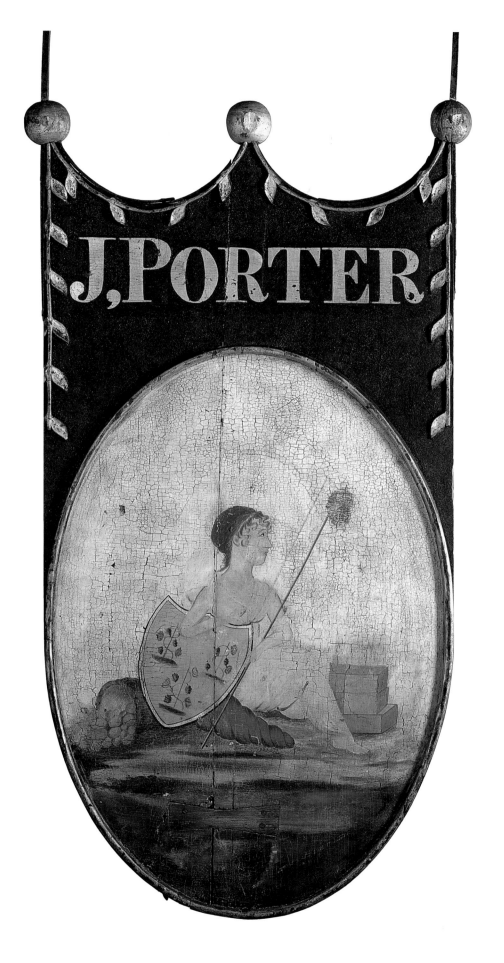

Cat. 27. Sign for Porter's Inn, circa 1820–25

Cat. 28. Sign for Daniel Loomis's Inn, signed by William Rice, circa 1820

Cat. 29. Sign for Cady's Hotel, circa 1820s

Cat. 30. Sign for the Chesebro Hotel, dated 1821

Cat. 31. Sign for Abbe's Inn and the Lion Hotel, signed by William Rice, circa 1822, and by Luther Terry Knight, dated 1866

Cat. 32. Sign of the Grapes, dated 1822

Cat. 33. Sign for Carter's Inn, circa 1823

Cat. 34. Sign for Dyer's Inn, signed by William Rice, circa 1823

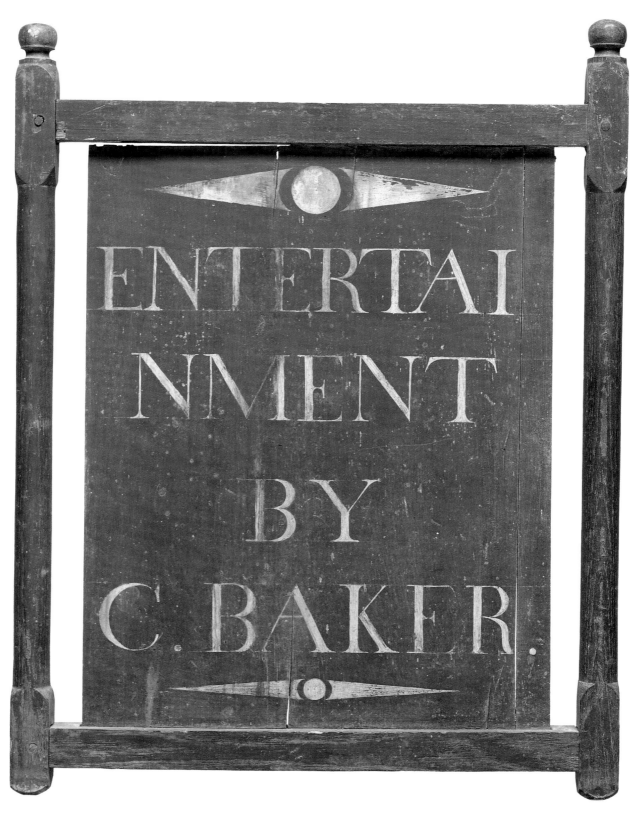

Cat. 35. Sign for Baker's Inn, circa 1820–38

Cat. 36. Sign for Williams's Inn, dated 1803 and 1826

Cat. 37. Sign for Arah Phelps's Inn, signed by William Rice, circa 1826

Cat. 38. Sign for Wedgwood's Inn, dated 1827 and 1836

Cat. 39. Sign for Hayes's Inn, dated 1828

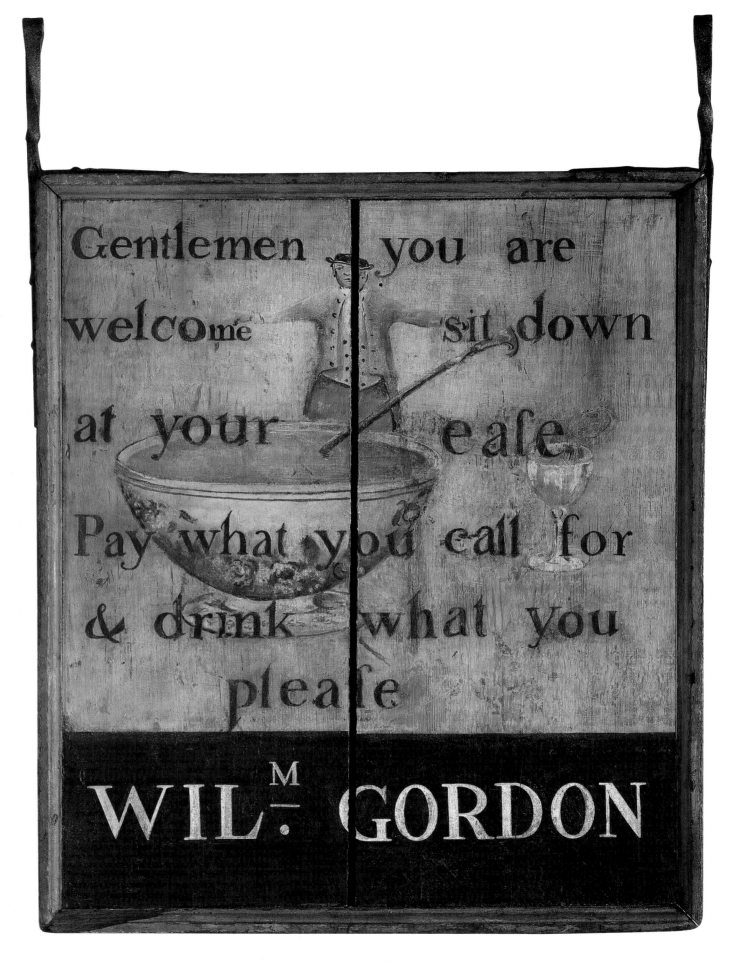

Cat. 40. Sign for Gordon's Inn, circa 1790–1830

Cat. 41. Sign for Stiles's Inn and the Thompson Hotel, dated 1831, repainted circa 1902

Cat. 42. Sign for Collins's Hotel, circa 1825–35

Cat. 43. Sign for Harrington's Inn, dated 1833

Cat. 44. Sign for Mechanics' Hotel, dated 1834

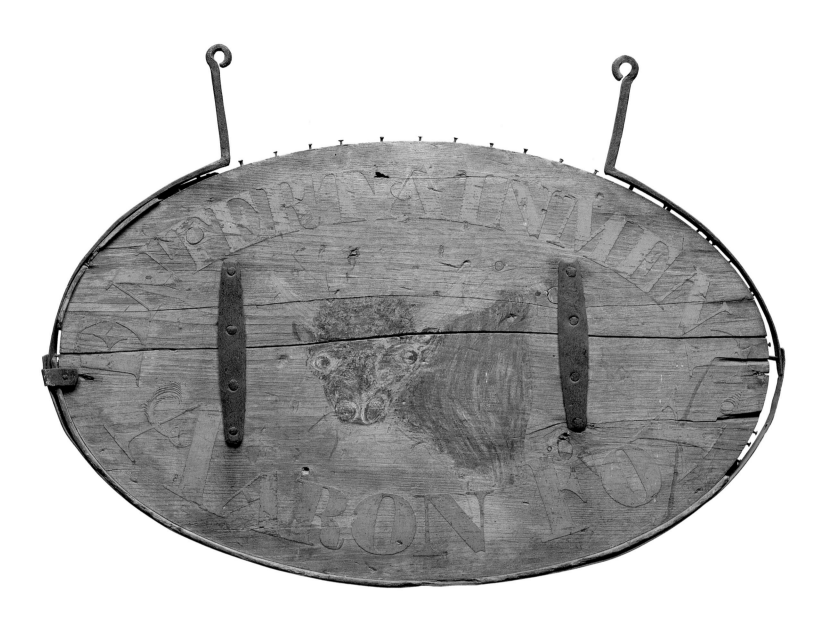

Cat. 45. Sign for Fox's Inn, circa 1834

Cat. 46. Sign for the Vernon Hotel, signed by William Rice, dated 1834

Cat. 47. Sign for the Hannah Hotel, circa 1836

Cat. 48. Sign for Fitch's Inn, circa 1834

Cat. 49. Sign for Hemingway's Tavern and Churchill's Inn, dated 1838, probably made circa 1836

Cat. 50. Sign for Warner's Hotel, signed by William Rice, dated 1836

Cat. 51. Sign for Mason's Inn, 1830s or later

Cat. 52. Sign for Bailey's Hotel, signed by George Crossingham, dated 1837 or 1857

Cat. 53. Sign for Mallett's Hotel, probably 1840s

Cat. 54. Sign for the Temperance Hotel, circa 1826–42

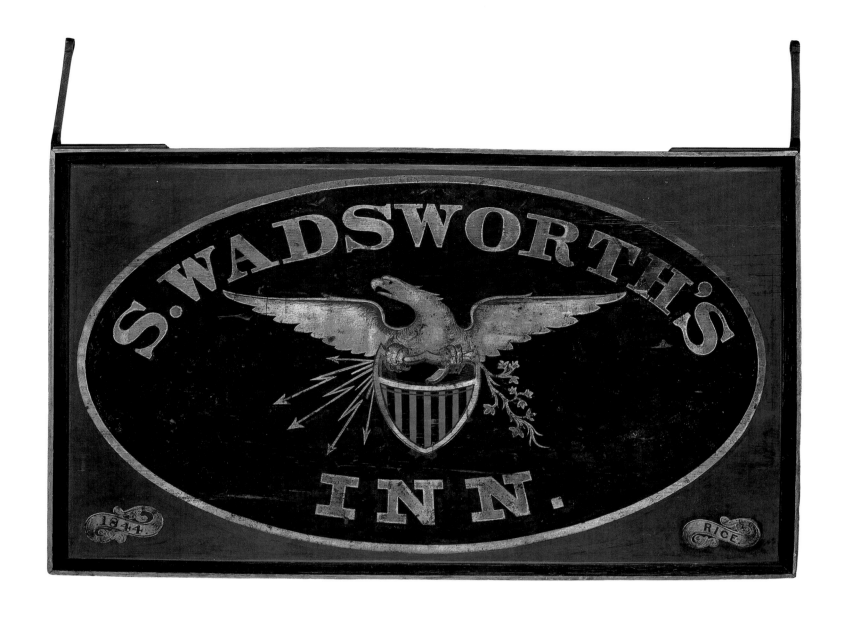

Cat. 55. Sign for Wadsworth's Inn, signed by William Rice, dated 1844

Cat. 56. Sign for Curtis's Woodbury House, circa 1882 or earlier

Cat. 57. Sign for Cooper's Hotel, circa 1850–1900

Cat 58. Sign for the Chafee House, circa 1865–89

Cat. 59. Sign for Crofut's Inn, circa 1892 or earlier

Cat. 60. Sign for the Grosvenor Inn, circa 1772–86, signed by Augustus Hoppin, 1894

Cat. 61. Sign for the Van Der Hayden Inn, dated 1796

Cat. 62. Sign for the Windham Inn, dated 1783 and 1891

Cat. 63. Sign for Pettibone's Tavern, circa 1810–24, repainted circa 1939

Cat. 64. Sign for H. Rust, early 20th century

Cat. 65. Sign for Palmer's Inn, 1780–1815

Fig. 110. Stanley Sweet, *Portrait of Morgan Bulkeley Brainard*, oil on canvas, 1941.

Morgan B. Brainard, 1879–1957, and the Brainard Tavern Sign Collection

By Ellsworth S. Grant

Morgan and Newton Brainard were both presidents of The Connecticut Historical Society. They had other things in common: education at Hartford Public High School and Yale University, a love of farmland and Long Island Sound, salmon fishing, and especially a passion for collecting antiques. Like their uncle, Morgan G. Bulkeley, they represented old-fashioned republicanism. But in other respects they differed. Morgan Bulkeley was a dominating figure in Connecticut politics for decades, having served as mayor of Hartford, governor and U.S. Senator. Newton Brainard served only as mayor of Hartford for two years, while Morgan Brainard's career was the Aetna Life Insurance Company, of which his energetic uncle had been president for more than forty years. Armed with a law degree from Yale, Morgan Brainard joined the Aetna in 1905 and became president in 1922. Under his guidance the company made big strides, and even in the Great Depression his calmness and common sense carried it through with minimum loss. Of equal significance for the welfare of Hartford was his bold decision to build a new home office on a twenty-two-acre site that once belonged to Thomas Hooker.

In the eyes of the city's business leaders Morgan Brainard was regarded as a "godfather" who had earned the prestige of his uncle. At one time or another he served as a director of thirteen different corporations. Notwithstanding his eminence, he always retained the image of the "aw shucks" country lad who pursued the simplest pleasures. One of these was a devotion to Connecticut's heritage. The executive offices on Aetna's eighth floor were furnished with antiques. The pine wall panels and floors were taken from an eighteenth-century house in Torrington. The directors' mahogany table was supposed to have once belonged to Thomas Jefferson. But during the 1920s he concentrated on collecting old Connecticut tavern signs, and soon they cluttered his office, home, garage, and summer cottage in Fenwick.

He called it an eccentric taste inspired by three different memories:

The first was when as a boy I remembered the window of Brooks' restaurant and saloon on Main Street in Hartford . . . and in the window was a carved figure of an infant Bacchus astride a wine

cask. This was known as the Windham Bacchus, and the story is that it was carved by a British prisoner during the Revolutionary War and used as a sign for Backus' tavern.

Then, I was fascinated by a sign that hung in front of the old Robbins homestead in Rocky Hill, and on close examination I discovered that the figure on it represented the duke of Cumberland on a prancing charger [fig. 111].

And the third was another boyhood memory of a sign that hung from the stables of the Wadsworth tavern . . . at the corner of Albany Avenue in Hartford, half a block from my own home [cat. 55]. In collecting, one thing leads to another and, through some rather ridiculous feeling that if no one preserved these useless objects they would soon be chopped up for firewood I proceeded to acquire them when opportunity offered.

(Letter to Robert W. Carrick, associate editor
of *House & Garden*, 7 May 1941)

In a 1934 article written for the Society for the Preservation of New England Antiquities in Boston, Morgan Brainard had more to say about the Wadsworth Tavern and tavern signs in general:

the genial proprietor was Daniel Wadsworth, a huge man who must have weighed over 300 pounds and whom I can remember traveling around the city in a low-hung buggy. . . . He apparently was . . . an ardent student of natural history, on which subject he had collected a library of sufficient importance to be sold by a New York auction house. . .

He seemed to have been well liked, and in size and geniality to have fulfilled completely one's mental picture of a tavernkeeper. As the city grew and outlying real estate became more valuable, moral standards increased correspondingly, and what was tolerated when land was cheap was frowned on. . . . He (Wadsworth) was finally convicted of selling intoxicating liquors . . . [and] sentenced to serve a term in jail. There he presented even a greater problem than when he was at liberty. No cell was big enough to hold him, and after a few days he was given his freedom. . .

Fig. 111. *Sign of the Duke of Cumberland*, dated 1753(?) and 1773, as repainted by Louis James Donlon, dated 1914, Rocky Hill, Conn. CHS, cat 2, side 2.

After the proprietor had died and I learned that the property was to be sold, I made up my mind that the sign should be preserved, and after some difficulty I found that it still existed and secured it. [see fig. 27]

Mr. Brainard's collection had to remain in his possession until The Connecticut Historical Society was able to move from the Wadsworth Atheneum in 1950 to the Veeder residence on 1 Elizabeth Street and the Hoadley Auditorium was completed six years later. At that time Newton Brainard was president. Thompson R. Harlow, who had become the Society's sixth Librarian in 1940 and later assumed the title of executive director until his retirement in 1980, helped Newton to per-

suade his brother to donate the collection, then numbering sixty-six tavern and trade signs. No doubt the convincing argument was that the signs would be prominently and safely displayed along the walls of the auditorium, where they have remained ever since. The catalog of Brainard signs was published in 1958 with an introduction by Tom Harlow. In 1970, the first time material from the Society was sent abroad, ten signs were shown at Japan's World Exhibition.

(Excerpted from Ellsworth S. Grant's report, "The Tavern Signs of Morgan B. Brainard, Connecticut Historical Society, Hartford, Connecticut," 1997.)

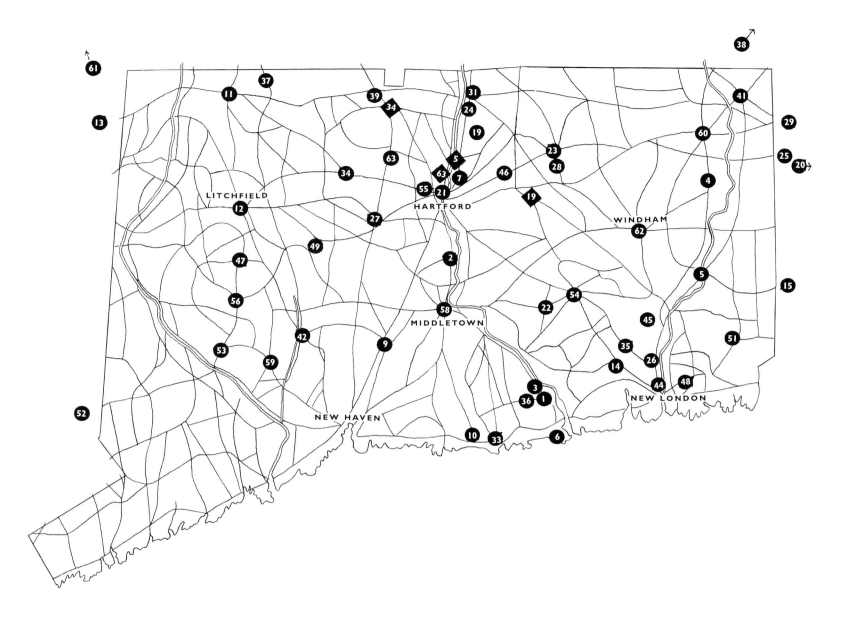

Fig. 112. Locations of tavern, inn, and hotel signs illustrated in this book.
Numbers within circles represent catalogue numbers;
numbers within diamonds represent figure numbers.
Based on Henry Schenck Tanner, *Map of Connecticut,* 1839 (fig. 38).

Catalogue Entries

NOTES ON THE CATALOGUE

Both catalogue entries and catalogue plates are arranged chronologically, with the goal of providing a visual overview of changes in sign form and decoration. Some anomalies occur, due to the relatively common practice of painting new imagery on old signboards. One side of each sign is illustrated in the catalogue plate section; in general, this side is considered side 1. Side 2, if significantly different, is generally represented by a text illustration, referenced by a figure number in the catalogue entry. Signs are not shown to scale. Due to the page format, vertical signs appear relatively larger than horizontal signs.

All dimensions are stated in inches, with height preceding width. Dimensions include only the body of the sign, excluding any hardware that extends beyond the sign itself.

Identification of wood and other materials is by eye, unless otherwise specified.

Any and all information not specifically cited is compiled from historical data, conservation reports, and object records, assembled in the museum object research files and in a computerized data base of Connecticut innkeepers, at The Connecticut Historical Society.

Identified places of origin of signs illustrated in this catalogue are indicated on the map on p. 181.

*An asterisk beside the catalogue number indicates that the sign was included in the exhibition *Lions & Eagles & Bulls: Early American Tavern & Inn Signs from The Connecticut Historical Society.*

KEY TO CITATIONS

Aetna 1939
Aetna Casualty Room, National Association of Insurance Agents' Convention, Boston, October 1939.

American Heritage 1960
Rudolf A. Clemen, " 'Shall I not take mine Ease in mine Inn?' " *American Heritage*, vol. 11, no. 4 (June 1960): 60–63.

Antiques 1928
Mabel M. Swan, "Early Sign Painters," *Magazine Antiques*, May 1928, pp. 402–5.

Benes
Peter Benes, *Two Towns: Wethersfield and Concord. A Comparative Exhibition of Regional Culture, 1635–1850* (Concord, Mass.: Concord Antiquarian Museum, 1982).

Chapin
Howard M. Chapin, "Rhode Island Signboards," *Rhode Island Historical Society Collections* 19, no. 1 (Jan. 1926): 20–32; no. 2 (April 1926): 53–64.

Collier
Christopher B. Collier and Bonnie B. Collier, "The Literature of Connecticut History," *The Connecticut Scholar*, Occasional Papers No. 6 (Hartford: Connecticut Humanities Council, 1983).

CHS
The Connecticut Historical Society.

CHSB
Connecticut Historical Society Bulletin.

Conn. Furniture 1967
Connecticut Furniture: Seventeenth and Eighteenth Centuries (Hartford: Wadsworth Atheneum, 1967).

Conn. Guide
Workers of the Federal Writers' Project of the Works Progress Administration for the State of Connecticut, *Connecticut: A Guide to its Roads, Lore, and People*, American Guide Series (Boston: Houghton Mifflin, 1938).

Courant
Connecticut Courant [newspaper], Hartford.

Crofut
Florence S. M Crofut, *Guide to the History & Historic Sites of Connecticut* (New Haven: Yale University Press, 1937).

DAB
Dictionary of American Biography.

Decorator 1960
Muriel E. Baker, "Tavern Signs," *The Decorator*, Journal of the Esther Stevens Brazer Guild of the Historical Society of Early American Decoration, Inc., 15 (Fall 1960), pp. 4–7.

Earle
Alice Morse Earle, *Stage-Coach and Tavern Days* (New York: MacMillan, 1900).

Forbes

Allen Forbes and Ralph M. Eastman, *Taverns and Stagecoaches of New England,* vol. 2 (Boston: Printed for the State Street Trust Company, 1954).

Fowble

E. McSherry Fowble, *Two Centuries of Prints in America, 1680–1880; A Selective Catalogue of the Winterthur Museum Collection.* (Charlottesville: University Press of Virginia for The Winterthur Museum, 1987).

Garvin

Donna-Belle Garvin and James L. Garvin, *On the Road North of Boston: New Hampshire Taverns and Turnpikes, 1700–1900* (Concord: New Hampshire Historical Society, 1988).

Grant

Ellsworth S. Grant, "The Tavern Signs of Morgan B. Brainard: The Connecticut Historical Society, Hartford, Connecticut" (unpublished report, The Connecticut Historical Society, 1997).

Great River

The Great River: Art & Society of the Connecticut Valley, 1635–1820 (Hartford: Wadsworth Atheneum, 1985).

Hamilton

John D. Hamilton, *Material Culture of the American Freemasons* (Lexington, Mass.: Museum of Our National Heritage, distributed by University Press of New England, Hanover, N.H., and London, 1994).

House and Garden 1941

"From Old Inns of Connecticut," *House and Garden Magazine*, July 1941.

Japan 1970

Folk Art exhibit, United States Pavilion, Japan World Exposition, Osaka, 1970.

Kane

Patricia E. Kane, et al., *Colonial Massachusette Silversmiths and Jewelers* (New Haven: Yale University Art Gallery, distributed by University Press of New England, Hanover and London, 1998).

Larwood and Hotten

Herman Diedrik Johan van Schevichaven [Jacob Larwood] and John Camden Hotten, *The History of Signboards, From the Earliest Times to the Present Day* (London: John Camden Hotten [1866]).

Lathrop

Elise L. Lathrop, *Early American Inns and Taverns* (New York: McBride, 1926).

Lipman and Winchester

Jean Lipman and Alice Winchester, *The Flowering of American Folk Art: 1776–1876* (New York: Viking, in cooperation with the Whitney Museum of American Art, 1974).

Little, *Painting*

Nina Fletcher Little, *Paintings by New England Provincial Artists: 1775–1800* (Boston: Museum of Fine Arts, 1976).

Little, *Wall Painting*

Nina Fletcher Little, *American Decorative Wall Painting* (New York: Dutton, 1989).

Lord and Foley

Priscilla Lord and Daniel J. Foley, *The Folk Arts and Crafts of New England*, rev. ed. (Radnor, Pa.: Chilton, 1975).

MBTS

The Connecticut Historical Society, *Morgan B. Brainard's Tavern Signs* (Hartford: The Connecticut Historical Society, 1958).

Nutting

Wallace Nutting, *Furniture Treasury*, 2 vols. (New York: Macmillan, 1928).

Rice

Kym S. Rice, *Early American Taverns* (Chicago: Regnery Gateway, in association with Fraunces Tavern Museum, New York, 1983).

Seymour 1958

George Dudley Seymour's Furniture Collection in The Connecticut Historical Society (Hartford: The Connecticut Historical Society, 1958).

Spinning Wheel 1955

Clarence T. Hubbard, "Old Tavern Signs," *Spinning Wheel*, May 1955, pp. 10–12.

Terry

Marian Dickinson Terry, ed., *Old Inns of Connecticut* (Hartford: Prospect Press, 1937.

Vincent

"Connecticut Inns and Hotels and Their Signboards, 1750–1850," (unpublished research report, The Connecticut Historical Society, 1999).

Wood

Frederic J. Wood, *The Turnpikes of New England, and Evolution of the Same through England, Virginia, and Maryland* (Boston: Marshall Jones, 1919).

Cat. 1*

Sign for Bull's Inn, dated 1749
CENTERBROOK, CONNECTICUT

Innholder: Edward Bull (active ca. 1749–64)
Attributed to Saybrook sign maker (active ca. 1749–71)

Images: On both sides, profile of riderless black horse, centered on board but facing in opposite directions on each side, white ground. No underlying images.
Text: On both sides, on pediment, "EB."; under image, "ENTER-TAINMENT. / FOR MAN &. HORS"; on apron, "1749". Side 2 differs in having reversed numeral "7". No underlying text.

Paint on pine board, oak frame, iron hardware, 48-1/2" x 31-3/4"
Collection of Morgan B. Brainard, Gift of Mrs. Morgan B. Brainard, 1961.63.9

Illustrated: color plate 1 (side 1), fig. 21 (side 2)

This sign is the only American tavern sign, firmly dated prior to 1750, that is known to have survived without repainting.[1] Image and text appear here in the most common mid-eighteenth century arrangement, with the legend below a single large image, rendered in profile. Eighteenth-century New England inn signs do not generally use the words "inn" or "tavern"; as in this example, they typically display the innholder's initials, a date (usually the year in which the innholder received his or her license), and a pictorial motif. Some include the words "Entertainment," or "Entertainment for Man and Hors" (often without the "e")—a direct reference to the colonial legislation that explicitly required that each town arrange for the "entertainment" of travelers and their horses, the word entertainment being used to mean simply, the "hospitable provision for the wants of a guest" (*OED*). Given the traveler's complete dependence on his mount, provision of stabling or pasturage was a crucial part of an inn's services: surviving bills and accounts list oats, grain, or "horse-keeping" in addition to board, lodging, eating, and a selection of strong drink for the master (see fig. 29).

Not surprisingly, the horse seems to have been one of the most popular "logos" for colonial inns, figuring in names significantly more often than other traditional emblems such as trees, stags, lions, swans, or bulls (which one might expect an innholder named Bull to display). Horses may have had a particular, local significance for patrons of this inn, located along the western fringes of the Narragansett region, home of the first recognized American-bred horse. Narragansett pacers were highly desirable riding horses, prized for their endurance, speed, and smooth gait (created by moving right, then left legs together, rather than in the diagonal action of a common trotting horse). Narragansett pacers made up a significant proportion of Rhode Island's exports between 1725 and 1760, sold to discerning and well-heeled riders throughout the mainland English colonies and the West Indies.[2]

In its overall design, the Bull signboard shares recognizable features with other decorative arts of the early eighteenth century,

particularly such baroque-inspired passages as the bold "S," or ogee, curves; the molding profiles, and the boldness and complexity of the post turnings. Specific details relate it to two other signs originating in the Saybrook area of southeastern Connecticut (cat. 3,6). Shared construction methods, related turnings, and the use of the same molding plane to shape the horizontal rails suggests production in the same shop, as yet unidentified.[3] One notable construction element distinguishes this early sign from the other two in the Saybrook group. All three exhibit horizontal rails joined into the vertical posts by two parallel tenons. In this earliest example, each rail is a solid piece of wood, into which a long rectangular slot, or mortise, has been cut through to hold the central board. This technique required that each end of each rail be carved into two projecting parallel tenons (two tenons were necessary to prevent the possibility of a single, centered tenon sheering off because of the long mortise cut for the signboard). In the later signs, the maker simplified construction by replacing the single rails with paired half-rails, separated by spacer blocks to create a slot for the signboard. The projecting ends of each half-rail formed one of the parallel tenons, thus reducing the amount of laborious woodcutting (see figs. 16–17 for diagram of construction features).

Innholder: Capt. Edward Bull (1717–82) was the only son of Edward and Mary Post Bull of Saybrook. In 1739 he married Temperance Clark (1715–86), also of Saybrook. The couple removed in 1739 from Saybrook Point, along the shoreline, to the town's Second Society, a relatively new settlement five miles north, also known as Pautapaug and later Centerbrook (short for Center Saybrook). Bull held numerous local offices and served as Captain of the militia, 1753–60. He inherited extensive landholdings as an infant and died a rich man, with holdings valued at nearly £ 1600. Exact dates of Bull's tavern licenses are unknown, but he probably retired by 1764, when references appear to Benjamin Williams as the innholder in Centerbrook.

Original location: Bull's inn is said by family tradition to have been at the intersection of what is now Rt. 153 and Ingham Hill Road, a site that seems rather inconveniently distant from the eighteenth-century highway. Perhaps this was a later residence, occupied by Bull after his retirement from tavernkeeping in the 1760s. Bull also owned properties in the center district of Centerbrook, a more likely site for an inn. Centerbrook Village is now part of Essex Township.

Provenance: The absence of repainting suggests that this sign was not used after Bull's retirement. It remained in Centerbrook as late as 1920, probably owned by the innkeeper's great-great grandson, John E. Bull.[4]

Construction notes: Single board, with single molded, horizontal rails, and turned posts. Board is set vertically and hand-sawn at top and bottom to create decorative pediment and skirt profiles; board passes through full-width mortise cut through each rail and is held by nails. Each rail is tenoned through the turned posts with two parallel tenons and secured at each joint by two pins.

Surface notes: This sign displays only one paint layer on each side; side 2 is more weathered. The horses are identical in outline, suggesting use of a template, which was reversed from one side to the other. Lettering appears to have been executed by hand within guidelines scribed into the board. Both images and lettering, painted black, are raised above the lead-white ground, which has largely worn away. Rails and posts may have been painted gray.

Condition and treatment notes: Original iron hangers have been reversed from their original positions, perhaps to avoid reusing nail holes. Sign was disassembled at some time. On side 1, the horse's chest has been marred by five bullet holes. Treatment at WACC, 1999–2000, included surface cleaning.

Related signs: Sign for Hayden's Inn, 1762 and 1766, Essex, Conn. (cat. 3); Sign of the Black Horse, ca. 1771, Saybrook Point, Conn. (cat. 6).

Publications: *MBTS*, p. 22.

1. The only other American example dated pre-1750 is a restored sign said to be from the Daggett Tavern at Slater Park, Pawtucket, Rhode Island, bearing the date 1725; Chapin, pp. 22, 54
2. John Dimon, *American Horses and Horse Breeding* (Hartford: By the Author, 1895), pp. 52–55; for period testimony to the popularity of Narragansett pacers, see James McSparren, *America Dissected* (Dublin, 1753), cited in W.H. Gocher, "The Narragansett Pacers," *American Horse Breeder*, 3 May 1933, p. 143.
3. The other two signs display scroll pediments of slightly later style, commensurate with their dating.
4. B.F. Case to Morgan Brainard, East Granby, Conn., 16 Sept. 1920 (CHS museum object files).

Cat. 2

Sign of The Duke of Cumberland,
dated 1753(?), 1773, and 1914
ROCKY HILL, CONNECTICUT

Innholders: Oliver and Mary Pomeroy (licensed 1761–73); John and Sarah Robbins (licensed 1773–86)
Maker unidentified; side 2 overpainted by Louis James Donlon, 1914

Images: On both sides, three-quarter view of leaping black horse, with rider dressed as cavalier, centered against white ground. Side 2 is overpainted, with grass added beneath horse's feet.
Text: Side 1 has two sets of initials on pediment, "I R·S" over "O P M"; above the image, "The Duke of Cumberland" (badly worn); below the image, "ENTERTA / INMENT"; on the apron, "1773" over "1753" (badly worn). Side 2 is overpainted, displaying the same text, except as follows: on the pediment, "OPM" has been overpainted, over earlier initials, and spacing has been altered to "ENTERT / AINMENT".
Signed: "Restored 1914 Louis James Donlon", on top edge of sign.

Paint on pine board, ash posts, 40-5/8" x 20-1/4"
Collection of Morgan B. Brainard, Gift of Mrs. Morgan B. Brainard, 1961.63.43

Illustrated: color plate 2 (side 1), fig. 111 (side 2)

Before the Revolutionary War, portraits of British nobility, military heroes, or other popular leaders ornamented numerous American tavern signs. Oliver Pomeroy, a young and enterprising merchant, must have paid a premium for the elaborate equestrian portrait identified on this sign as the Duke of Cumberland. The original image was evidently quite sophisticated, both in composition and execution. Horse and rider are shown in a conventional pose, widely repeated in contemporary military imagery, and the specific design is almost certainly based on a contemporary print or book illustration, yet to be identified.[1] Tack or pin holes evident in each corner of the panel indicate the use of a template. However, the scale of the figure is probably too large (almost 18" high) for the template to have been traced

directly from a print source. The relatively naturalistic depiction of the galloping steed, the sense of motion, and particularly the slightly foreshortened angle of view, demanded the hand of an accomplished artist. The earlier date, 1753, corresponds to Pomeroy's building a new dwelling house and presumably obtaining a tavern license (not located).

His Royal Highness, William Augustus, Duke of Cumberland (1721–65) was a younger brother of King George III. He was renowned among English Protestants for his crushing defeat of Bonnie Prince Charlie, Catholic pretender to the throne of Scotland, at the battle of Culloden in 1746. Benjamin Franklin described him, in *Poor Richard's Almanack* for 1749, as "our glorious Billy, of Cumberland, another among the modern [heros],"[2] and his flying cape and jaunty cocked hat epitomized mid-eighteenth-century gallantry. Even though Cumberland fell from official favor during the Seven Years War (when his command of British forces in Europe ended in an ignominious surrender to France), his earlier victory over the Scottish pretender remained memorable, considered by many a triumph of parliamentary government over royal absolutism. An additional connection to local interests may be found in the fraternity of Freemasonry; in January 1766, amidst the Stamp Act controversy, the St. John's Lodge No. 4, in Hartford, honored Cumberland with an effusive eulogy, praising him as a glorious prince, one of the "greatest Ornaments" of the Masonic brotherhood, and a "true and cordial Friend to [American] Rights & Liberties."[3]

Few American signs with royalist imagery survived the Revolution unscathed, and this one contains several musket ball holes. Despite this disfigurement, the sign remained at the Robbins house, fascinating the boy, Morgan Brainard.[4] Long exposure heightened the sculptural effect of black lettering, horse, and rider, raised in shallow relief above the white background. Where paint layers protected the wood from erosion, weathering has rendered the surface an exquisitely detailed, almost fragile, incarnation of the original image.

Inn name: Eighteenth-century references designate this inn by owners' names; no period references have been located to the pictorial motif on the inn sign as a name.

Innholders: Lt. Oliver Pomery (1729–76) was the son of Capt. John and Rachel Sheldon Pomeroy of Northampton, Mass. In 1750 in Wethersfield, Conn., he married Mary Lyman (1729–76), also of Northampton, Mass. Oliver Pomeroy became a prosperous merchant, owning and operating a wharf on the Connecticut River. Although the tavern license was recorded in Oliver's name, the sign displays the initials of the couple: "OPM".

Capt. John Robbins (1716–98) was the son of Richard Robbins. He served as Rocky Hill's militia captain for four years prior to obtaining his tavern license; he subsequently represented the town at various sessions of the Connecticut General Assembly during the 1780s. Sarah Boardman Wright (1731–84) was a widow when she married John Robbins in 1770, becoming the second of his three wives. Although John remarried in 1784, he did not update the initials "JRS" on the sign.

Original locations: This sign hung at two separate structures within the Stepney Parish of Wethersfield, which was incorporated as Rocky Hill in 1843. The Pomeroy house, referred to by antiquarians as the "Long Tavern," was a frame structure, probably built in the 1750s, on the river landing in Rocky Hill, near Pomeroy's wharf. It is no longer extant.

When Robbins became tavernkeeper, he evidently acquired the Pomeroy sign and moved it to his own house, located on the hill above the landing, along the main road from Middletown to Hartford. Robbins was among the wealthiest men in Connecticut, and his brick residence, built in 1767, was one of the most expensive houses built anywhere in the Connecticut River Valley prior to the Revolution. Both substantial and stylish, it introduced into the area such cosmopolitan Georgian features as a Palladian-style window and cornice with modillion blocks and flutings.[5] That Robbins did not commission a new sign to hang in front of his handsome house suggests that the image on Pomeroy's old sign may have held a particular significance for him, as for his predecessor. Robbins's house remains standing on its original site, now fronting a side street parallel to Rt. 99 in Rocky Hill.

Provenance: Preserved by Robbins family descendants, the sign remained in the Robbins house in Rocky Hill until purchased by Morgan Brainard.[6]

Construction notes: Single board, with applied moldings. No structural frame. Board is oriented vertically and hand-sawn at top and bottom to create decorative pediment and skirt profiles. Double moldings make a rectangular frame for the central image. The ogee-profiled inner moldings are applied to both faces of the signboard and nailed with hand-wrought nails; corners are mitered. The outer moldings consist of thick boards with rounded ("bullnose") edge profiles, applied to the side edges and to the top and bottom faces of the signboard. At the corners, the outer horizontal moldings are contoured to fit around the shaped vertical moldings. Wood is *Pinus strobus*, Eastern white pine, identified by analysis (Hoadley, March 2000).

Surface notes: Side 1 is heavily weathered, although brushwork, following the contours of the horse, remains visible in the black paint; no other colors were found remaining in the image. Lettering was executed between scribed guidelines. Side 2 was overpainted by Louis James Donlon in 1914; the repainted image has heavy black outlines surrounding areas of vivid, rather flat colors. A patch of grass was added beneath the horse, although there is no evidence of such a background element on side 1.

Condition and treatment notes: Original hanging hardware is missing. Holes bored into the top edge of the pediment indicate that there were originally three finials (as on cat. 7), which are also missing. Damage from musket balls includes a large hole, between the "T" and "E" on side 1, which ripped away adjoining wood fragments, as well as smaller holes with surrounding paint losses. Two outer moldings are missing from side 2. Earlier treatment (1914) included filling musket ball holes with white lead, from side 2, and repainting side 2. Treatment at WACC, 2000, included surface cleaning; removal of black overpaint from edges, only where visible from side 1; and installation of new hanging hardware, stamped "WS" and "2000", fabricated by blacksmith William Senseney, Williamstown, Mass., based on outline of original hardware, visible in raking light.

Exhibitions: Wethersfield Historical Society, 1998–99, 1982–83; "Two Towns: Concord & Wethersfield," Concord (Mass.) Antiquarian Museum, 1982; Aetna 1939 (side 2).

Publications: *MBTS*, p. 61 (side 1), cover (side 2); Smith, *Tavern Signs*, p. 13; Benes, *Two Towns*, p. 119 (side 1); Lord and Foley, p. 151; *Decorator* 1960, p. 4 (side 1); *Spinning Wheel* 1955, p. 12 (side 2); *CHSB* 11 (Oct. 1946): cover (side 1); Terry, *Old Inns*, p. 135 (side 2); Henry R. Stiles and Sherman W. Adams, *The History of Ancient Wethersfield, Connecticut*, 2 vols. (New York: Grafton Press, 1904), vol. 1. p. 845. Textbooks, various editions: Davidson, *The American Nation*; Conlin, *The American Past* (Harcourt, Brace, Jovanovich); Hodgins, et al., *Adventures in American Literature* (Holt, Rinehart, & Winston) (side 2).

1. See, for example, the engraving, "A Perspective View of the Glorious Battle, after J. Hamilton, published in 1746; Peter Harrington, *Culloden 1746: The Highland Clans' Last Charge*, Campaign Series 12 (Osprey Publishing Co., 1998), p. 73.
2. July 1748; quoted in *Poor Richard: The Almanacks for the Years 1733–1758* (New York: Heritage Press, 1964), p. 152. Few objects known to have been American-owned make reference to the Duke of Cumberland.
3. Eulogy quoted in George S. Dunkelberger, comp., *An Early History of St. John's Lodge, No. 4, A.F.&A.M, Hartford, Conn. 1762–1937* (Hartford: Case, Lockwood & Brainard Co., 1937), pp.104–5. Since the Masonic Lodge in Hartford was not formed until 1762, Pomeroy or Robbins might have been initiated elsewhere; membership records have not yet been located. Both would certainly have been likely candidates for membership and would have been acquainted with many Masons.
4. Brainard to Robert W. Carrick, *House & Garden Magazine*, 7 May 1941; cited in Grant, p. 3.
5. *Great River*, pp. 100–2.
6. "Tavern Visited by George Washington," *Hartford Daily Courant*, 16 January 19[07]; CHS museum object files; Terry, *Old Inns*, p. 137.

Cat. 3*

Sign for Hayden's Inn, dated 1762 and 1766

ESSEX, CONNECTICUT

Innholders: Uriah and Ann Hayden (licensed 1766–90)
Attributed to Saybrook sign maker (active ca. 1749–71)

Images: On side 1, a three-masted frigate, known locally as the "Old Ship," centered on board. On side 2, English royal coat of arms, centered on board. No underlying images.
Text: On both sides, on pediment, two sets of initials, "VHA" over "IAR"; under image, "Entertainment"; on apron, two dates, "1766" over "1762".

Paint (traces remaining) on yellow or tulip poplar board, pine frame, iron hardware, 42" x 30-7/8"
Gift of Miss Susan M. Loomis, 1896.7.0

Illustrated: color plate 3 (side 2), fig. 24 (side 1, detail of ship's rigging), fig. 67 (side 1, conjectural rendering of original color scheme)

During the 1760s and 1770s, Hayden's shipyard on the Connecticut River was among the busiest in the district. His most notable production was the *Oliver Cromwell*, a twenty-gun state ship authorized by the colony of Connecticut in January 1776 and often called "the first United States warship." When the *Oliver Cromwell* sailed to New London in August 1776, she became the largest vessel to pass over Saybrook bar, at the mouth of the Connecticut River. Hayden's occupation—and ambitions—as a shipbuilder and West Indies trader suggest an obvious rationale for his selection of a fully-rigged ship as an emblem for his inn, which opened in 1766.[1]

Given to the Connecticut Historical Society in 1896, this extraordinary early sign escaped "freshening" by Colonial Revival enthusiasts. Severe weathering has transformed it from a brightly colored, almost garish, two-dimensional object into an exquisitely subtle sculptural relief, best viewed by raking light (compare fig. 67 with fig. 24). The surface relief observed in this sign has occasioned considerable debate among curators and conservators, with the majority opinion concluding that the evidence (especially the absence of edge tool marks) points to weathering rather than carving as the primary factor in relieving the surface. The colored paint on the figures and lettering, evidently thicker or more durable, protected the underlying wood in these areas, while the thinner background color—probably white—weathered away, exposing raw wood to accelerated erosion.[2]

Although traditionally said to have been imported from England, the frame of this sign displays construction techniques, turnings, and molding profiles closely related to those on two other signs from the Saybrook area of southeastern Connecticut (cat. 1, 6), arguing for production in a single local woodworking shop. Moreover, laboratory analysis has recently identified the wood as yellow poplar, *Linodendron tulipifera*, a locally available species. The exceptional pictorial decoration on this signboard contrasts with the simpler black horses on the other two signs and may suggest the hands of different painters. Whereas the black horse signs repeat the same motif on both sides, evidently from a template, the Hayden sign displays two very different designs: the English royal coat of arms and a three-masted frigate under full sail and flying a British flag.[3] Both arms and ship were considerably more complex, and thus more time consuming to execute, than the elegant, but comparatively simple, horse silhouettes. The ship, in particular, is rendered in intricate detail, from its five flags to its eleven gun ports, from its fancy stern carving and lamp to the shrouds on each mast; like the Duke of Cumberland and General Wolfe (cat. 2, 4), Hayden's ship was likely copied from a print source. The symbolic message is also quite different from the two other Saybrook area signs. On the black horse signs, both image and text communicate function: "entertainment [for travelers]." On the Hayden sign, only the text carries this functional message; both king's arms and ship express identity, both public (citizen of the British Empire) and private (shipbuilder and merchant).

There are indications that this sign was used briefly prior to the Haydens' acquisition of it. As originally created, it evidently displayed the initials "IAR", the date "1762", and the ship and the royal arms above the word, "Entertainment," executed in a rather elaborate script. The artisan who adapted it for the Haydens' use executed the overlying initials, "UHA", in much simpler and more angular style than that used in the earlier lettering, and the final "6" in "1766" is squeezed rather awkwardly in front of the "2" in the earlier date. The location of unused nail holes underneath the bottom rail, revealed by X-rays, suggests that the frame was taken apart at the time and reassembled with the bottom rail installed upside down, thus reversing the profile (see construction notes).[4]

Innholders: Uriah Hayden (1731–1810) was the son of Nehemiah Hayden of Saybrook. He married Ann Starkey (1736–1813). Hayden purchased numerous properties in the 1760s, became Captain of the local militia in 1770, and was chosen a member of the local Committee of Correspondence in 1774. No local couple has been identified to match the earlier set of initials, "IAR".

Original location: A two-story frame dwelling, built in 1766, at the foot of Main Street, on the Connecticut River bank in what is now the village of Essex. The building survives and is now owned by the Dauntless Club. At least two reproductions of the old sign have hung in front of the club, the earlier installed before 1937, and a new one created ca. 1999.

Provenance: Descended to the donor through the family of original owner.

Construction notes: Single board, with double, molded, horizontal rails and turned posts. Board is set vertically and hand-sawn at top and bottom to create decorative pediment and skirt profiles. Board is held by nails between paired molded rails. Each rail is tenoned into the turned posts and secured with two pins. The frame does not fit the signboard well. The top rail covers over both the top flag of the ship and the bottom of the initial, "H". The bottom rail cramps the placement of the numerals on the skirt. The rails of this sign differ from those in other two Saybrook group signs in that the orientation of the lower rail molding repeats rather than reverses the profile of the upper rail. Style analysis suggests that this example is the second of the three made by this unknown maker, a chronology confirmed by the documentary evidence on tavern licensing. Woods are *Liriodendron tulipifera*, yellow or tulip poplar, for the central panel, and *Pinus strobus*, eastern white pine, for the rails and turned posts; identified by analysis (Hoadley, March 2000).

Surface notes: This sign is heavily weathered, with almost all paint worn off side 1. Side 2 retains slightly more color, with evidence of a white ground, black lettering, and image colors of ochre, red, and dark brown. Based on visible paint traces, WACC Paintings Conservator Sandra L. Webber painted a conjectural rendering of the original color scheme of the brig on side 1 (fig. 67). The surface history of this sign is particularly complex. The word "Entertainment" was possibly added after original production; the layout and line work is not as well executed as the images. These letters do show evidence of relief-carving with edge tools, as do certain areas around the heraldic crest on side 2. This work, evidently intended to clarify portions of the image, may have been carried out at the time other alterations were made, very early in the sign's history, including the addition of new owners' initials and date, "VHA / 1766". With the exceptions of these areas, there is no evidence of carving "set in" or tool marks, particularly in such areas as the jewels of the central crown, where traditional wood carving techniques would have left traces. In addition, late wood growth rings, which run continuously *across* image outlines, would have been cut through had the images originally been carved with edge tools.

Condition and treatment notes: Hardware may be of later date. Terminations of the pediment scrolls are missing. Holes in the pediment were probably made to affix hanging wire shown in an early twentieth-century photograph. One turned post was broken and repaired below the upper mortise block. Treatment at WACC, 1999–2000, included stabilization of wood support and hardware, surface cleaning and removal of old oil surface finish.

Related signs: Sign for Bull's Inn, 1749, Centerbrook, Conn. (cat. 1); Sign of the Black Horse, ca. 1771, Saybrook Point, Conn. (cat. 6).

Exhibitions: Old State House Museum, Boston, 1994–95 (photographic reproduction).

Publications: *MBTS*, p. 44; Rice, *Early American Taverns*, p. 69 (side 2); Louis F. Middlebrook, *History of Maritime Connecticut during the American Revolution, 1775–1783*, 2 vols. (Salem, Mass.: Essex Institute, 1925), vol. 1, opp. p. 97; Earle, *Tavern Days*, p. 28.

1. Information on the Oliver Cromwell compiled by CHS Curator of Technology, Richard C. Malley.
2. For further discussion of "preferential weathering," the environmental interaction between painting and weathering, see Carlisle, "Weather It Is," Chapter 7.
3. Other King's Arms inn signs are recorded, all from seaports (Boston, Salem, Newport); none of these have been located. See CHS museum research files; Chapin, pp. 25–26; Terry, *Old Inns*, p. 151. A board painted with the royal

coat of arms, ca. 1726, originally hung in the Connecticut Assembly and is preserved at CHS.
4. Radiography performed by Frederick U. Conard, Jr., M.D.

Cat. 4*

Sign of General Wolfe, ca. 1768
BROOKLYN, CONNECTICUT

Innholder: General Israel Putnam (licensed 1768–76)
Maker unidentified

Images: On both sides, full-length profile portrait of General James Wolfe, in red military uniform, with right hand upraised and index finger pointing forward, centered on board, with green background below horizon line. No underlying images
Text: On both sides, "Gen¹. WOLFE". No underlying text.

Paint on pine, 30" x 24-1/4"
Gift of Rufus S. Mathewson, 1841.11.0

Illustrated: color plate 4, fig. 55.

The subject and owner of this sign were both military heroes to their contemporaries, their faces made familiar through prints, magazine illustrations, and paintings. British Major General James Wolfe (1727–59) won international fame for the success of his audacious plan to surprise the French army at Quebec by scaling the unguarded cliffs behind the city. Wolfe's troops defeated the French, unsettling the latters' hold on Canada, but both he and the French commander, the Marquis de Montcalm, were killed in the encounter. Israel Putnam was likewise a celebrated hero, albeit on a smaller scale.[1] He had fought under Wolfe's command, serving with Major Robert Rogers's Rangers. At the conclusion of Putnam's military service, he returned to his extensive farmlands in eastern Connecticut, but he can hardly be said to have settled down. According to tradition, entertaining Putnam's former comrades became so expensive that his wife suggested applying for a tavern license. Although undocumented, the story rings true: Putnam's license dates to 1768, shortly after he married the wealthy widow, Deborah Lothrop Avery Gardiner, and the couple set up innkeeping in the residence she had inherited from her first husband.[2] The burdens of entertaining former military comrades, moreover, are attested to by even so wealthy a man as George Washington, who once called Mount Vernon his "well-resorted tavern."[3]

Putnam's choice of a British "redcoat" as his standard bearer has often been viewed as being at odds with his support of the American Revolution. Oral history holds that disgruntled patriots vandalized the sign by firing buckshot at its British redcoat.[4] Although this possibility exists, it is more likely that Putnam's selection of Gen. Wolfe was not an unfortunate choice but a deliberate choice, grounded in the complicated political terrain of the late 1760s. Wolfe died an Anglo-American hero well before the onset of pre-Revolutionary crises, and there is no evidence that Putnam's patriotism was ever questioned. By the time he opened his tavern in 1768, Putnam had already established himself as a active patriot, having joined the Sons of Liberty during the Stamp Act crisis of 1765–66. His affiliations made his tavern a recognized "rendezvous of ex-soldiers and patriots."[5] In this context, Wolfe represented not British tyranny, but its opposite, traditional British liberties, which American patriots believed to have been abrogated by current royal ministers. (Notably, Wolfe's contemporary, British statesman William Pitt [1708–78], became an American hero at this time, because of what colonists viewed as his efforts to uphold traditional British liberties).[6] An engraving published by Nathaniel Hurd in Boston in 1762 underlines this symbolism, presenting George III as an opponent of "Evil and Corrupt Ministers"; supporting the king in this contest are former prime minister Pitt, holding the "Magna Charta of Liberties," and James Wolfe, "the British HERO."[7] As key architects of British victory in the Seven Years War, Pitt (on the homefront) and Wolfe (on the battlefield) also embodied the political and cultural ascendancy of the British empire, an accomplishment in which British subjects on both sides of the Atlantic took justifiable pride. Wolfe's death on the outskirts of Quebec effected his apotheosis into a pantheon of heroes; safely above imperial politics, he epitomized a halcyon moment of shared Anglo-American triumph. Having served under Wolfe's command, Putnam and his former military comrades presumably felt a strong connection to their fallen leader. From their perspective, he embodied not only remembrances of youth and adventure, but also such classical, republican virtues as valor, honor, daring, and self-sacrifice. Finally, Putnam's choice of Wolfe as standard bearer suggests a deliberate play on words, a rebus for one of his own most celebrated exploits: shortly after his arrival in Connecticut, the young Putnam had rid the local community of a ravaging wolf by descending into its den and killing it.[8]

Wolfe's glorious victory and tragic death quickly became one of the most celebrated events of the tumultuous years leading up the American Revolution. Representations of the fallen hero inspired a wide variety of visual productions, from monumental history paintings to handcolored mezzotints to watch-papers and tavern signs. "The Death of Wolfe," painted by American-born artist Benjamin West in London in 1770, became the most influential history painting of the late eighteenth century. For middle-class audiences, London printmakers turned out portraits in a variety of sizes, and these in turn eventually reached American consumers, including innkeepers and sign painters. In December 1762, Boston engraver Nathaniel Hurd advertised a new set of three small medallion portraits: "a striking likeness of his Majesty King George the Third, Mr. Pitt and General Wolfe fit for a picture or for Gentlemen and Ladies to put in their watches."[9] While Hurd's medallion style portrait inspired a General Wolfe tavern sign, dated 1768, in Newburyport, Massachusetts, Nancy Finlay has persuasively demonstrated that the artist of the Putnam sign worked directly from the initial, full-length London version, based on a sketch by Wolfe's fellow officer, James Hervey (fig. 54).[10] Even with a printed source as guide, the successful enlargement of Wolfe's full-length standing figure on Putnam's sign was unquestionably the work of a comparatively well-trained and talented artist. The execution is skillful, not only copying carefully such details as the ruffled white shirt cuff, the exact placement of buttons and buttonholes, the wrinkles in the coat sleeves, but also achieving more difficult technical effects such as proper proportion and articulation of limbs and body, the use of contour shading to suggest three-dimensionality, the sense of arrested motion conveyed by the shift of weight onto one foot, and the hint of wind blowing through Wolfe's hair.

Putnam's General Wolfe sign is among the most sophisticated and well-painted signs surviving from the eighteenth century; indeed, it fares well in comparison with any figure painting done in America prior to 1770. Only a handful of painters possessing the requisite skills have been identified in eastern Connecticut as early as 1768. One intriguing candidate is the Boston-born painter William Johnston (1732–72), considered the first professional artist to have worked in Connecticut.[11] Portraits by Johnston survive of sitters from New London, New Haven, Hartford, Middletown, and even Windham, only a few miles from Brooklyn. Johnston's three-quarter-length view of Windham's leading citizen, Eliphalet Dyer, echoes certain aspects of the Wolfe figure, particularly the arrangement of the right hand and the handling of costume details. Although primarily known today as a portraitist, Johnston had extensive connections to sign and ornamental painting. His father, Thomas Johnston, practiced engraving, japanning, and heraldic painting, teaching these arts to several apprentices, including at least three sons. John Johnston, Williams' younger half-brother, apprenticed to Boston coach and ornamental painter John Gore in 1767; in 1797, he painted the Sign of the Good Samaritan for the Boston Dispensary. This sign, like General Wolfe, is a relatively sophisticated composition, directly based on an engraving from the early 1770s. Finally, one of Thomas Johnston's engraving clients was Jacob Hurd, father of the Boston engraver who had copied Wolfe's portrait in 1762; the Johnston-Hurd connection may have provided direct access to the full-length London version.[12]

Innholder: Israel Putnam (1719–90) was born in Salem Village, Massachusetts (now Danvers), where his parents, John and Elizabeth Porter Putnam, had been the principal protagonists in the notorious witchcraft trials of 1692. He arrived in Connecticut in 1739, with sufficient wealth to purchase a sizeable estate of 514 acres. At the opening of the Revolution, he was widely considered one of America's preeminent military leaders. His exploits were the stuff of legend: he survived Indian capture in 1758 and fought in Pontiac's War in 1764. He is also said to have been Connecticut's first brewer and to have introduced the first cigars, after being shipwrecked off the coast of Cuba in 1762. After the death of his first wife, Hannah Pope Putnam in 1765, he married Deborah Lothrop Avery Gardiner (b. 1716). She brought to the partnership both substantial wealth and impeccable social credentials: the daughter of Samuel and Deborah Crow Lothrop, widow of the Rev. Ephraim Avery, the first ordained minister at Brooklyn, and after his death, John Gardiner, proprietor of Gardiner's Island, in Long Island Sound. In addition to providing the house that the tavern occupied, Deborah Putnam must have taken an active role in daily operations, presumably assuming sole responsibility during her husband's frequent absences (records of the Masonic lodge in Hartford show Israel Putnam to have been a frequent visitor, despite the distance of more than forty miles). In 1772–73 Putnam participated in an exploring expedition in West Florida; in 1774, he drove a herd of livestock to Boston to relieve the British siege; and in April 1775, he abandoned his plow in the field to take up arms after receiving the news of conflict at Lexington and Concord, thus becoming known as "the American Cincinnatus." Israel Putnam was thenceforth almost continually in the field, until a paralytic stroke ended his career in 1779; Deborah is reported to have accompanied him until her death in 1777, at his command in the New York Highlands. Thus, although the tavern license was renewed in June 1775, it could hardly have been very active in its last year.[13]

Original location: Putnam's tavern is sometimes confused with his farmhouse, which he occupied from 1739 until after his remarriage in 1767 to Deborah Lothrop Avery Gardiner. The Putnam farm lay in the northwestern section of Brooklyn, near the Pomfret town line, on what is now Route 93—five miles distant from the main road. The Genl. Wolfe was situated much more conveniently, on the green in Brooklyn, in a house inherited by the second Mrs. Putnam from her first husband, the Rev. Ephraim Avery. The road through Brooklyn carried travelers bound from Boston and Worcester, Massachusetts, to Norwich and New London, Connecticut. Although neither Putnam's farmhouse nor the tavern house remain standing, their locations are marked by stone tablets. A three-story house, built ca. 1778 by Putnam's daughter Mehitable and her husband, General Daniel Tyler, was later the site of another well-known tavern, Mortlake House or Manor; it can be seen in many views of the Putnam monument on the Brooklyn green.[14] The village of Brooklyn was in Putnam's time part of the town of Pomfret, from which it was incorporated in 1786.

Provenance: The sign was evidently taken down at some time after Putnam returned to arms in 1775, and stored at the Putnam homestead, which had been taken over by Israel Putnam, Jr., in 1767, after his father's remarriage and removal to town. Israel, Jr., inherited the property in 1790 and sold it five years later to Joseph Matheson, Esq. The farmstead descended to Matheson's grandson, Rufus S. Mathewson, who acquired it in 1834 and seven years later sent the sign to The Connecticut Historical Society, "as a memento of the olden time & as having belonged to one so distinguished" as "Gen. Israel Putnam of Revolutionary & wolf-den memory."[15]

Construction notes: Single board, raised and fielded on both sides, one side with a wider bevel.

Surface notes: This sign displays only one paint layer on each side; side 2 is more weathered. Several details of the uniform and sword-belt are raised above the surface plane, with opinions differing on whether this effect is the result of partial relief carving, or of preferential weathering, which wore away the thinly painted white areas more quickly than more heavily coated, colored areas. Mylar tracings reveal that the two portrait figures are identical, pointing to the use of a template. Letters are partially raised or recessed and may have been carved; they appear to have been executed free-hand. The background, applied after the figure was painted, displays broad, undulating brush strokes.

Condition and treatment notes: The frame into which this panel fitted is missing, and with it, any original hardware and date or owner's initials that might have existed. Evidence of vandalism includes disfigurement of the face on both sides and 30–40 buckshot holes on each side, shot from various angles, including overhead. Two lead shot pellets remain embedded. Treatment at WACC in 2000 consisted of consolidation of the wood structure and surface cleaning; and selective inpainting of gouges in the face on side 2, to re-establish the eye and profile, using as guide the face on side 1 and known portraits of Wolfe. In order to provide support for the panel, a reproduction frame was created by Alexander Carlisle, using as a model the period frame on the Sign of the Pine Tree, a contemporary sign with contiguous provenance (cat. 5). Replacement hardware, stamped "WS / 2000", was blacksmith-forged by William Senseney, Williamstown, Mass., using a sympathetic but neutral design.

Exhibitions: "Drums A'Beating, Trumpets Sounding: Artistically Carved Powder Horns in the Provincial Manner, 1746–1781," Concord Museum, Concord, Mass., 1994; Brooklyn Historical Society, Brooklyn, Conn., 1994 (photographic reproduction).

Publications: *MBTS*, p. 70; Earle, *Tavern Days*, p. 211; F.W. Salem, *Beer: Its History and Its Economic Value as a National Beverage* (Hartford: F.W. Salem, 1880).

1. *DAB*, vol. 15, pp. 281–82; for additional references to Putnam, see Collier, *Literature*, p. 318.
2. The first published appearance of this widely repeated story may be Ellen D. Larned, *History of Windham County*, 2 vols. (Worcester, Mass.: Charles

Hamilton, 1874–80), vol. 2, p. 6.

3. Cited in *Mount Vernon: Yesterday, Today, Tomorrow,* 13 (Winter 1998), p. 17.
4. Recorded in CHS museum object files.
5. *DAB,* vol. 15, p. 281.
6. New Yorkers erected a marble statue to Pitt in the Battery in 1770. In 1786, Charles Willson Peale executed an oil portrait followed by a mezzotint, enti-tled "Worthy of Liberty, Mr. Pitt scorns to invade the Liberties of other People." Pitt's pose in this portrait echoes Wolfe's.
7. Fowble, *Prints,* pp. 295–96.
8. Putnam's Wolf's Den became a popular nineteenth-century tourist attrac-tion, and is still preserved as a state park, located off Route 44 in Pomfret; see Christopher P. Bickford and J. Bard McNulty, *John Warner Barber's Views of Connecticut Towns, 1834–36* (Hartford: The Acorn Club and The Connecticut Historical Society , 1990), p. 79.
9. Kane, *Silversmiths,* p. 617.
10. Finlay, "Lions and Eagles," Chapter Five. The Newburyport tavern sign bearing Wolfe's image is much less skillfully executed than Putnam's; see Earle, *Tavern Days,* pp. 145–46; for other Wolfe signs, see Garvin, *North of Boston,* p. 130; and Jean-Claude Dupont and Luc Dupont, *Les enseignes d'hier à aujordh'hui (*Quèbec: Musée de la civilisation, 1998).
11. Other candidates include John Durand (active 1765–82, who is known to have painted portraits in New Haven and Norwich in 1768 and 1772, and Winthrop Chandler (1747–90), who trained as a house painter, but also exe-cuted numerous portraits and ornamental paintings (primarily overmantels and fireboards) for clients in towns around Brooklyn, especially Woodstock and Scotland, Connecticut. Unlike Johnston and Durand, Chandler made less use of print sources for his compositions, and his earliest identified works date to 1770; see Elizabeth Mankin Kornhauser, *Ralph Earl: The Face of the Young Republic* (New Haven and London: Yale University Press and Wadsworth Atheneum, Hartford, 1991), pp. 6–8, 102–4; Kornhauser and Christine S. Schloss, "Paintings and Other Pictorial Arts," *Great River,* pp. 135–36. Even more speculative candidates are two women, both from Lebanon, Connecticut, and both said to have exerted artistic influence on the noted painter John Trumbull (1756–1843): Sibyl Huntington May (1734/5–98) and Faith Trumbull Huntington (1743–75). May, reputed to have been John Trumbull's first teacher, painted a landscape overmantel for the East Haddam, Connecticut, parsonage, ca. 1758; *Great River,* pp. 149–50. Faith Trumbull is credited by her younger brother, John Trumbull, with several oil paintings (location now unknown) in addition to needlework pic-tures in the collections of The Connecticut Historical Society and the Lyman Allyn Museum of Connecticut College, New London; see Betty Ring, *Girlhood Embroidery: American Samplers & Pictorial Needlework, 1650–1850,* 2 vols. (New York: Knopf, 1993), vol. 1, pp. 54–58; CHS museum object files.
12. Little, *Paintings,* pp. 22, 138–45; Kane, *Silversmiths,* pp. 81–82, 615–17, 1020–21. Little also identifies a group of interior wall panels from Brooklyn as being the work of an as yet unidentified painter; one of these panels was said to have come from the Israel Putnam house, although its style seems to bear little relationship to the Wolfe sign; see Little, *Wall Painting,* pp. 53, 68, 137.
13. *DAB,* pp. 218–20; Putnam, *History of the Putnam Family,* pp. 87–126.
14. Crofut, *Guide,* vol. 2, pp. 832–36, 839.
15. Mathewson to Henry Barnard, Woodstock, Conn., 3 May 1841, CHS museum object files; Crofut, vol. 2, p. 839.

Cat. 5*

Sign of the Pine Tree, dated 1768
LISBON, CONNECTICUT

Innholder: probably Joseph Read III (licensed 1769–70)
Maker unidentified

Images: On both sides, a round disc, centered in pediment, over stylized pine tree, centered on board. No underlying layers.
Text: On side 1, below image, "Entertainment: For / Man & Hors" ; on apron, "1768". Side 2 differs only in having a period after "Hors.", but no colon after "Entertainment". No underlying layers.

Paint on pine board, iron hardware, 42" x 23"
Collection of Morgan B. Brainard, Gift of Mrs. Morgan B. Brainard, 1961.63.42

Illustrated: color plate 5, fig. 51 (watercolor rendering)

The pictorial elements in this sign may have been intended as a coded message with political connotations. Reading the sign as a rebus, or pictorial representation of words or syllables, the com-bination of yellow, circular orb (sun) over a stylized pine tree may have been intended as a veiled reference to the Sons of Lib-erty, an extra-legal resistance organization that had adopted as its symbol the Liberty Tree. The motif of the stark, symmetrical pine tree was a familiar element of colonial New England's visual culture, made famous in part by the pine-tree shilling minted in Boston from 1667 to 1682. Authorized by the Massachusetts Bay General Court in 1652, during the Cromwellian protectorate, the Massachusetts mint produced coins displaying the letters "NE" for New England, a willow and oak tree as well as the more famil-iar pine.[1] Three decades later, when the British crown revoked the Massachusetts Charter, minting money was one of several "grievances" cited; the pine tree, struck on colonial coinage in place of the usual sovereign's portrait, thus connoted alterna-tives to British royal authority. The 1768 date of this sign coin-cides with the enactment of the Townshend Acts, which ignited a new wave of colonial resistance.

Innholder: Joseph Read III (b. 1709) was the son of Joseph Read II (1681–after 1759) of Norwich. The younger Read married Thankfull Andrus in 1740. A descendant of the first settler in Newent (the section of Norwich township that later became Lisbon), Joseph Read III became an extensive landholder, with at least eight tracts located along the Quinebaug River northeast of Norwich. Two relevant tavern licenses are known: the earlier license (1769) names Joseph Read rather than Joseph Read III; however, Joseph Read II would have been nearly ninety, if still alive; he is thus a much less likely candidate than his son. Other documents are known to refer to the son as simply Joseph Read. Read may have kept tavern for only a few years; he is not listed as a tavernkeeper in the 1797 and 1798 tax lists for Norwich.

Original location: Read's tavern may have been located at what was still known as the "Read homestead" as late as 1868, on the road east of Newent center (later Lisbon). Period references suggest that Read's tavern was less important than the one operated by Benjamin Burn-ham, located on more heavily traveled Norwich road.

Provenance: A label previously attached to the sign indicates that it was owned by A.F. Read, a descendent of the original owner, before being acquired by Morgan Brainard.

Construction notes: Single board, fielded on both sides, set vertically into grooves of joined frame. Horizontal rails have integral pediment and skirt (e.g., vertical extensions, which are hand-sawn to create dec-orative profiles). The frame construction is conceptually flawed. The vertical stiles are tenoned through the top and bottom rails, thus reversing the nearly universal practice of horizontal rails tenoned into stiles (see fig. 16). Consequently, the entire weight of panel, stiles, and bottom rail rests on the wooden pins that secure the vertical tenons into the rails. Straps from the hanging hardware reinforced the top joint, but the lower joints required reinforcement at a later date.

Surface notes: This sign displays only one layer of paint on each side. Its original color scheme featured yellow suns, bright green trees, and white lettering set off by a barn-red background. Laboratory examina-tion revealed that the pigment used for the trees was a copper-based verdigris, which has oxidized to black or brown, leaving traces of green only in tiny surface fissures. The absence of any repainting suggests that this sign was probably in use for only a short period.

Condition and treatment notes: Structurally, this sign survived in relatively unaltered condition. Sheet metal straps were added at a later date to one side of the frame, reinforcing the lower mortise and tenon joints. The iron hanging hardware is original. Corrosion of this hardware was accelerated by a substantial sodium sulfate deposit, similar to airborne sea salt combined with air polutants. Treatment at WACC in 1998–99 included removal of this deposit from all wood and metal surfaces and consolidation of flaking paint on the tree motifs.

Related objects: Watercolor rendering, by Alfred Parys, ca. 1940, *Index of American Design*; National Gallery of Art, 1943.8.7743.

Publications: *MBTS*, p. 60; *Antiques* 1928, p. 405.

1. All coins were dated 1652, the date of authorization of the Massachusetts mint. On coinage as a design source for this sign, see Finlay, "Lions and Eagles," Chapter Five.

Cat. 6*

Sign of the Black Horse, ca. 1771
SAYBROOK POINT, CONNECTICUT

Innholders: Ambrose Kirtland (active ca. 1771–80)
Attributed to Saybrook sign maker (active ca. 1749–1771)

Images: On both sides, profile of riderless black horse, centered on board, white ground. No underlying images.
Text: On side 1, below image, "EntertaInment"; on skirt, "177__". On side 2 (repainted), below image, "EntertaInment"; on skirt, "17".

Paint on pine board, possibly oak, iron hardware, 47" x 28-3/4"
Collection of Morgan B. Brainard, Gift of Mrs. Morgan B. Brainard, 1961.63.8

Illustrated: color plate 6 (side 1), fig. 8 (side 2)

Distinctive molding profiles, construction techniques, related turnings, and histories of use in the Saybrook area of southeastern Connecticut suggest this sign was made by the same craftsman or workshop as Edward Bull's 1749 Black Horse sign and the Hayden inn sign of 1762 and 1766 (cat 1,3). Several stylistic features corroborate its dating as the latest of the group: the fully developed scroll pediment (replacing the baroque S-curves of Bull's sign), the simplified turnings on the posts, and the distinctive shape of finials, which echo those on late eighteenth-century New London-area case furniture.[1]

In contrast to the similarity of construction features, the decoration of these three signs is almost certainly by three different hands, as yet unidentified. Placement of the horse in the middle of this signboard leaves ample room for a name or wording in the space above, although no evidence of lettering or scribed guidelines exists. It is possible that this sign represents a ready-made example—that is, a sign made in anticipation of eventual purchase by an innkeeper rather than one made to a specific order. By definition, ready-mades had to be generic designs to which names and dates could be added easily.

Inn name: Period sources refer to this inn by the proprietor's name: "at the dwelling-house of Mr. Ambrose Kirtland, innholder." No period references have been found using the image on the sign as a name for the inn.

Innholder: Ambrose Kirtland (1737–1816) married Elizabeth Gibson (ca. 1729–87). Eighteenth-century tavern licenses for Saybrook are unlocated; however, Ambrose Kirtland is documented as an innkeeper by a notice in the *New London Gazette,* 7 July 1780.

Original location: Kirtland's house still stands on North Cove at Saybrook Point and has been extensively documented. Deed research supports local tradition that it was built by John Burrows between 1712 and 1759. Kirtland acquired the property in 1771, and deeded it in 1794 to his son Daniel (1766–1829). It was a seaport tavern, oriented to water traffic but not convenient to any major roads. While many similarly situated inns declined in the nineteenth century, this one experienced a revival of business, becoming a profitable transfer point between steamboats landing at the wharf to its rear and the Connecticut Valley Railway.[2]

Provenance: The sign remained with the house as late as 1937, despite a fire that badly damaged the house itself.[3] Photographs taken in the mid-1890s depict the sign hanging in situ during ownership of the house by the Potter family (CHS, Graphics Collection, X1950.4.2, 15).

Construction notes: Single board, with double, molded, horizontal rails and turned posts. Board is set vertically and hand-sawn at top and bottom to create decorative pediment and skirt profiles. Board is held by nails between paired, molded rails. Each rail is tenoned into the turned posts and secured by two pins at each joint.

Surface notes: The figure of the horse is slightly elevated, but no defining knife cuts are visible, indicating that the relief results from weathering of the background. The lettering, in contrast, is flush with the surface, suggesting that it may have been added after the background had been substantially weathered. The horse appears to have been laid out from a template, while the lettering is painted within scribed guidelines; the "I" in "Entertainment" is, anomalously, a capital with a dot above it. Side 1 is heavily weathered, with significant paint losses; side 2 and the turned posts are repainted.

Condition and treatment notes: Hanging hardware is original. The ends of each scrolled pediment arch are missing, and one upper post block is shattered and split. Both sides display numerous scratches, probably due to vandalism. Treatment at WACC in 2000 included surface consolidation and cleaning, repair of damaged post block.

Related objects: Watercolor rendering (side 1), by John Matulis, ca. 1940, *Index of American Design*, National Gallery of Art, 1943.8.16463; published Hornung, pl. 239, p. 77; Christensen, no. 161, p. 65.

Exhibitions: Japan 1970; "The Horse in Art," Fine Arts Gallery of San Diego, 1962–63.

Publications: *MBTS*, p. 21; Terry, *Old Inns*, p. 158.

1. See *Connecticut Furniture* 1967, no. 99, p. 59. The scalloped profile of the sign's lower rail appears on two mid-eighteenth-century chairs, one of which has a history of ownership in New Hartford, Conn., too distant from Saybrook to suggest any historical link; Seymour, p. 68; Nutting, no. 1924.
2. *Connecticut Guide,* p. 291.
3. Lathrop, p. 148.

Cat. 7*

Sign of the Bull's Head, dated 1760 and 1797, possibly made ca. 1777; repainted 1797 and 1804; overpainted ca. 1910–20

EAST WINDSOR, CONNECTICUT (NOW CALLED EAST WINDSOR HILL, IN SOUTH WINDSOR)

Innholders: Aaron Bissell, Sr. (active ca. 1760–87); Dorothy Stoughton Bissell (licensed 1788–94); Epaphras Bissell (licensed 1795–96); Aaron Bissell, Jr. (licensed 1797–1803 and 1806–13); John Alderman (licensed 1804–09)
Maker unidentified

Images: On both sides, head and neck of horned bull, extending to edge of board, with tree trunk, grass, flying birds, sky in background. Side 2 has been repainted.
Text: On side 1, on pediment, "1797" over "1760"; on apron, "J. ALDERMAN" over "A. Bissell." Side 2, repainted ca. 1910–20, has three sets of dates on the pediment, "1760" over "1797" over "1760"; and three names on the apron, "A Bissell." over "J. ALDERMAN" over "A. Bissell".

Paint on pine board, iron hardware, 56" x 36-1/2"
Collection of Morgan B. Brainard, Gift of Mrs. Morgan B. Brainard, 1961.63.7

Illustrated: color plate 7 (side 1), fig. 49 (side 2)

On 29 February 1836, the *Connecticut Courant* advertised for sale "all of the Real Estate which belonged to Aaron Bissell, deceased," including ample farm acreage and timber lands, farm buildings, and "the place so long and so well known as Bissell's Tavern." Located at the intersection of the main road north from Hartford, with the east-west road leading to the Connecticut River ferry, Aaron Bissell's was evidently a well-known landmark, cited in newspaper ads by travelers who arrived there only to discover they had lost something along the way. Its guests included John Adams, who noted in 1771 that he "reached Bissills of Winser . . . just as they had got their Indian Pudding and their Pork and Greens upon the Table."[1]

Efforts to unravel the history of this sign are complicated by the presence in East Windsor of numerous Bissells, extensive property holdings, and for a short time, two different Bissell taverns. The sign bears the date 1760, the year in which Capt. Aaron Bissell, Sr., took up tavernkeeping. However, the image, construction, and configuration of wooden elements all argue for a slightly later date. Period illustrations and surviving examples of the 1740s through 1760s indicate that American inn signs of this period generally displayed a single, centrally placed device surrounded by a monochromatic background (cat. 1–6). The extension of the Bissell bull's head to the edge of the signboard and the inclusion of background elements such as the tree trunk, grass, and flying birds are unusual features for the period. This configuration relates closely to a sign, dated 1794, from the Eleazar Bates inn in Haddam, Connecticut. (The Bates sign, not examined, may have originated somewhat earlier, based on its turnings and overall profile.)[2]

The design and construction of wooden elements on the Aaron Bissell sign are virtually identical with a second East Windsor sign, from the inn established by David Bissell in 1777 (fig. 63). Both East Windsor signs are well-conceived pieces of woodworking, each with a large center finial, supported by gently arched scrolls and smaller side finials and broad, somewhat shallow pediments with high centerlines. On both, cylindrical columns, marked at each end with torus moldings, hold the composition together. Both signs share the same pediment profiles, "L" shaped iron hardware, picture frame molding, and thin, columnar posts that are tenoned into the horizontal rails with gravity-defying vertical tenons (see fig. 16 for diagram contrasting this distinctive feature to the usual, and more structurally sound, practice of tenoning horizontal rails into the posts). These commonalities point strongly to production in the same woodworking shop, relatively close in time.

Why would Aaron Bissell, Sr., have ordered a new sign in the late 1770s? Although signs typically stood up to use for longer periods than the two decades Bissell had been in business, there is always the possibility of accidental or intentional damage. The opening of David Bissell's inn in 1777, however, introduces the possibility of competition for name recognition. Whereas travelers' recommendations to "Bissell's" would no longer suffice as identification, distinctive visual imagery could.[3] According to early descriptions, David Bissell's sign, now in the collection of the Wadsworth Atheneum, originally featured a portrait of George Washington surrounded by thirteen interlacing rings and the legend: "The 13 United States / Entertainment by David Bissell, A.D. 1777". This relatively elaborate emblem was evidently modeled on the new paper currency designed by Benjamin Franklin and authorized by the Continental Congress in 1776.[4] Aaron Bissell, in contrast, chose a more traditional emblem, perhaps suggesting that his inn was the more established; his sign is also noticeably larger than his cousin's. The bull's head may also have conveyed pride in the family's extensive and successful farming operations, as well as specific historical associations. According to local tradition, John Bissell, the progenitor of the family in America, had substantially aided the Connecticut Colony in its early days, bringing from England a much-needed herd of "17 cows and a bull . . ."[5]

John Alderman acquired the sign from Aaron Bissell, Jr., probably in 1804, when Bissell temporarily left tavernkeeping and would no longer have needed the sign. Although Alderman had operated a tavern in East Windsor from 1797–1800, it was presumably in someone else's premises, as he is not recorded as owning property in East Windsor until 1804. Alderman had his own name painted on the sign, but did not alter the date, perhaps because 1797 corresponded to his own start as an innkeeper, even though at a different site. Although complicated, this chronology is supported by physical evidence: the style of lettering used in Alderman's name is significantly different from that used in the date, and the apron retains substantially more of the white ground than the rest of the sign, suggesting that this lower section was repainted more recently and thus received less exposure to the elements. Aaron Bissell, Jr., resumed innkeeping in the family homestead, in 1806, but must have hung a new sign. Two years later, Alderman sold out and moved on to take up innkeeping in Vernon, Connecticut. The old sign shows no further evidence of updating until it became collectible in the early twentieth century, when repainting one side subtly but significantly altered the image, producing a quaint effect similar to that popularized in book illustrations, posters, and advertising art.

Inn name: Period references designate this inn by owners' names: "at the dwelling-house of Mr. Aaron Bissel, Innholder," "landlord Bissell's tavern," "Captain Bissell's tavern," or simply "Bissell's." References to "Bissell's Hotel" begin to appear in the late 1820s. No period references have been located to the pictorial motif on the inn sign as a name.

Innholders: Capt. Aaron Bissell, Sr. (1722–87), was born in Windsor, a fifth-generation member of one of the oldest families in one of the three oldest towns in Connecticut. In 1757, he married Dorothy Stoughton, also of East Windsor. In addition to tavernkeeping, Bissell cultivated extensive acreage and held the rank of Captain in the local militia. He was succeeded as tavernkeeper by his widow and sons, Epaphras and Aaron Bissell, Jr.(1761–1834). The brothers prospered in trade and farming. By 1813–15 both had moved their families into new brick residences close by, turning over to others the operation of Bissell's Tavern, still in the old homestead.

John Alderman (1768–1856) was born in East Granby, Conn., and married Hannah Westland, of East Windsor, Conn., in 1802. According to town records, he obtained a tavern license in 1798, "in place of Daniel Hayden, who refused." He was subsequently licensed in East Windsor in 1799–1800 and 1804–08. He operated an inn in Vernon, Conn., for several years, but moved to Hamilton, New York, ca. 1820, remaining there the rest of his life.

Original locations: The town of East Windsor was separated from Windsor in 1767; in 1845 the section known as East Windsor Hill became part of the new town of South Windsor. Auction notices for Aaron Bissell, Jr.'s, estate in 1836 provide a detailed description of his extensive landholdings, which ran from the Hartford road to the Connecticut River on the west and the Scantic River on the north, with "the road to Bissell's Ferry running across said land." South of the Ferry road "is the place so long and so well known as Bissell's Tavern; 105 acres of land, with a House, three large barns, and out-Buildings convenient for a large Tavern, and as good a place for such an establishment as any in the country." North of the Ferry road, opposite the old homestead, was Bissell's "country seat," a two-story brick house built in 1813. The inn was purchased by Daniel Gilbert Sperry and continued in business as "Sperry's Hotel" through at least the mid-1840s.[6]

David Bissell's inn (during the ten-year period of its existence) was located at the ferry landing itself, presumably drawing off some of the river traffic.

John Alderman's inn was located three doors south of Aaron Bissell's, on the Hartford road, possibly on Bissell property. Alderman is not recorded as owning a house in East Windsor. His only known property was a 1-1/2 acre lot on the west side of the road, where he set up a distillery.

Construction notes: Single board with single, molded, horizontal rails and columnar posts. Board is set vertically and hand-sawn at top and bottom to create decorative pediment and skirt profiles. Board passes through full-width mortise cut through each rail, with rails held in place by nails. Thin, columnar posts are tenoned vertically into both top and bottom rails. Three turned finials are saddled over the top of the board, with triangular extensions added to finish the lower points

of the pediment. Turned drops are doweled into the lower ends of the posts. Moldings are applied to the top and bottom of both faces and to the side edges of the signboard, creating a rectangular "picture frame."

Surface notes: Side 2 (with buckshot punctures) was overpainted in the early twentieth century, using a thick, glossy paint in highly contrasting shades of black, white, green, blue, and brown. The overpainting altered side 2 significantly, reinstating the earlier date and name, and creating a streamlined, hard-edged, modernistic counterpart to the softly weathered original. On the turned columns, horizontal rails, and framing moldings, repainting extended only to the picture plane, leaving these sections curiously two-toned when viewed directly on edge. The bull's heads are "mirror images," and may have originally been drawn with a template, although the overpaint makes accurate reading difficult.

Condition and treatment notes: Hanging hardware is original. The center scrolls of the pediment have broken and been reattached. Finials and drops are replaced. Treatment at WACC in 1999 included consolidation of the wooden support, hardware, and paint layers, and surface cleaning. Laboratory x-rays revealed that the existing hardware was insufficient to bear the weight of the sign, due to fabrication cracks and metal corrosion. Strong lightweight steel cable was discretely attached to the sign internally to provide hanging support.

Related signs: Sign for David Bissell's and Joseph Phelps's inn, dated 1777 and 1801, East Windsor, Conn. (Wadsworth Atheneum; see fig. 63); Sign for Eleazar Bates's inn, dated 1794, Haddam, Conn. (present location unknown).

Related objects: Watercolor rendering (side 1), by John Matulis, ca. 1940, *Index of American Design*, National Gallery of Art, 1943.8.8089; published Hornung, pl. 233, p. 75.

Exhibitions: Japan 1970; "American Folk Painting and Sculpture," Museum of American Folk Art, New York City, 1966.

Publications: *MBTS*, p 20; Smith, *Tavern Signs*, p. 11 (side 2); Alexandra Grave, *Three Centuries of Connecticut Folk Art* ([New Haven]: Art Resources of Connecticut, 1979), fig. 90 (side 1); *Welcome to Felicity's World, 1774: Life in Colonial America* (Middletown, Wisc.: Pleasant Co., 1998) p. 32 (side 2).

1. John Adams journal, 10 June 1771, cited in Richard J. Buel, Jr. and J. Bard McNulty, ed., *Connecticut Observed: Three Centuries of Visitor's Impressions* (Hartford: The Acorn Club, 1999), p. 38.
2. Present location unknown, formerly Historical Society of Greenfield, Massachusetts; CHS museum research files.
3. For recommendations to "Bissell's" as one of the "best Stages or Houses to put up at," see Nathanael Low, *An Astronomical Diary; or, Almanack* (Boston, 1770); Bickerstaff's *Boston Almanac* (Boston, 1775).
4. Connecticut engraver Amos Doolittle employed a similar composition for his "A Display of the United States of America," 1791. David Bissell's sign was repainted in 1801 by East Windsor painter and engraver Abner Reed with a medallion bust of Liberty on one side and an eagle on the other; see fig. 63. The original imagery is described in Earle, *Tavern Days*, pp.150–51. David Bissell's sign is 6" shorter and 5" narrower than Aaron Bissell's.
5. Henry R. Stiles, *The History and Genealogies of Ancient Windsor, Connecticut* (Hartford: Case, Lockwood & Brainard Co., 1891), p. 462. The explicit patriotism of David Bissell's sign makes it tempting to read Aaron Bissell's bull as a figure for John Bull, a conventional personification of England. However, Aaron Bissell was also a patriot, and John Bull does not emerge as a pictorial figure until the Napoleonic era.
6. *Conn. Courant*, 29 Feb. 1836, p. 3, col. 5; Stiles, *Ancient Windsor*, pp. 762–66;

Cat. 8

Sign of the Bird-in-Hand, dated 1786

LOCATION UNIDENTIFIED, PROBABLY CONNECTICUT
OR SOUTHERN NEW ENGLAND

Innholder and maker unidentified

Images: On both sides, a gloved hand holding a bird, framed within an oval outline, centered on a Prussian Blue background (now faded nearly to white). No underlying images.
Text: On both sides, below the image, "Entertain_ / _ment, by [erased]"; on the apron, side 1, "178[6]"; on the apron, side 2, "[17]86". No underlying text.

Paint on pine board, pine rails and moldings, chestnut posts, iron hardware, 47-1/4" x 27-3/4"
Collection of Morgan B. Brainard, Gift of Mrs. Morgan B. Brainard, 1961.63.6

Illustrated: color plate 8, fig. 69 (detail).

"Entertainment," the act of receiving guests and providing for them, was probably the most common word used on eighteenth-century tavern signs. The vignette of gloved hand holding a bird functions as a rebus for the familiar maxim, "a bird in hand is worth two in the bush," and the original background color—a welcoming shade of robin's egg blue—may have been intended to enhance not only the cream-colored lettering but also the bird motif. The "bird-in-hand" was a common tavern sign motif throughout the British North American colonies, as well as in as England (see cat. 23). Tavern sign historians Larwood and Hotten underscore the appropriateness of this image to tavern use by associating its message—the advantages of present, known circumstances over future, unrealized possibilities—with prompt payment for food and drink.[1]

One of the most conspicuous features of this sign is the obliteration of the innkeeper's name, leaving a badly marred section along the bottom. What little evidence of lettering remains coincides with a pencil notation below the image on one side, reading "Isaac Woodward 1786." Presumably Woodward's name was removed in order to update the sign for a new owner, a process that was never completed. Although the bird and the hand are identical in outline on both sides, their alignment changes: a mylar tracing made from one side can be lined up on the other side with either the hand or the bird, but not both simultaneously. Presumably the pattern(s) or template(s) used to lay out the design slipped during the transfer process, producing two slightly different versions.

Innholder: Although two Isaac Woodwards (grandfather and grandson) lived in Canterbury, Conn., the town tavern licenses do not record either of them as grantees.

Construction notes: Single board with flat, shaped rails and turned posts. Board is set vertically and tenoned into top and bottom rails. The rails have integral pediment and skirt (e.g., vertical extensions, which are hand-sawn to create decorative profiles). Rails are tenoned horizontally through the turned posts, with some of these joints wedged in addition to being pinned. Decorative moldings, mitered at the corners, are nailed to both faces of the signboard. The sign frame employs an extended baluster shape for the posts, rather than bisymmetrical balusters flanking a central ring, which is the more common eighteenth-century treatment. A little ring, or "collerina," punctuates the long neck of the baluster. Wood used in the turned posts is *Castanea dentata*, American chestnut, identified by analysis (Hoadley, March 2000).

Surface notes: This sign displays only one layer of paint on each side. The oval image area was originally executed in dark red, blue-green, black, and white. Traces of blue paint visible at the signboard edges were sampled and determined by FTIR and PLM analysis to contain Prussian blue pigment; a sample from the green-colored area of the oval vignette contained a very small amount of Prussian blue, resulting in the green hue still visible. The name of the tavern owner was removed mechanically using some sort of small blade; guidelines scribed into the wood for the height of the letters remain visible. The scalloped oval border around the central vignette seems to have been laid out with a pattern, which evidently shifted in process (like the misaligned bird-in-hand).

Condition and treatment notes: Hanging hardware appears to be original. The pediment contained a severe break and one ogee-shaped lobe is missing from skirt. The top of one post was split. Treatment at WACC in 1999 consisted of surface cleaning, removal of a streaky later oil or resin coating , consolidation of the pediment break and split post, and replacement of an applied molding missing from the top of one side.

Publications: *MBTS*, p. 19.

1. Larwood and Hotten, *History of Signboards*, pp. 446, 449.

Cat. 9

Sign for Bement's Inn, ca. 1786–1810

WALLINGFORD, CONNECTICUT

Innholder: Deodate Bement (licensed ca. 1786–1829)
Maker unidentified

Images: Both sides display images of saddles on saddle blankets. The more elaborately ornamented saddle, on side 1, is a sidesaddle, with double horns to facilitate riding aside. No underlying images.
Text: On both sides, below image, "Entertainment / Deo^t. Bement". No underlying text.

Paint (traces remaining) on yellow or tulip poplar board, iron hardware, 55-7/8" x 27-1/2"
Collection of Morgan B. Brainard, Gift of Mrs. Morgan B. Brainard, 1961.63.12

Illustrated: color plate 9 (side 1), fig. 77 (side 2), fig. 88 (detail, sidesaddle on side 1)

According to a manuscript family history, Deodate Bement's older brother, Meakins Bement (1743–1826) of East Hartford, was a saddler.[1] This association may somehow have accounted for the use of saddles here, perhaps making this sign a double advertisement, acquainting visitors, to one brother's inn, of the other's saddle shop. Conspicuous double horns mark the saddle on side 1 as a sidesaddle: the upright top horn supports the rider's right leg, while the lower, curved horn (called a leaping horn) serves as a brace for the left leg. Display of the sidesaddle suggests a deliberate appeal to women, who were traveling in rising numbers as roads and stage lines improved after the Revolution. A humorous notice in the *Connecticut Courant* for 5 June 1797 called attention to this phenomenon, under the heading, "Caution to Tavern-Keepers." A party of women and mares, it recounted, continued on to the next inn after encountering an old-fashioned sign offering, "Entertainment for Man & Hors."[2]

The elaborate ornamentation of the sidesaddle suggests that it must once have been painted in polychrome colors, as black and white would probably not have been sufficient to articulate such rich detail. Almost none of the original paint remains, however, focusing attention on the lively silhouette and vibrant sculptural qualities of this sign. Its bold pediment and skirt profiles represent two-dimensional versions of contemporary furniture ornament, with attenuated scrolls flanking an abstracted urn and drop (the urn might also be viewed as an abstracted wine glass). In comparison to standard prototypes in architecture and furniture, the scrolls are appealingly unorthodox—stiff, overly vertical, up-right, even misshapen. They also vary left to right, indicating less-than-masterful workmanship. In contrast to the uneven execution of the signboard itself, the raised lettering and images are very accomplished.

Inn name: Referred to by proprietor's name ("Beemont") in *Stafford's Almanack* (New Haven, 1786).

Innholder: Deodate Bement (1751–1836) was the son of Edmond and Abigail Meakins Bement of Enfield, Conn. The family name is sometimes given as Beaumont. After serving in the Revolutionary War, Deodate Bement married Mary Parsons (d. 1790) of Wallingford in 1780, moving to Wallingford in that year. In 1790, Bement married Lucina Rose.

Original location: Bement owned several properties in Wallingford. His tavern was probably located on his earliest acquistion, deeded 1780 and 1783: a one-acre house lot, near the church in the center of Wallingford, along the post road from Hartford to New Haven.

Construction notes: Single board with applied moldings; no structural frame. Board is oriented vertically and hand-sawn at top and bottom to create decorative pediment and skirt profiles. Applied moldings, mitered in corners, are nailed to front and back faces. Wood is *Liriodendron tulipifera*, yellow or tulip poplar, identified by analysis (Hoadley, March 2000).

Surface notes: Traces of original black paint survive on the lettering of one side; the Prussian blue visible on pediment and skirt may or may not be original.

Condition and treatment notes: One hanging strap may be original. The wood of the main board is aged and severely desiccated, in some areas, to the point of punkiness. Sodium sulfate accretions were found embedded in the wood pores and iron strap. Two vertical side moldings on side 1 may be original; all other applied moldings appear to be old replacements, with some later additions and repairs. The top and bottom moldings on both sides have been relocated one width toward the center, covering over the top of the upper horn of the sidesaddle on side 1, and leaving a row of nail holes visible on both sides. Additional nail holes along the outer edges of the sides indicate former presence of some kind of molding strip. Treatment at WACC in 1999 included surface cleaning, resecuring of the surviving hanging strap, and installa-

tion of a new hanging strap, blacksmith-fabricated to match the existing one and stamped "1999".

1. J. Granville Leach, "Chronicles of the Bement Family in America for Clarence Sweet Bement," manuscript, CHS Library; cited in CHS museum object files.
2. Cited in Vincent, "Connecticut Inns and Hotels," p. 7.

Cat. 10*

Sign for Blatchly's Inn, dated 1788 and 1794;
repainted, possibly ca. 1920
EAST GUILFORD, CONNECTICUT (NOW MADISON)

Innholder: Moses Blatchly, Jr. (licensed 1792–1802)
Maker unidentified

Images: Both sides have two layers of imagery. On side 1, an allegorical female figure of Justice, over a fully-rigged sailing vessel. On side 2, an American flag, over a standing figure of a sailor leaning on an anchor, framed by panels of drapery.[1]
Text: Both sides have multiple layers of text, which are quite difficult to disentangle. On side 1, the pediment has two dates, "1794" over "1788.", and one name, "M. BLATCHLY"; the skirt has "ENTERTAINMENT" over "Entertainment / M.B."; the main part of the sign has two legends, "The Scale of Justis", which presumably refers to the upper image of the allegorical figure, and "The Charming PatroNes", which presumably refers to the lower image of the sailing vessel. On side 2, the pediment has two dates, "1794" over "1788", and one name, "M. BLATCHLY"; the skirt has "ENTERTAINMENT" over "Entertainment / MB"; the main part of the sign has two legends, "The Cantine," which presumably corresponds to the upper image of the flag, and "Hope on the Anchor", which presumably refers to the lower image of the sailor.

Paint on pine board, unidentified hardwood frame, iron hardware, 35-1/4" x 23-3/4"
Collection of Morgan B. Brainard, Gift of Mrs. Morgan B. Brainard, 1961.63.10

Illustrated: color plate 10 (side 1), fig. 26 (side 1, with overlay of underlying image)

The history of the Blatchly sign is somewhat difficult to reconstruct. It evidently displays two layers of eighteenth-century artwork, which were jumbled together in a twentieth-century repainting by an unidentified restorer (an early photograph, preserved in Morgan Brainard's papers, depicts side 1 prior to this repainting). Moreover, the frame is a later replacement, although it suggests evidence of age.

The earliest painted surface indicates this sign was made in 1788 for "M.B.," whom the overlying redecoration identifies more completely as M. Blatchly. The first image, visible under raking light, was a sailing vessel with the legend "The Charming Patrone[s]" linked to a pennant flying forward from the main mast. No ship of that name has surfaced yet in historical records of the New England and Mid-Atlantic regions. The opposite side of the sign continues the maritime theme with a sailor leaning on an anchor, traditionally a symbol of hope.

Two entirely different images were painted over the original maritime compositions, possibly for Moses Blatchly, Jr., who continued the family establishment after his father's death in 1791. A female allegorical figure, with the legend "Scales of Justis" covers the brig on side 1, while an American flag overlies the anchor on side 2. The word "Entertainment," the inn-keeper's name, and the date were evidently repainted at this time as well.

Such re-uses were commonplace, as surfaces wore away or establishments changed hands. However, several details seem anomalous. The allegorical figure of Justice typically holds scales in one hand and a sword in the other. If one of the two hands is raised, the higher hand holds the scales—not the lower as in this sign. Justice's headdress tends to be tightly woven, while the loose wreath of laurel leaves seen here recalls Indian Princess headdresses.

Innholders: Moses Blatchly, Jr. (1762–1826), was born in East Guilford, the son of Moses Blatchly, Sr. (1722–91), and Huldah Munger. The dates on the sign do not appear to correspond with dates known for either Blatchly. No tavern licenses are recorded for Moses Blatchly, Jr., before his father's death in 1791, and none at all for Moses Blatchly, Sr.

Construction notes: Single board, with single, molded, horizontal rails and turned posts. Board is set vertically and hand-sawn at top and bottom to create decorative pediment and skirt profiles. Board passes through full-width mortise cut through each rail and is held by nails. The rails are tenoned through the turned posts and secured at each joint by one pin. An original half-round appliqué is added at top of the pediment.

Surface notes: Early twentieth-century restoration included complete overpainting of the allegorical figure on side 1, using heavy, opaque, shiny paints on both figure and lettering. Repainting confused the sign by making simultaneously visible text from both eighteenth-century layers. Posts and rails were painted a bright turquoise blue, with a blue and red border added to the signboard.

Condition and treatment notes: Three features indicate that the frame (which exhibits evidence of woodworm) is a replacement: changes in surface color and texture suggest that slightly wider rails once covered the signboard, the lower rail partially covers the earlier lettering, and each rail covers a set of unused nail holes in the signboard, created by a former frame. At the time of the early twentieth-century repainting, the frame was evidently taken apart and reassembled backwards; the missing lower section of one post was also replaced. During treatment at WACC in 1999, the twentieth-century overpaint was removed from side 1, using a pre-restoration photograph as a guide to the earlier appearance.

Exhibitions: Aetna 1939 (side 1).

Publications: *MBTS*, p. 23. Textbooks, various editions: Henretta, *America's History* (Bedford/St. Martin's Press); Henretta, *America: A Concise History* (St. Martin's Press); Brinkley, *The Unfinished Nation* (McGraw-Hill); Brinkley, *American History*, (McGraw-Hill); *The American Nation* (Simon & Schuster); Davidson, *A History of the Republic: The United States* (Prentice Hall).

1. The sequence of images on side 2 is particularly difficult to ascertain. It is possible that the flag is the lower layer.

Cat. 11

Sign for Lawrence's Inn, ca. 1797
NORFOLK, CONNECTICUT

Innholder: Ariel Lawrence (active 1785–99)
Maker unidentified

Images. On both sides, a similar array of Masonic iconography. No underlying imagery.
Text: On both sides, below iconography, "A=Lawrence,s Inn". No underlying text.

Paint on pine board, smalt (used as a colorant, not for texture), gold leaf, iron hardware, 20"x 50"
Collection of Morgan B. Brainard, Gift of Mrs. Morgan B. Brainard, 1961.63.32

Illustrated: color plate 11 (side 2)

This horizontal sign displays an extensive vocabulary of Masonic symbols. The Order of Freemasonry was organized in the early eighteenth century as an international organization of men who pursued social experiences and moral instruction through secret rituals and ceremonies. From the mid-eighteenth-century on, Masonic symbolism appears in the decoration of furniture, ceramics, textiles, and other objects used in Masonic lodges or in the homes of members.[1] Lawrence's sign is among the earliest surviving examples of Masonic imagery made for public display. Lawrence joined the Montgomery Lodge at Salisbury in 1790, five years after he was first licensed to operate a tavern. He became a charter member of Western Star Lodge No. 37, Norfolk, established 18 May 1796. Local historians report that Lawrence built a tavern in 1797, and a newspaper ad of that year documents his removal from an earlier establishment.[2] Given the focused theme of the sign and Lawrence's interests, the inn was a likely meeting place for the new lodge; his office, as Junior Deacon, was to escort candidates and visitors into the lodge. To remain a viable business in such a modestly sized community as Norfolk, located in the northwesternmost section of Connecticut, however, Lawrence could hardly have limited his services exclusively to Masons.

Among the more visible elements in the sign are the two pillars of King Solomon's Temple with initials for Boaz ("in strength") and Jachin ("God will establish"). Between the pillars, the square and compass, painted below "G" for God, symbolize reason and faith; to the sides, the sun and moon represent the "jewels," or badges of office of the Senior and Junior Deacons, respectively, and the crossed keys are the treasurer's jewel. The anchor, painted in the left center, indicates hope and comfort for the weary, a most appropriate symbol for this sign but incidental in its design. All of the symbols and the tavern owner's name are executed freehand, within scribed lines and centering marks that aid in positioning. Despite careful spacing and arrangement, the individual symbols fail to cohere as a composition; they recall instead the random assemblage of motifs on some needlework samplers. The lettering also looks unschooled, both in the unintentionally wavering thickness of lines and in the concentration of distinguishing curved elements at the tops and bottoms of each letter. The proportions of this sign are among the narrowest known in tavern signs, although they are similar to those seen on trade signs of the period.

Inn name: Known period references all use proprietor's name.

Innholder: Ariel Lawrence (b. 1743) was the son of Samuel and Patience Bigelow Lawrence of Killingly, in eastern Conn. The family moved to Simsbury, northwest of Hartford, ca. 1755. Ariel married Lucy Wilcox of Simsbury in 1762 and moved to Norfolk. He left the area in 1799, possibly moving to Oneida, New York, where the name appears on the census of 1800.

Original location: Lawrence's house remains extant, on the northwest corner of Route 44 and Mill Street in Norfolk. The house became Norfolk's first post office in 1804 and was subsequently operated as a tavern by James Shepard (active 1821–46).

Construction notes: Thick, single, rectangular board, oriented horizontally. Applied moldings, mitered at corners, are nailed to the faces of both sides. The top molding strips overlay hanging straps that extend nearly the full height of the board and are painted the same blue as the background. No structural frame, no pediment or skirt.

Surface notes: This sign displays only a single paint layer on each side. Background is blue, with smalt (a blue glass additive) used to establish the color. Letters are in gold leaf and the symbols are white, with gold used in the sun's rays.

Condition notes: Hanging hardware is original. One vertical molding strip is missing from side 1, as is top molding strip from side 2. Side 2 has later red paint blotting out three Masonic symbols. Both sides are heavily weathered.

Publications: *MBTS*, p. 48; *Stories from the Freedom Trail*, videotape, Connecticut Public Television, 1998.

1. Hamilton, *Material Culture of the American Freemasons*; for further discussion of the Masonic influence on inns and inn signs in Connecticut, see Vincent, "Some suitable Signe," Chapter Four.
2. *Conn. Courant*, 8 May 1797: p. 4, col. 3.

Cat. 12

Sign for Marsh's Inn, ca. 1785–1810
NORTHWESTERN CONNECTICUT, POSSIBLY LITCHFIELD OR NEW MILFORD

Innholder: possibly Ebenezer Marsh, Jr. (licensed 1786–94 in Litchfield), or Elihu Marsh, Jr. (licensed 1806–30 in New Milford) Maker unidentified

Images: On side 1, the Connecticut state seal (a shield containing three grape vines). On side 2, a decanter and glasses within a vertical oval.
Text: on both sides, in name band below image field, "E. MARSH" over "E. Marsh's" over "D.H[otchkiss?]". On side 1, "SIGILL. REIP. / CONNECTICUTENSIS" around the seal.

Paint on pine board, oak frame and iron hardware (both replaced), 64" x 27-5/8"
Collection of Morgan B. Brainard, Gift of Mrs. Morgan B. Brainard, 1961.63.35

Illustrated: color plate 12 (side 1)

Federal-style design features, notably the framing oval and glass decanter and stopper painted on side 2, suggest a production date in the 1790s or early 1800s. The lettering around the state seal on side 1 corresponds to an alteration enacted by the Connecticut Assembly in 1784.[1] This dating is at odds with the previously published identification of the innholder as Col. Ebenezer Marsh, Sr., of Litchfield, who was licensed 1752–72 and died in 1773. More likely candidates emerge from subsequent generations of the Marsh family in northwestern Connecticut, notably Marsh's son, Ebenezer, Jr., in Litchfield, or a cousin, Elihu, in nearby New Milford.

Although the frame of this sign has been entirely replaced, it is likely to have originally had a similarly-constructed frame. However, the original frame probably had turned posts and finials, rather than the present square elements, which evoke the Arts and Crafts Movement. The shaped pediment and skirt boards of this sign resemble some contemporary federal-style looking glasses in outline and proportions.[2] The federal-style decanter and stopper on side 2, half filled with red wine and flanked by single wineglasses, belong to a long tradition of images signaling the function of the buildings they ornament.[3]

Inn name: References to the inn during the tenure of the senior Marsh consistently use the name of the proprietor, "at the dwelling-house of Col. Ebenezer Marsh, innholder" (1766). No period references have been found using the imagery of the sign as a name.

Innholders: Ebenezer Marsh, Jr., (ca.1738–1807) was the son of Deborah and Col. Ebenezer Marsh, Sr. (ca. 1701–73) of Litchfield. Both father and son were licensed as tavernkeepers in Litchfield, and this sign has previously been published as belonging to Ebenezer Marsh, Sr. However, physical characteristics of the signboard indicate that it could hardly have been produced until well after the senior Marsh's death in 1773. In addition to Ebenezer Marsh, Jr., an Elihu Marsh, Jr. is also documented as an innkeeper in New Milford, ca. 1806–30, a date range that fits nicely with the physical attributes of the sign. "D. H[otchkiss?]" remains unidentified.

Construction notes: Single, rectangular board, oriented vertically. The pediment and skirt boards are horizontally-oriented boards, sawn to create decorative profiles and nailed to the rails. The remainder of the sign is evidently a late nineteenth-century construction, made to hold the old signboard. Paired, horizontal rails are tenoned through the stiles, with single pins on top and double pins on the bottom. The plinth for the central finial is cut to fit over the pediment.

Surface notes: Side 2 is largely repainted, although thick, aged paint layers exist in the central element of the decanter itself. The bright green field surrounding the state seal on side 1 has also been repainted. Faint evidence shows through of a guilloche- or ribbon-like arc at the top of the seal, suggestive of borders on some versions of the state seal.

Condition notes: Hanging hardware is replaced. The joined rails and stiles and the central finial are replacements, in the Arts and Crafts style of the late nineteenth century. The pediment and skirt boards show old damage and repairs, pre-dating the current frame. The lower two inches of one lobe of the apron is replaced, as is the central projection on the pediment.

Publications: *MBTS*, p. 52.

1. "The Connecticut State Seal," *Connecticut State Register & Manual* (1998), pp. 830–31.
2. Other signs echoing the profiles of federal-style looking glasses include the sing for Banner's inn, dated 1806, in Smith, *Tavern Signs*, p. 34, and the sign for Bean's inn, dated 1824, at the Winterthur Museum (acc. no. 60.218). See Zimmerman, "Reading the Signs," Chapter Three.
3. Sign for David Loomis's Inn, 1811 (cat. 22); Sign for Stratton's inn, in Smith, *Tavern Signs*, p. 36.

Cat. 13

Sign for Hinman's Inn, ca. 1795–1815

FARMINGTON OR SOUTHBURY, CONNECTICUT

Innholder: Amos Hinman (licensed 1789–1804) in Farmington, or Aaron Hinman (licensed 1796–1807) in Southbury
Maker unidentified

Images: On both sides, a radiant sun with facial features, centered on oval panel. No underlying imagery.
Text: On side 1, in banner above sun, "A. HINMAN."; in banner below sun, "Inn." On side 2, in banner above sun, "A. HINMANS,"; in banner below sun, "Inn."

Paint on hardwood, probably black cherry board, oak bracket, iron hardware, 44-1/2" x 28"
Collection of Morgan B. Brainard, Gift of Mrs. Morgan B. Brainard, 1961.63.31

Illustrated: color plate 13

The most notable feature of this sign is its gloriously curved frame, which visually wraps around the oval signboard. To accomplish this effect, the rails are cut with incurving arcs at each end, so that the tenons enter the posts at points below and above the center line of the rails. No other examples of offset rails have been noted. Although the majority of surviving oval or shield-shaped signboards date to the 1810s, the form is known in New England as early as 1795, replacing earlier, vertically-oriented rectangles.[1] Most oval boards swing freely from the upper rails, while this one is held stationary within the frame; whether this feature is a factor of chronology or simply a particular shop tradition remains undetermined. The post turnings employ opposing balusters above and below a central element in a combination typical of eighteenth-century signs, in contrast to the attenuated or otherwise streamlined turnings of most federal-era signs. Accordingly, the Hinman sign may date relatively early among oval signs. It is unusual in retaining its original overhead support beam. The fact that only one end is shaped probably indicates that the beam extended from a single post or from a building.

Innholder: Connecticut tavern licenses record several innkeepers named A. Hinman. The most likely owner of this sign is Amos Hinman of Farmington, who obtained a license for a tavern on the Litchfield Road in 1789, replacing "Capt. Youngs who hath neglected and refused to take license." In May 1815 Amos Hinman announced his intention to "move out of this holy state," inviting "all enterprising men" to inspect his 400-acre farm in the western part of Farmington, warranted "to be good for raising Burdock, Skunks' cabbage, and Itch weed."[2]

Construction notes: Single board, cut into smooth-edged oval shape, with flat horizontal rails and turned posts. The board is oriented vertically and is attached with wooden dowels to the centerpoints of the rails and posts. Rails are cut from single boards, with shaped profiles on both edges, joined to posts with offset, double tenons mortised into posts and secured with wooden pins.

Surface notes: The yellow pigment used for the sun has been identified as a pale litharge-based color, probably Patent or Montpellier's Yellow, used by house painters until the introduction of Chrome Yellow around 1815; the background was white, now largely worn off. Both sides display centering holes and compass arcs used to lay out the sun's disk, with divider holes marking the spacing of rays. The name banner, with white letters on a black band, resembles work on later signs, as the Sign for Wightman's Inn, ca. 1815–24 (cat. 26).

Condition and treatment notes: The signs retains not only its original hanging hardware, but also the oak bracket from which it originally hung. The central panel has split near the restraining frame attachments as it dried and aged. Splitting also occurred in the offset rails at points of stress. Treatment at WACC in 1999 included resecuring failed joints and horizontal splits in the rails; removal of dark oil or varnish surface coatings.

Publications: *MBTS*, p. 47.

1. See the Wilkins tavern sign, 1795, in Garvin, p. 35; the M. Root sign at Memorial Hall Museum, Pocumtuck Valley Memorial Association, Deerfield, Mass., carries a 1795 date that may be original, illustrated in Smith, *Tavern Signs*, p. 31. A photograph of the Sun Tavern sign, dated 1798, location unknown, appears in the CHS museum research files.
2. "Hartford County Nominee List" for 1789; *Courant*, 17 May 1815, p. 3, col. 6.

Cat. 14

Sign for Caulkins's Inn, dated 1769, 1798?, and 1839,

probably made ca. 1790s
FLANDERS, CONNECTICUT (SECTION OF EAST LYME TOWNSHIP)

Innholders: Dr. Daniel Caulkins (active ca. 1781–90); Elizabeth Smith Moore Caulkins (active 1790–1816); Elisha Caulkins (active 1816–32)
Maker unidentified

Images: On both sides, landscape scene with tree on left, rising sun on right, possibly underlying versions of the same composition.
Text: On both sides, in pediment, "1769" over "1839" over "1798?", in name band at bottom, "E. CAULKINS." in gold leaf over "E. CAULKINS" in yellow paint.

Paint on pine board, gold leaf, 43-1/4" x 28"
Collection of Morgan B. Brainard, Gift of Mrs. Morgan B. Brainard, 1961.63.13

Illustrated: color plate 14

This sign is one of only a few surviving examples that can be confidently associated with a tavern operated by a female innkeeper. Elizabeth Smith Moore Caulkins held a tavern license in her own name for twenty-five years, from the death of her husband until the marriage of her youngest son (the fact that the son, then age twenty-seven, did not take over until he had married suggests strongly the importance of female contributions to the enterprise of innkeeping).

Dating of this sign is complicated by the presence of three dates, applied in non-chronological sequence. The lowest date is from the 1790s (although the final digit is difficult to read), a period appropriate to the overall shape of this sign. The steeply vertical pediment scrolls, in particular, recall similar features on the Bement sign, made ca. 1786–1810 (cat. 9). The second date, in order of application, is "1839," which corresponds to the year of Elizabeth Caulkins's death (although her children had long since taken over the official management of the inn). The uppermost date on the sign is "1769", applied in gold leaf, presumably a commemorative date added for unknown reasons much later in the sign's history.[1] The name, "E. Caulkins," identifying both mother and son, served its purpose for over four decades, although it had to be freshened at least once, in gold leaf matching that on the 1769 date.

The landscape scene depicts a tree with the sun rising over what appears to be the water's edge, perhaps combining features of the inn's actual setting—at the head of the Niantic River, fronted by large willow trees—with the traditionally popular motif of the rising sun; on side 2, seven stars, originally gilded, arc across the sky over the sun.[2] Stylistic features link this composition to the second date, 1839. Its painterly, naturalistic, and romanticized qualities relate to mid-nineteenth-century landscape painting, and landscape motifs are rarely seen on American inn signs prior to the 1810s (cat. 23, 27). If the rising sun theme continued an earlier tradition associated with the Caulkins tavern, the sign might be expected to have had an earlier version of this emblem—perhaps a large, stylized sun in the center of the board. Surprisingly, however, no evidence of an underlying design has been found.

Inn names: All known references prior to 1800 designate this inn by proprietor's name: "at the dwelling-house of Mr. Daniel Calkins, innholder" or "at the dwelling house of widow Elizabeth Caulkins, innholder." In 1800–10, the terminology shifts to "Caulkings's Tavern" or "Mrs. E. Caulkin's tavern." Between 1816–30, the enterprise is referred to as "Caulkins' Tavern," "Caulkins's Inn," or, somewhat more formally, the "Inn of E. Caulkins." No references from this period have been found using the pictorial motif (rising sun) as a name for the inn.

Innholders: Dr. Daniel Caulkins (1746–90) was the son of Amos and Mary Caulkins of New London. He moved to the Flanders section of East Lyme in 1777, with his first wife, Mary. She died later that year, and in 1778 he remarried Elizabeth Smith Moore (1749–1839), widow of Elisha Moore (d. 1773). Dr. Caulkins purchased a dwelling house and lot in 1779 and was operating a tavern by at least 1781. He died at age forty-four, according to the local newspaper, of "a kick of a horse in his bowels the preceding day, leaving a disconsolate widow and eleven children."

Elizabeth Smith Moore Caulkins (1749–1839) took over the inn after her husband's death and continued to operate it in her own name for the next quarter-century. She did not remarry.

Elisha Caulkins (1789–1869) was the youngest son of Daniel and Elizabeth Caulkins. In 1816, he married Abby Chapman (1794–1880) of East Haddam, Conn. The following year, he succeeded his mother (then nearing seventy) as innkeeper. Other members of the Caulkins

family continued to operate the inn until the 1840s or 1850s.

Original location: The Caulkins family chose its property well, and the inn's enviable site may in part explain its longevity. Not only was it located in the Flanders town center, on the New York to Boston post road, but also at the crossroads of the Niantic road (now Connecticut Rt. 161), and at the head of the Niantic River. It was thus convenient for both local and traveling customers, and both land and water-borne traffic. Although the house itself is gone, the site retains part of its original function as a McDonald's restaurant.

Construction notes: Single board, grain oriented vertically, hand-sawn at top only to create decorative pediment profile. No skirt and no structural frame. Applied moldings, mitered at corners, are nailed to the outer edges of board on the sides and bottom, and across the faces of both sides at the top.

Surface notes: The 1769 date and the lettering are executed in gold leaf, using a stencil. The 1839 date is yellow, as is the trim on the black frame and an earlier version of the lettering. The ground layer seems to be gray; the sun may originally have been gilded, as were the stars arcing overhead. Side 1 is heavily weathered, with 25–30% paint loss. The tree and sun are well raised above the background, with evidence of repainting guided by the raised outlines. The extent of wear suggests that the sign hung outdoors for many years, consistent with the inn's long operation by the same family. Side 2 had been obscured by a layer of black, possibly spray, paint.

Condition and treatment notes: Original hanging straps had been reset approximately one inch higher, and cracked scroll ends in pediment had been resecured at an unknown time. The top of the central finial is broken away. Treatment at WACC, 2000, included surface cleaning and reduction of black overpaint on side 2; securing of loose wood elements and hanging hardware.

Publications: *MBTS*, p. 26.

1. There was already a dwelling-house on the property when Daniel Caulkins purchased it in 1779; the date 1769 might commemorate either the construction of the house or its opening as a tavern by the previous owners, Daniel and Ruth Way.
2. *New London Gazette*, 20 Aug. 1828, p. 3, col. 5; the willow trees are noted in J.L. Chew, "Famous Taverns of New London," *New London County Historical Society Records* (1890–1912), vol. 2, pt. 1: pp. 69–85. The combination of large tree and rising sun also appears on a sign for the Simonds inn, dated 1810; see Forbes and Eastman, *Stagecoaches and Taverns*, vol. 2, p. 115.

Cat. 15

Sign for Perkins's Inn, dated 1830, probably made ca. 1800–20
WEST GREENWICH, RHODE ISLAND

Innholder(s): probably Shapley Morgan; Thomas T. Hazard; possibly Elliot Lee Perkins
Maker unidentified

Images: On both sides, near-profile view of brown and white bull's head, extending to edge of board on viewer's left, landscape background. No underlying images.
Text: On both sides, on top rail, "E L PERKINS." over "T. T. Hazard" over "S. Morgan", on bottom rail "INN", on skirt "1830".

Paint on pine board, smalt, gold leaf, 47-1/4" x 28-1/4"
Collection of Morgan B. Brainard, Gift of Mrs. Morgan B.
Brainard, 1961.63.39

Illustrated: color plate 15

The bull pictured on the Perkins inn sign stares out with a commanding eye as if from the window of a barn. This pose narrows
the distance between viewer and subject. In other contexts, the
words "close" or "intimate" might describe this portrait appropriately. Overall, the painting style appears more modern than
prevailing practices of the early nineteenth century, particularly
among sign painters. Except for the eye, and to a lesser degree
the horns and nose, the bull's features are rendered in
"painterly" fashion, using broad brush strokes.

Two other names painted successively underneath Perkins's indicate that the sign itself predates 1830, the date associated with
Perkins's proprietorship. All the essential features of design and
construction of this sign were in use by the end of the eighteenth
century and continued to be used through the first decades of
the nineteenth. The Perkins tavern stood just inside the Rhode
Island border, along the Shetucket turnpike connecting Norwich
and Providence; it was, from a Connecticut perspective, "the end
of the line" and thus a welcome stopping point. Increased traffic
anticipated from the incorporation of the turnpike in 1829 may
have provided an impetus for Perkins's taking up tavernkeeping
and for sprucing up the old sign.[1]

Innholders: The first name on this sign, "S. Morgan", was probably
Shapley Morgan, who appears in West Greenwich census records for
1820 and 1830.

The middle name, "T.T. Hazard", is identified as Thomas T. Hazard
(1792–1874), son of John Hazard. Thomas Hazard married Mary
Tillinghast (before 1823) and in 1843, Esther L. Tillinghast. He was
a prominent local figure, representing West Greenwich in the Rhode
Island State Assembly for 32 years.

The uppermost name on this sign may be Elliot Lee Perkins (1806–64),
who married Mary H. Congdon (1808–67), and resided in South
Kingston, Rhode Island.

Construction notes: Two boards, grain oriented vertically, set into
grooved edges of flat rails and stiles. Horizontal rails are tenoned
through stiles and double pinned. Thin, applied molding strips,
mitered at corners, are nailed to the face of the panel, along the
slightly protruding edge of the frame. The pediment and skirt are separate boards, oriented horizontally and sawn to create a decorative
profile at top and bottom; these boards are nailed to the top and bottom rails.

Surface notes: Side 2 is more severely weathered. The Perkins name is
stenciled in gold leaf over a black band textured with smalt. Some of
this later surface survives on the green and yellow paint decoration of
the pediment and skirt. The bull exhibits less wear than the painted
surfaces of the frame; the image may have been repainted more
recently than the name and date bands.

Condition and treatment notes: Hanging hardware appears to be original. The pediment and skirt boards have split apart and been repaired.
Treatment at WACC, 1999, included paint consolidation and removal
of later varnish layers.

Related objects: Watercolor rendering (side 2), unidentified artist, ca.
1940, *Index of American Design,* National Gallery of Art, 1943.8.76913.

Publications: *MBTS,* p. 57; *Decorator* 1960, p. 6; Terry, *Old Inns,*
p. 241.

1. An early twentieth-century history of Griswold, Conn., two towns west of
   West Greenwich, commented that the Shetucket Turnpike "ended, as far as
   Connecticut was concerned, near the Tom. T. Hazard Tavern, a noted
   hostelry, just over the line in Rhode Island"; Daniel L. Phillips, *Griswold—
   A History . . .* ([New Haven]: Tuttle, Morehouse & Taylor Co., 1929), p. 279.

Cat. 16

Sign for the Griswold Inn, ca. 1800–25

PROBABLY NEW YORK STATE

Innholder and maker unidentified

Images: On side 1, standing allegorical figures of Liberty and
Justice, holding a shield displaying a sun and mountain peaks. The
shield is topped by an eagle perched on a globe. On side 2, a pair of
eagles. No underlying images.
Text: On both sides, "GRISWOLD."

Paint on pine board, gold leaf, 33-1/8" x 26-5/8"
Collection of Morgan B. Brainard, Gift of Mrs. Morgan B.
Brainard, 1961.63.26

Illustrated: color plate 16 (side 1)

This sign has traditionally been assigned to Lyme or Killingworth, towns in southeastern Connecticut, based on Brainard's
collecting in that area, and on the presence of numerous Gris-
wolds licensed as innkeepers in those towns between 1765–75.
However, the dark name band along the bottom is a design convention that does not appear until the end of the eighteenth-
century. The presence of imagery closely resembling the New
York State seal suggests a New York origin, as yet unspecified.

Construction notes: Single board panel, with narrow bevels at edges,
presumably to ease fitting board into a frame, now missing. Unpainted
margins along the edges indicate that the board originally floated
within grooves or channels cut into the frame. The absence of nail
holes along the edges (except for a few that appear to represent later
repairs) suggests that the missing frame was probably constructed of
substantial rails and stiles assembled by mortise-and-tenon joints.

Surface notes: Although weathered and repainted, the decoration is
accomplished. A particularly attractive feature is the elegant ribbon
that underscores the seal on side 1 and provides a perch for the
opposed eagles on side 2. The images have been repainted, but fine
crackling in the paint and other evidence of age suggest that the
repainting campaign is old. Repainted sections follow existing outlines
defined by weathering and erosion of the background. Sharp, raised
edges of the primary images suggest possible carving. The gilded letters of the Griswold name are scribed out individually, set within horizontal scribe lines partially visible through the deep blue name band
(now darkened nearly to black). Inexplicably, the name is placed
higher on side 1 than on side 2.

Condition notes: A split through the panel has been resecured with corrugated staples nailed into the top and bottom. Both sides look equally weathered.

Publications: *MBTS*, p. 41.

Cat. 17

Sign of the Punchbowl, dated 1803
PROBABLY SOUTHERN NEW ENGLAND

Innholder and maker unidentified

Images: On side 1, punchbowl, centered against white background. On side 2, indecipherable. No underlying imagery.
Text: On both sides, in name band above lower rail, "O . D". On side 1, incorporated into what appears to be a tablecloth beneath the punchbowl, "1803".

Paint on pine board, frame of maple or visually similar wood, 46-1/2" x 23-1/2"
Gift of Helen E. Royce, 1959.32.94

Illustrated: color plate 17

This sign was previously assigned to Oliver Dickinson of Wallingford, based on information provided by the donor, Helen E. Royce (1873–1962), a collector and dealer in American antiques who operated the Nehemiah Royce house in Wallingford as private museum. Extensive documentary research, however, has failed to locate an Oliver Dickinson in Wallingford. Neither the initials nor the construction and design elements provide sufficient evidence to suggest alternative owners or even locales. The distinctive scrolled pediment, drawn without a central finial, recalls similar designs on other signs; unfortunately, these comparisons lack any geographical commonality.[1] The elongated baluster turning with a ring, or "collarina," of the frame posts is too common a decorative device to be diagnostic, as are the ball finials and drops. However, the relatively unusual technique of using notched shoulders above the long mortise in the lower rail to hold the signboard in place may someday help identify the sign maker.

The painted images of this sign are almost completely worn away on both sides, leaving only the chalky white-lead ground. The initials "O.D", executed in the same black paint as the joined frame, lie centered within a name band along the bottom. Paint evidence is sufficient to determine that the punchbowl on side 1 was white, with a blue scallop-decorated rim and blue floral sprays on the body, and filled with a red wine or punch. A band of bluish-green scrolled decoration along the bottom, immediately above the name band, suggests the ornamented border of a tablecloth, but the image is inconclusive. The 1803 date is tucked into this composition below the punch bowl as if it had been embroidered onto the tablecloth. The upper half of the sign plane is even more difficult to discern. It appears to be empty except for another band of bluish-green waves or scroll-like elements across the top quarter. Blue scrolls and borders decorate the pediment.

Innholder: Documentary research has not yet identified an innkeeper with appropriate initials active in Connecticut ca. 1803.

Construction notes: Single board, hand-sawn at top and bottom to create decorative pediment and skirt profiles, with single, molded, horizontal rails and turned posts. Board is set vertically through long mortises cut through rails. These mortises are slightly shorter than the width of the board, and the resulting notches or shoulders in the signboard prevent movement. The thick, bead-molded rails are single-tenoned through the turned posts. Marks from a four-part chuck are still visible on the bottoms of the turned posts. The skirt has a semi-circular profile.

Surface notes: This sign displays only a single layer of paint on both sides.

Condition notes: Both tenons of the top rail are replacements, as are both scroll terminations of the pediment. The posts and rails show some evidence of woodworm. There is no evidence to indicate how hanging hardware was attached.

1. Sign for Wightman's Inn, ca. 1815–24 (cat. 26); Sign for Bowen's inn, 1811, Coventry, R.I., in Chapin, p. 28; the 1802 Cutter sign from Jaffrey, N.H., in Earle, *Tavern Days* pp. 153, 412; the 1795 Root sign of unknown origin, Pocumtuck Valley Memorial Association, Deerfield, Mass.; and the Cady sign, also of unknown origin, at Shelburne Museum, previously owned by the Sheldon Museum of Middlebury, Vt., both illustrated in Smith, *Tavern Sign*, pp. 31, 33.

Cat. 18

Sign for Lewis's Inn, ca. 1805–20
PROBABLY CONNECTICUT

Innholder and maker unidentified

Images: On both sides, the United States seal. No underlying imagery.
Text: On both sides, in a name band on the upper rail, "C.B. LEWIS.", on the banner held by the eagle, "E. PLURIBUS UNUM". No underlying text.

Paint on pine board, posts and bottom rail are chestnut or ash (replaced), gold leaf, iron hardware, 56" x 30"
Collection of Morgan B. Brainard, Gift of Mrs. Morgan B. Brainard, 1961.63.33

Illustrated: color plate 18

Although a fragmentary survival, the Lewis sign nonetheless merits study as a relatively rare, neo-classical example of a suspended, scalloped oval signboard. The swinging oval signboard, upper rail, and pediment are original, as is the painted eagle. The unusual profile of the pediment combines a double-lobed central element with flanking swan's necks or scrolls; pediments typically employ one treatment or the other, but not both simultaneously. The pediment terminates at each side with small bulbous elements, a distinctive treatment also seen on the Spencer sign, dated 1810 (cat. 21). The rarity of this decorative element, combined with the similarity of scalloped signboards suspended from a rail, suggests the likelihood of common origins.

Innholder: No individual named C. B. Lewis has been identified in Connecticut before 1860.

Provenance: Reported to have been displayed for a time, as an antique, at the Pettibone Tavern in Simsbury, Conn. (CHS museum object files).

Construction notes: Single board, suspended from top rail; square stiles and bottom rail (replaced). Board is cut into an oval shape with scalloped edge; oriented vertically. Rails are tenoned through stiles and pinned. Top rail, or header, has applied moldings, mitered in the corners, nailed to each face. Pediment is applied to the top edge of the header.

Surface notes: Edges of the oval show evidence of gilding. The eagle is raised above the surface of the background, possibly by relief carving. The use of a sans serif alphabet suggests a later date for the lettering in "C.B. LEWIS".

Condition notes: Hanging hardware is missing. Chestnut or ash posts and bottom rail are replacements (the posts are appear to be wheelbarrow handles). Pediment has been reinforced at a later date by screwing boards on to one side. Panel is darkened with age and later protective coatings and may have been damaged by fire or heat. Serious paint losses have occurred on both sides.

Related signs: Sign for Spencer's Inn, 1810, possibly Hartford (cat. 17); Sign for Holcomb's Inn, ca. 1802, East Granby, Connecticut (St. Mark's Lodge No. 36, Simsbury; fig. 34).

Publications: *MBTS*, p. 49.

Cat. 19*

Sign for Tarbox's Inn and Village Hotel,
dated 1807 and 1824, overpainted possibly ca. 1831
SCANTIC, CONNECTICUT (SECTION OF EAST WINDSOR TOWNSHIP)

Innholders: Thomas Tarbox (licensed 1807–24); Ephraim Ely (licensed 1824–28); Isaac G. Allen (licensed 1831–33)
Signed by William Rice (1777–1847)

Images: On both sides, top rail, a five-pointed star with square and compass. On side 1, main board, U.S. seal. On side 2, main board, text over eagle with Connecticut state seal.
Text: On both sides, top rail, "1824" over "1807"; on bottom rail, "E. Ely." over "T TARBOX". On side 2, main board, "VILLAGE HOTEL".
Signature: on side 1, "Rice" in bottom of shield

Paint on pine board and frame, sand, smalt, gold leaf, iron hardware, 50-1/2" x 25"
Collection of Morgan B. Brainard, Gift of Mrs. Morgan B. Brainard, 1961.63.21

Illustrated: color plate 19 (side 1, after removal of overpaint); fig. 36 (side 1, during removal of overpaint); fig. 102 (side 2)

The federal eagle depicted on this sign represents the earliest known work signed by William Rice, Hartford's leading sign painter during the second quarter of the nineteenth century; it predates by more than a decade Rice's previously authenticated work (cat. 28). The appearance of a characteristic Rice eagle on a shield-shaped sign adds a new dimension to Rice's oeuvre, since all previously identified signs appear on horizontal, rectangular boards, a slightly later sign style.

When Thomas Tarbox obtained his tavern license in 1807, William Rice had just opened a new shop, advertising gilding, varnishing, sign painting and house painting—in Worcester, Massachusetts.[1] It is possible (although currently undocumented) that Rice painted the Tarbox sign while testing the Hartford market as an itinerant, perhaps simply adding name and date to a prepainted assemblage; he could even have sold the innkeeper a prepainted shield, to be hung into a frame constructed by a local woodworker. (It is also possible that Rice painted the Tarbox eagle a decade later, in 1816–17, just after he had moved his family and business to Hartford. This date would coincide with Tarbox's remarriage and construction of a larger dwelling. However, the shield shape was by then well established and thus seemingly out of character with the enthusiasm for novelty documented in Rice's many advertisements.)

The Tarbox eagle had been revealed by an earlier, uncompleted attempt at removing the Village Hotel paint layer; however, the Rice signature was only discovered when removal of this layer was completed during treatment at the Williamstown Art Conservation Center in 1999–2000. Under the intact Village Hotel paint on side 2, raking light reveals the outlines of another eagle, this one with a Connecticut state seal. The juxtaposition of federal and state seals is also seen on Rice's next earliest known work, the Daniel Loomis inn sign, ca. 1820 (cat. 28). Notable similarities include the outline of the eagle's wing (particularly its long, straight top line), the articulation of the feathers, the angular hooked beak and open mouth, the position of the head and neck, and the rounded outline of the shield on the Connecticut state seal.[2]

No other Rice signs display frames of the type seen here. The scrolls of the pediment rail are flat in comparison to counterparts in furniture or architecture, and the inverted cusp in the center is delightfully unconventional. The scalloped base is bold but simply conceived. The posts are almost devoid of decoration. The columnar segment between the rails has an incised ring in the center, a meager visual reference to a long tradition of dividing long posts into opposing sequences of turnings. The posts terminate in simple, ovoid finials and drops.

It is possible that Rice's decoration is a second-generation image, painted onto Tarbox's board in 1824, when Ephraim Ely became Scantic's tavernkeeper after Tarbox's death. Examples do survive of Rice compositions over earlier imagery, however, no evidence of earlier imagery has been found on this sign.[3]

Tarbox's 1824 probate inventory listed an estate valued at $1797.44, including "1 sign" worth 25 cents. The sign does not appear in the list of property that his widow chose as her dower share, and there is no indication that she continued to operate the inn, although she did remain in the homestead. In 1824 Ephraim Ely acquired a tavern license, and Tarbox's sign, which he moved to his own inn, located in rental property. Ely's alterations to the sign were probably minor, updating the rails with his own name and license date and possibly adding the Masonic emblems of star and square and compass. No documentary references to the name, "Village Hotel," have been found until after Ely's tenure as innkeeper.

The final repainting of the sign most likely occurred in 1831, when Isaac G. Allen, whose name is written in pencil on the "V" in Village, was first granted a tavern license. The arched "Village" name banner, the gilded lettering, and the dark, sand-laden, background paint resemble other signs of the 1830s (cat. 42, 47, 49). The new style of naming rendered the old practice obsolete, and the rails were completely overpainted with white paint. By this time, moreover, the fraternal organization of Freemasonry had come under attack, and was declining in Connecticut. The Morningstar Lodge No 28, of Enfield, reportedly survived this period "by meeting not more than two or three times a year, secretly, in the woods near town." Masonic insignia would evidently no longer have been desirable emblems for an enterprising innkeeper to display.[4]

Inn name: Period newspaper notices refer to "at the dwelling-house of Thomas Tarbox, inn keeper," and "at the house of Ephraim Ely," or "Ephraim Ely's Tavern" (1826). No references have been located prior to 1828 to the eagle motif or to the name, "Village Hotel."

Innholders: Thomas Tarbox (1776–1824) was the son of Jonathan and Lydia Bill Tarbox of Hebron, Connecticut. He bought property (half-interest) in Scantic in 1801; five years later he bought out his partner and shortly thereafter, took up tavernkeeping. His first wife, Lucy, died in 1816, the same year in which he remarried Clarissa Collins.

Ephraim Ely [Jr.] (1785–1848) was probably the son of Ephraim Ely [Sr.] of East Windsor. Ely and his wife, Lora (d. 1853), moved from East Windsor to nearby Ellington in the 1830s.

Isaac G. Allen was licensed in Enfield in 1831–33, and subsequently in East Hartford, then two towns to the south, in 1835–36.

Original location: In 1801 Tarbox bought a half-share of a small, half-acre lot in Scantic, a settlement in the northeastern section of East Windsor. Over the next five years, he and his partner, John Felshaw, increased the value of the lot by building several structures on it, including a dwellinghouse, which Felshaw operated as a tavern, 1802–06. At the time of Tarbox's death in 1824, the property had grown to two and one-half acres, with a large, gable-end dwelling house, a blacksmith shop, a horse shed, and a barn. It was located on the west side of Scantic road, just south of the Meeting House lot. A small building remains on the site, commemorated as "Tarbox's Tavern"; this is not the substantial dwelling, erected in 1816, that is depicted in the estate papers, but it may be the blacksmith shop that stood on the property when Tarbox acquired it in 1801.

Ely's tavern evidently occupied a different site, as yet unidentified, as Clarissa Tarbox continued to occupy the family homestead.

Construction notes: Single board, grain oriented vertically, cut into shield-shape and suspended by iron hinges from upper rail; single, flat, shaped, horizontal rails and turned posts. Each rail is tenoned through the posts and doubled pinned. The rails extend up and down and are cut at top and bottom to create scrolled pediment and scalloped skirt profiles.

Surface notes: The original painting scheme had an off-white background, with names and dates painted in black. Tarbox's name appears in Roman capitals; Ely's in an elegant script. The green foliage

of the eagle's olive branch was executed in copper green paint, which has now partially oxidized and darkened. Both sets of names and dates were painted over with white paint, evidently at the same time the eagle was completely covered with a new ground layer of red-brown paint, now darkened to almost black. This second ground layer incorporates white sand as a texturing agent. The Village Hotel name banners are set within scribed lines and the lettering is gilded.

Condition and treatment notes: Hanging hardware is a later replacement. The tips of the post finials and drops appear to have been sawn off. An earlier restoration effort, of unknown date, had effectively destroyed the Village Hotel layer on side 1. Treatment at WACC in 1999–2000 included removing the remnants of the Village Hotel layer on side 1, and consolidation of wood splits and paint surface.

Publications: *MBTS*, p. 36.

1. On Rice, see Vincent, "Sign Painters," Appendix 1, q.v.
2. Similar eagles appear on the Treat inn sign, dated 1818, Historical Society of Glastonbury, Conn; Benes, *Two Towns*, no. 236, p. 120; and an unidentified New England sign, likely to be by Rice, Westmoreland Museum of Art, Greensburg, Pa; Smith, *Tavern Signs*, p. 39.
3. Sign for the Griswold inn, 1836, now at the Torrington Historical Society.
4. Dorothy Ann Lipson, *Freemasonry in Federalist Connecticut* (Princeton: Princeton University Press, 1977), p. 327; see Vincent, "Some suitable Signe," Chapter Four.

Cat. 20

Sign for Angell's Inn, dated 1808
PROVIDENCE, RHODE ISLAND

Innholder: probably Richard Angell
Maker unidentified

Images: On both sides, an eagle holding a laurel branch and anchor, centered on the signboard. No underlying images.
Text: On both sides, in pediment, "1808", under eagle, top line, "Entertainment · by", bottom line, "R·ANGELL· " over "R A" over "R [ANG]ELL".

Paint on pine board, iron hardware, 28-1/2" x 17-3/4"
Collection of Morgan B. Brainard, Gift of Mrs. Morgan B. Brainard, 1961.63.2

Illustrated: color plate 20

The highly individualistic design of this sign has long been celebrated as a folk art masterwork. The central eagle is curiously heart-shaped, lending it a overstuffed quality, exacerbated by limp wings and scrawny feet. Covering its body are nine white and eight red bars—one stripe for each state in the Union in 1801—alluding to the national seal. Instead of the usual arrows, however, the eagle grasps a laurel branch and an anchor (a major element of the Rhode Island state seal). The free-hand lettering is more accomplished than the bird; "Entertainment", which is guided by horizontal scribe lines, is especially fluid. In contrast, the date in the pediment meanders. The pediment itself is another highly individualistic interpretation, possibly inspired by round-headed pediments on some rural case furniture of the region.

Provenance: Purchased by Brainard in 1928 from T. C. Stapleton of New York City, who stated that he had located it in a garret in Brooklyn, Conn., ca. 1926.

Construction notes: Single board, hand-sawn to create decorative profile at top only. Applied moldings, mitered in the corners, are nailed to the faces of both sides. No structural frame.

Surface notes: The eagle is rendered in dark red and white, with at least two paint applications. Traces of earlier lettering bleed faintly through the white background: a bold "R A" centered between the two existing lines of text, and yet another version of "R · ANGELL" positioned within scribe lines below the present name. Given the naive quality of this sign painting, the maker may have redone the lettering to adjust and improve spacing of text and image.

Condition notes: Hanging hardware appears to be original. The tip of one pediment scroll is missing.

Related objects: Watercolor rendering, by John Matulis, ca. 1940, *Index of American Design*, National Gallery of Art, 1943.8.8110; published Hornung, pl. 68, p. 229; Christensen, no. 371, p. 189; *American Heritage* 1960, p. 62.

Exhibitions: "Signs of the Times," Rhode Island Historical Society, 1989–90; "Hunters of the Sky," touring exhibition organized by The Science Museum of Minnesota, 11 venues, 1994–98 (photoreproduction); Japan 1970.

Publications, *MBTS*, p. 15; Philip M. Isaacson, *The Amerian Eagle* (Boston: New York Graphic Society, 1975), pp. 180–81. Textbooks, various editions: *America: The People and the Dream* (Scott, Foresman).

Cat. 21

Sign for Spencer's Inn, dated 1810
HARTFORD, CONNECTICUT

Innholder: John Spencer (licensed 1810–11)
Maker unidentified

Images: On both sides, the state seal of Pennsylvania (an eagle atop a shield displaying a ship, a plow, and three sheaves of grain). No underlying imagery.
Text: On side 1, on upper rail, "1810" over "1810", on lower rail, "I, SPENCER" over "I, SPENCER". On side 2, both rails have thick black paint layer over "1810" and "I, SPENCER".

Paint on unidentified softwood board, frame of ash or chestnut, unidentified hardwood, gold leaf, iron hardware, 46-1/2" x 20-3/4"
Collection of Morgan B. Brainard, Gift of Mrs. Morgan B. Brainard, 1961.63.46

Illustrated: color plate 21

This sign is accompanied by family history linking it to Hartford innkeeper John Spencer. Spencer's grandson, who was nearly an adult by the time of his grandfather's death in 1860, attested to its provenance in 1918. However, close examination reveals several ambiguous and conflicting physical features. Its

shape, construction, and materials support the painted date of 1810. The urn finials are excellent examples of neo-classical design, as are the attenuated columns marked with a ring or collarina near the top, which suggestively marks off space for a capital. The distinctive pediment profile and the shape of the scalloped oval panel closely resemble features on the Lewis sign (cat. 18) and the Holcomb sign, from East Granby, Connecticut, ca. 1802 (fig. 34). However, the swinging oval panel displays considerably less wear than the frame, suggesting that either the frame may have been reused, or the panel replaced. The hardware that attaches panel to frame fits poorly and may not be original, although it has clearly been in place many years. The glossy black paint on the date and name bands is sloppily applied, and appears to be painted over another version of the same date and name, a curious coincidence. Finally, the presence of imagery drawn from the Pennsylvania state seal seems anachronistic on an inn sign owned by a Hartford innkeeper descended from an old, local family.

Innkeeper: John Spencer (1781–1860) was the son of John and Mary Spencer of Hartford. In 1814 he married Olive Rogers (b. 1794). The Spencers moved to Windsor and took up farming sometime during the decade of the 1840s.

Original location: On the Windsor Road north of Hartford, near the Windsor town line.

Provenance: Acquired by Brainard from Josiah Cleveland ("Cleve") Capen (b. 1843), grandson of Hartford innkeeper John Spencer.

Construction notes: Single board, suspended from top rail; horizontal rails with integral pediment and skirt; turned posts. Board is hand-sawn into an oval shape with scalloped edge; oriented vertically. Board has two battens, tapered along the edges and from end to end, inset across one side to counteract warpage, a practice occasionally encountered in furniture and painted panels. Battens appear to be original to the board. Each horizontal rail is tenoned through the turned posts and secured with two pins. The rails extend up and down to form a decoratively-shaped pediment and skirt (now missing). Applied moldings are nailed to the faces of the rails, forming a rectangular frame for text.

Surface notes: The surface of the center panel displays less wear than the frame. The rails were repainted, sloppily, with bronze letters and black paint, apparently in an effort to increase the legibility of areas that had flaked severely; the original color may not have been black. The poorly drawn letters and numerals and the use of bronze paint suggest that this repainting may have been done by an amateur or owner.

Condition and treatment notes: Hanging hardware is missing. The hardware securing the oval panel to the upper rail does not fit well on the panel and is probably not original to it (although the painted decoration extends over the hardware). The skirt is missing along the bottom edge of the lower rail, except for small half-round elements at each end. One pediment scroll is missing, as are three molding strips from the upper rail, side 2. Displacement of the wooden pins suggests that the frame has been taken apart and reassembled. The paint on the posts shows more wear than the paint on the image board. Treatment at WACC, 1999-2000, included surface cleaning, consolidation of flaking, glossy black and bronze paint on text bands on side 1, removal of upper layer on side 2 only, and removal of later bronze paint on finials. New hanging hardware installed, using original attachment locations; fabricated as a simple generic interpretation of period ironwork, by blacksmith William Senseney, Williamstown, Mass., stamped "WS / 1999".

Related signs: Sign for Lewis's Inn, ca. 1805–20, location unidentified, (cat. 18); Sign for Holcomb's Inn, ca. 1802, East Granby, Conn., (St. Mark's Lodge No. 36, A.F.&A.M., Simsbury, Conn.; fig. 34)

Related objects: Watercolor rendering, by John Matulis, ca. 1940, *Index of American Design,* National Gallery of Art, 1943.8.16490; published Hornung, pl. 77, p. 238; Lord and Foley, p. 4; *House and Garden* 1941, p. 20.

Exhibitions: "Signs of the Times," Rhode Island Historical Society, Providence, 1989–90; Japan 1970.

Publications: *MBTS*, p. 64; *American Heritage* 1960, p. 62; Terry, *Old Inns*, p. 37.

Cat. 22*

Sign for David Loomis's Inn, dated 1811
WESTCHESTER, CONNECTICUT

Innholder: David Loomis (licensed 1811–21)
Maker unknown

Images: On both sides, a decanter and four wine glasses, silhouetted against white background. No underlying imagery.
Text: On side 1, above image, "D, Loomis.", below the image, "iNN *1811*". Identical on side 2, except that a period replaces the comma after the initial "D.". No underlying text.

Paint on pine, iron hardware, 25-1/2" x 32-1/2"
Museum purchase, 1958.10.1

Illustrated: color plate 22

The Loomis sign boldly displays a decanter flanked by pairs of wine glasses, a clear reference to drinking, one of several activities associated with taverns and inns. At the time this sign painting was made, a "cheerful glass" of wine was thought to improve one's humor and sociability, a theory later reversed by proponents of the Temperance Movement. The shapes of the glass objects, executed in gray, are contemporary with the 1811 date on the sign. Their rounded bottoms suggest domed feet, raised to prevent sharp pontil marks underneath from scratching table surfaces. The black lettering, executed free-hand within scribed guidelines, is proficient but lacks the flourish and precision encountered in some other examples of this time. In keeping with a somewhat untutored style, the 1811 date appears, seemingly as an afterthought, unbalancing the design.

Several elements of the idiosyncratic lettering of this sign appear on another sign, attributed to the same unidentified maker: the distinctive capitalization of "iNN," the interchanging of comma and a period, the upside-down "s", the continuation of the written message in italics in the lower right corner (fig. 19). Simply but strongly designed and executed in white and black paint, this second sign pictures a crescent moon above the text, "E, Fitch[s] / iNN". Elijah Fitch operated a tavern in Bolton, located fifteen miles north of Westchester, from 1810 to 1842. The Fitch sign, probably made in 1810, is vertically oriented and uses a different construction system.

Inn name: A printed "Public Ball" ticket of 1819 refers to this establishment as "Mr. David Loomis' Hall" (CHS Library).

Innholder: David Loomis (ca. 1774–1842) was the son of Solomon and Prudence Robbins Loomis, both of Colchester, Conn. He married Clarissa Williams (ca. 1775–1838). In 1819, the inn was under the management of O. Carriers and A. Loomis, probably David's son, Alfred Isham Loomis (1796–1882).

Original location: Along the East Haddam-Colchester turnpike in Westchester, a village approximately 4 miles west of Colchester center. The house remains extant, but was moved to Old Lyme in recent years and extensively remodeled.

Provenance: The sign remained in the Loomis house and descended in the family until 1958, when it entered the collection of The Connecticut Historical Society.

Construction notes: Two boards, oriented horizontally and encased in moldings. Moldings are mitered at corners and nailed to edges of boards. Iron support straps are recessed flush with the image plane and painted over.

Surface notes: This sign displays only one paint layer on each side. Plane chatter marks, caused by vibrations of a long plane used to smooth the surface of the pine boards, are evident over much of this sign.

Condition and treatment notes: The hanging hardware is original. The larger board has split in two, and nails securing the side moldings have caused chips to split away. Treatment at WACC, 1998–2000, included surface cleaning and consolidation, and replacement of missing section of top molding. Discolored segments of the iron hanging straps were inpainted to increase legibility. Reversible steel pins were inserted through the boards to support both the original join and the subsequent split, which precluded safe handling.

Related signs: Sign for Fitch's Inn, ca. 1810, Bolton, Conn. (Collection of The New-York Historical Society; fig. 19).

Exhibitions: Japan 1970.

Publications: CHS *Annual Report,* 1959, p. 31.

Cat. 23*

Sign for Rose's Inn, ca. 1813, repainted ca. 1940
COVENTRY, CONNECTICUT

Innholder: Horace Rose
Signed by Harlan Page (1791–1834)

Images: On both sides, identical genre scene, depicting a man holding a bird, with two additional birds hidden in a large bush. The version on side 2 was repainted early in the twentieth century. At the bottom of each side is a square and compass.
Text: On both sides, at top of scene, "H. ROSE.", and immediately below scene, "A bird in the hand is worth / two in the bush."
Signature: "H Page" painted in the grass at the lower right of the scene.

Paint on pine board, iron hardware, 33-1/2" x 23-1/4"
Collection of Morgan B. Brainard, Gift of Mrs. Morgan B.

Brainard, 1961.63.44

Illustrated: color plate 23

The painter of this sign, Harlan Page, was born in Coventry in 1791 and trained as a joiner. This may be the only inn sign he painted. In 1814 he experienced a religious conversion and turned his energies to preaching and religious proselytizing. He subsequently became a prolific illustrator, producing drawings and engravings for American Tract Society publications. Page's Tract Society work consists primarily of moralistic scenes illustrating familiar maxims, much like the "bird-in-hand" scene depicted here.[1] The man holding the bird is drawn in a flat, two-dimensional manner, suggesting modest artistic skills. Faint scribe lines cut into the wood panel guide the free-hand lettering. The square and compass at the bottom of the sign is a Masonic device, symbolizing faith and reason. Innkeeper Rose, like many of his neighbors, may have been a member of Warren Lodge No. 50, founded in 1810 in nearby Andover. In this case, the square has ten inches marked on it and is actually ten inches long, suggesting that Page may have traced his own tools.

Ovals and shield-shaped panels, both drawn from contemporary neo-classical designs, were especially popular for inn signs from shortly after 1800 until the early 1820s. The shaped boards were typically hung within a wooden frame, sometimes fixed in place (cat. 13, 30), and sometimes allowed to swing freely (cat. 18, 19, 26). The iron straps on this signboard terminate in eyes, from which it was presumably suspended. Although it is possible that this sign never had a wooden frame, the lack gives it an unfinished appearance, much as a painted canvas looks incomplete without a frame.

Innholders: Horace Rose (1788–1862) was the son of Jehiel and Mary Ripley Rose of Coventry. He married Marcia Edgerton (1789–1875) of Lebanon, Connecticut. Jehiel Rose was licensed as tavernkeeper from 1800–12; after his death in 1813, his sons continued the enterprise in the family homestead, with Horace licensed 1813–14, and his older brother, Roderick, 1817–18. During the 1820s, Horace and his family emigrated to Otsego, New York; Roderick was declared insolvent; and the house was sold to pay debts, lending a certain poignancy to the inn sign's motto.

Original location: On Ripley's Hill, along the north-south road, in what was then the business section of Coventry, northeast of Wangumbaug Lake.

Provenance: After the homestead was sold out of the Rose family in the 1820s, the sign was apparently stored in the attic, where it is said to have been found by a later owner in 1936.

Construction notes: Three boards, cut to a shield shape, oriented vertically.

Surface notes: Side 1 displays only a single layer of paint; side 2 was heavily overpainted, probably ca. 1940. A mylar overlay dawing of side 1 indicates that a template was used to replicate the entire composition, including the lettering.

Condition and treatment notes: A thin metal strap applied to the outside bottom edge appears to be a later repair, stabilizing a split through the larger board of the sign. The hanging straps are original; however, the connecting straps may have originally extended across

the top edge of the shaped board (as on cat. 27). The board probably hung within a wooden frame, which is now missing. Treatment at WACC in 1999 included surface cleaning and consolidation, removal of later resinous coating, and stabilization of vertical split in wood.

Related objects: Watercolor rendering, by Alfred Parys, ca. 1940, *Index of American Design*, National Gallery of Art, 1943.8.8026; published Hornung, pl. 71, p. 226.

Publications: *MBTS*, p. 62; Smith, *Tavern Signs*, p. 16 (side 1); Lord and Foley, p. 151; *Spinning Wheel* 1955, p.12; Terry, *Old Inns*, p. 241.

1. Vincent, "Sign Painters," Appendix 1, q.v.

Cat. 24

Sign for Field's Inn and Abbe Inn,
ca. 1814–20 and ca. 1914
ENFIELD, CONNECTICUT

Innholders: Peter Reynolds Field (licensed 1814–23); William A. Abbe (active ca. 1914–18)
Possibly painted originally by Luther Allen (1780–1821)

Images: On side 1, eagle with outswept wings, centered on board. On side 2, text on black background, over eagle with outswept wings.
Text: On side 1, in band at bottom, "*P R FIELD*", on side 2, "ABBE INN AND TEA ROOM," dispersed across board, over "*P R FIELD*".

Paint on pine board and moldings, gold leaf (side 2 only), iron hardware, 31-1/2" x 50"
Collection of Morgan B. Brainard, Gift of Mrs. Morgan B. Brainard, 1961.63.1

Illustrated: color plate 24 (side 1); fig. 78 (side 1, under raking light)

Separated in space by one and one-fourth inches of wood, the two sides of this sign are separated in time by almost one hundred years. The contrast between Peter Field's spread-winged eagle and the austere gold-on-black lettering of the "Abbe Inn and Tea Room" introduces a fascinating history. Although the signboard is of a size and form that first became popular in the 1810s, the concept of a "tea room" substantially post-dates the Civil War.[1] The Field and Abbe names locate the sign in place and time. The first owner, Peter R. Field, was licensed as tavernkeeper in Enfield, north of Hartford, from 1814–23. After a succession of owners and tenants, his homestead passed into the Abbe family in the early 1840s. William Abbe operated it as the Abbe Hotel, beginning about 1850, and acquired a much larger signboard, ornamented with William Rice's trademark lion and eagle (cat. 31). Peter Field's sign, by then antiquated, was presumably relegated to the attic, where it was rediscovered by William A. Abbe (William Abbe's son) in the early 1910s. Abbe had it repainted and hung it outside the old homestead, which he had by 1914 reopened as the "Abbe Inn and Tea Room." Abbe also continued to use his father's sign, treating tourists in search of the antique to not one, but two (more-or-less) authentic, "ancient" signs.[2]

The presence of the earlier image (visible in outline under the tea room lettering, fig. 78) made this sign a tantalizing mystery—and a conservation dilemma. On the one hand, the text painting, "Abbe Inn and Tea Room," is of considerable interest in its own right. As a Colonial Revival example, it represents the intersection of American moderism and American historicism in the field of graphic design. On the other hand, it obscures an earlier, and thus historically privileged, art work. Fortunately, because both sides of the twentieth-century painting were identical, it was possible to compromise: during treatment at the Williamstown Art Conservation Center, the Abbe Inn layer was removed from one side only. The sign is thus preserved for the future as a multi-generational object, side 1 displaying its original, early nineteenth-century decoration, and side 2, its early twentieth-century reincarnation.

Extensive research into local history and genealogy suggests Field's neighbor, Enfield painter Luther Allen, as the most likely painter of the Field sign. In 1801, Allen advertised "Sign painting, lettering with gold leaf, and smalting." Allen likely continued to work as an itinerant until about 1820; he subsequently left the area, dying in Ithaca, New York, in 1821.[3]

Inn name: Period newspaper notices consistently refer to the early nineteenth-century inn as "at the dwelling-house of Peter R. Field, innholder." No references have been found using the pictorial motif (eagle) as part of the name. William A. Abbe's early twentieth-century establishment is referred to as "Abbe House" or "Abbe Inn and Tea Room."

Innholders: Peter Reynolds Field (b. 1774) was the son of Dr. Simeon Field, Sr., and Margaret Field of Enfield. In 1801 he married Hannah Prudden (1777–1854). In 1823 Peter and Hannah Field moved to Colebrook, New Hampshire, and in 1837, to Beloit, Wisconsin.[4]

William A. Abbe (b. 1858) was the son of William Abbe, also an innkeeper (see cat. 31). The Abbe family was large and well established in Enfield, with several members engaged in innkeeping at various times.

Original location: The Field homestead remains standing on its original site: the northwest corner of the intersection of the main north-south road between Hartford and Springfield (now Enfield Street, or Rt. 5), and the east-west road leading to the newly erected toll-bridge across the Connecticut River at Enfield (now Bridge Lane). The land was acquired by Simeon Field, Sr., in 1761, and the house was presumably built shortly thereafter. In 1807 Simeon Field, Jr., sold a strip of land on the south edge of the property, for the road to the bridge then being built. A kitchen ell was added in 1811, two years prior to Peter Field's first known tavern license. The property was described in an 1826 newspaper ad as "the valuable Tavern Stand in the center of the town of Enfield, formerly occupied by Peter R. Field, and now in the occupation of Stephen O. Russell."[5] The railroad station erected at the river terminus of Bridge Road later provided a new source of customers.

Construction notes: Single board, grain oriented horizontally. Encased in moldings (quarter round and hollow, each bordered by fillets) applied to both faces, mitered in the corners. No structural frame. The board is unusually large (32" wide) and the thickest (1-1/4") in the entire collection.

Surface notes: The surfaces of the eagle and Field text are raised slightly above the background. Very little paint remains on the newly revealed eagle, which retains traces of browns, white, black, and ochre (on talons and beak, matching the earlier frame moldings); background was white or light gray. The italic letters for Field's name were scribed into the surface prior to being painted in white, against the dark text band. The Abbe Inn text shows evidence of gold leaf and the use of stencils, but very little trace of weathering. Some small passages in the Abbe Inn text were water-gilt instead of the usual oil-gilt.

Condition and treatment notes: Hanging hardware is original. During treatment at WACC, 1999–2000, Abbe Inn paint layer on side 1 was documented, then removed; later moldings on side 2 were removed and replaced with tulip poplar moldings matching the original profile. One bent hanging strap was straightened.

Publications: *MBTS*, p. 14.

1. See Ames, "Signs of the Past," Chapter 9.
2. Only the William Abbe sign (cat. 31) is visible in a published view of the Abbe Inn and Tea Room, ca. 1917, see *Memorial of Captain Thomas Abbey* (East Orange, N.J.: Abbey Printshop [1917]), p. 77.
3. *Courant*, 19 Jan. 1801, p. 3, col. 5; on Allen, see Vincent, "Sign Painters," Appendix 1, q.v.
4. Enfield Church Records, excerpted in Francis Olcott Allen, *The History of Enfield, Connecticut*, 3 vols. (Lancaster, Pa.: L. Wickersham Printing, 1900), vol. 1, p. 1465.
5. *Courant*, 20 March 1826, p. 3, col. 5.

Cat. 25

Sign for Hammon's Inn, dated 17?? and 1818,
probably made ca. 1790–1800
FOSTER, RHODE ISLAND

Innholders: Almedus Wilkinson (active ca. 1810–17); Reuben Hammond (active ca. 1818–28)
Maker unidentified

Images: On side 1, Rhode Island state seal (anchor). On side 2, United States seal.
Text: On both sides, in band under image, top line, "R. HAMMON" over "A. Wilkinson", bottom line, "*INN*.", on skirt, "1818", on side 1, over "17??".

Paint on pine board and frame, iron hardware, 42" x 23-3/8"
Collection of Morgan B. Brainard, Gift of Mrs. Morgan B. Brainard, 1961.63.27

Illustrated: color plate 25 (side 1); fig. 9 (side 2)

The Hammon Inn sign combines official seals of Rhode Island and the United States. Each of the images has been repainted, but raised paint layers beneath the uppermost decoration indicate that the visible images follow earlier, and most likely original, paint schemes. However, the more modern painting style is softer and less precise than the earlier style, notably in the sponge-decorated lower corners of each side. Heavy outlining, evident in the eagle's banner and elsewhere, seems to deaden some forms and exaggerate others, as in the flukes of the anchor. Two features of the sign are relatively unusual. The pediment, sawn to shape from the top of the signboard, incorporates a two-dimensional central finial, the outline of which resembles a turned and carved "cork-screw and urn" finial commonly used in large pieces of case furniture.[13] The second feature is the continuation of the ogee curves at the corners of the top and bottom, a little detail that animates the shape of this sign. Although some signs display a small volute or other element, as the now-damaged Spencer sign or the Windham Inn sign (cat. 17, 62), most signs end with a simple horizontal termination.

The two names on this sign locate it in Foster, Rhode Island, just across the border from Killingly, Connecticut, on the stage line to Providence. The earlier owner, Almedus Wilkinson, also operated taverns in North Scituate and Providence, Rhode Island, as well as Brooklyn, Connecticut. His brother, Brownell Wilkinson (1785–1861) was licensed in both Plainfield and Killingly, Connecticut. The extent of the Wilkinson family's innkeeping operations provides an indication of how irrelevant political borders might be, especially for those active in transportation-related businesses. Traces of an underlying date, "17??" on side 1, suggest that the sign may have originally been constructed, some time before 1800, presumably for Almedus Wilkinson's father, Joseph Wilkinson, who was also an innkeeper.

Innholders: Almedus Wilkinson (1787–1861) was the son of Joseph Wilkinson (1750–1814) a farmer and tavernkeeper in North Scituate, Rhode Island, just on the edge of Foster.

Col. Reuben Hammond (1787–1828) was the son of Rev. John Hammond of Foster. Reuben Hammond was a merchant, blacksmith, cooper, and farmer, as well as innkeeper. He married Abbey Ailsworth.

Provenance: Purchased by Morgan Brainard at the Macfarlane auction, Willimantic, 1918.

Construction notes: Single board, grain oriented vertically, hand-sawn at top and bottom to create decorative pediment and skirt profiles; no structural frame. Applied, ogee-profiled molding strips, mitered at corners, are nailed to both faces, forming a rectangular image frame. Pediment has scrolls flanking central finial shape; skirt has double ogee lobes.

Surface notes: Text is well executed, with calligraphic flourishes flanking the word, "Inn"; lettering is placed within ruled guidelines. Both anchor and eagle have multiple layers of paint on what appears to be the same design, on a white ground. On side 1, the upper layer of paint on the anchor is brown and gold; the lower layer, mostly black and white. The upper corners of side 1 had striped spandrels, now buried under white paint. On side 2, the eagle's upper layer is red and black, with some sponge decoration. The moldings display fewer layers of paint than the board itself.

Condition notes: Hanging hardware appears original. The top frame molding may have been relocated.

Exhibitions: "Signs of the Times," Rhode Island Historical Society, 1989–90.

Publications: *MBTS*, p. 42; Terry, *Old Inns*, p. 242; *Antiques* 1928, p. 405 (side 2).

1. A similarly-outlined central finial appears on the sign for the J. Angell Center Hotel, of Centerdale, Rhode Island, some fifteen miles east of Foster near Providence; Nina Fletcher Little, *Little by Little: Six Decades of Collecting American Decorative Arts* (New York: Dutton, 1984), p. 107.

Cat. 26

Sign for Wightman's Inn, ca. 1815–24
WATERFORD, CONNECTICUT (QUAKER HILL SECTION)

Innholder: Asa Wightman (active 1815–36); Mercy Smith Wightman (active 1837–39)
Maker unidentified

Images: On both sides, on central board, profile view of walking lion, with slightly different positioning of tail from side to side. On pediment scrolls, cornucopia.
Text: On both sides, in banner above lion, "A. WIGHTMAN'S"; in banner below lion, "INN". Identical on both sides except that side 1 has reversed "N's". No underlying text.

Paint on pine board and frame, sand, gold leaf, iron hardware, 55-3/4" x 31"
Collection of Morgan B. Brainard, Gift of Mrs. Morgan B. Brainard, 1961.63.51

Illustrated: color plate 26 (side 1)

Asa and Mercy Wightman operated taverns at two separate locations within the town of Waterford, Connecticut. This sign may have hung at both, or only at the second Wightman inn. From 1815 until 1824, the Wightman inn was located near the Rope Ferry Bridge, the post road crossing over the Niantic River, a high-traffic area from which Wightman, a master mariner and coastal trader, could profitably have carried on numerous trade operations. In 1824, they relocated to a farmstead at Smith's Cove, an inlet off the Thames River north of New London. The major factor in assigning the sign to the second inn has been its name: the Quaker Hill inn subsequently became known as the Red Lion, while the first was remembered as the Blackfish. No period references to either name have thus far been located.

The form of the sign could date as early as 1815: it combines an eighteenth-century style structure of vertically-oriented frame with an early nineteenth-century, neo-classical oval panel, suspended from the frame by iron pintal hinges (see cat. 18, 21).[1] Much of the sign has been repainted; however, the image follows (imperfectly) the raised outlines of earlier name bands and lions. No traces of a different image have been observed. The stylized cornucopia in the pediment appear to be part of the original decoration. They resemble ornament painted on the backs and crests of inexpensive "fancy" chairs; only a few examples of painted pediment decoration have been noted on signs. One charming incongruity of this sign is the reversal of all of the letter "N's" on side 1.[2]

Inn name: Period newspaper notices refer to the inn by the proprietor's name, "at the house of Asa Wightman's" or "at the house of Mrs. Mercy Wightman." No period references have been located using the pictorial motif of the sign as part of the name of the inn.

Innholders: Capt. Asa Wightman (1784–1836) was the son of Timothy Wightman. Born in East Lyme, he married, in 1811, Mercy Smith (1789–1872). Wightman was a master mariner, engaging in coastal trade along the Atlantic seaboard. He served in 1813 in the Connecticut militia, with rank of captain.

Mercy Smith Wightman (1789–1872) continued the inn for four years after being widowed at about age forty-seven.

Original location: The Wightmans' first tavern was located at Rope Ferry Bridge, at the bar of the Niantic River. In 1824 Wightman bought a six-acre property with a new house and outbuildings, located in Waterford at the head of Smith's Cove, on the New London-Norwich turnpike. By 1837–39, when Mercy Wightman advertised (repeatedly) to sell or lease the property, the crossroad was known as the "old Colchester road."

Construction notes: Large center board with thin additions nailed to each side edge, cut to oval shape. Flat, horizontal rails with pediment and skirt extensions, chamfered posts. The board, with grain oriented vertically, hangs by iron straps from the pediment rail, which is constructed of two horizontal boards set edge-to-edge, the seam lying just above the iron hanging loops. The upper board extends up to form a pediment, hand-sawn to create decorative scrolls. The bottom rail appears to be a single board, which extends down to form a skirt, hand-sawn to create decorative cusps. The upper and lower rails are joined to the chamfered posts with double through-tenons and double-pinned. Narrow horizontal moldings are applied to both top and bottom rails.

Surface notes: The frame was previously dark green but has been overpainted in black. The lion and background are repainted, with sanded paint around the lettering. The letters are gilded. The cornucopia in the pediment are executed in a more polished manner than other elements. The lion resembles illustrations in accounts of lion hunting and travel in Africa, published in the 1820s, although an exact prototype has not yet been located.

Condition and treatment notes: Some hardware is replaced. The lower section of the top rail is replaced, but the upper section appears consistent with the rest of the frame. The top of one post is replaced and spliced into the original section. Finials and drops are missing, and appear to have been sawn off the posts. The bottom point of one skirt cusp is missing; the other is replaced. An old metal strap repair stabilizes a crack through the signboard, with paint on this strap extending into surrounding wood areas. Iron brackets have been attached to stabilize the lower corners inside the frame.

Exhibitions: Japan 1970.

Publications: *MBTS*, p. 69; John Tarrant Kenney, *The Hitchcock Chair* (New York: Clarkson N. Potter, 1971), p. 132 (side 1); United States Information Agency, *United States Pavilion Japan World Exposition* (Osaka, 1970); Robert L. Bachman, *An Illustrated History of the Town of Waterford* (Waterford, Conn.: Morningside Press, 1967), p. 91.

1. For other examples of oval-panel signs of the 1810s, see the Lewis inn sign, dated 1812 and the Stratton inn sign, ca. 1815, both in Smith, *Tavern Signs*, pp 36, 46; the Beemer inn sign, dated 1815, in Lipman and Winchester, *Flowering of American Folk Art*, p. 222; and the Patch inn sign, dated 1816, in Benes, *Two Towns*, no. 233. For pre-1800 examples of this type, see cat. 18, n. 1.
2. For similar painted ornament, see Cynthia V.A. Schnaffner and Susan Klein, *American Painted Furniture, 1790–1880* (New York: Clarkson Potter, 1997), pp. 91, 153, 181; John Tarrant Kenney, *The Hitchcock Chair* (New York: Clarkson N. Potter, 1971), pp. 182, 184, 205; Zilla Rider Lea, *The Ornamental Chair: Its Development in America, 1700–1890* (Rutland, Vt.: Charles E. Tuttle, 1960), pp. 58, 90–92. For other signs with painted pediment decoration, see the Patch inn sign, dated 1816, in Benes, *Two Towns*, no. 233; Angell's Center Hotel sign, ca. 1824, Nina Fletcher Little, *Little by Little: Six Decades of Collecting American Decorative Arts* (Boston: Society for the Preservation of New England Antiquities, distributed by University Press of New England, Hanover, N.H., and London, 1998), p. 107; the Red Lion Inn sign, ca.

1825, in Carolyn J. Weekley, *The Kingdoms of Edward Hicks* (Williamsburg, Va.: Abby Aldrich Rockefeller Folk Art Center, in association with Abrams, New York, 1999), p. 75. Kenney also compares the Wightman sign to Hitchcock chair stencils with backwards "N's", Kenney, *Hitchcock Chair*, pp. 129–32. Information on lion imagery from Nancy Finlay, CHS Curator of Graphics.

Cat. 27*
Sign for Porter's Inn, ca. 1820–25
FARMINGTON, CONNECTICUT

Innholder: Joseph Porter (licensed 1820–22)
Maker unidentified

Images: On side 1, landscape with seated female allegorical figure, over traces of earlier version of same motif, framed in vertical oval. On side 2, landscape with large tree on left, small house on right, over traces of slightly different buildings, framed in vertical oval. Text: On both sides, "J, PORTER". No underlying text.

Paint on pine board, smalt, gold leaf, iron hardware,
46-1/4" x 24-3/8"
Collection of Morgan B. Brainard, Gift of Mrs. Morgan B. Brainard, 1961.63.41

Illustrated: color plate 27 (side 1); fig. 13 (side 2)

Among the more creative and unusual of Connecticut signs, the Porter sign combines neo-classical shapes and decorative devices in a refreshingly novel way. The sign is cut from a single board into a shield, with applied, gilded moldings that define a central, oval, pictorial panel. Gilded vine leaves, reminiscent of bright-cut decoration on silver, hang from gold balls along the edge of the black field.[1] The image painted within the oval on side 1 shows a seated, female allegorical figure representing Liberty.[2] In her left hand she grasps a staff with an indistinct Liberty Cap, while her right arm holds a shield with the arms of the State of Connecticut. A large cornucopia, signifying the bounty of the land, lies on the ground in front of her, while several bales or boxes, presumably representing manufactured goods, lie behind her. More delicately drawn and colored than the majority of inn sign images, the neo-classical image on this sign was undoubtedly based on an engraved source, for which several possibilities exist. The general motif of a seated female figure ornamented numerous coins used in America beginning in the 1740s, personifying either a country or a concept—Britannia, Hibernia, Columbia (after the creation of the new United States), Justice, or Liberty. The Connecticut one-cent pieces, or "coppers," designed by Connecticut engraver Abel Buell and minted in New Haven, 1787–93, featured, on the reverse, a seated female figure of Liberty, based on Britannia. She holds a pine-tree like laurel branch and a staff; a shield bearing the arms of Connecticut rests against her side in some issues.[3]

Even more closely related to the Porter sign—both pictorially and historically—is a seated goddess with staff, Liberty cap, and Connecticut shield, engraved on currency issued by the Mechanics Bank of New Haven. Notably, the Mechanics Banks was chartered specifically to finance the building of a canal through

Farmington, an enterprise that raised great expectations locally.[4] Organization of the Farmington Canal Company in 1822 may have been an inducement for Porter's acquisition of a new inn sign, just as it inspired the building, nearby, of a new brick, Union Hotel (now part of Miss Porter's School). Whatever its exact source, the Porter sign localizes the iconography of the early Republic, celebrating Connecticut as a land of liberty and prosperity, founded on agriculture, manufactures, and trade.[5]

The image on side 2 is less explicitly symbolic: a large tree overhanging a small, somewhat naive one-and-one-half story house. Landscape scenes are fairly uncommon on extant tavern signs; however, those that do survive include several with a large tree at the edge of the board, sometimes overhanging a relatively smaller house.[6] The house on this sign does not correspond with descriptions of the Porter homestead, and it is certainly possible that it is simply a generic vignette. Given the highly allegorical content of side 1, however, it would seem surprising that side 2 would not also have a symbolic dimension. Perhaps side 1 represents the public face of Connecticut's bounties, and side 2, the domestic counterpart.[7] It is also possible that the tree, an aging specimen with distinctive, laterally-extended branch, may be a generalized reference to Connecticut's famous Charter Oak, celebrated as a symbol of liberty for its role in preserving the Connecticut charter from confiscation by officers of the crown in 1687.[8]

Inn name: Designated in period sources by proprietor's name, "at the house of Joseph Porter, innkeeper."

Innholders: Capt. Joseph Porter (1766–1826) was the son of Ensign Joseph and Abigail Smith Porter. He descended from one of the founders of Farmington. In 1790 he married Susanna Langdon (1768–1843).

Original location: Porter's homestead stood in Farmington center, at the northeast corner of New Britain Avenue and High Street. Reportedly built in the first decade of the eighteenth century, the structure burned in January 1886.[9]

Provenance: Owned in 1904 by Farmington historian, Julius Gay, who described the sign as having "a picture of a house on one side and on the reverse that of a goddess armed with helmet, spear, and shield, in apparel better befitting the heat of summer than the blasts of winter. She was doubtless the first goddess to bear on her shield the three grapevines of Connecticut."[10]

Construction notes: Single board, grain oriented vertically; cut into a shield shape, with applied oval molding and stylized laurel vine. No structural frame. Gilded balls are made in halves and glued around iron hanging straps.

Surface notes: Infra-red photographs and visible pentimenti indicate the existence of two or three paint campaigns on both sides, the upper two being similar in design. On side 1, an earlier version of the female figure was slightly larger and placed higher within the oval. A photograph of side 1 published in 1906 shows the present paint scheme in place and in visibly aged condition, with the woman's cheek damaged and the shield darkened. At some time between 1906–28, both cheek and shield were retouched, the latter with bright green vine clusters on a vivid yellow ground. Microscopic examination of paint stratigraphy in the shield indicates that the body of the shield was originally painted white, then overpainted first with red, then with a new white ground, followed by the present yellow. Patches of the same red paint were also found in the damaged area of the face, on the Liberty cap, in

the sky (both sides) and elsewhere, possibly the effects of vandalism or an early attempt at restoration. Notably, the existence of the vine clusters are documented in Gay's description of 1904, indicating that enough of the original image survived to serve as a reliable guide for subsequent repainting of the Connecticut seal. On side 2, infra-red photographs reveal a slightly different building arrangement beneath the present one. No evidence was found confirming earlier speculation that this underlying imagery was a federal eagle. Paint stratigraphy also indicates three layers in the lettering, the lowest and top layers incorporating gold leaf. The smalt surrounding the letters may be associated only with the uppermost paint scheme, probably dating ca. 1830–50, when smalt was most commonly used.

Condition and treatment notes: Hanging hardware appears to be original. The board had split apart vertically and been repaired with two large butterfly patches, on the top and bottom of opposite sides; these patches were covered by the uppermost layer of paint and had evidently been in place many years before 1906. Each leaf applique evidently had a counterpart that originally projected beyond the edge of the sign; only those pointing inward survived, and some of these, in addition to sections of the vine stem, had been replaced at some time. The paint surfaces are desiccated and had been harshly cleaned at some point in the past; the paint possesses aged characteristics, including lack of solubility. Treatment at WACC, in 1998–99, included surface consolidation and cleaning, insertion of reversible steel pins to stabilize the broken board (preserving the early butterfly patches), and replacement of missing molding sections and several inpointing leaves, following outlines visible in the black ground.

Related objects: Watercolor rendering (side 1), by Alfred Parys, ca. 1940, *Index of American Design*, National Gallery of Art, 1943.8.7767; published Hornung, pl. 71, p. 225, Lord and Foley, p. 4.

Exhibitions: Japan 1970.

Publications: *MBTS*, p.59; *American Heritage* 1960, p. 62; Terry, *Old Inns*, p. 243; *Antiques* 1928, p. 403; Arthur L. Brandegee and Eddy A. Smith, *Farmington, Connecticut: The Village of Beautiful Homes* (Farmington, 1906), p. 155. Textbooks, various editions: Hodgins, et al., *Adventures in American Literature* (side 2).

1. Similar diagonally-placed leaves appear on numerous early nineteenth-century picture and looking glass frames found in the Hartford area.
2. Frank H. Sommers, "The Metamorphoses of Britannia," *American Art: 1750–1800, Towards Independence*, ed. Charles F. Montgomery and Patricia E. Kane (Boston: New York Graphic Society for Yale University Art Gallery, New Haven, and the Victoria and Albert Museum, London, 1976), pp. 40–49.
3. Wyman W. Parker, *Connecticut's Colonial and Continental Money*, Connecticut Bicentennial Series 18 (Hartford: American Revolution Bicentennial Commission of Connecticut, 1976), pp. 46–47. Earlier versions of a similar figure appeared on Hibernia coins, 1722–24; Hibernia-*Voce Populi* coins, 1760; Massachusetts coppers, 1776; "Washington pieces," 1783–84, and other issues; see R.S. Yeoman, *A Guide Book of United States Coins*, ed. by Kenneth Bressett (Golden Books, 1999).
4. Nancy Finlay noted the resemblance to the Mechanics Bank note (CHS x1993.6.30); Julius Gay, "The Canal: An Historical Address Delivered at the Annual Meeting of the Village Library Company of Farmington, Connecticut," 1899, reprinted in Gay, *Farmington Papers* (Hartford: Case, Lockwood & Brainard Co., 1929), pp. 177–79.
5. Several elements of the Porter design appear in a popular allegorical print, *America Guided by Wisdom*, drawn by John J. Barralet and engraved by Benjamin Tanner in Philadelphia, circa 1815. The principal figure represents "The Genius of America"; she holds a staff flying the American flag and a shield with the U.S. seal; at her feet lies a cornucopia. In the middle distance is a seated female figure, identified as Ceres, goddess of Agriculture, accompanied by Mercury, emblem of Commerce, and surrounded by sheaves of grain and barrels and bales of goods, destined for trading ships in the harbor; E McClung Fleming, "From Indian Princess to Greek Goddess: The American Image, 1783–1815," *Winterthur Portfolio* 3 (1967), p. 50.
6. Similar tree and house configurations appear on the Wedgwood inn sign, ca.

1827 (cat. 38) and the Chadwick inn sign, ca. 1797–98; Smith, *Tavern Signs*, p. 28. Large trees surround a five-bay house in the sign for Smith's inn, Heritage Plantation of Sandwich, Mass.; Smith, *Tavern Signs*, p. 33.

7. The Barralet/Tanner engraving of *America Guided by Wisdom* features a woman spinning at the doorstep of a small cottage overhung by large trees at the edge of the picture.

8. Two views of the Charter Oak were painted in 1818 by Hartford carriage-maker George Francis, and a spate of inexpensive views for the popular market soon followed; Robert F. Trent, "The Charter Oak Artifacts," *CHSB* 49 (Summer 1984): 123–27. The Charter Oak appears on the sign for Mason's inn, ca. 1830s or later (cat. 51).

9. Julius Gay, *Old Houses in Farmington: An Historical Address, delivered at the Annual Meeting of the Village Library Company of Farmington, May 1, 1895* (Hartford: Case, Lockwood & Brainard Co., 1895), p. 19.

10. Julius Gay, "Farmington Two Hundred Years Ago: An Historical Address delivered at the Annual Meeting of the Village Library Company of Farmington, Connecticut," 1904, reprinted in Gay, *Farmington Papers*, pp. 273–74.

Cat. 28

Sign for Daniel Loomis's Inn, ca. 1820
COVENTRY, CONNECTICUT

Innholder: Daniel Loomis, Jr. (active 1820–29)
Signed by William Rice (1777–1847)

Image: On side 1, eagle with Connecticut state seal, twenty-two stars, and military gear. On side 2, eagle with U.S. seal, twenty-two stars, and military gear.
Text: On both sides, in banner curving through lower part of image, "DANIEL LOOMIS".
Signature: On both sides, in lower right corner, "Rice."

Paint on pine board and moldings, smalt, gold leaf, iron hardware, 43-7/8" x 57-3/8"
Collection of Morgan B. Brainard, Gift of Mrs. Morgan B. Brainard, 1961.63.34

Illustrated: color plate 28 (side 2); fig. 58 (side 1); fig. 76 (color, side 1); fig. 80 (detail, side 1)

On each side of this sign, a cannon barrel, rifle, and sword—weapons associated with the artillery, infantry, and cavalry—flank the seals of the United States and the State of Connecticut. Cannon balls lie in two stacks along the bottom. Although a more specific symbolism is also possible, the prominent military iconography suggests the correlation between militia rank and tavernkeeping in colonial and early nineteenth-century America. As Vincent notes in "Some suitable Signe," tavernkeepers tended to be prominent members of local militia, giving credence to the old saying that a militia captain was expected to provide drinks for the company.[1] Assuming that the number of stars follows the pattern of the American flag, it is notable that Alabama became the 22nd state in December 1819, and Maine the 23rd in March 1820. This time-frame corresponds to Loomis's first license, taking over the inn previously run by his father and grandfather. This sign is the earliest identified example of a pattern that was repeated at numerous country inns around Hartford: the acquisition of a new sign, painted by the enterprising Hartford sign painter, William Rice, corresponding to the transfer of management to a new generation of an established family operation.[2]

Innholders: Daniel Loomis III (1789–1844) was the son of Daniel II (1765–1835) and Mary Hibbard Loomis, and the grandson of Daniel Loomis I (d. 1806); all three Daniel Loomises were innkeepers in Coventry. In 1815 Daniel Loomis III married Jerusha Richardson (ca. 1792–1849); his grandfather having died a decade earlier, he was designated by contemporary references as Daniel Loomis, Jr. It is possible that the middle Daniel Loomis was still active as an innkeeper at age 55 in 1820, and thus the original owner of this sign. However, it is more likely that he had turned the operation over to his son, Daniel Loomis III, who had married and set up housekeeping five years earlier, and who, as a new proprietor, might be inclined to acquire a new-style sign. According to a family genealogy, both Daniel Loomis II and III were bridge builders; the elder was also a road contractor.[3]

Original location: The Loomis inn was located about seventeen miles east of Hartford, along the Providence turnpike (now Rt. 44).

Construction notes: Three boards, grain oriented horizontally, joined with splines or featherboards set in grooves. Applied moldings are nailed to the outer edges of board. The ends of the top and bottom moldings are cut to the shape of the inside contour of the side moldings, so that the side moldings can slide over the ends as the large signboard expands and contracts across the grain with changes in humidity (see fig. 18). No structural frame, no skirt or pediment.

Surface notes: Heavily weathered, with approximately 50% paint loss, especially to the gray background, leaving the image slightly raised. The cannon barrel projecting into the composition from the side is an unusual feature. Several elements on side 1 appear to be later repaintings of earlier designs, including the smalt treatment and a sloppy application of red paint to the name banner. The vines in the Connecticut seal may have originally been gilded. The leaf size of the gold sheets used for gilding is evident on the eagle. The two eagles were probably laid out with a template, although slight variations are visible; strips in the shield on side 2 were marked off in equal widths with dividers.

Condition and treatment notes: Hanging hardware is replaced. Entire sign is desiccated, with splits and checking. Moldings are loose, with at least three large losses; somewhat disintegrated and furry in the lower molding. Treatment at WACC in 1999 included surface cleaning and replacement of missing spline in joint between top and center boards.

Publications: *MBTS*, p. 50.

1. No records of regular military service by Daniel Loomis have been located, and the name is too common in the militia records to ascertain a specific identity.
2. Other nineteenth-century Connecticut establishments exhibiting this pattern include the Abbe inn, Enfield (cat. 31); the Phelps inn, Simsbury; Griswold's inn, Torrington; the Viets inn, Granby; and Pettibone's inn, Norfolk; see Vincent, "'Some suitable Signe,'" Chapter Four, n. 46.
3. Elais Loomis, *Descendants of Joseph Loomis in America . . .*, rev. by Elisha S. Loomis (N.p., 1908), pp. 287–88, 417.

Cat. 29

Sign for Cady's Hotel, ca. 1820s
GLOUCESTER, RHODE ISLAND

Innholder: Hezekiah Cady (active ca. 1807–57)
Maker unidentified

Images: On both sides, four horses pulling a stage coach, over a square and compass.
Text: On both sides, "H. CADY'S HOTEL." over "J. Converse / HOTEL".

Paint on pine board, ash or hickory banding, 32-3/8" x 44-3/4"
Collection of Morgan B. Brainard, Gift of Mrs. Morgan B.
Brainard, 1961.63.18

Illustrated: color plate 29

The shape and painted border of Cady's Hotel sign suggest a date in the 1820s, despite Cady's having taken up innkeeping over a decade earlier. Horizontal oval signs continued to be made through the 1830s, but these later versions often had decorative iron mounts and/or decorative nailing patterns on the wooden banding that wrapped around the sign board (cat. 48, 49). The initial layer of imagery, associated with the unidentified innkeeper, J. Converse, featured a masonic square and compass with a border of circles and ovals, neatly scribed with a compass. The upper layer, painted in a looser manner, depicted a stagecoach drawn by four horses. Remnants of the coach profile, now severely weathered, suggest a vehicle pre-dating the popular "Concord coach," first introduced in 1827.[1] Assuming the sign to have been created for Converse, ca. 1820, then Cady must have acquired it and had it repainted relatively soon after its original production. The chartering of a new turnpike in 1825, with a tollgate located at or near Cady's Hotel, suggests a likely motivation for updating the inn sign with imagery appealing explicitly to long distance travelers.[2] Increasingly through the nineteenth century, hotel owners marketed their establishments and services to specific types of customers. In addition, growing opposition to the Masonic movement may have made such Masonic iconography as the square and compass much less advantageous for an enterprising innkeeper to display.[3]

Innholders: Hezekiah Cady (1785–1857) was the son of Col. Joseph and Lucy Leavens Cady, of Killingly, Connecticut. In 1810 he married Ann Greene Cook. The Cady family had residences and businesses in eastern Connecticut and in nearby Rhode Island towns. Hezekiah reportedly took over innkeeping from his brother, Joseph, who had operated an inn in Pomfret, Conn., before moving to a new operation in West Gloucester, located just across the state border into Rhode Island. According to family tradition, Joseph's wife, Susanna Kingsbury Cady (1777–1857) was "a famous cook, which was a strong factor in giving the house a good reputation."[4]
J. Converse has not yet been identified.

Original location: Cady's hotel was located along the Rhode Island and Connecticut Central Turnpike, chartered in 1825, with tollgates on the western and eastern sides of Gloucester. The western tollgate was opposite Cady's hotel.

Construction notes: Two boards, grain oriented horizontally, joined by three inset, or floating, tenons. Assemblage is cut into oval shape. Wood banding is nailed around the outside of the entire sign. No structural frame.

Surface notes: Weathering has worn away the upper image so severely that it is difficult to untangle from the remains of a completely different paint scheme underneath. The Cady text, set within a black name band at the bottom of the oval, covers border decoration that is integral to the design and layout of the Converse Hotel image, thus establishing Converse as the earlier name. Similarly, the deteriorated picture of four horses pulling a stage coach lies over the faint outlines of a large compass and square—Masonic symbols that were part of the earlier Converse scheme.

Condition and treatment notes: Hanging hardware appears original. Treatment by Peter Arkell, Branford, Conn., in 1988, included replacement of rotted floating tenon joining the two boards and fabrication and installation of two iron reinforcement braces.

Exhibitions: "Signs of the Times," Rhode Island Historical Society, 1989–90.

Publications: *MBTS*, p. 33.

1. *The Carriage Collection* (Stony Brook, New York: The Museums at Stony Brook, 1986), p. 104. Cady's coach appears quite similar to that on the 1826 sign for the Williams inn, Centerbrook, Conn. (cat. 36); other coach and fours appear on the Keeler Hotel sign, ca. 1815–27, Ridgefield, Conn., and the 1828 sign for the Jacobs inn, East Thompson, Conn., repainted but probably following the original image, both in Smith, *Tavern Signs*, pp. 21, 46.
2. Richard M. Bayles, ed., *History of Providence County, Rhode Island* (New York: Preston, 1891), p. 530.
3. The Masonic imagery on Thomas Tarbox's sign, ca. 1807, also appears to have been painted out by the early 1830s (cat. 19).
4. Orrin Peer Allen, *Descendants of Nicholas Cady . . .* (Palmer, Mass: By the Author, 1910), pp. 74, 154–56.

Cat. 30

Sign for the Chesebro Hotel, dated 1821
PROBABLY STONINGTON, CONNECTICUT

Innholder: Probably Amos Chesebro
Maker unidentified

Images: On side 1, eagle with upraised head. On side 2, eagle with downturned head; possibly an earlier image layer, now indecipherable
Text: On both sides, around perimeter of board, "A. CHESEBRO / HOTEL." over an earlier name, largely indecipherable, "P. Pi_____"; on bottom rail, "1821".

Paint on ring-porous hardwood, possible traces of gold leaf, iron hardware, 45-1/8" x 25-1/2"
Collection of Morgan B. Brainard, Gift of Mrs. Morgan B. Brainard, 1961.63.15

Illustrated: color plate 30

The profile of the lower rail provides compelling evidence that contemporary furniture was an important design source for woodworkers who made signs. The rail duplicates a common skirt profile found on American federal chests made from about 1800 through the 1820s.[1] The finials on the sign are reminiscent of some late-eighteenth century turned seating furniture produced in southern New England. The columnar posts are long cylinders that lack any degree of taper indicating top or bottom, but they end in customary, decorative reels and rings that visually separate the mass of the round column from the square blocks at either end.[2]

Innholder: Census records list many Chesebroughs in New London County, with six whose first names begin with A living in Stonington, the easternmost town along the Connecticut coastline. The most likely candidate is Amos Chesebrough (1773–1846), son of Samuel and Mary Slack Chesebrough, of Stonington. In 1801, Amos Chesebrough married Phebe Denison (1782–1846) of Stonington.

Construction notes: Single board, grain oriented vertically, cut to oval shape, with single, flat horizontal rails and turned, columnar posts. Projecting tenons at top and bottom attach board to horizontal rails. The rails extend up and down to form pediment and skirt, cut at top and bottom to create decorative profiles. Rails are joined to posts with through-tenons and double pinned.

Surface notes: The Chesebro name and eagle decoration are later repainting campaigns over another image that is no longer decipherable. The lettering is yellow and more skillfully executed than the image, which is sloppily painted, in yellow, black, red, blue, and white on a black background. The 1821 date is raised above surface, from weathering, possibly carving, or a combination of the two, and most likely records the year the sign was originally made. Underlying letters, "P. Pi_____", are painted in large script lettering along scribed guidelines.

Condition notes: Hanging hardware appears original. Pediment rail is split in half along grain of wood, and arches of both pediment scrolls are missing. A hole in the center of the pediment indicates a missing finial. One upper joint into the post is broken.

Exhibitions: Japan 1970.

Publications: *MBTS*, p. 28

1. One such chest was owned by Laura Wells Churchill of Newington, Conn.; *Seymour*, pp. 50–51. Two other chests with the same skirt, labeled by Joseph Rawson of Providence, R.I., the regional design center east of where the sign was probably used, are illustrated in Eleanore Bradford Monahan, "The Rawson Family of Cabinetmakers in Providence, Rhode Island," *Magazine Antiques*, July 1980, p. 137, figs. 7–8.
2. The Chesebro sign resembles one for Healy's inn, dated 1819; Hamilton, *American Freemasons*, p. 27.

Cat. 31

Sign for Abbe's Inn and the Lion Hotel,
ca. 1822, repainted 1866
ENFIELD, CONNECTICUT

Innholders: Daniel Abbe, Jr. (active 1804–14 and 1822–28); Robert M. Abbe (active 1832–34 and 1845–53); Daniel P. Abbe (active 1836–40); William Abbe (active 1853–71); William A. Abbe (active ca. 1914–18)
Signed by William Rice (1777–1847) and Luther Terry Knight (b. 1844)

Images: On side 1, lion, with body in profile, head facing forward, wrapped in chains, standing on grass-tufted ground. On side 2, eagle with U.S. shield and seventeen stars in sky, inside central oval outline. U.S. arms in shield are painted over Connecticut arms.
Text: None.
Signatures: On side 1, in lower right corner, "L. Knight" over "Rice". On side 2, in lower right corner, "L. Knight 1866" over "Rice".

Paint on pine board and moldings, iron hardware, 54" x 76-3/4" x1986.8.0

Illustrated: color plate 31 (side 1), fig. 37 (side 2)

Measuring four and one-half feet high by over six feet wide, and weighing ninety pounds, this impressive sign is among the largest inn signs known.[1] The immense lion on side 1 is approximately two-thirds life-size, occupying the entire signboard and leaving no room for a name band. At least four other signs inscribed or attributed to William Rice display this particular lion—facing directly toward the viewer, usually wild-eyed and chained, and standing on grass-tufted ground (see related signs, below). Side 2 displays other characteristic Rice features, especially the framing oval, ornamented with alternating triglyphs and flowers, and thunderbolts in place of arrows in the eagle's claw.

The history of this sign is intertwined with that of at least two other signs, three sign painters, two properties, and several innkeepers, in the Connecticut River town of Enfield, about sixteen miles north of Hartford. It was created by Hartford sign painter William Rice, probably about 1822, for Daniel Abbe, Jr. Like many purchasers of Rice signs, Abbe was the scion of an established innkeeping family. His father, Daniel Abbe, Sr., had been licensed from 1773–1804, at a location near the Enfield ferry across the Connecticut River. Succeeding to the family business about 1804, Daniel Abbe, Jr., participated in the effort to erect a bridge, which opened in 1807. In that year, Abbe paid Enfield ornamental painter and handyman, Stephanus Knight, for "Painting a Sine," possibly refurbishing Daniel Abbe, Sr.'s old sign.[2] Several factors make it highly unlikely that the present sign could be the one painted or repainted by Stephanus Knight in 1807: its Rice signature and characteristic moldings and lion/eagle motifs as well as its extraordinarily large size and horizontal format (features dating at least a decade later). Presumably the sign painted by Knight passed out of use during the period 1814–22, when Daniel Abbe, Jr., was not granted a tavern license.[3] The local tavernkeeper during this period was Peter R. Field, who dwelt at the intersection of the Hartford road with the road to the river bridge. Field was licensed 1814–22 and had his own sign, which survives in the Connecticut Historical Society collection (cat. 21).

The physical features of the present sign support a production date of ca. 1822, when Daniel Abbe, Jr., resumed innkeeping at a new site, nearer the river bridge (in 1817 he had purchased the houselot just north of Peter Field's inn). The sign presumably passed to his sons, Daniel Pease Abbe and Robert Morrison Abbe, who were recorded as innkeepers in the 1830s and 1840s. Robert Abbe's tavern reportedly burned in the 1850s, and he evidently left the business, as no further licenses are recorded.[4] His sign survived, however, and was subsequently acquired by William Abbe, a distant cousin, who moved it one house south, to the old Field residence, which he had acquired some years earlier. William Abbe received a license in 1853 and began innkeeping in the old Field homestead, convenient to both the old bridge and the newer railroad station, erected at the river terminus of Bridge Road. In 1856, William Abbe's establishment was listed as the "Lion Hotel" in the Connecticut Business Directory. Ten years later, he had the sign repainted by Luther Terry Knight. Although Knight's work seems to have consisted primarily of repainting or strengthening the original composition by William Rice, he did make one notable change—conspicuously nationalizing the iconography by painting the stars and bars over the Connecticut grapevines originally displayed on the eagle's shield on side 2.

An 1896 photograph shows the sign nailed to a tree in front of the Abbe Hotel, located in the old Field homestead; at this time it had a smaller, secondary board, suspended from the main board, with the name "W^M ABBE'S HOTEL."[5] Although the name plaque is now missing, the iron hanging strap that held it in place remains bent around the bottom of the surviving sign. William Abbe appears to have left the hotel business in favor of the tobacco business; between 1871–95, no published references have been located to the property as a hotel, although it may have continued to house boarders. After William Abbe's death in 1895, the Field Inn/Abbe Hotel property passed to his son, William Arthur Abbe, who reopened it as the Abbe Inn and Tea Room. A photograph of 1917 documents that the William Abbe Hotel name band had been removed, and the sign rehung, on a bracket extending out from a different tree in front of the same house. William A. Abbe also found, repainted, and rehung Peter Field's century-old inn sign (cat. 21).

Inn name: After Daniel P. Abbe's death in 1840, the property was offered for lease as "The Hotel lately occupied [sic] by D.P. Abbe, . . . being the best and most convenient Tavern stand in the town."[6] In the late 1840s, the establishment was consistently called "the Hotel of Col. Robert M. Abbe." In 1856–71, William Abbe's establishment was listed as the "Lion Hotel" in the *Connecticut Business Directory*. On an 1869 Enfield School District map, it appears as "Wm. Abbe's Hotel." William A. Abbe's early twentieth-century establishment is referred to as "Abbe House" or "Abbe Inn and Tea Room."

Innholders: Daniel Abbe, Jr. (1775–1833) was the son of Daniel Abbe, Sr. (1749–1815) and Sarah Pease Abbe of Enfield. In 1795 he married Elizabeth Morrison (1772–1842) of Enfield. Licenses are recorded for him for the years 1804–14, 1822, and 1824–28.

Robert Morrison Abbe (1797–1883) was the son of Daniel Abbe, Jr., and Elizabeth Morrison Abbe. In 1822 he married Maria Norcott (1800–57) of East Windsor; in 1860 he married Mary M.S. Meade. He died in LeRoy, New York. Licenses are recorded for him for the years 1823, 1832–34, 1845, 1847, and 1853.

Daniel Pease Abbe (1809–40) was the son of Daniel Abbe, Jr., and Elizabeth Morrison Abbe, and the brother of Robert Morrison Abbe. Licenses are recorded for him for the years 1836 and 1838–39.

William Abbe (1817–95) was the son of Timothy Abbe (first cousin to Daniel Abbe, Jr.) and Rhoda Prudence Clark Abbe of Enfield. In 1849 he married Caroline Markham (ca. 1826–before 1903).

William A. Abbe (b. 1858) was the son of William and Caroline Markham Abbe of Enfield. In 1886 he married Alice Phelps of Enfield.

Original locations: This sign evidently hung at two separate locations in Enfield. From ca. 1822–50, it marked the Abbe family inn, located on the west side of the main north-south road, one houselot north of the east-west road to the river bridge and about sixty rods south of the Enfield meeting house. From ca. 1853–1918, it hung in front of the old Peter Field homestead, renamed the Abbe or Lion Hotel, and subsequently the Abbe Inn and Tea Room. The Field/Abbe structure remains standing on its original site (one houselot south of the Abbe property), which occupies the northwest corner of the intersection of the main north-south road between Hartford and Springfield (now Enfield Street, or Rt. 5), and the east-west road now called Bridge Road.

Provenance: Entered the Connecticut Historical Society's collections at an unknown date, well before 1959; possibly acquired at the Abbe Inn liquidation sale, Enfield, 24 May 1918.

Construction notes: Two boards, grain oriented horizontally, set within grooved moldings that are nailed to the edges of the signboard. The ends of the top and bottom moldings are cut to the shape of the inside contour of the side moldings, so that the side moldings can slide over the ends as the large signboard expands and contracts across the grain with changes in humidity (see fig. 18 for detail of this characteristic feature, on another Rice sign). No structural frame, no skirt or pediment.

Surface notes: On side 2, the eagle composition seems to float against a sky with puffy white clouds and seventeen stars, rather sloppily gilded; red and white stripes have been painted over the three grapevines of the Connecticut arms. The coved interior of the frame is painted bright yellow over an earlier scheme of white and black serrations. Both sides are obscured by a heavy, darkened varnish (probably dating to the Knight refurbishing), which make it difficult to see the painted decoration clearly. Some areas on both sides look baked and desiccated as if from fire, corroborating reports of the Abbe inn burning in the 1850s.

Condition notes: Two sections of the moldings on side 2 have split off. The bottom ends of the hanging hardware have been bent ninety degrees and are now screwed into the bottom molding, thereby preventing movement of that element. Originally, these straps extended straight below the bottom molding and supported a separate sign band bearing the legend, "W^M ABBE'S HOTEL."

Related signs: Sign for Phelps's inn, ca. 1826, North Colebrook, Conn., signed, with lion and eagle (cat. 37); sign for Goodwin's inn, undated, Hartford, signed, with lion on each side, probably repainted (Wadsworth Atheneum), in *Great River*, 173–74; sign for Hawley's inn, possibly Sandisfield, Mass., ca. 1825–30, signed, with lion and eagle (Abby Aldrich Rockefeller Folk Art Center); sign for unidentified inn, probably New England, possibly by Rice, with lion (front half only) and eagle (Westmoreland Museum of Art, Greensburg, Pa.), in Smith, *Tavern Signs*, p. 39.

Publications: *MBTS*, p. 72; C. Terry Knight, "Enfield: Some Beauties Natural and Sketches Historical of an Old New England Town," *Connecticut Quarterly*, vol. 2, no. 4 (Oct.–Dec. 1896), pp. 370 (side 2), 371 (side 1, in situ in front of the William Abbe Hotel, which had earlier been Peter Field's inn and would later become the Abbe Inn and Tea Room); *Memorial of Captain Thomas Abbey* (East Orange, N.J.: Abbey Printshop [1917]), p. 77 (side 2, in situ in front of the Abbe Inn and Tea Room).

1. Two other very large signs by Rice have survived: the Vernon Hotel sign, ca. 1834, is slightly larger, measuring 75-1/4" x 63-3/8" (cat. 46); the Goodwin tavern sign, ornamented with a similar lion, is slightly smaller, measuring 49-1/2" x 74-3/4" (Wadsworth Atheneum), *Great River*, pp. 173–74.
2. Knight, mss. account book, 1795–1809, p. 112, CHS Library. Stephanus Knight was married to Agnes Pease, a cousin of Daniel Abbe, Jr.'s, wife, Sarah Pease. On Knight, see Vincent, "Sign Painters," Appendix 1, q.v.
3. The 1807 sign painted by Stephanus Knight for Daniel Abbe, Jr., is not known to have survived.
4. Franklin J. Sheldon, *Nonsense, Common Sense, Incense* (Enfield: By the Author, 1925 and 1926; Enfield Historical Society), p. 13.
5. C. Terry Knight, "Enfield: Some Beauties Natural and Sketches Historical of an Old New England Town," *Connecticut Quarterly*, vol. 2, no. 4 (Oct.–Dec. 1896): 370.
6. *Courant*, 27 February 1841, p. 3, col. 6.

Cat. 32

Sign of the Grapes, dated 1822
LOCATION UNDETERMINED

Innholder: J. Williams
Maker unidentified

Images: On both sides, a grapevine with three bunches of grapes, centered on board.
Text: On both sides, on top rail, "1822"; on bottom rail, "J. WILLIAMS."

Paint on pine, 57-1/2" x 32-7/16"
Collection of Morgan B. Brainard, Gift of Mrs. Morgan B. Brainard, 1961.63.17

Illustrated: color plate 32

The design of the wooden components of this sign is consistent with the painted date of 1822. Certain qualities of the sign demonstrate the maker's familiarity with furniture-making refinements, and some features conform to woodworking practices in the greater Hartford region, although they are not exclusive to that area. Notable features include the well-shaped and proportioned scrolled pediment and double-ogee skirt, as well as the elongated finials that incorporate urn-like elements below narrow ovoid cones. The finials recall chair finials of the early nineteenth century, and the gracefully swelled, turned columns manifest the capabilities of a well-trained turner. Comparisons to documented chair or other finials on furniture may one day help identify a geographic origin. The painted image of grape clusters and vine is an unambiguous allusion to wine and wine-drinking, an appropriate symbol for a tavern; its specific configuration rather loosely recalls the grapevines on the Connecticut seal. In comparison to the large letters and numbers, the grapevine looks undersized; if the present surface is a repainting of an earlier image, it is possible that some design element—perhaps an encircling oval border—was omitted.

Innholder: Too many J. Williamses exist in the historical record in the early 1820s to suggest any particular place of origin.

Construction notes: Single board, grain oriented vertically. Flat, horizontal rails with pediment and skirt extensions and turned, columnar posts. Board is tenoned into rails. Rails are tenoned through turned posts and doubled pinned. Rails extend vertically and are hand-sawn at top and bottom to create decorative pediment and skirt profiles. Applied molding strips are nailed to both faces of board.

Surface notes: Grapes are blue, green, and brown, molding and lettering are black, background is white. Evidence of blue and red paint under the white on the posts, as well as the surface qualities of the grape clusters, suggest that this sign has been repainted. There is a disparity in the paint layering and wear in different areas of the sign. The lettering is of higher quality craftsmanship than the present image. Possible charring of surfaces now covered by the uppermost paint layer indicate that the sign may have been in or near a fire. The sequence of charring followed by painting is also consistent with a cleaning technique, described in nineteenth-century painters' manuals, which involves burning away old paint prior to repainting (see Webber, "Signs Faithfully Executed," Chapter Six).

Condition notes: Original hanging hardware is missing; nail-hole evidence indicates that hanging straps were once applied to outer sides of posts at the juncture of the top rail. One pediment scroll, the central finial, and a lower section of applied molding are missing; the second pediment scroll has broken and been nailed back. Entire sign is covered with silted grime.

Cat. 33*

Sign for Carter's Inn, ca. 1823
CLINTON, CONNECTICUT (THEN PART OF KILLINGWORTH)

Innholder: Jared Carter (active 1823–28)
Possibly painted by Jones & Bush, Middletown, Connecticut (active ca. 1823–25)

Images: On side 1, two men drinking at table. On side 2, a couple with a driver in a carriage pulled by two horses. No underlying images.
Text: On both sides, above the image, "STRANGERS, RESORT"; below the image, "J, CARTER". No underlying text.

Paint on pine board and moldings, smalt, gold leaf, iron hardware, 23-3/4" x 42-1/2"
Collection of Morgan B. Brainard, Gift of Maxwell L. Brainard, Charles E. Brainard, Mrs. Edward M. Brainard, Mrs. Morgan B. Brainard, Jr., Mrs. H. S. Robinson, Jr. (Constance Brainard), 1971.30.1

Illustrated: color plate 33 (side 1), fig. 2 (side 2), fig. 70 (detail, side 2)

Carter's sign achieves an unusually high level of artistry and evokes a new kind of hotel by both its wording and its imagery. The term "resort" was new in the lexicon of American inn signs when Jared Carter first advertised his establishment in 1823, implying a destination rather than mere accommodation along a journey. Carter described his "house" as "pleasantly situated upon the stage road . . . , about eighty rods from the water, commands an extensive view of the [Long Island] sound, and will be a pleasant and healthful resort for valetudinarians who may wish the benefit of the sea air."[1] Moreover, the phrase, "Strangers, Resort," suggested efforts on the part of the innkeeper to provide a polite setting that welcomed strangers. Although social nuances are doubtless lost with the passage of time, side 1 shows a military officer and a civilian gentleman enjoying dinner together (each with his hat hanging on the wall and his dog lying behind him on the carpet). On the opposite side, a coachman driving a well-dressed couple in a calash (a light carriage with a folding top) extends the subtexts of prosperity and destination. This vehicle is pointedly not a public stagecoach.

In keeping with the elite messages conveyed by the words and pictures, the ambitious painting of this sign incorporates an exceptional level of detail, varied coloration, and compositional balance. On the carriage side, the signpainter unifies the image with "S," or ogee, curves, prominent in the darkened outlines of the horses as they arrive in lock-step at the front of the inn.[2] The shape of the carriage and the large and small wheels echo this artistic theme. On the other side, the painter plays with diagonals, which dominate the painted floor covering, but also appear in the crossed utensils on the plates and in the posture of the two gentlemen. Both images relate to contemporary British caricatures, iconographically and stylistically, and were probably based upon existing artwork, laid out with the aid of a mechanical transfer device. The scene of the men dining, for example, closely resembles numerous period interior scenes in watercolor: seated figures, facing each other across a table, surrounded by domestic accoutrements, patterned carpet, and pets.[3] Slight outlines tracing the image details suggest the possible use of either a pantograph or camera obscura (fig. 70). A compass was used to perfect and align the wheels and spokes on the carriage. The sign appears to have been given a protective coating of varnish at the time of its making, a practice rarely seen on surviving signs but appropriate here because of the thinness and delicacy of the paint layer. The minimal amount of wear and absence of repainting on this sign indicate that it had little exposure to the outdoor elements. By 1828, Carter was out of business, and the sign went into the family attic.

Inn name: Newspaper notices refer to the inn by the proprietor's name, "at the dwelling house of Jared Carter" or "the Inn of Jared Carter." Carter himself announced it as simply a "House for Public Entertainment." No period references have been found using the pictorial image or the phrase, "Strangers, Resort" as part of the name.

Innholder: Jared Carter (1797–1829) was the son of William and Polly Wilcox Carter of Middletown. In 1818 he married Mary (Polly) Dibbell. Their son David (b. 1821) married Mary J. Chittenden, whose family subsequently operated the Chittenden or Killingworth Hotel, probably located in the Carter premises and depicted in a John Warner Barber view of the 1830s.[4]

Original location: Carter's inn was located in what was then the First Society of Killingworth, at the crossroads of the Middletown Turnpike and the post road from New York to Boston, along the Connecticut shore. Carter sold the property in 1828, and the structure is now gone; the site can be identified as the southwest corner of Commerce and Main Street. This section of Killingworth incorporated as Clinton in 1838.

Provenance: Descended to Jared Carter's son, David Carter (b. 1821), who loaned it to the 250th anniversary celebration of Guilford in 1889. Purchased by Morgan Brainard in 1929. According to Morgan Brainard's grandson, this sign hung in the dining room of the Brainard farmhouse on Avon Mountain in West Hartford, Conn.

Construction notes: Single board, grain oriented horizontally. Applied moldings, mitered in corners, nailed to the outside edges. No structural frame, no pediment or skirt.

Surface notes: Details in the images were thinly and delicately painted, with gold leaf used to highlight such details as buttons, epaulets, the tray beneath the decanter. Unfortunately, the application of varnish dulled the metal. The letters were laid out with stencils and less expertly executed than the images. The ground is grayish-white. The smalt on this sign is the largest and most three-dimensional found on any sign in the collection, measuring roughly 1/16" to 1/8" in diameter.

Condition and treatment notes: Hanging hardware appears to be original. Varnish had yellowed, pooled, and dulled the metal leaf. Otherwise, the sign is remarkably well preserved, owing in large part to limited outdoor exposure. Treatment at WACC in 1998–99 consisted of surface cleaning and a light application of matte varnish, except over the gold leaf.

Related objects: Watercolor rendering, by John Matulis, ca. 1940, *Index of American Design,* National Gallery of Art, 1943.8.8054 (side 1); 1943.8.8050 (side 2); published Hornung, pl. 240, p. 77 (side 2); Alice Ford, *Pictorial Folk Art from New England to California* (New York: Studio Publcations, 1949), p. 138; *House and Garden* 1941, p. 20.

Exhibitions: "Three Centuries of Connecticut Folk Art," Art Resources of Connecticut, New Haven, 1979.

Publications: *MBTS,* p. 25; *Art of the State* (Abrams, 1999); Nicholas O. Warner, *Intoxication in Nineteenth-Century American Literature* (Norman: University of Oklahoma Press, 1997), jacket; Ogden Tanner, *Everyday Life in Colonial America* (New York: Reader's Digest, 1993); Patricia M. Tice, *Altered States: Alcohol and Other Drugs in America* (Rochester, New York: The Strong Museum, 1992), p. 26; Jean Lipman, et al., *Five Star Folk Art: One Hundred American Masterpieces* (New York: Abrams, in association with the Museum of American Folk Art, 1990), p. 84; Shirley Abbot, *The Art of Food* (Birmingham, Alabama: Oxmoore House); Jean Lipman, et al., *Young America: A Folk-Art History* (New York: Hudson Hills, in association with the Museum of American Folk Art, 1986), p. 86 (side 1); Alexandra Grave, *Three Centuries of Connecticut Folk Art* (New Haven: Art Resources of Connecticut, 1979); Lipman and Winchester, *Flowering of American Folk Art,* p. 223. Textbooks, various editions: Hodgins, ed., *Adventures in American Literature*; George Tindall and David Shi, *America: A Narrative History* (Norton).

1. *Middletown Gazette,* 24 April 1823, p. 3, col. 5.
2. The horses are similar in profile to those on the Bradley inn sign, dated 1817, from nearby Guilford, Conn. (Shelburne Museum).
3. For example, Eunice Pinney, *Two Women,* ca. 1815, Windsor, Conn., and numerous double portraits by Joseph H. Davis, such as, *Page and Betsy Batchelder,* 1836, Maine or New Hampshire; both in Lipman and Winchester, *Flowering of American Folk Art,* pp. 43, 47. Easel paintings reminiscent of side 2 are also known, for example, *The Yellow Coach,* artist unknown, ca. 1825, in Nina Fletcher Little, *The Abby Aldrich Rockefeller Folk Art Collection* (Williamsburg, Va.: Colonial Williamsburg, distributed by Little, Brown, Boston, 1957), p. 107. For British caricatures, see *Catalogue of Political and Personal Satires Preserved in the Department of Prints and Drawings in the British Museum,* 11 vols. (London, 1870–1954).
4. "Clinton: West View of Killingworth (Central Part)," in Christopher P. Bickford and J. Bard McNulty, ed., *John Warner Barber's Views of Connecticut Towns, 1834–36* (Hartford: The Acorn Club and The Connecticut Historical Society, 1990), p. 54.

Cat. 34*

Sign for Dyer's Inn, ca. 1823
CANTON, CONNECTICUT

Innholder: Zenas Dyer (active 1823–51)
Signed by William Rice (1777–1847)

Images: On side 1, plow and beehive with bees, centered inside horizontal oval band. On side 2, a small floret, centered inside an oval wreath, inside horizontal oval band.
Text: On side 1, inside top of oval, "HOLD or DRIVE."; inside bottom of oval, "Z. DYER." On side 2, inside top of oval, "STRANGERS HOME."; inside bottom of oval, "Z. DYER." Signature: On both sides, in lower right corner, "Rice".

Paint on pine board, 40-7/8" x 62-1/2"
Collection of Morgan B. Brainard, Gift of Mrs. Morgan B. Brainard, 1961.63.20

Illustrated: color plate 34 (side 1), fig. 81 (side 2)

The phrase "Hold or Drive" on Dyer's sign refers to a well-known moral maxim, urging industriousness and attention to business, popularized in the eighteenth century by Benjamin Franklin's *Poor Richard's Almanac* and widely repeated during the early nineteenth century: "He that by the Plow would thrive, himself must either hold or drive."[1] Both beehive and plow were popular symbols of industry, in the general sense of diligence and earnest effort. Like the U.S. eagle, the beehive and plow motif was available as a standard type ornament, which early nineteenth-century newspapers used frequently to mark notices of agricultural interest. The beehive was also used as a symbol of industry in Masonic iconography, but no evidence has been located thus far to suggest that Dyer's inn had particular Masonic associations. In Dyer's sign, painter William Rice enclosed the central image inside a band of ornamental patterns drawn explicitly from the vocabulary of classical architecture, with alternating triglyphs and acanthus leaves. Side 2 offers, instead of moral instruction, a message of welcome, conveyed by both the legend, inviting "Strangers Home," and the imagery, an eight-petaled central flower enclosed by a simple oval wreath. Both sides display an unusual, mottled green background with a textured surface, created by flocking, a technique usually associated with wallpaper but promoted by Rice as a fancy, special effect on signs.[2]

While the iconography of this sign departs from Rice's more typical lions and eagles, it seems aptly suited to Dyer's particular circumstances. The inn occupied a crossroads in Canton, a rural village about fifteen miles, or half a day's journey, northwest from Hartford along the main road to Albany (now Route 44). The beehive and plow presumably aimed at local customers, the neighboring farmers and tradesmen who might attend the annual agricultural fair, which Dyer hosted every other year, featuring displays of cattle and other stock for "those desirous of exchanging, buying, or selling the different kinds of animals" (the alternating site was Abraham Hosford's inn).[3] The floral motif on side 2, in contrast, might have been aimed at traveling customers, genteel "city folk" who might be enticed to stop for their mid-day meal.

Inn name: Contemporary newspaper notices designate the inn by the proprietor's name, occasionally as "at the house of Capt. Zenas Dyer", but far more commonly, as "at the Inn of Zenas Dyer." No period references have been found using either pictorial motifs or slogans from the sign as part of the inn name.

Innholder: Zenas Dyer (1788–1856) was the son of Daniel and Sarah Northway Dyer. He married, before 1817, Sarah Chidsey (1794–1887). Licenses survive for the years 1821–43 and 1846–51. Upon Zenas Dyer's death, his widow inherited the property, but there is no evidence that she continued innkeeping. According to the 1860 census, son Daniel had taken up residence in the old homestead, with his mother listed as a domestic residing at a nearby house, a poignant suggestion of declining circumstances.

Original location: The Dyer inn occupied a rise overlooking the Farmington River Valley, along the heavily traveled Albany-Hartford Turnpike (now Route 44). The dwelling still stands on Dyer Cemetery Road, a small side road parallel to Route 44, just east of Route 179 (the widening and straightening of Route 44 moved the main road away from the old inn). The house remained in the possession of the family until at least 1956, when it displayed a sign, "Margaret's Salteds," announcing Margaret Dyer's thriving business in fudge and salted nuts.

Construction notes: Two boards, grain oriented horizontally. Set within the channels of plain board moldings, mitered at corners, and nailed to the edges with a quarter round molding nailed on the inside edges. No structural frame, no pediment or skirt.

Surface notes: Surfaces show evidence of weathering and extensive repainting, evidently following the weathered outlines and color scheme of earlier versions. The plow, beehive, and most of the bees are raised above the surrounding background, probably as a result of weathering. The ovals were laid out with the aid of a mechanical device; centering holes are visible on side 2. The design is painted in two shades of green and an ocher brown, on a green background; lettering is currently bronze paint with glossy black outlines. The flocked surface, made by adding dry pigment to a mordant layer, has not survived well, tending to wash away under outdoor conditions.

Condition and treatment notes: Original hanging hardware is missing. Original moldings are missing and had been replaced at an unknown date. Modern dowels reinforce the glue joint that holds together the two boards of the sign plane. Treatment at CHS, by WACC staff, in 2000, consisted of surface cleaning.

Related signs: Sign for the Griswold inn, Torrington, Conn. (Torrington Historical Society).

Publications; *MBTS*, p. 35.

1. *Poor Richard's Almanack*, December 1747, quoted in *Poor Richard: The Almanacks for the Years 1733–1758* (New York: Heritage Press, 1964), p. 142.
2. Flocking appears on at least two other surviving Rice signs, the Vernon Hotel sign (cat. 46) and the Griswold inn sign, Torrington, Conn. (Torrington Historical Society). The Griswold sign also displays similar triglyph and acanthus banding and very similar lettering, evidently gilded, with thin, black outlines. On Rice's use of flocking, see Webber, "Faithfully and Promptly Executed," Chapter Six.
3. *Courant*, 29 September 1834, p. 3, col. 3

Cat. 35

Sign for Baker's Inn, ca. 1820–38
MONTVILLE, CONNECTICUT

Innholder: Caleb Baker (active 1820–38)
Maker unidentified

Images: None
Text: On both sides, "ENTERTAI / MENT / BY/ C. BAKER.".
No underlying text.

Paint on pine board, ash or chestnut posts, 29-1/2" x 22-1/2"
Collection of Morgan B. Brainard, Gift of Mrs. Morgan B. Brainard, 1961.63.5

Illustrated: color plate 35

Although conventional in form, Baker's inn sign is almost modernist in its stark dependence upon abstract geometrical forms, reduction of color to creamy white lettering on a dark green background, and random division of a word to fit into a vertical format. The unrelieved cylindrical shape of the turned posts is strikingly simple, in contrast to the usual fashioning of posts into balusters, with ornamental turned rings and/or reels in seemingly endless variety. Although simpler objects often represent less effort on the part of the maker, this sign gives evidence of good workmanship in both construction and design. The signboard attaches to the top and bottom rails with three tenons—in the center and at each edge—set into open mortises. Little splitting of the signboard has occurred because the mortises are wide enough to absorb most of the expansion and contraction caused by humidity changes. In contrast to some other simple signs, the lettering has been measured and arranged carefully. Faint lines scribed into the wood mark the tops and bottoms of the letters as well as the spacing between them.

Inn name: Designated in period sources by proprietor's name, "at the Inn of Mr. Caleb Baker," or, more commonly, "at the house of Caleb Baker."

Innholder: Caleb Baker (1773–1848) was the son of Joshua and Abigail Bliss Baker. Atypically for an innkeeper, Caleb Baker was unmarried.

Original location: Located in New London County, in southeastern Connecticut, probably on one of the roads between New London and Colchester. The relative frequency of contemporary notices suggests that Baker's inn was not as well-frequented as the other Montville inn, Houghton's, which was located a mile north of Uncasville and prospered as the half-way stop between New London and Norwich.

Construction notes: Single board, grain oriented vertically, with single, square rails and turned, columnar posts. A one-inch wide strip has been nailed to one vertical edge of the board, evidently to widen it. Board is joined to each rail with three through tenons set into open mortises. Rails have single, shouldered tenons mortised through posts, wedged and single pinned. No pediment or skirt.

Surface notes: The lettering displays a rust-colored staining, evidently a chemical reaction and possibly related to a salt air environment.

Condition notes: Original hanging hardware is missing; an imprint in the wood indicates that it was affixed by a metal plate screwed into the top of the top rail. One top rail tenon sheared off and has been replaced. Side 2 is more heavily weathered.

Publications: *MBTS*, p. 18.

Cat. 36

Sign for Williams's Inn, dated 1803 and 1826
CENTERBROOK, CONNECTICUT

Innholders: Benjamin Williams (active 1803–22?); Humphrey Williams (active 1826–30)
Maker unidentified

Images: On side 1, exterior scene of stage coach with two horses, off-center in oval outline, over a central rising sun. On side 2, interior scene of one man seated at a table with decanters and drinking glasses (presently illegible but documented photographically in 1900).

Text: On both sides, in pediment, "1826." over "1803"; in name band below image, "H.W." over earlier initials, not decipherable.

Paint on pine board, unidentified hardwood columns, possibly maple, gold leaf, iron hardware, 54-3/4" x 35-1/8"
Collection of Morgan B. Brainard, Gift of Mrs. Morgan B. Brainard, 1961.63.48

Illustrated: color plate 36 (side 1)

In 1900 this sign inspired the cover design of Alice Morse Earle's *Stage-Coach and Tavern Days*. Earle identified it as being from the Williams tavern, located in Centerbrook Village, along the Middlesex Turnpike, which was incorporated in 1802 and opened in 1804.[1] Benjamin Williams, Jr., obtained a tavern license in 1803, the earlier of two dates painted on the pediment. The sign at this time featured a single emblem of the rising sun, probably gilded, centered against a blue-green-gray background. Two decades later, when Benjamin Williams's son, Humphrey Williams, took over as innkeeper, changes in sign styles as well as changing patterns of travel occasioned the replacement of sign imagery as well as updating the name band and date. Covering over the old rising sun, Humphrey Williams ordered new, up-to-date images—an exterior view of a stagecoach on side 1 and an interior view of a man at table on side 2. While the combination recalls the Carter inn sign, ca. 1823, about ten miles away, in Clinton (cat. 33), differences are notable in both content and execution. The carriage on the Williams sign depicts a stagecoach loaded with at least five passengers and driver—clearly a public conveyance—whereas the Carter sign depicts a private vehicle. Similar depictions of stagecoaches appeared on the Cady Hotel sign and other examples dating to the 1820s (cat. 29), suggesting the extent to which enterprising innkeepers sought to attract stage passengers, as stage lines increasingly replaced earlier reliance upon water travel. Between 1818–25, the construction or consolidation of several roads connected Centerbrook directly with Guilford to the west, Lyme to the east, and Norwich to the northeast, substantially increasing the traffic passing by or near the Williams door.[2]

The off-center placement of the imagery on both sides of the Williams sign strongly suggests that the painter was used to working in an entirely different format—other stagecoach images of the 1820s are almost always found on horizontal, oval signboards. Faced with redecorating the generation-old Williams sign, the painter adapted currently popular motifs. He painted fashionable oval outlines to frame the images, but oriented them vertically to fill the maximum space on the vertically-oriented signboard. Rather than reduce the size of the coaching motif to fit the width of the signboard, he evidently made do with an existing template or pattern, which extended off the edge of the board. The resulting composition decapitated the two horses and completely eliminated the second pair (a four-horse team would have been needed to pull this loaded coach). The result is curiously appealing: the off-center positioning and cropped image creates a sense of motion, and the oval outline functions as a kind of portal, through which the viewer sees the coach driving past. According to an early illustration of side 2, it also appears to have been cropped from a larger composition, in which the lone man seated on one side of a table would have been balanced by a companion (as in the Carter sign), thus accounting for the large number of drinking vessels depicted.[3] The paint scheme originally used red extensively as an accent, on the finials, drops, and the shading of the gold leaf letters. The fluting in the columns is a further refinement, rarely seen on signs.

Innholders: Benjamin Williams, Jr. (1752–1822) was the son of Benjamin Williams, Sr., and Libbie Dickinson Williams of Centerbrook. He married Patience Pratt (1753–1820). In addition to his innkeeping, he carried on blacksmithing and operated a saw and gristmill. Inn licenses survive for the years 1803–07.

Humphrey Williams (1793–1870) was the son of Benjamin Williams, Jr., and Patience Pratt Williams of Centerbrook. He married Roxanna Bushnell (b. 1795). According to local history, Humphrey Williams kept the family tavern only a few years, after which he concentrated on farming and milling.

Original location: Located in Centerbrook center, along the Middlesex turnpike, which ran from Hartford to Saybrook, and about a mile and one-half west of the Connecticut River landings.

Provenance: Owned by George F. Ives, Danbury, Conn., in 1900.

Construction notes: Two boards, grain oriented vertically. Thin, bull-nosed, horizontal rails, and fluted, columnar posts. The two boards are joined with four dowels, which appear to be original. The frame is ornamental rather than structural, and is unusual in that it is not tenoned together. Instead, the posts pass through square holes in the rails, which are held in place by nails. Pediment is a separate board, grain oriented horizontally, hand-sawn to create decorative profile and nailed to top rail. Applied moldings, mitered at corners, are nailed to both faces of board. Thin bullnose strips are nailed to side edges of board.

Surface notes: The ground of the upper paint layer is gray-white. The dotted oval outlines continue onto edges of adjacent moldings. The underlying layer of paint on the pediment featured an elaborate foliage design, now painted over.

Condition and treatment notes: Two large holes under the bottom rail indicate that the sign once had a skirt board, balancing the pediment board. Nail or screw holes around the perimeter of the pediment and name band suggest that date and name plaque(s) were affixed there by subsequent owner(s). Paint surfaces were blistered and bubbled, possibly due to exposure to excess heat or chemicals; areas of paint loss are curiously free of weathering, which may suggest that paint loss occurred after sign was removed from exterior use. Large section of bullnose edge of lower rail is missing. Treatment at WACC, 1998–99, included surface cleaning and consolidation, stabilizing joinery, and replacing missing end of top rail.

Exhibitions: Aetna 1939 (side 1).

Publications: *MBTS*, p. 66; Earle, *Tavern Days*, p. 396 (side 2), p. 400 (side 1).

1. Earle, *Tavern Days*, pp. 152–53, 396, 400; Wood, *Turnpikes,* pp. 368–69.
2. Wood, *Turnpikes*, pp. 389, 391–92; Crofut, *Guide*, vol. 2, p. 482.
3. Earle, *Tavern Days*, p. 396.

Cat. 37*

Sign for Arah Phelps's Inn, ca. 1826

NORTH COLEBROOK, CONNECTICUT

Innholder: Arah Phelps (active 1798–99, 1826–39)
Signed by William Rice (1777–1847)

Images: On side 1, lion, with body in profile, head facing forward, no chains. On side 2, eagle, in profile, poised for flight. No underlying imagery.
Text: On both sides, below image, "A.Phelps' Inn." No underlying text.
Signature: On both sides, in lower right, above name band, "Rice."

Paint on pine board and moldings, iron hardware, 30-3/4" x 44-1/4"
Gift of Nancy Phelps (Mrs. John A.) Blum, Jonathan Phelps Blum, and Timothy Alexander Blum, 1977.105.0

Illustrated: front cover and color plate 37 (side 1), fig. 28 (side 2)

Captain Arah Phelps exemplified key traits found among Connecticut innkeepers during the early national era—activity in the militia, the Masonic fraternity, and local and state politics.[1] After serving in the Continental Army during the Revolution, Phelps moved to the new town of Colebrook (incorporated in 1779), in northwestern Connecticut, where his grandfather had long owned property. He built a dam and sawmill on Sandy Brook, as well as a dwelling-house nearby; upon his grandfather's death in 1791, he inherited 630 acres in joint tenancy with two cousins. He subsequently served in a variety of local offices, including surveyor of highways, committee for roads and bridges, constable, selectman, as well as representative to the state assembly and the state constitutional convention of 1818. He became captain of the militia in 1793 and a charter member of Western Star Lodge No. 37, Norfolk, in 1796. Although Phelps is documented as a tavernkeeper in 1798–99, no further evidence of innkeeping appears until 1826, when he was granted the first of many annual tavern licenses. It is possible that he leased the inn to other operators during the intervening period (Daniel Phelps and Enos North are listed as licenseholders). His resumption of personal oversight may have been related to the opening of the Sandy Brook Turnpike in 1825, presumably increasing traffic through North Colebrook.[2]

The physical features of this handsome sign are consistent with a production date of 1826, displaying such typical Rice characteristics as the distinctive coped moldings (see fig. 18) and the lion and eagle imagery. The delineation of the lion—with body in profile and head turned directly toward viewer—closely resembles several surviving Rice signs (see related signs, cat. 31). In contrast to the wild-eyed ferocity of Rice's other lions, however, this lion has soft, almost languid eyes, while its posture and tail seem playful rather than threatening. While Rice's lion recalls lions painted by Edward Hicks, a Quaker preacher and ornamental painter working primarily in Pennsylvania, no connection between Hicks and Rice has yet been documented. A more likely explanation is that both drew on widely disseminated print versions of similar lion imagery—in books, prints, news-papers, and on broadsides, including those posted in taverns, advertising the "curiosities," namely exotic animals, offered by itinerant entertainers and traveling circuses. In contrast to the rather wistful air of Phelps's lion, the eagle on side 2 is large and particularly ferocious, its great, powerful talons and tensed, poised-for-flight pose suggesting a natural history source, rather than the formal heraldic model, based on the Great Seal, used in all other Rice eagles presently known.[3]

The juxtaposition of lion and eagle on numerous Rice signs has traditionally been interpreted as political allegory, with the strong, independent American eagle triumphant over the docile, often chained, British lion. How obvious or important were these political references to tavernkeepers and their customers? Symbols of the new nation and inherent pride and patriotism abound in sign paintings; in some cases, the meaning seems almost impossible to miss, as in a sign from an unidentified inn, ca. 1800, depicting, a (French) cock, or rooster, crowing "Liberty" as it stands upon a prostrate (British) lion.[4] In the case of the Phelps sign, political symbolism seems considerably diminished by the lion's lack of chains and the conspicuous absence of the seal and other heraldic emblems usually held by the eagle.

Inn name: Period newspaper notices refer to the inn by the proprietor's name, "at the house of Capt. Arah Phelps, Inn-keeper."

Innholder: Capt. Arah Phelps (1761–1844) was the son of Josiah Phelps III of Harwinton, Conn. He was raised by his grandfather, Josiah Phelps II, in the family homestead in Windsor. In 1792 he married Wealthan Mills, daughter of Samuel Mills, his nearest neighbor in North Colebrook.

Original location: The Phelps house still stands at its original site in the village of North Colebrook, on the east side of Route 183, leading to Colebrook center, about two miles south. The Phelps inn was reportedly the meeting point for stages operating between Hartford-Albany and New Haven-Albany, with four stages stopping daily for dining, changing horses, and exchanging passengers.

Provenance: Descended in the Phelps family to the donors.

Construction notes: Single board, grain oriented horizontally, set within channels in moldings applied to outside edges. The ends of the top and bottom moldings are cut to the shape of the inside contour of the side moldings, so that the side moldings can slide over the ends as the large signboard expands and contracts across the grain with changes in humidity (see fig. 18 for detail of this characteristic feature, on another Rice sign). No structural frame, no pediment or skirt.

Surface notes: Both eagle and lion images are raised above the gray background surface, probably as a result of weathering. There is no evidence of repainting. Scribe lines are visible outlining the lion and separating the name band from the image. The yellow lettering is skillfully executed, apparently freehand.

Condition and treatment notes: Hanging hardware is original. Cove molding at lower right of side 1 is reattached or replaced. Treatment at WACC, 1999–2000, included surface cleaning and minor strengthening of structural elements.

Related signs: See cat. 31, related signs.

Related objects: Watercolor rendering (both sides), by Martin Partyka, ca. 1940, *Index of American Design*, National Gallery of Art,

1943.8.8033 (side 1), 1943.8.17125 (side 2); published Hornung, pl. 230, p. 74; Christensen, no. 122, p. 65.

Publications: Nancy Phelps Blum, *One Old House: Its People and Its Place* (Colebrook, Conn.: Colebrook Historical Society, 1997)*; Connecticut League of Historical Societies Bulletin* 9 (Winter 1956–57), cover.

1. Biographical information drawn largely from Nancy Phelps Blum, *One Old House: Its People and Its Place* (Colebrook, Conn.: Colebrook Historical Society, 1997).
2. Wood, *Turnpikes*, p. 394.
3. Peter Benes, "Itinerant Entertainers in New England and New York, 1687–1830," and Richard W. Flint, "Entrepreneurial and Cultural Aspects of the Early-Nineteenth-Century Circus and Menagerie Business," both in *Itinerancy in New England and New York*, ed. Peter Benes (Boston: Published for the Dublin Seminar for New England Folklife by Boston University, 1986), pp. 114–15, 132–35, 145, 149; *Great River*, pp.173–74. Such popular publications as *The New-England Primer*, in which "L is for lion," also illustrated docile lions. For further discussion of print sources, see Finlay, "Lions and Eagles," Chapter Five.
4. Metropolitan Museum of Art, in Smith, *Tavern Signs*, pp. 25–26.

Cat. 38

Sign for Wedgwood's Inn, dated 1827 and 1836

LOCATION UNDETERMINED, POSSIBLY PORTSMOUTH, NEW HAMPSHIRE

Innholders: J. Thomas and J. Wedgwood
Maker unidentified

Images: On side 1, meeting house with steeple, flanked by small trees, over a (possibly incomplete) landscape with at least one tree. On side 2, landscape scene with large tree on left, overhanging house on right, over a fully-rigged ship flying an American flag. Text: On both sides, on top rail, "1836" over "1827"; on bottom rail, "J. WEDGWOOD" over "J. Thomas".

Paint on pine board and frame, iron hardware, 50-3/4" x 29-1/4" Collection of Morgan B. Brainard, Gift of Mrs. Morgan B. Brainard, 1961.63.50

Illustrated: color plate 38

The origins of this unusual sign remain ambiguous. No Connecticut innkeeper named Wedgwood has been identified, but the name is common in the vicinity of Portsmouth, New Hampshire. Both sides display at least two layers of imagery, which are badly worn and thus difficult to disentangle. The upper layer on side 1 depicts a meeting house with primary entrance through the bell tower, topped by a codfish weather vane (a decorative feature usually associated with coastal areas from Boston north to Maine), and ornamented with green-louvered Gothic arches over the three large windows as well as neo-classical tracery under the eaves of the roof. The building originally was painted white. However, the white paint has been worn away, uncovering the blue of the sky, which was painted onto the entire top section of the board prior to adding the meeting house. A large tree appears to underlie the meeting house. Side 2 shows the faint image of a three-masted merchant ship flying the American flag, visible through a dominant and later landscape of a house and large tree. The earlier image layer on both sides contained a two-inch wide margin marked by a painted line with quarter-round insets in the corners, a common decorative technique in federal, or neo-classical, furniture and architecture.

Innholders: The earlier name of Thomas is too common throughout New England to suggest a geographic origin.

Construction notes: Single board, grain oriented vertically. Thick, flat, horizontal rails with pediment and skirt extensions, square posts with integral turned ends. The board is set into grooves in the rails and posts. Decorative moldings are run on the inner edge of the rails and applied molding strips are nailed to the inside edges of the posts on both sides of the sign. The massive, two-inch-thick rails are tenoned through the posts and pinned. The top joints are single-tenoned and the bottom joints are double-tenoned. The top rail extends upward slightly into a central projection supporting a finial. The broad lower rail extends down and is sawn to form two rounded lobes.

Surface notes: This sign displays extensive paint loss. Scribe lines can be seen for the underlying name, which is evenly spaced. The upper date, 1836, is painted free-hand in gold. The upper name is painted black, against a cream background; letters are uneven in spacing and poorly executed. Posts and upper rail are black. The leaves and branches of the trees flanking the meeting house on side 1 appear to have been created by daubing with sponges or similar applicators.

Condition and treatment notes: Hanging hardware appears to be original. Both turned drops are missing from the bottoms of posts. The center finial and one side finial had been replaced at an unknown date; the other side finial was missing. One vertical molding strip is missing from side 1. Prior to treatment at WACC, 1998–99, both posts exhibited severe rotting and shattered joints. Treatment included consolidation of decayed wood and insertion of replacement parts as necessary to stabilize joined frame, replacement of missing finial, and surface cleaning and consolidation.

Exhibitions: Aetna 1939 (side 1).

Publications: *MBTS*, p. 68; Terry, *Old Inns*, p. 242.

Cat. 39

Sign for Hayes's Inn, dated 1828
GRANBY, CONNECTICUT

Innholder: Obadiah Hayes, Jr. (licensed 1828–42)
Maker unidentified

Images: On side 1, eagle's head and upper body atop outline of globe, centered on oval board with serrated border; on top rail, a leafy sprig. On side 2, eight-petaled floret, centered on oval board with plain band border.
Text: On side 1, on bottom rail, "HAYES' INN". On side 2, on top rail, "1828"; on bottom rail, "O. HAYES."

Paint on pine board, maple or birch rails and stiles, probably ash banding wrapped around board, unidentified hardwood moldings on frame, gold leaf, iron hardware, 28-1/8" x 33-1/4"
Collection of Morgan B. Brainard, Gift of Mrs. Morgan B. Brainard, 1961.63.30

Illustrated: color plate 39 (side 2); fig. 40 (side 1)

Unlike most signs known from the 1820s or 1830s in northern Litchfield and Hartford Counties, the Hayes inn sign was not painted by William Rice. This distinction is even more notable given the fact that its owner, Obadiah Hayes, Jr., was a second-generation innkeeper, matching the profile of the typical Rice patron.[1] Several features of the Hayes sign represent distinct alternatives to contemporary Rice productions, especially the overall configuration of horizontal, oval board set in a joined, rectangular frame and the motif of an eagle atop a globe. (Rice typically worked on boards encased in moldings, rather than joined frames, and painted full eagles, with or without national or state insignia). Despite these differences, similarities between Hayes's eight-petaled floret and that on Dyer's inn sign, ca. 1823, from nearby Canton, suggest the possibility that Rice's work may have influenced the unidentified painter of Hayes's sign.

Inn name: Period newspaper notices refer to the inn by the name of the proprietor, "at the Tavern kept by Mr. Obadiah Hayes."

Innholders: Obadiah Hayes, Jr. (1781–1844) was the oldest son of Obadiah Hayes, Sr. (1754–1817) and Ahinoam Holcomb Hayes (1779–1844). He married Catherine Selden (ca. 1797–1883) of West Hartford, Conn. Obadiah Hayes, Sr., was licensed as innkeeper at the same location as his son, from 1803–06 and 1809–16. Obadiah Hayes, Jr., did not evidently take up tavernkeeping for some years after his father's death, as his first license was not issued until 1828, the date painted on the sign.

Original location: The Hayes homestead remains on its original site, opposite the North Granby cemetery.

Construction notes: Single oval board, grain oriented horizontally, sawn into oval shape. Flat, horizontal rails and flat, rectangular stiles. Oval board is wrapped in an ash or hickory band, curved to shape and nailed to board. Large spikes, set in place before the sign was assembled, hold the oval board to the frame at the center of top, bottom, and both sides. Rails are joined to stiles with single through-tenons and double-pinned. Bullnosed strap moldings are nailed to the top and bottom edges of each rail. No pediment or skirt.

Surface notes: Paint colors are primarily black and gold, with detailing in red, yellow, and blue (side 2 only). All design elements have gold leaf. Background is a thin black wash. Stars, numbers, and possibly letters are stenciled. A compass or dividers was used for centering the image. On side 1, letters are unevenly spaced and are outlined in yellow paint on top of gilding.

Condition notes: Hanging hardware appears original. Surface has darkened.

Publications: *MBTS*, p. 46.

1. Vincent, "Some suitable Signe," Chapter Four.

Cat. 40*

Sign for Gordon's Inn, ca. 1790–1830
LOCATION UNDETERMINED

Innholder and maker unidentified

Images: On side 1, a standing male figure, with punch bowl, wine glass, and ladle. On side 2, a standing male figure with plate of oysters, knife, and fork.

Text: On side 1, interspersed with punch bowl image, "Gentlemen you are / welcome sit down / at your ease, / Pay what you call for / & drink what you / please"; in black band below image, "WIL^M. GORDON" over "WIL^M. SPALDING". On side 2, interspersed with oyster plate image, "Here I stand / in wind & rain / True blue will never / stain"; in black band below image, " WIL^M. GORDON".

Paint on yellow pine board and moldings; 29" x 24-5/8"
Collection of Morgan B. Brainard, Gift of Mrs. Morgan B. Brainard, 1961.63.24

Illustrated: color plate 40 (side 1), fig. 23 (side 2)

This visually appealing sign presents several puzzles. Its long, rhyming verses have few, if any, parallel among American inn signs. In the Connecticut Historical Society collection, only the sign for Rose's inn, 1813, with its bird-in-hand motto awkwardly lettered below the narrative picture, approaches this sign in concept (cat. 23). The visual humor implicit in the little man stirring the large punch bowl is also unusual. The abbreviation of William as "WIL^M.", and particularly the small superscript "M" over a period are typically English usages; on Connecticut signs, the expected form would be simply a "W" for William.

Identification of owners and geographic origin remains unconfirmed, although the Gordon sign has traditionally been said to come from the area of New London, Connecticut. Although a "William Gorton" has been documented in Waterford, Connecticut, in 1827, no evidence has been found indicating that he was an innkeeper.[1] Moreover, the only William Spalding identified as innkeeper in Connecticut appears near Hartford in the 1830s, too late to have his name painted under Gordon's.

Construction notes: Two boards, grain oriented vertically, joined with tongue-and-groove joint. Encased within moldings, mitered at corners, that are nailed to the edges of board. No structural frame, no pediment or skirt. Wood used on the central panel is from the southern yellow pine group; identified by analysis (Hoadley, March 2000).

Surface notes: Side 2 retains its original surface, with severe paint loss making the rhyme almost indecipherable. Side 1 was substantially repainted, with rather bright colors, probably in the twentieth century, evidently following the outlines of the existing design. On side 1, the white paint comprising Wilm. Gordon's name, together with the associated black background layer, is extremely soluble, suggesting application much later than the underlying layer; however, the name Wilm. Gordon also appears on side 2, where it is not repainted, and is as heavily weathered as the image. Scribe lines are visible on both sides as guides for lettering. The rhymes are lettered in black, against a white ground.

Condition and treatment notes: Hanging hardware appears to be original. Treatment at WACC, 1999, included surface cleaning, removal of soluble overpaint from image on side 1, slight strengthening of letters on side 2 with watercolor, and structural consolidation.

Related objects: Watercolor rendering, by John Matulis, ca. 1940, *Index of American Design*, National Gallery of Art, Washington, D.C., 1943.8.8112.

Exhibitions: "Altered States: Alcohol and Drugs in American Society," The Strong Museum, Rochester, New York, 1996 (photoreproduction).

Publications: *MBTS*, p.39; Smith, *Tavern Signs*, p. 12; *We Americans* (Washington, D.C.: National Geographic Society [NGS], 1999); *Exploring America's Historic Places* (Washington, D.C.: NGS, 1999); *The World Book of America's Heritage* (Chicago: World Book, 1991); *The Country Traveler: Exploring the Past at America's Outdoor Museums* (New York: Time-Life, 1990), p. 28; National Geographic Society, *America's History Lands: Touring Our Landmarks of Liberty* (Washington, D.C.: NGS, 1962); *American Heritage* 1960, p. 60. Textbooks, various editions: *A More Perfect Union* (Houghton Mifflin); John A. Garraty, *The American Nation: A History of the United States to 1877* (Harper & Row); *Elements of Literature* (Holt, Rinehart & Winston); Hodgins, et al., *Adventures in American Literature*; Mary Beth Norton, *A People and a Nation* (Houghton Mifflin).

1. *New London Gazette*, 20 June 1827, p. 3, col. 4.

Cat. 41* *Exhibited only in Hartford*

Sign for Stiles's Inn and the Thompson Hotel, dated 1831, repainted ca. 1902
THOMPSON, CONNECTICUT

Innholders: Vernon Stiles (active 1831–49), Cornelius V. Chapin (active 1888–1904+)
Maker unidentified

Images: On both sides, landscape scene, with pair of white horses in center foreground, drawing open carriage with driver and male passenger, who stands, doffing his hat. Background depicts town scene with various dwellings and church.

Text: On both sides, on pediment, in drapery swag, "THOMPSON HOTEL"; below image, "VERNON STILES"; on skirt, "1831".

Paint on pine board and moldings, iron hardware, 44" x 66"
1998.5.0

Illustrated: color plate 41, fig. 3 (detail, side 1), fig. 65 (during conservation)

This sign is unusual in its intentional display of the names of two distinct establishments. All evidence indicates that this atypical feature resulted from Colonial Revival reuse of an early nineteenth century sign. The sign belonged first to Vernon Stiles, whose name appears prominently below the central image; Stiles purchased an existing tavern stand in 1831 and operated it for the next two decades. The Thompson Hotel, named in a drapery swag on the top border of the sign, did not open until about 1902, when it first appeared in local directories. It seems likely that the proprietor of the Thompson Hotel found the early sign, had the new name added but preserved the old name and image as relics of by-gone days, no doubt enhancing the appeal and authenticity of his country inn. Although multiple names are often visible today as accidents of time and exposure, the standard practice for reuse—documented by many examples—was for the names of new owners to replace the old, typically by application of a covering paint layer. The use of a secondary phrase complementing the innkeeper's name has many precedents, however, beginning with the frequent use of the word "Entertainment" on eighteenth-century signs. In the early 1820s, the Carter and Dyer inn signs incorporated the phrases, "Strangers Resort" or "Strangers Home," respectively, to convey a fuller impression of the establishment (cat. 33, 34). Innkeeper G. F. Bailey's addition of the word "Hotel" to his name was also probably an effort to upgrade the impression created (cat. 52).

Severe cracking and detachment of the painted surface from the wood substrate of this sign complicate deductions about the history of use. Lettering styles differ between the Thompson and Stiles name banners, as well as from one side to the other. An earlier pattern of painted scrollwork is barely visible under the present ornamentation of the sign border. This evidence combines to suggest that new borders were painted over the old when the Thompson Hotel name was added to the sign, presumably about 1902. Sometime later, both names had worn sufficiently on one side to require repainting. The central carriage scene may also have been reinforced, but it appears generally faithful to the original design. The coaching scene recalls the elegant calash pictured in Carter's "Strangers Resort" sign, intended to appeal to a wealthier sort of traveler (cat. 33). The execution of the scene is much less polished here than on Carter's sign, although some of the most glaring anomalies—the skewed carriage wheels and incorrect number of horses' legs—may have been introduced in repainting. The figure in the carriage has long been identified as the Marquis de Lafayette.[1]

The sign is unusual in being made of large boards joined at their edges and cut to a decorative shape. Hanging straps running the full height of the sign help hold the boards together. Somewhat similar construction appears in the Harrington sign, ca. 1833, with long bolts shot through the boards to secure them, and without the rectangular image field created here by the applied molding strips (cat. 43).

Interestingly, the sign makes no apparent reference to the popularity of the Stiles inn as a wedding destination. As the northeasternmost town in the state of Connecticut, Thompson offered easy access to couples in Massachusetts and Rhode Island, where state laws required a waiting period between the announcement of wedding banns and the actual ceremony. In Connecticut, couples could announce their intentions in the morning and wed that afternoon, a situation that, according to early local historians, made Thompson the "Gretna Green of New England."[2]

Inn name: Period sources of the 1830s designate the inn by the proprietor's name, "at Mr. Stiles' Inn."

Innholder: In 1831 Vernon Stiles, of Millbury, Worcester County, Mass., purchased the "tavern stand" formerly operated by the late Luther Bartlett, who had been an innkeeper in Thompson, 1828–30.

Leaving Thompson about 1850, Stiles reportedly emigrated to Racine, Wisc., where he died in 1863.

Original location: The Vernon Stiles Inn and Thompson Hotel remains standing, and in business as an inn, on its original site, at the intersection of the Boston-Hartford and Providence-Springfield turnpikes (now Routes 193 and 200).

Provenance: Ex. coll. The Vernon Stiles Inn Restaurant, Thompson, Conn. Acquired at auction, Skinner's, Bolton, Mass., January 1998.

Construction notes: Two one-inch thick boards, joined at the edges with four floating tenons, cut to create decorative profiles on all four edges. Molding strips, mitered at corners, are applied to each face to define a rectangular picture field, several inches inside the perimeter of the sign. No structural frame.

Surface notes: The entire board was evidently repainted at least once and perhaps twice. Analysis of a paint sample taken from the horses indicates that there are three white layers, typically used as a ground. The original background may have been greener and lighter in tone than the present black. Design elements are painted primarily in yellow, and letters are shaded in red on side 2. The central carriage scene, the Vernon Stiles name band, and the date appear to have been repainted over the same design elements, suggesting that these are part of the original decorative scheme. Overlay drawings made of both sides indicate the use of a template in laying out horses, carriage, and figures, although minor variations have been introduced through misalignment of the template and/or differences in the application of repaint layers. Repainting on side 1 appears to have followed underlying design elements more closely. Repainting on side 2, executed prior to 1926, altered the images slightly, moving the coach driver's head higher than its original position, giving him a top hat, for which there appears to be no earlier model, adding detail to the passenger's face and changing the position of his arm, and altering the window pattern of the inn in the background.[3] The ornament presently painted in the border outside the moldings seems to overlie an earlier foliated scrollwork of quite different design.

Condition and treatment notes: Hanging hardware is original. Curved lobes have split off both corners at one end. The upper corner at the opposite end had cracked through and had been awkwardly reattached. One vertical molding on side 2 was replaced. Paint was extremely desiccated and embrittled, with severe traction crackle, curling, and extensive flaking. Deterioration was more severe on side 1, which emitted an acrid odor, reminiscent of fire damage. Treatment at WACC, 1998–99, included structural consolidation, surface cleaning, and consolidation of paint.

Related signs: Sign for Bradley's Inn, dated 1817, Guilford, Connecticut (Shelburne Museum).

Publications: Smith, *Tavern Signs*, p. 47. The Stiles Inn and Thompson Hotel sign appears in situ, hanging from the corner of the inn, in Lathrop, *Early American Inns*, p. 101; Terry, *Old Inns*, p. 211 (side 2).

1. A vehicle identified as Lafayette's carriage does resemble the vehicle shown on the sign, especially in its scrolled ironwork detailing; Stephen Jenkins, *The Old Boston Post Road* (New York: Putnam, 1913), opp. p. 25.
2. Ellen D. Larned, *History of Windham County, Connecticut*, 2 vols. (Worcester, Mass: By the Author, 1874–80), 2:536. Gretna Green was a Scottish border village to which English couples traditionally eloped.
3. In 1926 this sign was described as having the faces unfinished and 'left blank" on one side, suggesting that the repainting on side 2 had been in place sufficient time to be no longer conspicuous as new work; Chapin, p. 25.

Cat. 42*

Sign for the Collins Hotel, ca. 1825–35

STRAITSVILLE, CONNECTICUT (SECTION OF NAUGATUCK)

Innholders: Ahira Collins (licensed 1811–33 and 1840), Ahira Collins & Son (licensed 1834–35), Sheldon Collins (licensed 1837–38)
Maker unidentified

Images: None.
Text: On both sides, top line, "COLLINS' " over "COLLINS", middle line, "1811," bottom line, "HOTEL." over "HOTEL".

Paint on pine board and moldings, smalt, gold leaf, iron hardware, 37-1/4" x 70-1/2"
Gift of Newton C. Brainard, 1957.66.1

Illustrated: color plate 42 (side 1), fig. 73 (side 2, with overlay)

The 1811 date boldly centered in this sign records the year of the inn's founding rather than the year in which the sign was made. The Collins Hotel, located about fourteen miles north of New Haven, along the road to Litchfield and Albany, was operated continuously by the Collins family from 1811 until the 1850s, when the railroad drew traffic elsewhere. Sign shape and construction both argue strongly against this sign having been made as early as 1811. Its overall proportions (about 1 to 1.9, vertical to horizontal) approximate those of the Carter inn sign, ca. 1823, and the Temperance Hotel sign, probably made in the late 1820s (cat. 33, 54). In contrast, signs of the 1810s and earlier were almost always oriented vertically.[1] The practice of encasing the outer edges of the signboard with large moldings also postdates 1820 on surviving examples. These comparisons suggest a likely production date in the 1820s or later.

Dating is further complicated by the fact that the painted decoration applied at the time of original construction is now obscured by a second layer of paint. On side 2, raised outlines visible under raking light indicate that in the earlier layer, the "COLLINS" name band was straight rather than arched, the word "Hotel" was placed higher on the panel, and there was no date present (fig. 73). Rows of three stars originally decorated the top and bottom margins, and scrolled devices ornamented the corners. These corner scrolls are incorporated into the redecoration on side 2, with the addition of a new, lower volute extending farther into the sign. The upper layer of decoration employs techniques and stylistic conventions of the 1830s and 1840s. The blue background is composed of smalt, a crushed glass that imparts a distinctive color, texture, and sparkle that appears in many signs of these decades. The gold block letters have red shading, a combination that is used as early as the 1826 redecoration of the Williams inn sign (cat. 36), although it is more typical of slightly later work, as are the leafy corner ornaments on side 1. The arched name band recalls similar design schemes on the redecorated Village Hotel sign of the early 1830s and the Hannah Hotel sign of about 1836 (cat. 19, 47). Comparing the physical evidence to the documentary evidence suggests a likely repainting date of about 1834, when the second generation entered into the family business under the title of Ahira

Collins and Son. The addition of the date, "1811," seems a deliberately commemorative gesture, perhaps staking a claim to precedence in the face of competition from newer inns.

Innholders: Ahira Collins (1785–1862), reported to have emigrated to Connecticut from Scotland with three brothers.
Sheldon Collins (b. 1814) was the son of Ahira Collins, of Naugatuck. In 1845 he married Lucy Newton of Albany, New York.

Original location: The Collins Hotel stood in an area known as Straitsville, where the New Haven-Albany road passes through a narrow defile between two rugged cliffs. Ahira Collins bought land and buildings there in 1809, a dozen years after the Straits Turnpike Company had been authorized, in 1797, to run regular stages from New Haven to Litchfield by way of Straitsville. The inn, erected ca. 1800–10, has traditionally been attributed to Waterbury-based architect-builder David Hoadley (1774–1839). It had an imposing, two-story colonnaded front, three front entrances opening into separate rooms, ballroom, tap room, and sitting rooms. In addition to the inn, the Collins family also operated the Straitsville post office and a general store with bowling alley in the basement. According to Lathrop, *Early American Inns*, the Collins inn sign "used to hang across the street suspended from long poles by chains."[2] The coming of the railroad in 1849 drew traffic away from Straitsville, and the inn closed at an undetermined date after 1850. Straitsville was a part of the town of Woodbridge until 1832, at which time it became part of the new town of Bethany. In 1844 it was added to the town of Naugatuck.

Provenance: A photograph published in 1926 depicts this sign in situ at the Collins house, hanging in a protected location under the front portico; however, the text states that the inn sign, bar and racks had been sold and removed from the house.[3]

Construction notes: Two boards, grain oriented horizontally. Boards are joined with four dowels, which appear original. Moldings are nailed to the outer edges and mitered in corners. The moldings are not grooved for the board.

Surface notes: The first decorative scheme was covered over by a thick layer of white lead paint in preparation for repainting. The second decorative scheme replicated the colors of the first, with a smalted background and a yellow size layer applied below the gilding. Some second-layer letters are slightly textured where they pass over smalted areas of the earlier layer. The corner flourishes are executed in yellow paint rather than gold leaf. The gilded letters are extremely bright in low ambient light, making them as visible as in full daylight.

Condition and treatment notes: Hanging hardware is original. Treatment at WACC in 1999 included structural consolidation, particularly of the bottom molding, which had been damaged by an earlier, presently inactive fungal attack, surface cleaning, and paint consolidation.

Related objects: A smaller sign, from the entrance to the Collins Hotel tap room, also survives at The Connecticut Historical Society (1957.66.2).

Exhibitions: Mattatuck Museum, Waterbury, Conn., 1982–98; Naugatuck Historical Society, ca. 1976–82; Deerfield Academy, Deerfield, Mass., ca. 1953–76.

Publications: *MBTS*, p. 30; Lathrop, *Early American Inns*, opp. 48 (in situ).

1. The Lawrence inn sign, ca. 1797 (cat. 11) is a notable exception to the prevailing verticality, but even so, its proportions are a narrower 1 to 2.5.
2. Lathrop, *Early American Inns*, pp. 56–57.
3. Ibid, p. 57, opp. 48.

Cat. 43

Sign for Harrington's Inn, dated 1833
LOCATION UNDETERMINED, NORTHEASTERN
UNITED STATES

Innholder: S. Harrington
Maker unidentified

Images: On both sides, eagle with head down and wings spread, centered on board beneath eleven stars, with four additional stars in volutes at corners of sign. No underlying imagery.
Text: On both sides, below eagle, top line, "S. HARRINGTON.", bottom line, "1833". No underlying text.

Paint on pine board, gold leaf, iron hardware, 35-7/8" x 57-1/8"
Collection of Morgan B. Brainard, Gift of Mrs. Morgan B. Brainard, 1961.63.28

Illustrated: color plate 43

Fabrication of this sign represents a simple, yet elegant construction and design strategy. The large signboard was fabricated from three boards, each 1-1/4" thick, glued edge-to-edge. The built-up board was then cut to an attractive shape with relatively little wastage, leaving an expansive area for the name and accompanying decoration. Long bolts set into holes drilled through all three boards ensured that the sign would hold together even if glue joints failed. Reddish-brown painted highlights added texture and definition to the dramatically posed, gilded eagle. Unlike several other signs of the first half of the nineteenth century, the number of stars in this sign—fifteen—does not correspond to the number of states in the Union at the time of manufacture.

The innholder's identity has not yet been established. There were two S. Harringtons in Connecticut in the 1830s—Simeon in Berlin and Stephen in Woodstock and Thompson—but neither has been documented as holding a tavern license. Numerous S. Harringtons lived in Rhode Island, Massachusetts, and New York in 1833, the probable date of manufacture of the sign. Neither construction nor design features point to any particular locale, especially as printed design sources for both the eagle and the style of lettering were widely distributed.

Construction notes: Three thick boards, with edges sawn to create decorative profiles on all four edges. No moldings, no structural frame, no pediment or skirt.

Surface notes: The background is black. Faint halos of gold deposits are evident, especially around stars. Stencils were used to lay out the letters between scribed guidelines. The numeral "8" may be stenciled upside-down.

Condition notes: Hanging hardware is original. One lower scroll has broken and is reattached with nails.

Exhibitions: Japan 1970.

Publications: *MBTS*, p. 43.

Cat. 44

Sign for Mechanic's Hotel, dated 1834
NEW LONDON, CONNECTICUT

Innholder: Asa Rathbone (active 1834), Carey Leeds (active 1835)
Maker unidentified

Images: None.
Text: On both sides, inside top of oval outline, "MECHANICS", inside bottom of oval outline, "HOTEL", in center of oval outline, "1834". No underlying text.

Paint on pine board and moldings, sand, gold leaf, iron hardware, 35-5/8" x 43-1/4"
Collection of Morgan B. Brainard, Gift of Mrs. Morgan B. Brainard, 1961.63.36

Illustrated: color plate 44

The Mechanics Hotel sign is one of the few in the Connecticut Historical Society collection known to have survived from an urban setting—the central district of the port city of New London. The hotel premises had been in operation as an inn since at least the Revolutionary War era, when it was reportedly one of the few buildings to survive the British burning of New London in 1781. The date 1834 links the sign to proprietor Asa Rathbone who presumably ordered the new sign to announce a new name and marketing strategy, aimed specifically at mechanics, the class of (predominantly urban) craftsmen and skilled laborers who ranked socioeconomically above unskilled day laborers but below the merchant and landowning members of society. Earlier attempts to appeal to specific clientele had included calling this same inn at least two other names: the New-London Coffeehouse (1790–1827) and the Farmer's Hotel (1827). There are subtle suggestions of declining fortunes. Despite being advertised for at least ten months in 1827, described as having "always been considered one of the best Stands in the city for a Public House, and . . . in good repair," the property failed to attract a new lessee, and reverted to the management of an earlier innkeeper.[1] Rathbone and his successor, Carey Leeds, each remained in business only a year. After 1835, the premises evidently ceased to be operated as an inn. In the 1840s, it reportedly served as a small fireworks manufactory and umbrella repair shop. In 1859, the local newspaper reported that "Ye Old 'Mechanics Hotel,'" had been torn down, having been in "unsightly and dilapidated condition" for "many years past."[2]

Despite its relatively small size and lack of pictorial motif, the Mechanics Hotel sign must have had considerable street presence, deriving dramatic visual impact from its bold moldings and vivid color scheme. Small areas protected from oxidation and wear indicate that the soft red color of the outer molding was originally a brilliant Chinese red, set off by a gold frame liner. The gilded oval band and lettering, blocked in black, stood out sharply against the green oval field and the dark—probably black—surround. The overall appearance of this sign recalls the larger, but similarly proportioned, signs produced by William Rice of Hartford.[3] It differs from Rice counterparts, however, in the specific configuration of molding profiles, in the construction techniques, and in the design of full-length hanging straps that wrap around the bottom to support the sign but lack a similar flange at the top.

Inn names: Newspaper notices of the 1780s refer to this inn by the proprietor's name, at "Mr. Pember Calkins's Tavern." Between 1790 and 1827, it is generally designated as a coffee-house, modified by the current proprietor's name. The terms inn, tavern, tavern house, public house, and hotel are also used during this period, with no evident distinction in meaning. In 1827, Peter Avery operated the inn briefly under the name, "Farmer's Hotel," but the well-established designation, "New-London Coffee-house" persisted as well. The name, "Mechanics Hotel," appears in newspaper notices in 1835, and the building continued to be called by that name, although its use as a hotel evidently ended by the mid-1840s.

Innholder: Asa Rathbone followed a long series of innholders at this premises. His last known predecessor was John Prentis, who operated the inn from 1821–27, returning in 1828 after a one-year sojourn in Hartford. Rathbone was briefly succeeded by Carey Leeds.

Original location: The house, said to have been built prior to 1750, stood on State (previously Court) Street, in downtown New London.

Construction notes: Single main board, grain oriented horizontally, with narrow boards glued to the top and bottom edges to increase the height of the sign. The sign board is encased in moldings, mitered at corners. Long dowels, gilded and nailed into place, serve as frame liners along the inner edge of the molding.

Surface notes: Stenciled and gilded letters contrast with the sand-paint background. On side 2, the lettering lacks black blocking and appears to have been overpainted.

Condition and treatment notes: Hanging hardware is original. Treatment at WACC, 2000, included surface cleaning and consolidation.

Publications: *MBTS*, p. 53.

1. *New London Gazette*, 9 April 1828, p. 3, col. 6.
2. James Lawrence Chew, "Famous Old Taverns of New London," *Records and Papers of the New London County Historical Society*, vol. 2, pt. 1 (New London, Conn.: New London County Historical Society, 1895): 80; *New London Daily Star*, 21 October 1859.
3. Especially the Pettibone inn sign, ca. 1829, Norfolk, Conn. (Norfolk Historical Society).

Cat. 45

Sign for Fox's Inn, ca. 1834

LEFFINGWELL, CONNECTICUT (SECTION OF NORWICH TOWNSHIP) OR EAST HADDAM, CONNECTICUT

Innholder: Probably Aaron Fox (active ca. 1834)
Maker unidentified

Images: On side 1, a bull's head and neck, centered on board. On side 2, an eagle with the arms of the United States.
Text: On both sides: at top of oval board, "Entertainment.", at bottom of oval board, "Aaron Fox."

Paint on pine board, probably ash wood banding, iron hardware, 24" x 36-1/8"

Collection of Morgan B. Brainard, Gift of Mrs. Morgan B. Brainard, 1961.63.23

Illustrated: color plate 45 (side 1), fig. 20 (detail, side 1)

The oval shape of this sign represents a design that, according to dated examples, seems to have been popular from the mid-1820s to the late 1830s (cat. 29, 48, 49). When originally made, this sign may have had metal scrolls applied to the outer band, as in the Churchill and Fitch signs (cat. 48, 49). Much of the evidence is now covered by a wrought-iron band, ending in hanging posts and eyes, that was probably applied several years later, perhaps when the iron-strap repairs were made to the crack through the center of the sign.

The lettering on this sign is finely drawn, with delicate, calligraphic flourishes on some elements, notably the capital "A's" and the period (see fig. 20). There are some indications that carving created the low relief of the lettering, as well as the stars and eagle's banner on side 2. However, severe weathering has obliterated some of the surface refinements, introducing uncertainty.[1] The bull's head on side 1 is among the more common tavern sign motifs in America and England (cat. 7, 15). In this case, weathering has obliterated the lower jaw, resulting in a rather ungainly appearance.

Innholder: Genealogical and local history research identifies two possible innholders. Aaron Fox (1794–1872) lived in Leffingwell, a small, rural community just inside the town of Norwich, near the border of Bozrah and Montville. Fox's principal occupation was farming, and no tavern licences or other records linking him to a tavern have been located. However, in 1834 he acquired property admirably sited for a public house, along the Norwich-Salem turnpike. Like many rural innkeepers, he may have augmented farm income with occasional room and board for travelers. The 1834 date conforms nicely to style analysis.

Aaron Fox (1763–1831) of East Haddam was previously identified as the original owner of this sign. He was married in 1795 to Eunice Beebe (ca. 1767–1833). The survival of similar, horizontal, oval signs dated 1826–28 (see cat. 29, n. 1) indicates that this sign could have been made during this Aaron Fox's lifetime, although he would have been in his 60s. Notably, the bull's head on this sign resembles one painted on an earlier sign from Haddam, Conn., just across the Connecticut River from East Haddam (see related signs, below).

Construction notes: Single board, grain oriented horizontally, sawn into oval shape. Applied banding with bead-molded edge is nailed to outer edge of board. This is in turn encased by iron strapping, in three sections, held by nails and screws. Ends of the top sections of the iron strapping are bent upwards to form the hanging hardware.

Surface notes: The lettering is painted yellow, with a layer of coppery green below. The bull's head is a mottled, or "pied," gray, and the lower jaw has worn off. The background color, probably off-white, has weathered away. The central images appear to be partially repainted or touched-up, especially the eagle on side 2.

Condition notes: Weathering is more severe on side 2. A split through the center of the sign is secured with old metal braces held in place by iron rivets. The top section of wood banding is missing. The iron strapping and hanging hardware is evidently a later replacement, probably added at the time the wood banding pulled off. A supplemental section of metal strapping on the proper right of side 1 may be a secondary, more recent repair.

Related signs: Sign for Eleazar Bates's Inn, dated 1794, Haddam, Conn. (present location unknown).

Publications: *MBTS*, p. 38.

1. On evidence of carving on this sign, see Zimmerman, "Reading the Signs," Chapter Three (fig. 20); for an alternative view, see Carlisle, "Whether It Is," Chapter Seven.

Cat. 46* *Exhibited only in Hartford*

Sign for the Vernon Hotel, dated 1834
MANCHESTER, CONNECTICUT, AND VERNON, CONNECTICUT (NOW ROCKVILLE)

Innholders: possibly George Rich, Manchester (active 1832–46); Alonzo Bailey, Vernon (active 1847–?)
Signed by William Rice (1777–1847)

Images: On both sides, in central panel, eagle perched on shield-like cartouche displaying the arms of Connecticut, with stars arcing in sky overhead; on side border panels, ornamental scrolls and drapery with fringe and tassels. Both sides are similar but not identical. No underlying imagery.
Text: On both sides, in name banner on top border panel, "VERNON" over "MANCHESTER"; in name banner on bottom border panel, "HOTEL." On side 2 only, above name band, "1834".
Signature: On both sides, center bottom, "RICE."

Paint on pine board and moldings, smalt, lead glass flakes, iron oxide, gold leaf, iron hardware, 75-1/4" x 63-3/8"
Gift of the Sabra Trumbull Chapter, Daughters of the American Revolution, Rockville, Conn., 1960.9.0

Illustrated: frontispiece (side 2), color plate 46 (side 1)

This masterpiece of signpainting is the largest example known of William Rice's work and was probably among the largest signs created in its time. Both sides are decorated with the Connecticut State seal in a composition that is as full and rich as an engraving: an eagle against a field of stars perches on an assymetrical cartouche that encloses three grapevine cluster devices (rendered more fully than those depicted in Rice's sign for Daniel Loomis, cat. 27). Cannon barrels project out at varying angles among fleshy fronds beneath the cartouche. An irregularly patterned, flocked surface, similar to that on the Dyer inn sign (cat. 34) is dimly visible in the field behind the seal. Several other special effects enhance the design—glittery glass flakes and green smalt as well as the usual blue, the rare use of low-relief carving on the letters and scrolls of the outer border on side 1, and an ingenious trompe-l'oeil passage. On the vertical borders of side 2, a pair of painted chains "hang" down from the upper scrolls, suspending the large scroll on the bottom border. Minor variations between the two sides of this sign include the positioning of the eagle's wings, the number of stars overhead, the color of the draperies on the side panels, the use of curved or straight name banners, and the placement of the artist's name.

The history of this grand sign has yet to be fully untangled. It was found, ca. 1900, in the attic of a Rockville house known locally as King's Stage House, after its first and most prominent proprietor, Hezekiah King (active 1821–28). Contrary to subsequent local histories, physical evidence indicates that the sign did not arrive at what had been the King tavern until after the tavern had passed into other hands. The sequence of names painted on the top border indicates that the sign was used at a hotel in Manchester, the next town west, prior to being repainted with the "Vernon" name. That sequence dates the initial production no earlier than the incorporation of Manchester in 1823, as there was no previous use of Manchester as a place name in Connecticut. The name was chosen deliberately in recognition of the area's development as a textile mill town (echoing the English textile manufacturing city of the same name), and this context may also explain the prominent display of drapery on the sign, a feature not observed on other known signs. The date, 1834, painted above the town name on side 2, in all likelihood represents the sign's production date. The manner in which the date is painted corresponds to the elaborate treatment of the original lettering for "Manchester Hotel," not to the simpler style of the overpainted word, "Vernon". In addition, the twenty-four stars surrounding the eagle correspond to the number of states in the Union between August 1821, when Missouri became the twenty-fourth state, to June 1836, when Arkansas followed as the twenty-fifth. The size and elaboration of the sign suggest a large and prosperous enterprise, and contemporary newspaper notices point to George Rich's Hotel as Manchester's preeminent hostelry in the 1830s. References to Rich's Hotel end in early 1847, the same year that Alonzo Bailey appears in Rockville (then part of Vernon) as proprietor of the former King tavern.

Inn name: Period documents employ the proprietor's name, referring to Rich's inn, tavern, public house, or hotel in addition to the phrase, "at the house of." No period references have been located using the names "Manchester Hotel" or "Vernon Hotel."

Innholders: George Rich was issued tavern licenses in Manchester 1832–43 and 1845–46. No licenses were issued in Manchester in 1844 due to the Temperance movement.

Alonzo Bailey (1800–67) of Vernon married Lucinda Pease (1816–67) of Enfield in 1836. In 1846 he acquired the tavern stand owned by Austin Tilden (active 1839–46), and before that, by Burt McKinney (active ca. 1838–89) and his brother-in-law, Hezekiah King (b. 1799).

Original locations: The site of Rich's Hotel in Manchester has not yet been determined. The King tavern was located about fourteen miles east of Hartford, along the Hartford and Tolland turnpike, which provided a through route to Boston by 1810. The brick tavern house was built ca. 1820–21 by Col. Lemuel King, reportedly for the use of his son, Hezekiah.[1] It passed to two additional proprietors by 1847, when it ceased operating as an inn. In 1867 it was purchased by the town of Vernon for use as the poor house. It was demolished ca. 1960. The northeast section of Vernon, including the King tavern site, was incorporated as the city of Rockville in 1889.

Provenance: The sign is documented in the attic of the King inn in 1912.[2] It was subsequently moved to the local high school, the public library, and the premises of Donald Fisk, Esq., where it was reported in 1955.

Construction notes: Two boards, grain oriented vertically, set within channeled moldings. The ends of the side moldings are cut to the shape of the inside contour of the top and bottom moldings, so that the ends of the side moldings can slide over the top and bottom moldings as the large signboard expands and contracts across the grain with changes in humidity (see fig. 18 for detail of this construction on another Rice sign). Four additional boards, sawn at their outer edges to create an elaborate decorative profile, are attached to the outside of the moldings. The top and bottom barge boards abut the moldings and are held in place by a few large, toed-in nails. Because the side moldings must move with the central panel as it expands and contracts, the side barge boards are secured to the moldings by long screws set in metal tabs in the long hanging brackets.

Surface notes: Ground layer is grayish-white. Guidelines were probably used for laying out lettering. Gold leaf was used for the stars, eagle, and names, including the artist's signature. Coarsely ground iron oxide was used to create the sparkly effect in the black spandrels. On side 1 the scrollwork on the outer border has been edged with a sharp tool and slightly relieved. A 1955 town history states that "Miss J. Alice Maxwell had [the sign] redecorated."[3] The extent of this redecoration may have been minimal, as painted the surface appears to be original except for small sections of in-painting and re-painting related to the name change.

Condition and treatment notes: Hanging hardware is original. Minor carpentry repairs were performed in 1960 to secure the center panel. Treatment, performed on site at CHS by WACC staff in 2000, included stabilization of joinery, and removal of later varnish and overpaint.

Publications: Smith, *Tavern Signs*, p. 17 (side 1); Vernon Historical Society, *Vernon, Our Town*, 2nd ed., rev. (Vernon: Vernon Historical Society, 1989), p. 41, (side 2). *CHSB* 25 (April 1960): cover (side 1).

1. "Rockville in Eighteen hundred and thirty-seven," [Letter from Hezekiah King to Asaph McKinney], published in *Rockville Journal*, 28 July 1887, p. 8, cols. 1–2.
2. Celia Prescott, *Vernon and Rockville in the Olden Time* (1912?), p. 7.
3. George S. Brooks, *Cascades and Courage* (Rockville, Conn.: Rady, 1955), p. 23.

Cat. 47*

Sign for the Hannah Hotel, circa 1836
BETHLEHEM, CONNECTICUT

Innholders: Gideon Crane (licensed 1836); Sarah Atwood Crane (licensed 1837); Edwin Hannah (active 1838–56)
Maker unidentified

Images: On side 1, a central rising sun, with face. On side two, a stylized cartouche with fleur-de-lis ends. No underlying imagery. Text: On both sides, above the central device, "E. HANNAH." over "G. CRANE'S."; below the central device, "HOTEL."

Paint on pine board, smalt, gold leaf, iron hardware, 30-1/8" x 38-5/8"
1966.122.2

Illustrated: color plate 47 (side 1), fig. 47 (side 2)

The rectangular shape and bold perimeter moldings of this sign as well as the style of lettering and the stenciled Greek Revival cartouche on side 2 suggest a time of manufacture in the 1830s or later. In this case, very precise dating can be established by fitting name evidence on the sign to historical circumstances. The letters in "E. HANNAH" are smaller and lack the graceful serifs of those in "HOTEL", suggesting that the two lines were painted by different hands. Traces of larger-sized letters are barely visible through the uniformly worn and oxidized black background surrounding "E. HANNAH." Tavern license records reveal that Gideon Crane, and subsequently his widow, Sarah Atwood Crane, operated a hotel in Bethlehem, preceding Edwin Hannah, who assumed control of the establishment upon marrying the widow Crane in 1838. The earliest license recorded for Gideon Crane is in 1836, the year he died, although he may have been in business slightly earlier (no licenses were recorded for Bethlehem, 1832–35). The lower quality of the relettering, prompted by change in ownership rather than weathering, suggests that it was probably executed by a less practiced local painter, rather than the accomplished sign painter, perhaps a regional specialist, who evidently produced the original sign.

Inn name: Period citations have been found using the proprietor's name, "E. Hannah's," and an alternate listing for the "Sun Hotel" (*Connecticut Business Directory*, 1856).

Innholders: Gideon Crane (1808–36) was the son of Phinehas and Irene Crane of Bethlehem, Conn. In 1828 he married Sarah Atwood (1811–89) of Woodbury, Conn.

Sarah Atwood Crane was married in 1838 to Edwin Hannah (1807–59), son of Col. Robert and Jerusha Hannah of Bethlehem. The Hannahs were descendants of Scotch-Irish emigrants who had settled in Voluntown, in eastern Connecticut, and then in Bethlehem, in western Connecticut, in the early eighteenth century.

Original location: The Crane/Hannah property was located on the east side of the main road through Bethlehem, near the church.

Provenance: Purchased from Avis and Rockwell Gardiner, Stamford, Conn.

Construction notes: Single board, grain oriented horizontally, set within channels of applied moldings, mitered at corners. Vertical moldings appear to be of oak whereas horizontal moldings are of pine. The oak moldings retain sharper edges, in keeping with the more durable qualities of that wood species. No structural frame, no pediment or skirt.

Surface notes: Letters and design elements were stenciled in place first, then the surrounding background was painted around them with a green and blue paint, textured with smalt particles.

Condition and treatment notes: Hanging hardware appears original. Treatment at WACC, 1999–2000, included structural consolidation, surface cleaning, and paint consolidation.

Publications: Smith, *Tavern Signs*, p. 14.

Cat. 48*

Sign for Fitch's Inn, circa 1834

LEDYARD, CONNECTICUT

Innholder: Russell Fitch (active 1834–47)
Maker unidentified

Images: Ornamental design, centered on board. No underlying imagery.
Text: On both sides, inside top of oval, "R. FITCH.", inside bottom of oval, "INN". No underlying text.

Paint on pine board, smalt, iron hardware, 21-1/4" x 32-3/4"
Collection of Morgan B. Brainard, Gift of Mrs. Morgan B. Brainard, 1961.63.22

Illustrated: color plate 48

The most appealing feature of this sign is the whimsical iron coils that seem to sprout from its perimeter. These coils are notable in being made of wrought iron, whereas other known examples use curled sheet iron to create such ornament (cat. 49). The coils on top of the sign end in disks, those on the bottom are shaped into leaves. Even the iron arms from which the sign hangs are angled to avoid intrusion of any straight lines into the composition. The placement of smalt on this sign is also unusual. Typically, smalt is found strewn on dark backgrounds to set off gold lettering. Here, the smalt is strewn on the lettering itself, which is painted brownish-black against a white background.

Russell Fitch operated at least two inns in New London County, in southeastern Connecticut. Stylistic comparisons to other oval signs with projecting metal ornamentation (cat. 49) suggest that this sign was more likely made in 1834 for Fitch's inn in Ledyard, rather than for the inn he opened in 1843 in nearby Preston.[1] The stylized ornament in the center is of a type that occurs repeatedly in other decorative applications, including printed graphics, in the 1830s and 1840s.

Innholder: Russell Fitch (1798–1884) was the son of Thomas and Elizabeth Fitch of Preston, Conn. In 1821 he married Julia A. Phillips (1800?–57) in Preston. After she died, he married Sarah A. Haskell (1813–1902). Fitch was licensed as tavernkeeper in Ledyard, 1834–38, and in Preston, in 1843 and 1847. He is not recorded as buying land in either community, so he may have operated in rented premises.

Construction notes: Thick, single board, grain oriented horizontally, cut into oval shape. The board is one of the thickest in the collection (1-3/8" thick). Board is wrapped by a strip of oak or ash banding attached to outer edges with nails set in decorative patterns. Wrought iron decorative coils are nailed to the top and bottom edges of the sign.

Surface notes: Faint oval layout lines define the upper and lower boundaries of the lettering, except at the sides where the "R" and "H" rise above the curve of the oval scribe line so that the name may be more easily read.

Condition and treatment notes: Both decorative and hanging hardware are original. This oval sign survives in excellent condition, suggesting that it may have hung outside only a relatively short time. Treatment

at WACC, 1999, consisted of surface cleaning and securing of ornamental ironwork.

Publications: *MBTS*, p. 37.

1. Dated examples with iron scrollwork include Howe's inn sign, dated 1829 (Henniker Historical Society, New Hampshire), Garvin, p. 35; the Fitts store and inn sign, 1832 (Museum of American Folk Art, New York), Jean Lipman, et al., *Five Star Folk Art: One Hundred American Masterpieces* (New York: Abrams, in association with The Museum of American Folk Art, New York, 1990), p. 83.

Cat. 49

Sign for Hemingway's Tavern and Churchill's Inn, dated 1838, probably made ca. 1836

PLYMOUTH AND HARWINTON, CONNECTICUT

Innholders: Allen Hemingway (active 1836–37); Lewis Churchill (active 1838)
Maker unidentified

Images: None.
Text: On both sides, inside top of oval, "L.CHURCHILL,S" over "HEMINGWAY", inside bottom of oval, "INN", over "TAVERN", in center of oval, "1838" over "STORE." / and"

Paint on pine board, smalt, sand or fine-grained smalt, possibly gold leaf, iron hardware, 25-5/8" x 44-1/2"
Collection of Morgan B. Brainard, Gift of Mrs. Morgan B. Brainard, 1961.63.16

Illustrated: color plate 49 (side 1), fig. 15 (side 2)

The presence of two sequential names on this sign place it in the towns of Plymouth and Harwinton, in northwestern Connecticut. Allen Hemingway of Plymouth was first licensed in 1836, providing a probable date for manufacture of the sign. He continued to operate a store in the Terryville section of Plymouth until at least 1850, but held no tavern licenses after 1837. He evidently sold the sign, as the second name corresponds to Lewis Churchill, who was licensed in Harwinton, one town north of Plymouth, in 1838.

The earlier decoration was rendered in black letters on a white background, similar to the color scheme of the sign for Fitch's inn (cat. 48). The repainted decoration of 1838 uses different materials as well as a new color scheme. The letters are yellow, stenciled over a thick paint, heavily textured with smalt or sand. The name band is greenish-brown, and the center oval is dark blue, a vivid change from simple black on white of the Hemingway decoration. Despite the heavy, dark coloration, the horizontal oval shape with a penumbra of metal C-scrolls lends an airy quality to the sign.

Innholders: Allen Hemingway (1808–86) was the son of Jacob Street Hemingway. In 1833 he married Marietta Linsley (1808–42) at Branford, Conn.; in 1843 he married Harriet Loisa Tyler (1819–95) at Branford. In addition to his store, he operated the post office for Plymouth, which was the home of the Seth Thomas Company and numerous other clockmaking concerns. In 1854, he removed to Norwood Park, Illinois, outside Chicago, where he went into business wholesaling clocks, presumably those produced by his former neighbors in Plymouth.

Lewis Churchill (1794–after 1860) was the son of Ellis and Patience Churchill of Plymouth. In 1817 he married Hannah Covington at Plymouth. Only one license has been located, from Harwinton in 1838, but he may have remained in business longer, as later licenses for the town were irregularly recorded. By 1850 he had moved to Southington, Conn., and identified himself as a farmer.

Construction notes: Single board, grain oriented horizontally, cut to oval shape. Applied banding with bead-molded edge (3/8") is nailed to outer edge of board. The banding is an unidentified, resinous wood, possibly a pine. Coiled C-scroll flourishes made of machine-rolled sheet-iron are nailed into the top and bottom edges of the sign.

Surface notes: A incomplete restoration attempted at an unknown date prior to 1939 removed much of the upper layer of paint on side 2, partially exposing the earlier decoration.

Condition notes: The hanging hardware, consisting of large, square spikes with eyes, appears to be original. One C-scroll is missing from the top center.

Exhibitions: Aetna 1939.

Publications: *MBTS*, p. 29 (side 2).

Cat. 50

Sign for Warner's Hotel, dated 1836
LOCATION UNDETERMINED, PROBABLY CONNECTICUT
OR MASSACHUSETTS

Innholder unidentified
Signed by William Rice (1777–1847)

Images: None.
Text: On both sides, inside top of oval outline, "WARNER'S" over "SMITH'S"; inside bottom of oval outline, "HOTEL"; centered in oval outline, "1836."
Signature: On both sides, in lower right corner, "RICE.", inside curving gilt banner.

Paint on pine board and moldings, smalt, iron oxide, gold leaf, iron hardware, 36" x 60-1/8"
1998.77.0

Illustrated: color plate 50 (side 1), fig. 64 (side 2)

Unlike most Rice signs, this one has no pictorial device to aid in catching the attention of passers-by. It relies entirely on graphics and color for visual impact. Like many other Rice signs, however, it employs an oval outline—more properly, an ellipse—to organize the design. The ellipse defines a central field within the sign plane and provides curved margins to guide lines of lettering. In keeping with Rice's skill, the graphic design of this sign is sophisticated. Although the overall organization of the two sides is quite similar, subtle differences in background colors and patterning produce quite different effects.

Side 1 has green spandrels and a black oval field, whereas side 2 has red spandrels and a green oval field. Both oval fields are irregularly patterned, using a mordant to affix a fine textured material, or "flocking."[1] On side 1, the letters and numerals are gilded. The date is shaded with painted gray sand. The letters are not shaded, but rather outlined with a thin black line. Side 1 also displays an unusual geometric pattern, which frames a small, red ellipse enclosing the central date. This pattern is composed of small red rectangles arranged in radiating pyramids to create an abstract sunburst effect, reminiscent of a modern skyline. This motif was originally even more dramatic, being painted over gold leaf, which has largely worn off.

On side 2, the blocked and serifed lettering is black, set off from the background by bright shading. The shading on each letter shifts from Chinese red on the bottom to gold on the side, creating the illusion of vibrant sunlight falling on the surface. Additional brilliance comes from the gilded outer and inner edges of the black, cove-shaped molding that frames the sign panel. In contrast to the relative severity of the decorative scheme, Rice used a very ornate signature band set into a gilded scroll, a device that also appears on his 1844 sign for Wadsworth's inn (cat. 55).

Innholders: This sign has not yet been firmly linked to a specific establishment. Numerous innkeepers named Smith and Warner have been identified, but not in an appropriate sequence.

Provenance: Ex. coll. Howard and Catherine Feldman, who acquired the sign in Pennsylvania. Auctioned at Sotheby's, New York City, October 1998.

Construction notes: Two boards, grain oriented horizontally. Signboard is set within channels of applied moldings, mitered at corners, and nailed to outer edges of boards (moldings are not contoured to allow movement, the usual Rice practice). Original hanging hardware wraps around top and bottom.

Surface notes: Lettering was laid out within scribed guide lines. Coarsely ground iron oxide was used to create the sparkly effect in the black areas. Both sides were overpainted at some time, evidently replicating the original design.

Condition and treatment notes: Treatment at WACC in 2000 included minor structural consolidation, surface cleaning, and paint consolidation.

1. Flocking also appears on Rice signs for the Dyer inn, Vernon Hotel (side 2) and Wadsworth inn (side 2) (cat. 34, 46, 55). See Webber, "Faithfully and Promptly Executed," Chapter Six.

Cat. 51

Sign for Mason's Inn, 1830s or later
PROBABLY NEW LONDON COUNTY, POSSIBLY COLCHESTER,
CONNECTICUT

Innholder: Andrew N. Mason (possibly active ca. 1840)
Maker unidentified

Images: On side 1, horse and rider with tree trunk. On side 2, landscape scene, with vignette in lower right of man hiding something in tree trunk.

Text: On both sides, below image "A.N. MASON".

Paint on pine board and moldings, gold leaf, iron hardware, 49-3/4" x 61"
Collection of Morgan B. Brainard, Gift of Mrs. Morgan B. Brainard, 1961.63.37

Illustrated: color plate 51 (side 1), fig. 109 (side 2)

In the shadowy darkness at the base of the large tree at the right of side 2 of Mason's sign, a man wearing a military officer's sword stealthily hides a rolled document in a hollow in the tree trunk. Connecticut residents of the nineteenth century would have immediately recognized this vignette as one of the most famous episodes in Connecticut history, the hiding of the colonial charter in 1687, a legendary act of resistance to British rule. Upon rising to the British throne in 1685, James II had revoked charters under which the New England colonies had enjoyed considerable self-government. In 1687, Royal Governor Sir Edmund Andros arrived in Hartford to complete formal annexation of the Connecticut Colony to the newly organized Dominion of New England. The colony submitted to Andros's rule "without any contest," but never surrendered its 1662 charter. According to legend, the charter was spirited away and hidden in the trunk of an already ancient oak tree, subsequently known as the Charter Oak.[1]

On side 1 of the Mason sign, a gentleman on horseback solemnly contemplates a large, hollow tree trunk. In contrast to the antiquated dress of the document-hider on side 2, this man wears a coat and hat of mid-nineteenth-century vintage. The apparent disparity of the two images prompts the question of how, or whether, they are related to each other. A survey of extant Connecticut signs reveals no clear pattern, with examples ranging from simple duplication of images in many eighteenth-century examples (cat.1) to no explicit relationships (cat. 54), and from thematic juxtapositions of national and state insignia (cat. 28) to possible contrasts of American eagles and British lions (cat. 31). The two images on this sign appear to be connected thematically. Inclusion of the tree trunk in each is a compelling common denominator, with the passage of time signaled by the change in clothing styles and the transformation of the full-sized tree to a hollow trunk. It is tempting to interpret this sign as a pictorial memento of both the oak and the historical event it commemorated, with the nineteenth-century gentleman on side 1 a visitor at the venerable shrine of liberty. Celebration of the Charter Oak as an icon of Connecticut history emerged early in the nineteenth century, prompting the production of Charter Oak images and souvenirs. The fad for Charter Oak relics peaked in the 1830s—with the Connecticut Bicentennial of 1836 followed by the Sesquicentennial of the Charter incident itself in 1837—and again in 1856 when the ancient tree finally fell in a windstorm.[2]

Innholder: Andrew N. Mason is listed in the Colchester census of 1840, although no tavern licenses have been located. Born in North Stonington, he married Janet Burdick of the same town in 1831.

Construction notes: Three boards, grain oriented horizontally, assembled with tongue-and-groove joints, held together by moldings nailed to the edges.

Surface notes: Ground layer is off-white. Lettering was skillfully executed in varnished gold or metal, although covered with bronze paint, now tarnished. The letter "A" has a distinctive curved mid-line on side 2. Letters were awkwardly retouched at some time in the past.

Condition and treatment notes: Hanging hardware may be original. Wood had rotted substantially at corners, requiring past reinforcement with modern metal brackets. Repairs to wood structure carried out by Peter Arkell, Hampton, Conn., in 1992. Treatment at WACC, 1999–2000, included structural consolidation, surface cleaning, removal of darkened varnish, and revarnishing.

Publications: *MBTS*, pp. 54–55; Smith, *Tavern Signs*, p. 15 (side 1); Terry, *Old Inns*, p. 243; *Antiques* 1928, p. 404 (side 1).

1. David S. Lovejoy, *The Glorious Revolution in America* (New York: Harper Torchbooks, Harper & Row, 1972), pp. 203–8; Christopher P. Bickford, "Connecticut and Its Charter," *CHSB* 49 (Summer 1984): 114.
2. Robert Trent, "The Charter Oak Artifacts," *CHSB* 49 (Summer 1984): 125–28.

Cat. 52

Sign for Bailey's Hotel, dated 1837 or 1857
SOUTH SALEM, NEW YORK

Innholder: George F. Bailey (active ca. 1850)
Signed by George Crossingham (possibly active 1828–43)

Images: On both sides, an eagle with outspread wings, perched on top of globe.
Text: On both sides, above the image, "LAKE GOWANUS HOTEL" over "HOTEL"; below the image, "G. F. BAILEY". Signature: On side 1, at lower right, "G Crossingham / (Croton Falls)". On side 2, at lower right, date, "1837" or "1857".

Paint on pine board and moldings, gold leaf, iron hardware, 37-1/8" x 40-1/2"
Collection of Morgan B. Brainard, Gift of Mrs. Morgan B. Brainard, 1961.63.4

Illustrated: color plate 52 (side 1)

A layer of recent overpaint obscures three earlier image layers, which in turn document changing circumstances surrounding this sign. The earliest image depicts an eagle with outswept wings, one up and one down. The eagle clutches in its beak a banner that unfurls across the top of the sign. Its talons grasp arrows and a laurel branch that lie above a wide name band identifying the innkeeper as G. F. Bailey, likely George F. Bailey of South Salem, New York, a sparsely populated area just west of Ridgefield, Connecticut. The second painting campaign introduced a new band across the top of the sign to display the word "Hotel." This band covered the unfurled banner and required repainting of the eagle slightly lower in the sign plane. In this second eagle, the up-and-down position of the wings is reversed. Because no evidence indicates any other name to accompany "Hotel," the band with Bailey's name, at the bottom of the sign, apparently remained unaltered. The name in the lower corner, presumably a painter's signature, is associated with this paint campaign, or possibly the next.

In the third paint scheme, the Hotel band above the eagle is covered over by a vermilion banner bearing the words, "Lake Gowanus Hotel," picked out in gilt letters. The painter of this layer may have introduced the blue background with stars to unify the new banner with the old eagle, which holds one end of the vermilion banner in its beak. Introduction of the new hotel name required obliteration of the old name band at the bottom of the sign. The painter covered Bailey's name with a globe on which the eagle now perched, a composition reminiscent of the New York State seal, but also in general use (cat. 39, 54). Unresolved is the sequence of another, smaller globe in this same location. If it belonged to the second campaign, it would have interfered with the Bailey name band. Finally, at an undetermined date, someone attempted to reinforce the faded and worn images. This uppermost paint layer mixes elements from different layers and obscures the archaeology of this sign.

The pieces of historical information thus far uncovered do not fit well with each other or with the paint sequence on the sign. The date painted on side 2 may be either 1837 or 1857. A George Crossingham appears in the New York City census records for 1830 and in the directories from 1828 to 1843, but he is not identified as a painter. No trade listing appears for him at all until 1837/38. In that year, he is listed as a baker at the same address where Thomas Crossingham is listed as a baker in 1833/34, suggesting a family business. Croton Falls, painted below Crossingham's name, is a village near South Salem, New York, where George F. Bailey was listed as an innkeeper in the census records of 1850. The proximity of the two villages places sign, painter, and patron in the same geographical vicinity. However, Bailey was listed as age 31 in 1850, making him too young to have commissioned a sign in 1837, and Crossingham cannot be documented as late as 1857.

Innholder: George F. Bailey was born circa 1819. His wife, Sarah A., was born circa 1829.

Construction notes: Two boards, grain oriented horizontally. Heavy, applied moldings, mitered at corners, are nailed to the edges of the signboard. Thin strips of wood line the inside of the moldings and further secure the signboard in place.

Condition notes: Hanging hardware appears original. Angled braces added later reinforce the bottom corners. Surfaces are heavily weathered. Nail holes around "Lake Gowanus" suggest that this name may have been covered over at some point.

Publications: *MBTS*, p. 17.

Cat. 53

Sign for Mallett's Hotel, probably 1840s
SOUTHFORD, CONNECTICUT

Innholder: Fenn Mallett (licensed 1848)
Maker unidentified

Images: None.
Text: On both sides, top line, "MALLETT'S" over "UNION," bottom line, "HOTEL."

Paint on pine board and moldings, smalt, gold leaf, 27-3/4" x 51-3/4"
Gift of Newton C. Brainard, 1957.59.1

Illustrated: color plate 53

This simply conceived sign typifies those of the 1830s and 1840s in its broad, horizontal orientation and its reliance upon lettering alone for ornament. The first generation of lettering, visible in "HOTEL.", is bold and angular, as evident in the octagonal "O" and square period. These letters were originally executed in gold leaf on a green painted ground. Subsequently, a redecorator scribed the Mallett name over the earlier "UNION", using a serifed letter style, and then filled in the outlines with gold paint. That same paint covers over the gilding on the letters of "HOTEL." Last, the redecorator applied a coating of blue smalt over the entire background. This coating did not adhere well to the original gilded letters, so that over time the granular paint coating has detached and fallen away, now partially revealing the Union name.

Innholder: Fenn Mallett (1811–51) was the son of John and Polly Mallett of New Milford, Conn. His father was of Huguenot ancestry. In 1837 Fenn Mallett married Susan C. Downs of Southbury. In 1848 he purchased property from M.M. Canfield, an earlier tavernkeeper, and obtained a tavern license. He was recorded as a taverner on the census of 1850 and as a farmer at his death in 1851. Whether his hotel failed or he combined vocations is unknown (census returns indicate that innkeepers in rural areas often listed themselves as farmers).

Construction notes: One or more boards, grain oriented horizontally. Thin boards with rounded molding profiles are nailed to the edges of the signboard forming a frame with mitered corners. Separate cove moldings, also mitered in corners, are nailed to the inside of the frame.

Condition notes: Hanging hardware is original. The molded edge of one side framing member is a replacement.

Exhibitions: Deerfield Academy, Deerfield, Mass., 1958–76.

Publications: *MBTS*, p. 51.

Cat. 54*

Sign for the Temperance Hotel, ca. 1826–42
PLAINFIELD AND COLCHESTER, CONNECTICUT

Innholders: J. Gladwin (licensed 1826–28); John Dunham and N. A. Brown (active ca. 1842)
Maker unidentified

Images: On side 1, a white horse pulling a chariot driven by a man in classical garb, with spear held in upraised right hand. On side 2, an eagle with upraised wings, perched on globe, flanked by the sun and moon with stars overhead.
Text: On both sides, below image, "TEMPERANCE" over "J. GLADWIN".

Paint on pine board and moldings, gold leaf, tin leaf, smalt, iron hardware, 39-1/8" x 76-1/4"

Collection of Morgan B. Brainard, Gift of Mrs. Morgan B. Brainard, 1961.63.47

Illustrated: color plate 54 (side 1), fig. 7 (side 2), fig. 68 (detail, side 1)

The commanding imagery of this sign may have been painted as early as the late 1820s, when Joseph S. Gladding (an alternate spelling for Gladwin, the earlier name on the sign) was licensed as a tavernkeeper in Plainfield, in eastern Connecticut. On side 1, the chariot reflects contemporary interests in classical antiquity, with counterparts in such diverse media as ceramics, molded plaster ornaments, metal furniture mounts, and typesetter's ornaments, in addition to more formal pictorial prints. The globe-topping eagle, its wings spanning 5-1/2 feet, enlarges upon similar motifs in numerous patriotic engravings and on other signs (cat. 39, 52). These vivid images have no known thematic or historical connection to the legend, "Temperance," which was painted over the Gladwin name band either by Gladding himself or by partners John Dunham and N.A. Brown, who reportedly hung the sign at the Temperance Hotel they opened in Colchester in 1842. The Windham County Temperance Report of 1838 lists Joseph Gladding among those who had adopted temperance principles, advocating the limitation or abolition of alcohol consumption.[1] During the peak of the Temperance movement in the 1840s, some Connecticut towns were so anti-alcohol that they refused to grant tavern licenses at all (see cat. 46). The pressure to limit or abolish alcohol consumption prompted some innkeepers, like Gladding and Dunham and Brown, to operate moderate or non-alchohol establishments, known as temperance taverns or hotels: in 1846, there were fifty-seven of these establishments reported in the state. In 1846, the Total Abstinence Society in New Haven reported that the town of Colchester had 400 temperance society members, "4 temperance stores, 1 rum tavern, 2 rum stores, 1 temperance tavern, 4 deaths from intemperance during the last two years."[2]

Inn name: Period newspaper notices refer to this establishment as "Temperance Hotel" or "Mr. Dunham's Temperance House."

Innholders: Joseph Sherman Gladding (1787–1872) was the son of Capt. Nathaniel Gladding of Providence, Rhode Island. In 1817, in Thompson, Conn., he married Susan Cady (1798–1874) of Plainfield, Conn. The Gladdings lived in Plainfield until at least 1846, moving to Hartford some time thereafter.

John Dunham and N.A. Brown advertised the opening of their "Temperance Hotel" in the *Connecticut Courant* for 6 August 1842. They are not otherwise identified.

Provenance: Purchased by Morgan Brainard from Mrs. S. P. Willard, who had purchased it from Mrs. Dr. Carrington of Hayward Ave., Colchester.[3]

Construction notes: Two boards, grain oriented horizontally, assembled by a tongue-and-groove joint. Moldings, mitered at the corners, are attached to the edges of the panel.

Surface notes: On both sides, the name band has been repainted in ocher paint with the word "TEMPERANCE" over larger, gold leaf letters used for Gladwin's name. Lettering and images are skillfully exe-

cuted. The ground layer is a thick, grayish white paint. On side 1, there are many drawing lines visible, some not used, which indicate that the chariot image was drawn free-hand, directly on the board (see fig. 68). A compass was used to lay out the wheel of the chariot. On side 2, details of the crescent moon, stars, eagle talons, and laurel branch were originally executed in tin leaf, now tarnished beyond recall. The red banner in the eagle's beak may have been part of an early version, apparently covered by the artist when he applied the smalt background.

Condition and treatment notes: Hanging hardware appears original. Both the signboard and moldings display old repairs in many locations. The upper corners and top moldings were restored at an unknown time. Treatment at WACC, 1999–2000, included repairs to wood structure, surface cleaning and consolidation, and inpainting of both earlier and new wood repairs.

Related objects: Watercolor rendering, by John Matulis, ca. 1940, *Index of American Design*, National Gallery of Art, 1943.8.17100 (side 1), 1943.8.16492 (side 2); published Hornung, pl. 237, p. 76 (side 1); Christensen, no. 119, p. 64 (side 1); *House and Garden* 1941, p. 20.

Exhibitions: "Altered States: Alcohol and Drugs in American Society," The Strong Museum, Rochester, New York, 1996 (photographic reproduction).

Publications: *MBTS*, p. 65; Arthur B. Kern and Sybil Kern, "Alcoholism and the Temperance Movement in Early American Folk Art," *Magazine Antiques*, February 1998 (side 2), p. 299; Smith, *Tavern Signs*, p. 17 (side 1); Lord and Foley, p. 147 (side 1); *Spinning Wheel* 1955, p. 10, Terry, *Old Inns*, p. 244; *Antiques* 1928, pp. 403–4. Textbooks: *The American Nation* (Holt, Rinehart & Winston).

1. *Windham County Temperance Report*, 1838.
2. Total Abstinence Society, *The Second Annual Report of the Connecticut Washington T[otal]. A[bstinence]. Society* (New Haven: Storer, 1846), p. 32. For additional discussion of temperance taverns in Connecticut, see Vincent, "Some Suitable Signe," Chapter Four.
3. Cyrus E. Pendleton, "Colchester Taverns of Other Days," unpublished report, 1938, p. 18 (CHS Library, on deposit from the Colchester Historical Society).

Cat. 55*

Sign for Wadsworth's Inn, dated 1844

HARTFORD, CONNECTICUT

Innholder: Elisha Wadsworth (licensed 1828–48); Sidney Wadsworth (active 1844–62)
Signed by William Rice (1777–1847) or Frederick F. Rice (1814–77)

Images: On side 1, lion, with body in profile, head turned to three-quarter view, no chains, with a yellow-green background. On side 2, eagle holding federal shield, centered inside oval field.
Text: On side 1, below image, "S.WADSWORTH." On side 2, inside top of oval, "S.WADSWORTH'S", inside bottom of oval, "INN."
Signature: On side 2, in lower right, "RICE.", in lower left, "1844". Both name and date appear in scrolled banners.

Paint on pine board and moldings, lead glass flakes, gold leaf, iron hardware, 35-1/2" x 60-1/8"
Collection of Morgan B. Brainard, Gift of Mrs. Morgan B. Brainard, 1961.63.49

Illustrated: color plate 55 (side 2), fig. 27 (side 1, as found in barn), fig. 50 (side 1), fig. 59 (side 2), fig. 75 (detail, side 2)

The Wadsworth's Inn sign is the latest example bearing the Rice signature in The Connecticut Historical Society's collections. Dated three years before William Rice's death, it exhibits the characteristic combination of a lion on one side and an eagle on the other. A similar arrangement of the eagle within a gilt-banded oval appears on at least three other known Rice signs, two of which also display the same placement of text (see related signs, below). In each case, however, the treatment of the eagle varies slightly. Here it has wings outstretched horizontally, and it clutches the federal shield as well as a single laurel bough, rendered in naturalistic detail. Thunderbolts shoot out from the other side, imparting more power to the image than conventional arrows. Variations seen on the other signs in this group include raised wings, which are accompanied by stars in the field above; claws extending below the shield instead of holding it, and different treatment of the laurel bough. Lettering may or may not be included within the oval, but the thunderbolt arrows seem to have been a characteristic Rice device, sometimes even replacing the laurel branch. Both lettering and eagle are enlivened by gold leaf, given a copper color by the addition of silver. Copper-colored leaf was a special effect advertised by William Rice's son Frederick. Although known advertisements date to the mid-1850s, the copper-colored leaf on this sign testifies to its use at least a decade earlier, during the period in which William and Frederick were working together under the firm name, "Wm. Rice & Co., Sign Painters." Morgan Brainard evidently regarded this sign as the work of Frederick Rice, noting that "it was one of the later types of signs painted by Rice, whose father before him was a sign-painter."[1]

In contrast to the recurrence of the Wadsworth eagle composition, the lion has no currently known counterparts in Rice's work. As demonstrated by Nancy Finlay in Chapter Five, Rice based the Wadsworth lion closely on a prototype drawn from Thomas Bewick's *Natural History of Foreign Quadrupeds*, published in England in 1809, and copied in America by wood engraver Alexander Anderson and countless others (see figs. 61–62). This lion is peaceful, almost tranquil. Its posture lacks the spring and tension visible in other Rice versions. The tail wraps around the lion's back in a gentle swish. Although powerful and heavily browed, the face looks forward, seemingly unmindful of the viewer. This lion has no need of the heavy chains found on some Rice lions.

As with numerous Rice signs, this one was evidently purchased by a second or third-generation innkeeper, for an establishment located along the Albany Turnpike west of Hartford. Sidney Wadsworth's father, Elisha, had been licensed as a tavernkeeper in Hartford since 1828, when he erected a brick house in a prime location, on a hill at the outskirts of Hartford. There is no evidence of an initial "E" underneath the "S", nor of any other painting under the present surface, indicating that the sign must have been acquired new in 1844. Although Elisha continued to hold a license until 1848, the sign suggests that Sidney had taken over active management by 1844.

According to recollections written by Morgan Brainard in 1934, this was the first sign he acquired, inspired by a boyhood memory of seeing it hanging from an outbuilding on the Wadsworth property, located less than a block away from his own home. When he learned of the impending sale of the property (in 1916), he recalled, "I made up my mind that the sign should be preserved, and after some difficulty I found that it still existed and secured it." Photographs in Brainard's papers depict the sign, presumably as he found it, in a barn or stable (see fig. 27).[2]

Inn name: Period newspaper notices refer to this establishment by the proprietor's name, "Elisha Wadsworth's brick Tavern."

Innholders: Elisha Wadsworth (1778–1854) was the son of Seth Wadsworth. In 1797 he married Lucy Woodford, whose father and three brothers were all innkeepers in Litchfield and Hartford Counties. Elisha Wadsworth first held a tavern license in Winchester, Conn., 1823–27, possibly taking over one of the Woodford family operations. In 1828 he returned to Hartford, where he held licenses dating 1829–41, 1845, and 1847–48.

Sidney Wadsworth (1813–87) was the son of Elisha and Lucy Woodford Wadsworth of Hartford. He married Eliza A. Sisson. He operated the tavern from about 1844 until 1862. He was a third generation innkeeper, counting from his maternal grandfather.

Lucy Wadsworth (1801–1900) was the daughter of Elisha and Lucy Woodford Wadsworth and sister of Sidney Wadsworth. According to a newspaper account of her ninety-fifth birthday, she was in charge of cooking for the tavern. Her obituary also states that she continued to operate it herself for some time after her brother, Sidney, discontinued hotelkeeping. She is further reported to have occupied the same room from 1828, when her father built the house, until her death seventy-two years later.[3]

Daniel Sydney Wadsworth (1848–1910) was the son of Sidney and Eliza Sisson Wadsworth. His obituary indicates that he was still engaged in tavernkeeping at the end of his life.[4]

Original location: The brick house built by Elisha Wadsworth still stands on the southeast corner of Albany and Prospect Avenues, on the Hartford side of the Hartford-West Hartford town line. The house was sold out of the Wadsworth family in 1916 and remodeled two years later. It has been turned to face Prospect Avenue instead of Albany Avenue, as it did originally. Later newspaper accounts state that it ceased operations as a hotel in 1862, presumably meaning that it no longer offered lodging. There are also references to the provision of food by Lucy Wadsworth after 1862 and to the provision of liquor (sometimes illegally) by Daniel Wadsworth as late as 1908.

Provenance: The sign remained on the property until after the death of Sidney Wadsworth's son, Daniel, in 1910. Morgan Brainard acquired it prior to the sale of the property in 1916.

Construction notes: Two or more boards, grain oriented horizontally. Board is held within grooves cut into moldings applied around the edges and mitered at the corners (moldings are not contoured to allow movement, the usual Rice practice). No structural frame, no skirt or pediment.

Surface notes: The surface shows relatively little weathering. The ground appears to be gray. Letters are stenciled. The sparkly effect on side 2 is created by lead glass flakes.

Condition and treatment notes: Hanging hardware appears original, but had been removed and reattached when earlier repairs were made to applied moldings. The moldings were removed, repaired at corners, and recut to fit the signboard, which had shrunken with age across the grain. Hardware was reattached using original holes on side moldings, with wood inserts used to fill in the resulting gaps between the horizontal arm of the hardware and the top molding pieces. Rotted wood in the moldings was repaired and inpainted in 1988 by Peter Arkell, Hampton, Conn. Treatment at WACC, 1999–2000, included surface cleaning and consolidation and resecuring of hardware.

Related signs: Sign for Hawley's Inn, ca. 1825–30, probably Sandisfield, Mass. (Abby Aldrich Rockefeller Folk Art Center); Sign for Robertson's Inn, dated 1831, Windsorville, Conn.; and Sign for Pinney's Hotel, dated 1836, Riverton, Conn. (both present location unknown).

Related objects: Watercolor rendering, by John Matulis, ca. 1940, *Index of American Design,* National Gallery of Art, 1943.8.7686 (side 1), 1943.8.16491 (side 2); published *House and Garden* 1941, p. 20.

Publications: *MBTS*, p. 67; Lord and Foley, p 152 (side 1); Terry, *Old Inns,* p. 34 (side 1, as found in barn), p. 244 (side 2).

1. Morgan B. Brainard, unpublished paper prepared for the Society for the Preservation of New England Antiquities, ca. 1934 (Morgan Brainard Papers, CHS Library).
2. Ibid.
3. *Hartford Daily Courant,* 11 December 1896 and 31 August 1900, p. 5, col. 2; clippings in CHS museum object files.
4. Newspaper clipping, ca. 1910, CHS museum object files.

Cat. 56

Sign for Curtis's Woodbury House, ca. 1882
or earlier
WOODBURY, CONNECTICUT

Innholder: Levi E. Curtis, active ca. 1874–1900
Maker unidentified

Images: None.
Text: On both sides, "WOODBURY, / HOUSE. / [L] . E . CURTISS".

Paint on pine board and moldings, gold leaf, iron hardware, 26-5/8" x 42-3/8"
1967.5.0

Illustrated: plate 56

Levi E. Curtis assumed proprietorship of the inn in Woodbury about 1882, following a long list of proprietors that can be traced back into the late eighteenth century. Curtis's advertising suggests that he actively promoted the age of his establishment as an inducement to guests: "Established 1754. / Curtis House, Main Street, Woodbury, Conn. / Quietly and pleasantly situated. First-class accommodations for both regular and transient guests."[1] About 1900, Curtis's successor, J. A. Sullivan, ordered "new and attractive signs" from Wallace Nutting (1861–1941), noted antiquarian, Colonial Revival pioneer, and reproduction furniture and hardware maker.[2] Nutting's signs, which apparently do not survive, were likely conscious imitations of earlier designs intended to recapture colonial sensibilities.

The Woodbury House sign relies on color and graphic design for its visual impact. Chinese red shading originally helped the block letters, now a faded gold, stand out from a bright blue background. The uppermost line forms a gentle arch with corner reserves, and the style of lettering varies from line to line. Placement of iron straps along the top and bottom of the sign indicate that it was bolted to the side of a supporting structure, either a post or a building, rather than attached from above.

Inn name: During Curtis's proprietorship, the establishment is listed in directories as "Curtis House."

Innholders: Levi E. Curtis (b. 1840) was the son of Stiles and Amelia Munrowe Curtis of Sherman, Conn. In 1870 he married Eliza Knapp of Pembroke, Conn. During the 1860s, he undertook a variety of businesses, operating as a cattle dealer in New Milford, Conn., and as a hat maker and a horse and produce dealer in Danbury, Conn. In 1874, he took up hotelkeeping, managing a hotel in Cornwall Bridge, Conn. In 1882 he sold the Cornwall Bridge hotel and purchased the Woodbury Hotel. There he followed a long series of innkeepers at the same location, stretching back to Damaria Gilchrist in the late eighteenth century.

Original location: According to local histories, the Woodbury House was built prior to 1736, when Rev. Anthony Stoddard, minister of the First Ecclesiastical Society of Woodbury, deeded the lot and house to his son. In 1882, Levi Curtis purchased "the McMurtree estate, known as the Woodbury Hotel." He subsequently raised the roof and added a third story and put in "modern conveniences."[3] The structure remains standing, and in operation as a hotel and restaurant, on the west side of Main Street (Route 6) in Woodbury.

Provenance: Purchased from Harold E. Cole, Woodbury, Conn.

Construction notes: Two or more boards, grain oriented horizontally, joined by a tongue-and-groove joint. Framing members, mitered at corners, are nailed to the outer edges of the signboard. Separate cove molding strips are set within the edges of the frame to complete the molding profile. No structural frame, no pediment or skirt.

Condition notes: Hanging hardware appears to be original. Surfaces are extremely worn.

1. *Barnes's Woodbury Directory of 1896,* p. 32.
2. Grace Curtis Sullivan, "The Curtis House," in Woodbury, Connecticut, Women's Club, *Woodbury and the Colonial Homes,* comp. by Mrs. Julia Minor Strong (N.p., 19??), p. 71.
3. *Biographical Review . . . Leading Citizens of Litchfield County Connecticut* (Boston: Biographic Review Publishing Co., 1896).

Cat. 57

Sign for Cooper's Hotel, 1850–1900
PROBABLY WESTERN CONNECTICUT

Innholder and maker unidentified

Images: None.
Text: On one side only, "COOPER'S. HOTEL."

Paint on pine board, sand or smalt, gold leaf, 6-3/8" x 58-1/4"
Gift of Newton C. Brainard, 1957.66.3

Illustrated: plate 57

Oral tradition links Cooper's Hotel sign to New Milford or Danbury, Connecticut, although no corresponding establishment has been located in the documentary record. The sign is significant as a generic example of an important change that took place in signage after the mid-nineteenth century. The board must be secured flat against a wall, where it is visible from the front only. Earlier, double-sided hanging signs, in contrast, displayed themselves to people approaching from either side.

Construction notes: Single board, grain oriented horizontally. Board is machine-planed and sawn to shape with cavetto, or hollow, molded edges. Two large holes at the board ends indicate that it was secured to a wall by nails or bolts.

Surface notes: The surface is worn. Gilded letters are imprecisely executed. Molded edges are painted red.

Publications: *MBTS*, p. 32.

Cat 58

Sign for the Chafee House, ca. 1865–90
MIDDLETOWN, CONNECTICUT

Innholder: George A. Chafee (active ca. 1865–1903)
Maker unidentified

Images: On both sides, relief-carved acanthus scroll.
Text: On both sides, above acanthus, "GEO.A.CHAFEE.", below acanthus, "'As we journey through / life, let us live by / the way'".

Paint on pine board, gold leaf, iron hardware, 27-1/4" x 36"
Collection of Morgan B. Brainard, Gift of Mrs. Morgan B. Brainard, 1961.63.14

Illustrated: color plate 58, fig. 79 (detail)

This sign differs from those made before the mid-nineteenth century in its reliance on graphic design and creative form. Its elaborate shape does not follow any particular tavern-sign convention, nor does it conform to the message verbalized by the sign. Instead, the lettering fills the available space. Applied ogee consoles, or brackets, fill the angular corners of the bottom and create a more cohesive, overall form. The bold lettering of the owner's name, arranged into a gentle arch, is the primary message by virtue of its size, placement, and clarity. The phrase below, rendered in a lighter italic, visually supports the arch. According to family history, the saying was a personal favorite of George Chafee's, but similar messages appear on other tavern-related artifacts, for example, a large English glass goblet, dated 1813, engraved with a tavern scene and the words, "In our Journey through life / May we live well on the road" (Currier Gallery of Art, Manchester, New Hampshire, 1981.4).

The central ornament is a scrolled acanthus leaf, a decorative device widely popularized in Victorian-era design books. Perhaps coincidentally, the particular form of this acanthus also resembles a ship's billethead, the ornamental wood carving fitted into the stemhead of the bow under the bowsprit, substituting for a more expensive figurehead. The resemblance to a billethead suggests the possibility of associations with maritime trade or clientele, perhaps production in one of Middletown's ship building or carving shops. George Chafee, the original owner of the sign, was also the owner of a steam packet, the *Geo. A. Chaffee*, registered 1870–72, operating between Middletown and New York City.[1]

The Chafee Hotel opened with much fanfare in 1889. "For the past score of years," a newspaper report commented, "Chafee has been a name well known to the traveling public and want of room on prior occasions has only been his defeat in entertaining." To remedy this lack, Chafee had renovated and expanded "the old Dr. Baker residence" on Court Street: "The new hotel is striking to the eye, neat in general appearance, and there is that home-like air to it that causes one to be greeted with an air of comfort, second to none except home. The new addition erected to the premises comprise the elegant dining room and sample room, with sleeping apartments overhead." Other amenities included a billiard room, reading room, and two "elegant parlors." "Each [sleeping] room is supplied with electric lights and bells, and stationery wash stands, with hot and cold water. Bath rooms are on each floor and numerous."[2]

Innholders: George Austin Chafee (1840–1903) was born in Bristol, Rhode Island, of Irish descent. He was married in Middletown, Conn., to Matilda Pitt of Birmingham, England. He eventually owned several enterprises in Middletown, beginning on College Street about 1865, with a "city restaurant and lager beer saloon," located just next to the Universalist Church (*Middletown Directory*, 1869/70). By the late 1880s, he expanded his hotel operations, running the Kilbourn House on Main Street for about a year and later opening the Chafee Hotel on Court Street. Throughout the period 1865–1900, the Middletown Directories list numerous members of the Chafee family in various tavern and hotelkeeping occupations.

Original location: According to Chafee's son, Charles A. Chafee, this sign hung first at Chafee's café on College Street and later "above the front steps of the Court street hotel." The Chafee Hotel was located in "the old Dr. Baker place on Court street," which Chafee remodeled and enlarged into a hotel building in 1889. Letterhead from Chafee's Hotel in the twentieth century shows what appears to be an early nineteenth-century (possibly earlier) five-bay, Georgian house, expanded substantially to the rear and updated with a porch running the full width of the façade and a fountain on the side. The only sign visible is a narrow, horizontal nameband reading "CHAFEE", mounted on the gable wall (similar to cat. 57).

Provenance: Acquired by Morgan Brainard from Charles A. Chafee, son of the original owner, and proprietor of Chafee's Hotel from 1903 until it closed in 1936.

Construction notes: At least four boards, grain oriented horizontally, are joined with tongue-and-groove joints and then cut into a decorative shape. Bullnose moldings are applied with nails to the outer edges.

Surface notes: Letters and central acanthus scroll are relief carved. A random repeating punched star pattern is seen throughout the gilded background. Microscopic examination indicates that there are two layers of gilding present and at least two layers of black paint on the letters, possibly three. The black surfaces of these letters were originally highlighted in gold designs, and possibly outlined in red. Coffee-colored paint on the outer moldings is a more recent application.

Condition and treatment notes: The tongue-and-groove joints between the boards had been glued during an earlier repair effort, of undetermined date, causing splitting along portions of the joins. Treatment at WACC, 1999–2000, included consolidation of wood, insertion of stainless steel dowels to increase structural stability, surface cleaning and consolidation.

Publications: *MBTS*, p. 27.

1. New London Customs House Records; M. W. Jacobus, *The Connecticut River Steamboat Story* (Hartford: The Connecticut Historical Society, 1956), pp. 100–2.
2. "Chafee's New Hotel," 1889, newspaper clipping, CHS museum object files.

Cat. 59*

Sign for Crofut's Inn, ca. 1892 or earlier
OXFORD, CONNECTICUT

Innholder: George E. Crofut (active 1892–1910 or later)
Maker unidentified

Images: On both sides, rebus with a crow in a tree and a foot suspended from the sky, above a house.
Text: On both sides, "'s" to the right of the foot, and "INN" on the roof of the porch of the house.

Paint, probably pine board and moldings, iron hardware, 37-3/4" x 37-3/4"
Collection of Morgan B. Brainard, Gift of Mrs. Morgan B. Brainard, 1961.63.19

Illustrated: color plate 59

This delightful, if somewhat unusual, sign painting is a rebus, or pictorial representation of a word or phrase. The crow and the foot in the heavens form the innkeeper's name, while the sprawling, gambrel-roofed building is labeled an inn. "Crow-foot's Inn" thus identifies Crofut's Inn, which operated in Oxford, a rural town in western Connecticut, from 1892 until at least 1910. A photograph taken in 1909 by Hartford photographer John Emery Morris depicts the inn with this sign projecting out over the front porch. A horizontal name band, similar to that of Cooper's Hotel (cat. 57), reads more conventionally, "CROFUT'S INN.", and is mounted along the roofline of the porch at the gable end of the house. The building shown in the photograph looks nothing like the building pictured on the sign.[1]

The age and origin of this sign are ambiguous. Materials, construction, shrinkage, and other physical features suggest that the signboard itself may be of late eighteenth- or early-nineteenth-century vintage. The paint surface does not appear to be as old as the signboard itself. It is possible that Crofut's father, also named George, may have used the signboard, as census records indicate that he was operating a boarding house in Middlebury, Connecticut, in 1880. Alternatively, the younger Crofut may have acquired a pre-existing signboard from almost any source, including England. In addition to the rebus, two features of this sign differ from typical Connecticut examples: its square shape and the thick, black mar-

gin surrounding the image. Similar borders occur on signs made elsewhere, including the sign for Wedgwood's inn, probably from the area of Portsmouth, New Hampshire (cat. 38).

Innholders: George E. Crofut (b. ca. 1859) was the son of George and Mary J. Crofut of New York. The Crofut family was living in Middlebury, Conn., at the time of the 1880 census.

Original location: The Crofut Inn was located on the west side of Southbury Road (Rt. 67) in Oxford. The house was operated as an inn by the widowed Maria Louisa McEwen Wilcoxson, ca. 1882–92. George E. Crofut bought the property in 1892 and continued operating it until at least 1911. The building was demolished during a highway widening about 1931.

Construction notes: Two boards, grain oriented horizontally, joined with a tongue-and-groove joint. Signboard is set within grooves of applied moldings, which are nailed to the edges and mitered at corners. Separate cove molding strips are applied to the inside recess between the signboard and frame, holding the signboard in place. No structural frame, no pediment or skirt.

Surface notes: Moldings have been repainted two or three times.

Condition and treatment notes: Hanging hardware is replaced. Original hanging system appears to have been large eye screws set into the top molding, extending into the upper board. Wood shrinkage has opened the join between the two boards. Side 2 had darkened, possibly through application of successive oil coatings. Side 1 was cleaned ca. 1960–62 and possibly recoated with glossy coating. Treatment at WACC, 2000, included surface cleaning, removal of varnish from both sides, consolidation of split top molding, and resecuring of hardware.

Exhibitions: Japan 1970.

Publications: *MBTS*, p. 34; Smith, *Tavern Signs*, p. 12; *CHSB* 27 (April 1962): cover (in situ); *Decorator* 1960, p. 5; Terry, *Old Inns*, p. 241; *Antiques* 1928, p. 402.

1. John Emery Morris, photograph of Crofut's Inn, Oxford, Conn., dated 1909 (Collection of the Historical Society of Glastonbury); illus. *CHSB* 27 (April 1962): cover.

Cat. 60

Sign for the Grosvenor Inn, dated 1765 and 1894,
probably made ca. 1772–86
POMFRET, CONNECTICUT (ABINGTON SECTION)

Innholders: Caleb Grosvenor (active ca. 1772–86); Ben Grosvenor (active ca. 1872–1923)
Maker unidentified, restored by Augustus Hoppin (1828–96)

Images: On side 1, profile view of riderless black horse, galloping on green ground. On side 2, profile view of white horse, also galloping on green ground and carrying a rider (possibly George Washington) holding an early version of the American flag.
Text: On both sides, on apron, "C*Grosvenor / 1765." Side 2 lacks the period after the date.
Signature: On side 2, at left end of upper rail, "Restored / 1894 / by A.H.", painted inside a circle.

Paint on pine board, posts of unidentified hardwood, iron hardware, 47" x 32-3/4"

Gift of Benjamin Grosvenor, Mrs. John P. Grosvenor, Mrs. Florence G. Connell and Miss Constance Grosvenor, 1963.52.0

Illustrated: plate 60 (side 1), fig. 93 (side 2)

Although the Grosvenor sign was entirely repainted and partially restored in the late nineteenth century, several physical features corroborate its eighteenth-century origin. The outer posts exhibit typical eighteenth-century turnings with centered rings in the same manner as the three signs attributed to the Saybrook sign maker (cat. 1, 3, 6). Additional scored rings flanking the mid-ring—barely visible beneath the heavy paint layers—exhibit a level of refinement associated with earlier turning. Some edges of the horse and equestrian figures, which may have been transferred to each side from a common pattern, appear to have been outlined with a cutting blade as was common in eighteenth-century sign decoration. Finally, the "C*Grosvenor" name across the lower rail is raised above the ground, a result of weathering generally associated with age. The use of both vertical stiles and vertical posts is an unusual feature, as is the double set of moldings framing the picture space: both stiles and rails have quarter round moldings run on their inner edges, as well as applied molding strips, which appear to be original. The combination makes up one the most complex assemblages of woodworking to survive on an eighteenth-century Connecticut sign.

Restoration work, dated 1894, evidently included the complete removal of earlier paint layers, as laboratory anaylsis indicates that all visible paint surfaces post-date the middle of the nineteenth century. Although the extent of multiple imagery on signs in the Connecticut Historical Society collection suggests that most sign painters simply painted over earlier work, not bothering to remove it, period manuals do describe several methods for effecting the complete removal of earlier paint layers (see Chapter Six). In any case, no evidence survives of the eighteenth-century imagery. The present equestrian figure suggests a portrait of George Washington, perhaps a reference to the first president's celebrated 1789 tour of New England, when he "bated the horses in Pomfret, at Colo. Grosvenor's" (presumably the inn run by Ebenezer Grosvenor, brother of Caleb, on the east side of town).[1] The display of the Grand Union flag, which flew over the patriot army in Boston until 1776, also suggests a commemorative gesture. The pediment was presumably added in 1894, as the thickness of wood does not match that of the upper rail to which it attaches. Its profile, exactly mirroring that of the skirt, is likely conjectural. Most eighteenth-century Connecticut signs feature pediments of much more elaborate profile than the skirts.[2] The numerals in the 1765 date were probably added during the 1894 restoration campaign. They are not raised, indicating that they are not as old as the letters in "C*Grosvenor". If there was a date on the eighteenth-century sign, it would likely have been located on the original pediment, now lost.

According to Grosvenor family history, this sign was found by late nineteenth-century innkeeper, Benjamin Hutchins Grosvenor, on property located along the old Hartford-Boston post road, west of Pomfret center, which had once been owned by Caleb Grosvenor, an eighteenth-century innkeeper from another branch of the same family. The date 1765, added in the 1894 restoration, does not correspond to known licensing dates for Caleb Grosvenor; it likely refers to the presumed construction date of the dwelling occupied by Benjamin Grosvenor's Colonial Revival inn, which the restored sign ornamented. Augustus Hoppin, who restored the sign in 1894, was a well-known illustrator of books and magazines and a member of Pomfret's summer colony.

Innholders: Caleb Grosvenor, [Sr.] (1716–88) was the son of Ebenezer and Ann Marcy Grosvenor of Pomfret, Conn., both descendants of long-established local families. In 1739 he married Sarah Carpenter (1720–93). When the Third Ecclesiastical Society built a new church for Abington, in the western section of Pomfret, in 1753, Caleb Grosvenor had the first choice of pews, in recognition of his payment of the largest amount of taxes.[3] Tavern licenses granted to Caleb Grosvenor of Pomfret survive from the years 1772–85.

Caleb Grosvenor, [Jr.] (b. 1751) was the son of Caleb and Sarah Carpenter Grosvenor of Pomfret. He may be the Caleb Grosvenor licensed in the nearby towns of Ashford, 1777–79, and Woodstock, 1787–89.

Benjamin Hutchins Grosvenor (1841–1923) was the son of John Williams and Phebe Spalding Grosvenor of Pomfret. Ben Grosvenor, as he was known, was the great-grandson of Amos Grosvenor (1723–90), a first cousin of Caleb Grosvenor, He served as a government Indian agent in Nebraska prior to marrying Anna Mathewson (1842–1927) of Pomfret in 1867.[4]

Original location: An advertisement in the *New London Gazette* for 10 March 1786 describes the Grosvenor tavern stand, located in the western section of Pomfret, known as Abington: "To be SOLD or LET, And entered immediately, A FARM containing about 300 acres, situated in Pomfret, Abington society, on the middle post-road leading from Hartford to Boston, with a large dwelling-house (which is now and has been for a number of years improved as a public house) and barn thereon. Said Farm is under good improvement, has an excellent orchard, which will make 80 barrels of cider annually, is well proportioned for mowing, pasturing, plowing and wood, and well watered. Said Farm will be sold for part hard money, part public securities, and part English or West-India goods, as may best suit the purchaser.—For further particulars, enquire of CALEB GROSVENOR, living on said Farm."

The Ben Grosvenor Inn opened ca. 1872 in a different farmhouse, located on the north-south Norwich-Worcester Turnpike, which was also known as Pomfret Street. The original two-story farmhouse had been built as a parsonage by the Rev. Aaron Putnam, circa 1758–62. It remained a private residence until purchased by Benjamin H. Grosvenor in 1871. Pomfret was then becoming a fashionable summer resort, and Grosvenor began taking in summer boarders the following year. By 1875 he was expanding the inn and its operations. He enlarged the inn, effectively enclosing the old homestead within a larger building with three-story, porticoed façade. The Ben Grosvenor Inn eventually provided housing for two hundred guests, with over nine hundred acres of farmland supporting the operation.[5] The Ben Grosvenor Inn ceased operations in the early 1940s and was sold to the Pomfret School in 1944. It was demolished in 1960.

Provenance: The sign was donated to The Connecticut Historical Society by Benjamin Grosvenor (grandson of Benjamin Hutchins Grosvenor), his mother, and sisters. According to the donors, Benjamin Hutchins Grosvenor found the sign stored behind a partition of a building on a farmstead, located on Ragged Hill Road, about three miles west of the Ben Grosvenor Inn. The Ragged Hill Road property, reportedly the site of Caleb Grosvenor's eighteenth-century inn, was one of several properties acquired by Ben Grosvenor in the late 1800s in support of his hotel operations.

Construction notes: Single board, grain oriented vertically, flat horizontal rails with integral pediment and skirt, vertical stiles, and also turned posts. The board is set into grooves in the inner edges of the stiles, which are in turn tenoned into the rails and double pinned. The rails extend up and down to form a decoratively-shaped pediment (now replaced) and skirt. Rails are tenoned through the turned posts and double pinned. The picture panel is framed by two sets of moldings: first, decorative moldings cut into the inner edges of the rails and stiles, and second, applied ogee-shaped molding strips, mitered at corners, nailed to the faces of the rails and stiles. The accuracy of the pediment profile, exactly mirroring the skirt, cannot be confirmed. No evidence of the original pediment shape survived the restoration, and may not even have existed at that time, prompting a conjectural design.

Surface notes: The two horses may have originated from a single drawing or template, as they are very close in form and positioning. Outlines appear to have been transferred onto the board using incised or scribed lines to indicate the forms prior to painting. The flag carried by the equestrian rider displays the design of the Cambridge or Grand Union flag of 1776.

Condition and treatment notes: The hanging hardware appears old and may be original, although it is looped rather than split and welded in typical eighteenth-century fashion. The pediment portion of the top rail is a late-nineteenth-century replacement. The lower portion of one bottom block of one turned post is missing. The opposite post is probably missing a turned drop. A section of the top applied molding on side 1 is missing. Treatment at WACC, 1998–99, included surface cleaning, paint consolidation, and inpainting of paint loss on horse's chest on side 1.

Publications: Smith, *Tavern Signs*, p. 14 (side 2); Lathrop, *Early American Inns*, p. 96; Earle, *Tavern Days*, p. 432; John Addison Porter, "Picturesque Pomfret," *Connecticut Quarterly*, vol. 2, no. 1 (Jan.–March 1896): 5 (side 2, with hanging bracket).

1. Quoted in Crofut, *Guide*, vol. 2, p. 857.
2. Similar pediment and skirt designs do appear on the Perkins inn sign, from West Greenwich, Rhode Island, some twenty-five miles southeast of Pomfret; however, even here the pediment is of slightly greater depth than the skirt (cat. 15).
3. Clarence Winthrop Bowen, *The History of Woodstock, Connecticut*, 8 vols. (Norwood, Mass., The Plimpton Press, 1935), vol. 6, p. 269.
4. Ibid., vol. 6, p. 333.
5. Crofut, *Guide*, vol. 2, p. 857.

Cat. 61

Sign for Van Der Hayden's Inn, dated 1796,
repainted ca. 1890–1920
PROBABLY WATERVLIET, NEW YORK

Innholder: John Van Der Hayden, Jr.
Maker unidentified

Images: On side 1, landscape scene with profile view of black horse, at walking pace, with male rider in eighteenth-century attire, probably George Washington. Side 2 is the same, except horse is prancing.

Text: On side 1, on pediment, "1796", below image, "Entertainment / B Y / John Van Der Hayden jun". On side 2, on pediment, "1796", below image, "Entertainment By / John Van der Hayden Junr."

Paint on pine board and moldings, iron hardware, 52-1/4" x 27-1/4"
Collection of Morgan B. Brainard, Gift of Mrs. Morgan B. Brainard, 1961.63.29

Illustrated: plate 61

Late nineteenth- or early twentieth-century overpaint almost completely covers an earlier, weathered image that survived in relief. Traces of scribed outlines used to design the original image are visible through the overpaint, which is applied in a crude, blotchy manner, perhaps intended to convey—or retain—an appearance of age. The overall construction echoes that of the Caulkins sign (cat. 14), supporting an original production date in the 1790s. The horseback rider, with white wig, three-cornered hat, sword, breeches, and riding boots, is presumably George Washington, whose likeness was everywhere and in all media in the new nation.

Innholders: John Van Der Hayden, Jr., was the son of John Van Der Hayden (b. 1725) of Albany, New York. The younger man married Annatje Perrie and evidently removed to nearby Watervliet, where he appears in the 1790 census. Both father and son used the anglicized form of the original name, "Johnannes Vanderheyden."

Construction notes: Three boards, grain oriented vertically, hand-sawn at top only to create decorative pediment profile. No skirt and no structural frame. Large, applied moldings, mitered at corners, are nailed to the side and bottom edges of the signboard. Smaller molding strips are nailed to the faces of the signboard at the top to complete the rectangular picture frame.

Surface notes: Both sides have a heavy, browning coat of varnish. Side 1 has slightly less overpaint, with small areas of older surface visible, as in saddle blanket. Board surfaces appear well weathered under the paint. Moldings are painted a reddish-brown on the outer edge, yellow on the inner. The pediment is a pale yellow green with thick, glossy black outline with leaf-like projections along its inner edge. The size of the name band and lettering differ slightly from side to side. The name band on side 1 is higher than that on side 2, and the lettering is on three lines, with the word "BY" in uppercase Roman letters. On side 2, the text occupies only two lines, with the word, "By" in script on the top line. A pattern of nail holes bordering the name band below "Entertainment By" suggests that another name plaque once covered the Van Der Heyden name, marking a change in ownership of the inn.

Condition notes: Hanging hardware appears to be original. Moldings have been reinforced with later nails.

Publications: *MBTS*, p. 45; Robert Bishop, *Folk Painters of America* (New York, Dutton, 1979), p. 32; *American Heritage* 1960, p. 62. Textbooks, various editions: *This Is America's Story* (Houghton Mifflin).

Sign for the Windham Inn, dated 1783 and 1891

WINDHAM, CONNECTICUT

Innholder: George A. Challenger (active ca. 1886–1928)
Maker unidentified

Images: On both sides, the arms of Scotland.
Text: On both sides, on pediment, "1783", on skirt, "1891".

Paint on wood, probably pine, gold leaf, iron, metal alloy,
69-3/4" x 43"
Collection of Morgan B. Brainard, Gift of Mrs. Morgan B.
Brainard, 1961.63.52

Illustrated: plate 62

A 1909 postcard depicts this sign hanging in front of the picturesque Windham Inn, a brick structure located on the green in
the northeastern Connecticut town of Windham. Use of this structure as a public house probably dates back to at least 1849, and it
evidently replaced an earlier inn on the same site. The early date
on the sign, 1783, appears to be too early for the construction of
the building depicted in the postcard, but it may relate to the earlier inn (Mercy Lathrop Fitch Carey took over operation of the tavern for the second time, after the death of her second husband, in
that year). The later date, 1891, corresponds to George Challenger's announcement, in the Willimantic Directory, that "This
fine House located in a beautiful old Town, has just been refur-
nished in a first-class manner, and is a fine residence for summer
boarders . . . [with] Horses and Pleasure Carriages to Let." Challenger had acquired the property about 1886, having previously
been an innkeeper in Scotland, Connecticut, less than five miles to
the east. The association with Scotland reappears in the otherwise
unexplained selection of the Scottish royal arms—a pair of unicorns flanking a central cartouche—as a pictorial device on this
sign. The two cast metal frogs atop the pediment are a reference,
both humorous and historical, to a local incident celebrated in
song, verse, and pageantry: the "Windham panic" of 1754 occurred
when an unnaturally loud clamor of frogs was thought to be either
advancing French and Indian troops or harbingers of the day of
judgment.[1]

Conflicting evidence makes dating problematic. Massive scale,
complex construction, and modern paint decoration convey the
sense of heightened colonialism that is a hallmark of Colonial
Revival products. Neither the overall design, notably the triangular pediment, nor the painted image have close counterparts
among documented late-eighteenth-century Connecticut signs.
The use of applied, split spindles rather than full, turned posts is
also atypical. No evidence of earlier imagery is apparent through
the layers of modern paint. However, the joinery, molding profiles,
and the turning of the split columns are consistent with earlier
work. Close examination reveals the presence of hand-forged nails
to secure applied moldings. The technique of using separate molding strips applied to the joined frame to produce an extra layer of
moldings also appears on the late-eighteenth-century Grosvenor

sign from Pomfret, a little more than twenty miles to the north
(cat. 60). The two signs are also similar in the use of a shallow half-
round ornamenting the pediment of one and skirt of the other. The
broken triangular pediment design of the Windham sign is not
characteristic of other Connecticut examples, but it does relate
closely to two large, early signs from Pennsylvania, which document the early use of this feature.[2]

Inn names: Directories for 1849–89 list the establishment as "Windham Hotel" or "Windham House." Beginning in 1890, it is consistently
listed as "Windham Inn."

Innholders: George Edward Challenger (1849–1928) was the son of
Samuel Challenger, Jr., and Charlotte Savage Wilcox. He was born
near Bath, England, came to the United States with his family at age
five, and worked in textile mills in Massachusetts and Connecticut
before becoming an innkeeper. He married Maria A. Finran of
Worcester, Mass.

Original location: A series of panoramic photographs of the Windham
Green, dating to the 1890s, depicts this sign in situ, hanging from the
branch of a large tree growing near the corner of the Windham Inn, a
white-painted brick house at the northeast corner of the Green. A
hotel had operated continuously on this site, along the main road from
Hartford to Providence, Rhode Island, from at least 1849, passing
through a series of proprietors. An earlier inn, possibly in a previous
structure, had been operated from circa 1755–1807, by related members of the Fitch and Carey families (John Fitch, Jr., active circa 1755;
his widow; Mercy Lathrop Fitch, active 1755–67; her second husband,
Eleazer Carey, active ca. 1767–82; and again Mercy Lathrop Fitch
Carey and her son, John Fitch, ca. 1783–1807). George Challenger
acquired the property about 1886 from the widow of the previous
hotelkeeper, B. S. Wilbur. He made extensive renovations, including
piping in spring water. In 1920, the Windham Inn was described as
drawing "a liberal patronage from city people during the heated
months of summer."[3] It continued to operate until 1942, but by 1950 it
had become a convalescent home.

Construction notes: Two or more boards, grain oriented vertically, with
flat horizontal rails and vertical stiles. The signboard is set within
channels on the inside edges of the rails and stiles. Rails are tenoned
into the stiles and secured with double pins set on a diagonal. The
inner edges of these framing members are molded and cut to miters at
the corners. Rails and stiles have additional moldings nailed to their
faces, along the outer edges. Split turnings, cut to fit over the hanging
hardware, are nailed to the outer edges of both stiles. The pediment
and skirt are made of separate boards, grain oriented horizontally,
which are nailed to outer edges of the rails. The pediment is cut to a
triangular "broken" pediment profile, with molding caps nailed to the
top edges. The skirt is cut to a decorative profile with two large central
lobes bordered by two smaller lobes at the outer corners.

Surface notes: The unicorns are executed in gold leaf on a blue background. The frame is painted white with black trim. The painting of
the two unicorns and the cartouche has been strengthened since the
publication of the sign in a photographic postcard about 1909 (CHS,
Graphics Collection). Dates and some decorative trim have also been
repainted. No evidence of an earlier image has been observed,
although the blue backround appears to contain remnant deposits of
smalt.

Condition notes: Hanging hardware appears to be original. Drops at
the bottoms of the split columns are missing, possibly sawn off. The
pediment cap may be a replacement.

Publications: *MBTS*, p. 71.

1. Ellen D. Larned, *History of Windham County, Connecticut*, 2 vols. (Worcester, Mass.: By the author, 1874), vol. 1, pp. 560–63.
2. Signs from the Three Crowns or Waterloo tavern, dated 1771, Salisbury Township, and the William Pitt sign, dated 1808, signed by Jacob Eicholtz, from Lancaster County, are of similarly large size and overall design. They also appear to share similar framing construction and molding configurations; Earle, *Tavern Days*, pp. 143, 156; Smith, *Tavern Signs*, pp. 24, 45. Of these two, only the Pitt sign has been examined first-hand. The Three Crowns sign is currently unlocated.
3. Allen B. Lincoln, ed., *A Modern History of Windham, Connecticut*, 2 vols. (Chicago: S.J. Clarke, 1920), vol. 2, p. 1448.

Cat. 63

Sign for Pettibone's Tavern, ca. 1810–24, repainted ca. 1939

SIMSBURY, CONNECTICUT (WEATOGUE SECTION)

Innholder: Jonathan Pettibone, Jr. (active 1776–1824)
Maker: possibly William Rice (1777–1847)

Images: On both sides, eagle based on the United States seal, with forty-eight stars overhead.
Text: On both sides, above the image, "PETTIBONE'S", below the image, "¹⁷⁸⁰ *TAVERN*."

Paint on pine board and moldings, gold leaf, iron hardware, 43" x 55-1/4"
Collection of Morgan B. Brainard, Gift of Mrs. Morgan B. Brainard, 1961.63.40

Illustrated: plate 63

This early nineteenth-century sign was repaired and completely repainted after incurring hurricane damage in 1938. Comparison with a photograph published in 1937 documents the replacement of the moldings, the appearance of a full-width, horizontal crack, changes to the field of stars, alteration of details in the lettering and eagle (although placement remained constant), and addition of the 1780 date commemorating erection of the original tavern. The present version has forty-eight stars, corresponding to the number of states in the Union in 1939. The earlier version had seventeen stars, corresponding to the number of states from 1803–12 and pointing to a possible production date in the midst of Jonathan Pettibone, Jr.'s, long tenure as innkeeper, from ca. 1775–1824.

Several features link this sign to the workshop of William Rice, including the large rectangular format and bold eagle with outswept wings (the eagle's beak and wings, as depicted in 1937, strongly resemble Rice examples). Moreover, assuming that the replacement framing elements followed the originals, the unusual method of cutting the moldings so that one piece slides over the other in the corners has thus far been found only on Rice signs. A disturbance in the heavy paint in the lower right of the red field on one side may represent a Rice signature. The pattern of disturbance conforms to the upper-and-lower-case lettering typical of his early style. Similar disturbances in the thick impasto, behind the eagle at shoulder height, provide evidence of a block-lettered name, not yet deciphered.

Innholders: Col. Jonathan Pettibone, Jr. (1741–1826) was the son of Col. Jonathan Pettibone. His tenure as innkeeper lasted nearly fifty years, from at least 1775 until 1824, when he was eighty-three years old. He was active in the militia and represented Simsbury in the state legislature. His son, Virgil, continued to operate a tavern, presumably at the same location, until at least 1845, perhaps later.

Original location: Jonathan Pettibone's tavern was strategically located at the crossing of the Farmington River, at the intersection of the road to Hartford with the main north-south road traversing the Farmington River Valley from Farmington to Granby. According to local histories, the structure was originally built about 1780, burned about 1800, and was subsequently rebuilt. It reportedly served as a stop on the Underground Railroad. It was acquired by Mrs. Sargent-Tilney in 1919 and restored for renewed use as an inn. It is now the Chart House restaurant, on the northeast corner of Routes 10 and 185.

Provenance: The inn and its sign remained in the Pettibone family until about 1870. When the property was sold, the sign apparently accompanied it. Photographs depict the sign hanging in situ in the 1890s.

Construction notes: One or more boards, grain oriented horizontally, are set within channels in the side, or upright, molding elements, which are nailed in place. The ends of the top and bottom moldings are cut to the shape of the inside contour of the side moldings, so that the side moldings can slide over the ends as the large signboard expands and contracts across the grain with changes in humidity (see fig. 18 for detail of this characteristic feature, on another Rice sign).

Surface notes: Thick coats of modern paint cover all surfaces. The present forty-eight stars were stencilled and have five points each. The earlier stars had eight points each. Traces of similar stars in slightly different locations are visible throughout the field above the eagle. The word "TAVERN" is executed in italic, the other text in Roman lettering. Some gold leaf appears on the eagle.

Condition notes: All of the moldings are replacements. Assuming the hanging hardware is original, it has been reattached to the new moldings. Sheet metal plates have been nailed to the upper corners.

Publications: *MBTS*, p. 58; "Stories From the Freedom Trail," videotape (Connecticut Public Television, 1998); *Spinning Wheel* 1955, p. 12; Terry, *Old Inns*, p. 51.

Cat. 64

Sign for H. Rust, early twentieth century

PROBABLY NORTHEASTERN UNITED STATES

Maker unidentified

Images: On side 1, profile of standing horse, with person in riding costume holding lead line. On side 2, eagle based on United States seal.
Text: On both sides, in band above the image, "H. RUST", in band below the image, "INN / 1820". On side 1, in the image field, above the horse, "POST ROAD", and below the horse, "Lady Madison 2.05". On side 2, in the image field, in banner above the eagle, "E. PLURIBUS UNUM", below the eagle, "POST ROAD".

Paint on pine board and moldings, iron hardware, 39-1/4" x 21-7/8"
Collection of Morgan B. Brainard, Gift of Maxwell L. Brainard,

Charles E. Brainard, Mrs. Edward M. Brainard, Mrs. Morgan B. Brainard, Jr., and Mrs. H.S. Robinson, Jr. (Constance Brainard), 1971.30.2

Illustrated: plate 64

At first glance, Rust's sign looks like yet another variation of late-eighteenth or early-nineteenth century work. A similar configuration of dark name bands above an image of a horse being held by a standing figure appears on an undated Rhode Island sign, published in 1926.[1] However, the delineation of costume of the figure leading the horse on this example strongly resembles artwork on early twentieth-century posters or magazine covers. The inscription underneath the horse is believed to be her name and track record, "Lady Madison 2.05." The eagle differs from early counterparts in numerous features, including such details as the banner and lettering, stars, and feather terminations, as well as its posture and the overall looseness with which it is handled. The exceptionally broad name band at the bottom has no known correlate.

Construction details corroborate an early twentieth-century production date. The signboard is a full inch thick, noticeably thicker than the usual 5/8" to 3/4" measurement. It is likely a fragment from an early building. The face moldings appear to be made from standard twentieth-century household cornice moldings. Wrought-iron barn door hinges with the top leaf shortened serve as hanging hardware. Surface details suggest an intentional effort to create an illusion of age and weathering, through the uneven application of paint and multiple coatings of darkened and muted paint and varnish.

Construction notes: Thick, single board, grain oriented vertically. Molding strips, mitered in corners, are nailed to the borders of each face. No structural frame, no pediment or skirt.

Surface notes: The handling of paint is not typical of sign painting technique. Letters and numerals are stenciled. There are four paint layers, all gray, brown or green, as well as a brush-applied "grime/patination" layer and evidence of distressing using sandpaper.

Publications: *MBTS*, p. 63.

1. Sign for Mowry's Inn, undated, Lime Rock; Chapin, p. 24; also Earle, *Tavern Days*, p. 57. Similar motifs of a standing figure holding a horse appear in the sign for Hays's inn, undated, Brattleboro, Vt., in Earle, *Tavern Days*, p. 65; on the sign for Dean's inn, undated, from Wickford, R.I. (Old Sturbridge Village); and on a sea chest, ca. 1825, which also displays a lion and a leaping horse with rider, similar to those painted on signs; Lipman and Winchester, *Flowering of American Folk Art*, p. 237. These objects have not been examined first-hand by the writers.

Cat. 65

Sign for Palmer's Inn, 1780–1815
PROBABLY ENGLAND

Innholder and maker unidentified

Images: On both sides, stylized floral border surrounds central motif of a floral wreath hanging from floral swags, with stylized pineapple below.
Text: On both sides, "ENTERTAINMENT / BY / W. Palmer".

Paint on pine board and frame, iron hardware, 42" x 30"
Collection of Morgan B. Brainard, Gift of Mrs. Morgan B. Brainard, 1961.63.38

Illustrated: plate 65

Several characteristics of this sign are strongly unlike signs made in Connecticut and elsewhere in the United States. The species of pine of which it is made exhibits large and numerous knots, not typically used in American woodworking of the nineteenth century. Construction, notably decorative moldings that double as battens, favors boards of narrow width, another non-American feature. The exclusive use of stenciling as a decorative technique is also highly unusual in American signs. Traces of paint suggest that this sign originally was white with blue and white decoration. The innkeeper's name, possibly painted in yet another color, is carefully executed above a diapered band across the panel. The side and bottom molding faces are decorated with meandering floral vines, and more diapered bands ornament the top and flank the iron hanging straps. Lively details add visual delight, including an inverted crescent above a six-pointed star in the center of the wreath, and small curved hearts used as periods in the text.[1] Even the edges are ornamented, with a rope motif.

Construction notes: Three narrow boards, grain oriented vertically, laid edge to edge and secured by broad, batten-like strips of wood nailed to each face with T-headed nails that extend through the three layers of wood and are clinched on the opposite side. The inner edges of these strips are shaped to a cove molding, mitered in the corners. Wood is identified as eastern white pine, by analysis (Hoadley, March 2000). This species identification by microscopic analysis contrasts with the macroscopic observation of non-American features, as described in the text of this entry.

Surface notes: The painted decoration is stenciled. The white or light-colored background paint has worn away almost completely except for small patches on one side and in the cove moldings under the top rails on each side.

Condition notes: Hanging hardware appears to be original. The surfaces of the sign appear to have been oiled.

Publications: *MBTS*, p. 56.

1. Similar to the asymetrical hearts seen in scrimshaw and other folk arts of northern New England, as well as the "bleeding heart" motif popular among Catholic French-Canadians; Richard C. Malley, *In Their Hours of Ocean Leisure: Scrimshaw in the Cold Spring Harbor Whaling Museum* (Cold Spring Harbor, New York: Whaling Museum Society, 1993), pp. 42–44.

Sign Painters in Connecticut, 1760–1850

By Margaret C. Vincent

With the exception of those painted by William Rice, most extant Connecticut tavern and inn signs bear no artist's signature. In an effort to identify possible creators of the many anonymous works, The Connecticut Historical Society has compiled documentation on artisans known to have painted signs in the state between 1760 and 1850. The biographies presented below summarize findings to date, which provide useful data about artisans active in particular areas at times when particular signs were made (see Tables 1 and 2).

This list of sign painters is admittedly incomplete. First, the artisans listed in the biographies have been identified largely through newspaper advertisements and directory listings, but a newspaper ad offering to paint signs does not prove that the individual did paint signs. Second, the list is geographically uneven, with more extensive research having been done for areas with heavier concentrations of signs in The Connecticut Historical Society's collection (see map, fig. 110). Coverage of the Hartford area is particularly strong, thanks in large part to the index of the *Connecticut Courant* from its beginning in 1764 through 1820. Third, it has been difficult to trace the movements of painters who were clearly itinerant during their times away from Connecticut.

Due to the parameters of research and the limitations of sources, many artisans were probably missed entirely. Others were investigated but are not included here due to inadequate documentation. Among these are locally and even nationally known artists—William Johnson, Winthrop Chandler, Ralph Earl, William and Richard Jennys, Richard Brunton—as well as less famous artisans such as Hartford coach manufacturer George Francis and other coach, furniture, house, and ship painters. Though most, if not all, of these individuals may have painted signs, no clear reference to such activity has yet been found, so they remain in our unpublished "pending" file. Undoubtedly, further research and input from other scholars will expand and refine the present list.

Key to Citations for Sign Painters' Biographies

Barbour Index
 Connecticut State Library, Barbour Index to Connecticut Vital Records (microfilm, CHS Library).

Bénézit
 Emmanuel Bénézit, *Dictionnaire Critique et Docuementaire des Peintres, Sculpteurs, Dessinateurs et Graveurs,* rev. ed. 8 vols. (Librarie Gründ, 1966).

CHSB
 Connecticut Historical Society Bulletin.

Conn. Gazette
 Connecticut Gazette [newspaper], New London.

Courant
 Connecticut Courant [newspaper], Hartford.

Dunlap
 William Dunlap, *History of the Rise and Progress of the Arts of Design in the United States,* 3 vols. (New York: George P. Scott, 1834).

Evans
 Nancy Goyne Evans, *American Windsor Chairs* (New York: Hudson Hills Press, 1996).

French
 H. W. French, *Art and Artists in Connecticut,* reprint ed. (1879; New York: Kennedy Graphics, Inc. Da Capo Press, 1970).

Gerdts
 William H. Gerdts, *Art Across America: Two Centuries of Regional Painting, 1710–1920,* 3 vols. (New York: Abbeville, 1990).

Groce and Wallace
 George C. Groce and David H. Wallace, *The New-York Historical Society's Dictionary of Artists in America, 1564–1860 (*New Haven: Yale University Press, 1957).

Hale Index
 Charles R. Hale, Connecticut Cemetery Inscriptions (microfilm, CHS Library).

Harlow
 Thompson R. Harlow, "Connecticut Engravers, 1774–1820," *CHSB* 36, no. 4 (October 1971).

Index Am. Ptgs.
 Index of American Paintings, Smithsonian Institution Research Information System.

Little, *Paintings*
 Nina Fletcher Little, *Paintings by New England Provincial Artists: 1775–1800 (*Boston: Museum of Fine Arts, 1976).

Little, *Wall Painting*
 Nina Fletcher Little, *American Decorative Wall Painting* (New York: Dutton, 1989).

Mercury
 American Mercury [newspaper], Hartford.

NEHGR
 New England Historical and Genealogical Register.

Luther Allen (1780–1821)
(active in Enfield ca. 1801–11)

Allen advertised in 1801 as a limner, practicing the arts of portrait painting in oil, pastels, or crayons, "from busts to full figures," miniature painting, hair work, coach and carriage painting, sign painting, with smalting and lettering in gold leaf, clock-face painting, and copperplate and typographical engraving. His age, twenty-one, suggests that he may have just recently completed an apprenticeship, and his wording suggests that he may have been working as an itinerant, using his home town of Enfield as a base. In 1803 Allen married Sally Pease Abbe, daughter of local innkeeper Daniel Abbe, Sr., and sister of innkeeper Daniel Abbe, Jr. (see cat. 31). Allen died in Ithaca, New York, at age forty-one.

Presently identified works include two undated engravings: a posthumous portrait of Longmeadow, Massachusetts, pastor, Rev. Stephen Williams (d. 1782), and a view of Newport in 1795. Four portraits are known, including miniatures of the artist and of his wife. No tavern signs bear Allen's signature, but in 1814 he was a close neighbor of Peter R. Field, and may have painted the eagle on Field's sign (cat 24).

References: *Courant*, 19 Jan. 1801, 8 May 1811; US Census; *Index Am. Ptgs.*; Harlow, pp. 99–100.

Isaac Allyn (1787–1839)
(active in New London 1809–12, St. Louis 1818)

In an 1812 New London advertisement, Allyn offered to paint ships and houses as well as signs. His shop produced both "coarse and fine" painting and was active enough to employ four men. Evans has identified a Windsor chair maker named Isaac Allyn working in nearby Preston, Connecticut, from 1809 to 1812. The name is not unique, but there is a strong probability that the painter and the chair maker are the same person. Evans further speculates that this may be the same man who worked as a chair maker in St. Louis, Missouri, in 1818.

References: *Conn. Gazette*, 22 April 1812; Evans, pp. 428, 642.

Chester Andross (dates unknown)
(active in Hartford 1807–22)

The Hartford firm that later became Chester Andross's was operated as early as 1805 by Lemuel Swift, who advertised as painter, glazier, and paper hanger. Andross may have been one of Swift's apprentices, becoming a full partner in 1807 with Lemuel and Zenas Swift. Swift and Co. advertised house, ship, and sign painting in addition to paper hanging and glazing. They also sold "Paints of all colours ground in oil, boiled Oil, Putty, Spanish White, etc." In 1811 the firm dissolved and Lemuel Swift became a grocer. The painting business was continued by Chester Andross and his new partner, Phipps Deming, a painter, glazier, and wall paper hanger previously working in Farmington, Connecticut. Andross and Deming continued in business until 1815, when Deming announced his intention of moving out of state. (He actually moved only to Avon, Connecticut.) Chester Andross took William

F. Andross into the business, but this new partnership lasted only until 1819 when the inventory and furnishings were liquidated.

Shortly thereafter, William Rice relocated to the Andross shop. Both Androsses may have moved briefly out of state—a firm of the same name has been found in Savannah, Georgia in 1818–19. However, Chester Andross returned to Hartford by June 1820, advertising sign-painting and fan lights. In 1821 he again offered a wide array of painting, including signs that were "As usual, cheap and neat." His latest known advertisement is dated 1822, when he was working "at the sign of the Porpus." Like his competitor, William Rice, Andross continued to paint signs, but concentrated on the new craze for fan lights.

References: *Courant*, 62 different notices beginning 3 April 1805 through 13 August 1822; *Mercury*, 12 May 1814, 21 May 1816, 30 Sept. 1817, 3 Nov. 1818.

William F. Andross (dates unknown)
(active in Hartford 1818–19)

see Chester Andross

John Sutcliff Barrow (dates unknown)
(active in Hartford 1793, Middletown 1804)

John Sutcliff Barrow may have been the same Barrow who, working in New York City in 1784, had painted a coach for prominent Hartford merchant Jeremiah Wadsworth. Other Barrows advertised in New York City as paint suppliers and coach, house, and sign painters, ca. 1777–92. John S. Barrow's Connecticut career began as early as 1793, when he advertised that he had taken part of Asa Allen's shop, near the Court House in Hartford, intending to practice coach, sign, and sleigh painting and gilding, and to teach drawing. The ad's acknowledgement "to his friends, for the encouragement he has already received" suggests that Barrow had already established a local clientele. Barrow used a similar phrase in his 1804 Middletown advertisement, in which he identified himself as a coach, house, ship and sign painter. His later history is uncertain, although a John S. Barrow and family were recorded from 1800–10, in Chatham, Connecticut, a ship-building center on the east side of the Connecticut River, across from Middletown. A John S. Barrows is also said to have married Olive Chase in Providence in 1827.

References: *Mercury*, 16 Dec. 1793; *Middlesex Gazette*, 30 March 1804; Rita Susswein Gottesman, *The Arts and Crafts in New York, 1777–1799* (New York: The New-York Historical Society, 1954), p. 339; [Patricia Kane] "Jeremiah Wadsworth's Coach," *CHSB* 28 (April 1963): 42; *NEHGR* 87 (1933): 327.

Beatty & Co.
(active in Norwich 1793)

Beatty & Co. advertised that they intended to open a shop "at Mr. Teel's Tavern, sign of General Washington" in Norwich, specializing in house, sign, coach, and heraldry painting and gilding. Additional services included varnishing of silk and linen (for hat and coach covers) and repairing of umbrellas.

References: *Norwich Packet,* 12 Sept. 1793.

Lucius Bidwell (1807–52)
(active in Middletown 1829–32)

Born in Wethersfield and raised in Middletown, Connecticut, twenty-two year old Lucius Bidwell partnered in 1829 with ornamental painter William Goodrich (q.v.). After the dissolution of this partnership in the same year, Bidwell opened his own painting studio in "a room over Mr. Joseph Warner's directly opposite the Post-Office in Middletown." There he offered his services as a house, ship, and sign painter. How long he remained a painter is uncertain, but he seems to have quit the profession by 1850, when he listed his occupation as "laborer."

References: *Middlesex Gazette*, 30 Sept. 1829, 18 April 1832; US Census.

Samuel Blydenburg (dates unknown)
(active in Hartford 1794–1803, New York City 1818–20)

Probably from New York or Long Island, Blydenburg came to Hartford before January 1794, when he was working with John Grimes (q.v.). By April 1796, he opened his own business, advertising primarily as a paper hanger, but also announcing his continuing painting business. By 1799 his painting services included ornamental and sign painting, and during the following few years Blydenburg expanded to include military regalia, fan lights, and looking glass repairs. He kept a supply of sign boards "ready painted, for lettering.—Tavern signs finished with various devices ready for the insertion of the name." Mindful of the cost of shipping signs, he offered to "Merchants and others who live at a distance . . . signs painted on canvass equal in all respects to those on board, and transported free of expence [sic]." In 1808 Blydenburg was manufacturing wallpaper in Brookfield, Massachusetts, and by 1818 he was working as a sign painter in New York City.

References: *Courant*, 25 April 1796, 20 May 1799, 15 July 1799, 25 Nov. 1799, 20 April 1801, 1 Feb. 1802, 8 June 1803, 31 Aug. 1803; *Massachusetts Spy, or Worcester Gazette*, 30 Nov. 1808; *Longworth's American Almanack, New-York Register, and City Directory* (New York: David Longworth, 1818, 1819, 1820).

Henry Bodge (1787–1827)
(active in Hartford 1811)

see Jonathan Hartshorn

John Coleman Bull (dates unknown)
(active in Hartford 1798–1805)

Coach painter John C. Bull worked at the "Sign of the Coach Body" near Hartford's South Church in 1798. Two years later he was offering the full range of ornamental painting, including signs, and was selling varnishes and "Japan Gold Size." In 1805 John C. Bull became a partner with Almarin and Alfred Janes. Their finer

work included military flags and coats of arms, and they painted signs on glass as well as wood.

References: *Courant*, 18 June 1798, 24 July 1805, 30 Oct. 1805; 2 July 1806; *Mercury*, 3 April 1800.

George Burnham (1800–68)
(active in Hartford 1828)

see Joseph J. Grant

Thomas K. Bush (dates unknown)
(active in Middletown 1823–25)

see Solomon Jones

Abial Canfield (dates unknown)
(active in Bridgeport 1823)

see William Curtis

Chauncey Case (1810–63)
(active in Hartford 1838–63)

Case was living in Hartford by 1834, and by 1838 he and Osmyn Case had formed the firm "C. & O. Case—House, Ship, and Sign Painters, Glaziers and Paper Hangers." The firm also sold paints and supplies. Osmyn left the business shortly thereafter, though he continued to work independently and rejoined Chauncey as a partner from 1851–58. Hartford City Directories record a number of associates, including George W. Smith, who joined Chauncey in 1840 but went out on his own a few years later, and "Mr. G. B. Pease," who offered "Graining neatly done" from 1852–57. Later, Osmyn teamed up with S. E. Hascall, under the name Case & Hascall. Three other Cases, Henry, Gordon G. and Joseph T., are listed as painters in the Hartford City Directory, and may be related. Chauncey Case worked until 1863 when he met an ironic end—he was struck in the head by a falling sign.

References: *Courant*, 3 March 1838, 5 Jan. 1839, 6 March 1841; *Hartford Times*, 5 Jan. 1839; *Hartford Courant*, 27 Nov. 1884; *Hartford City Directory*; U.S. Census.

Osmyn Case (d. 1860)
(active in Hartford 1838–60)

see Chauncey Case

Hiram Cauldwell (dates unknown)
(active in New Haven 1826–27)

Cauldwell's specialty, according to an 1827 advertisement, was drawing machine parts for patent applications. Like many contemporaries, he also painted military flags, Masonic regalia, and signs.

References: *Connecticut Herald*, 24 April 1827.

Abial A. Cooley (1782–1858)
(active in New London 1816)

Cooley was born in Bolton, Connecticut, in 1782, but had moved to New London by 1816. Located in John Maniere's New London hardware manufactory, Cooley painted signs, flags, and profiles. By 1828 he was living in Hartford, where he remained until his death in 1858. At first he was employed as a lumber and wood inspector, but by 1838 he worked as a druggist. A family genealogy reports that "Dr. Abiel A. Cooley . . . was a physician; also invented improvements in friction matches, an ingenious shingle-machine, and one of the first power presses in use. He was the first to apply the cam-movement to pumps."

References: *Conn. Gazette*, 4 Sept. 1816; *Hartford City Directory*; Mortimer Elwyn Cooley, *The Cooley Genealogy* (Rutland, Vermont: The Tuttle Publishing Co., 1941) p. 615.

Matthew Curtis (1783–1864)
(active in Bridgeport 1821–64)

Matthew Curtis and Samuel B. Middlebrooks were partners in Bridgeport, Connecticut, in 1821, advertising that, in addition to selling paint and supplies and making fanlights, "they have workmen so that they can Glaze and Paint any Building, per contract or otherwise; Sign and Ornamental Painting done as usual." The two partners continued to offer painting services at their "Bridgeport Paint Store" until Middlebrooks's death in 1838. In 1842, Curtis took a new partner, Theodore Drake. By 1850, Curtis was still painting houses, but in 1860, at age 78, he had retired, listing himself as a "Gentleman" with $28,000 in real and personal property. Middlebrooks's son, Charles (1820–85), and a Spencer Curtis (possibly Matthew's son) were also painters in Bridgeport in 1850.

References: *Connecticut Journal* (Bridgeport), 21 March 1821; *Republican Farmer* (Bridgeport), 17 Nov. 1824, 11 June 1828, 27 Jan 1829, 10 March 1831, 14 March 1832, 18 April 1832, 29 March 1842, 29 March 1942; US Census; Hale and Barbour Indexes.

William Curtis (dates unknown)
(active in Bridgeport 1823)

In 1823 William Curtis and Abial Canfield operated a chair factory in Bridgeport. As a sideline, they announced "Sign-Painting, Gilding, Ornamenting, &c. executed with neatness and elegance on the lowest terms at the same place."

References: *[Bridgeport] Courier*, 17 Sept. 1823.

Abraham Delanoy (1742–95)
(active in Charleston, South Carolina 1766, New York City 1767–71, New Haven 1784–87)

In 1766 New York-born Abraham Delanoy traveled to London to study painting with Benjamin West. On his return to America, he painted portraits in Charleston and New York City, before coming to Connecticut. His work in New Haven is known through a series of advertisements in the *Connecticut Journal*, including a 1784 example, announcing "Painting/ Portrait, Sign, Ornament and plain Painting, Gilding, &c. &c. performed by A. DELANOY, at low Prices." Further, he offered a "small Assortment of Paints, Sash and large Brushes for Painting, 6 by 8 Window-Glass, Linseed Oil and Whiting" from his house "in the New-Township, in the Street on a Line with the second Bridge from the Mouth of the Creek, opposite Capt. David Phipps." A 1785 *Connecticut Journal* ad offered "Likenesses painted on canvas, carriages painted, ornamented, gilt and varnished. Signs of all kinds. Plain house and ship painting carried on. . . . Paints mixt at short notice." William Dunlap, writing in 1834, remembered the artist during this period as "in 'the sear and yellow leaf' both of life and fortune. He was consumptive, poor, and his only employment sign-painting." Dunlap assisted Delanoy in this occupation by painting a portrait of Admiral Hood, from memory, on a sign. Delanoy remained in New Haven only a few years. By 1790 he was living in Westchester County, New York, where he remained until his death in 1795.

No signed ornamental work is known, but at least a dozen portraits are either signed by or attributed to the artist. Among these are portraits of Peter Livingston (1772) and various members of the Sherman family (ca. 1787).

References: *Connecticut Journal* (Bridgeport), 16 June 1784; Dunlap, 1:161; Groce and Wallace, pp. 172–73; *Index Am. Ptg.*; Gerdts, 1:101; Little, *Paintings*, p. 86; Little, *Wall Painting*, p. xix.

Phipps Deming (1784–1820)
(active in Farmington 1810, Hartford 1811–15)

see Chester Andross

Theodore Drake (dates unknown)
(active in Bridgeport 1842)

see Matthew Curtis

Isaac G. Farden (b. ca. 1810–12)
(active in Litchfield 1833, North Haven 1834, Massachusetts [unidentified towns] 1836, Hartford 1838, Bridgeport 1840, New Haven 1842, Connecticut [unidentified towns] 1843, 1845, Torrington 1850, Waterbury 1860)

Farden is identified as a sign painter through a single 1833 advertisement in the *Litchfield Enquirer*, in which he offered to "attend to Ornamental House and Sign Painting." Other activities included painting imitation wood and marble and hanging wall paper. His address, Sedgwick's Hotel, suggests that he was working as an itinerant. Directory, census reports, and vital statistics data place him subsequently in a number of Connecticut and Massachusetts towns and cities. Farden remained an artist—he is identified as such in the 1838 Hartford City Directory and in both the 1850 and 1860 census. His son, Isaac G. Farden, Jr., was also an artist, living in Middletown in 1860.

References: *Litchfield Enquirer*, 9 May 1833; US Census; *Hartford City Directory*; Barbour and Hale indexes.

David Finch (ca. 1799–1855)
(active in Bridgeport 1826–29)

Well-documented by Evans as a chair maker, David Finch also advertised sign and ornamental painting.

References: *Republican Farmer* (Bridgeport), 11 Oct 1826; Evans, pp. 451, 693.

Caleb Galpin (1771–1863)
(active in Berlin 1797–1803)

Galpin is documented as a sign painter in the account book of Giles Curtis, a Berlin merchant. In 1797 Curtis owed Caleb Galpin 1/10/ for "painting my sign & small cart." A year later, Galpin also painted Curtis's house, carriage wheels, and "chambers." In 1803, he painted frames for Curtis. No other details of Galpin's career are known, although details of his life are well established. He was born in Middletown and raised in Berlin, Connecticut, where he remained until at least 1840. By 1850 Galpin had moved to Scottsville, New York, a town near Rochester, where he died at age ninety-two.

References: Giles Curtis, mss. account book, part I, p. 67; part II, p. 53, cited in Wadsworth Atheneum, The Great River Archives (microfilm, CHS Library); US Census; Barbour and Hale indexes; Catharine M. North, *History of Berlin, Connecticut* (New Haven: Tuttle, Morehouse & Taylor Co., 1916), p. 208; William Freeman Galpin, *The Galpin Family in America* (Syracuse: Syracuse University Press, 1955), p. 23–25, 28.

William Goodrich (dates unknown)
(active in Middletown 1829–31)

In 1829 William Goodrich was partnered with Lucius Bidwell (q.v.). When the partnership dissolved in that year, Goodrich retained the Middletown shop and continued the business of painting, paper hanging, and glazing.

References: *Middlesex Gazette*, 22 July 1829, 14 April 1830, 27 Oct. 1830, 9 Feb. 1831.

Hugh Gourley (1798–1855)
(active in Hartford 1823–50)

Hugh Gourley emigrated from Ireland to Hartford before 1823, when he advertised in Hartford as a house, ship and sign painter, and paper hanger. His partner was Windham-born Norman Ormsby, who left the firm in the same year and subsequently moved to Oswego, New York. Gourley renamed his firm "H. Gourley and Co." and worked as a painter in Hartford until retiring in 1851. An 1831 newspaper ad featured sign painting, but also listed painting in imitation of wood and marble and the manufacture of fan lights, varnishes, and paints. By 1848, the year after William Rice's death, he occupied 10 American Row, in the same building as the Rice shop. Gourley's sons Daniel D. and Montgomery M.

both worked as painters in Hartford.

References: *Courant*, 12 Aug. 1823; 27 Sept. 1831; *Hartford City Directory*; US Census.

John Graham (dates unknown)
(active in Hartford 1798–1800)

Graham was listed as a painter in the 1798 Hartford tax assessment. During the following two years he placed a series of advertisements in the *Connecticut Courant* announcing the "business of Painting in its different branches." His work included the usual house, ship, coach, and sign painting, gilding, and glazing, but he also mentions carpets, clock faces, and window curtains. With the addition of a journeyman joiner, his firm offered house joinery. Like some of his contemporaries, Graham sold paints and window glass. His less typical sidelines included the manufacture of "Spouts and Conductors of different sizes and lengths" and offering rides in hot air balloons.

References: *Courant*, 1 April 1799, 20 May 1799, 16 Dec. 1799, 31 March 1800, 2 June 1800, 30 June 1800, 14 July 1800, 18 Aug. 1800.

Erastus Granger (b. 1813)
(active in Hartford 1838–55)

Born in New York State, Granger was listed as a painter in the Hartford City Directory in every year from 1838 to 1855. A single 1841 advertisement listed "Sign, Fancy and Ornamental Painting" in addition to his earlier notices for house painting and papering.

References: *Courant*, 27 Nov. 1841; *Hartford City Directory* 1838–1855; US Census.

Joseph Jennings Grant (ca. 1813–39)
(active in Hartford 1834–37)

Grant was born in Wapping, a village in South Windsor, Connecticut, the son of Sylvester and Nancy Pease Grant and the nephew of innkeeper Gustavus Grant. Perhaps he was the Mr. Grant working with housepainter George Burnham in Hartford in 1834. In 1837 Joseph J. Grant was working independently at house, sign, and fancy painting, as well as paper hanging and glazing. His 1837 advertisement thanked the public for past patronage and stressed that his sign painting "shall be executed in a style not inferior to that done at any other establishment in the City, notwithstanding the *mean* attempts of an individual (who has been long established in this branch of the business, in this city,) to injure him in business, by constantly ridiculing the execution of many of the Signs painted at his establishment." Though his critic went unnamed, it could only have been William Rice.

References: *Courant*, 5 May 1834, 13 May 1837; Arthur Hastings Grant. *The Grant Family: A Genealogical History of the Descendants of Matthew Grant of Windsor, Conn., 1601–1898* (Poughkeepsie, N.Y.: A.V. Haight, 1898), pp. 48, 99.

Jason Griffin (dates unknown)
(active in Middletown 1824)

Griffin advertised that he had rented a room in R. Chafee's Middletown store, "where he intends to execute the different branches of Wood, and Copperplate Engraving, House, Ship, Sign, and Ornamental Painting, and Gilding."

References: *Middlesex Gazette*, 28 April 1824.

William Griffin (possibly 1768–1833)
(active in Brooklyn, Connecticut, 1831)

Occupying a room under the Brooklyn courthouse, Griffin carried on "the business of House & Sign PAINTING—Papering, Glazing and Gilding." This single notice suggests that Griffin was itinerant, planning to stay in Brooklyn for only a short time. The artist could be the William Griffin who was born in Killingworth in 1768, is recorded in the Killingworth census in 1810, 1820, and 1830, and died in 1833. Circumstantially, he could be the painter of Vernon Stiles's Thompson Hotel sign (cat. 41) and the Minor Bradley sign from Guilford, now at the Shelburne Museum. The two signs are quite similar, but are dated nearly twenty years apart and hung in different parts of Connecticut.

References: *Windham County Advertiser*, 8 June 1831; US Census; Barbour and Hale indexes.

John Grimes (dates unknown)
(active in Hartford 1794–98)

In 1794 Grimes and Samuel Blydenburg (q.v.) were working in Ferry Street in Hartford carrying on the painting business "in the branches of House, Shop, Sleigh, Chaise, and Sign painting, Gilding and Glazing, &c." and selling paint, liquid ink, putty and other supplies. When Blydenburg left the partnership shortly thereafter, Grimes continued alone. For a short time beginning in 1796, Grimes took Youngs Hosmer into the business. Again independent, Grimes apparently met some financial difficulty, for early in 1798, he announced a sale of joiner's molding tools, window sashes, and other goods, adding that "if the above are not disposed of by the 10th March next, they will then be sold at Auction . . . . Cash, Flax-Seed, Linseed Oil, or any kind of Country Produce received in payment for any of the above articles."

References: *Courant*, 20 Jan. 1794, 25 Aug. 1794, 20 April 1795, 14 March 1796, 22 Aug. 1796, 5 Dec. 1796, 6 March 1797, 1 May 1797, 16 Oct. 1797, 12 Feb. 1798.

Jonathan Hartshorn (1778–1848)
(active in Hartford 1811–47)

Hartshorn ran a painting shop in Hartford in 1811 and 1812. The business was a typical one, offering house, ship, and sign painting, wall papering, and mixed paints. During these years Hartshorn briefly took a Mr. Henry Bodge into his painting business. No record has been found of Mr. Hartshorn from 1812–24, but in the latter year he again advertised the same mix of services. Although he remained in Hartford for many years, he may have eventually scaled back his business—from 1828–47 he is listed in the Directories only as a paper hanger.

References: *Courant*, 27 March 1811, 22 Aug. 1811, 8 Jan. 1812, 1 June 1824; *Hartford City Directory*.

Samuel Holt (1801–84?)
(active in Hartford 1824–25, 1841–45, 1853–57, 1864–84, Windsor 1860)

Born in Meriden, Holt "established himself in the city of Hartford" in 1824 as an ornamental painter. A second ad offered "Military, Standard, Fancy, Ornamental, Masonic and Sign PAINTING . . . LETTERING of every description, either plain, rich, neat, or ornamental, executed at short notice." His name does not appear in the 1828 Hartford City Directory. According to French, he received professional painting instruction, though the teacher and location remain unknown, and worked for some years as a miniaturist. According to Groce and Wallace, Holt's deteriorating eyesight obliged him "to abandon miniature painting for ornamental work." He returned to Hartford three times between 1841 and 1884, during which years the Hartford City Directory listed him variously as "painter," "artist," or "ornamental painter." When not in Hartford, he appears to have been in Massachusetts, where all his children were born. He lived in Windsor, Connecticut, in 1860, according to the U. S. census. His four sons—Samuel L., George C., Thomas R., and Channing A.—followed him as ornamental painters.

References: *The Times and Hartford Subscriber*, 16 March 1824, 10 Aug. 1824; Groce and Wallace, p. 323; French, p. 66.

Youngs Hosmer (dates unknown)
(active in Hartford 1796)

see John Grimes

Webster James (dates unknown)
(active in Norwich 1782–84, 1803–04, Hartford 1788)

In a 1782 advertisement, James announced that he carried on "the Painting Business, In all its Branches . . . Such as Carpeting, Sign-Painting and Guilding, also Coats of Arms, Miniature, and other fine Work." James may have come to the Norwich Landing area from Providence—a 1782 census records a Webster James in that city. According to Harlow, a 1784 ad in the *Connecticut Gazette* proves that Webster James was still in Norwich, where he "did carving as well as signs, coats-of-arms and miniatures." By 1788 he had moved his painting, gilding, and carving business from Norwich to Hartford, and he was still in that city in 1790. Eventually he returned to the Chelsea section of Norwich, where he sold paper-hangings.

References: *Connecticut Gazette and the Universal Intelligencer*, 30 Aug. 1782; *Courant*, 25 Feb. 1788; *Norwich Courier*, 21 Sept. 1803; *CHSB* 32 (Oct. 1967): 136; *NEHGR* 127 (1973): 304.

Alfred Janes (dates unknown)
(active in Hartford 1805)

see John Coleman Bull

Almarin Janes (dates unknown)
(active in Hartford 1805)

see John Coleman Bull

David T. Johnson (1800–76)
(active in Norwich 1824, Middletown 1830–35, New York 1840, New Haven 1843–76)

Johnson was living and working in Norwich by 1824, having taken a room "under the Hotel." He offered "ALL KINDS OF Military and Masonic WORK, In the line of Painting, Gilding, Bronzing, and Etching./ ALSO./ Carriage, Sign and Chair Painting, Picture Coloring and Framing, Map Trimming, and Varnishing &c./ House and Ship PAINTING./ Ornamental Ship Work in particular." He was living in Middletown at the time of his 1835 marriage, in New York at the birth of a son (1840), and back in Connecticut at the birth of a daughter (1843). In 1850 the family was living in New Haven; the census of that year lists Johnson as a "Laborer" living next door to "Coach Painter" George W. Stebbings. In an 1861 New Haven Directory, Johnson listed his occupation as "carriage maker." He was still in New Haven at his death in 1876.

References: *Norwich Courier*, 29 Sept. 1824; *Middlesex Gazette*, 16 June 1830, 16 Feb. 1831; New Haven City Directory, 1861–62; US Census; Barbour and Hale indexes.

Solomon Jones (1799–1853)
(active in Middletown 1823–26, Marlborough 1850)

Jones was born in Connecticut, probably in Hebron or Marlborough, but by 1823 he had moved to Middletown, where he painted, gilded, and bronzed military flags and Masonic regalia. The militia and the Masons were friends as well as clients—Jones was a sergeant in the local trainband and a member of Middletown's St. John's Lodge No. 2. By 1823 Jones formed a partnership with Thomas K. Bush and placed a very large advertisement in the *Middlesex Gazette* for their "Painting, Gilding, &c." business located north of the Washington Hotel (see fig. 35). Jones and Bush's work for the Masons is recorded in two Middletown account books. One of these suggests that they were not fabricating their own signs, though they are known to have possessed certain cabinet making tools. In addition to the military and Masonic work, they offered to paint carriages, signs, chairs, clock dials, "pictures," houses, and ships and to engrave wood and metal.

Jones and Bush advertisements were large and frequent until the dissolution of the firm in 1825. Money was apparently a problem, since the firm turned over not just their "Books, Notes, [and] Accounts" but also "all other property" to Charles Dyer, the main seller of paint and artists' supplies in Middletown, undoubtedly

the biggest creditor of Jones and Bush. An announcement for the subsequent auction listed, among other materials, "2 [sets]. Painters Job Brushes; 1 do. Engraving Tools; 28 Vols. containing a full set of Plates of Encyclopedia; 10 Masonic Aprons, gilt; 9 Frame pictures; 1 do. Macdonough's Victory; 1 Box Water Colours; 200 Coffee Mills . . . one box Prusian Blue; 1 do. Chrome Yellow; 20 Tin Plates; 2 sets Bits and Braces; 1 Drawing Machine, &c."

Two months after the sale, Bush surfaced "over the Store of Messrs. Chittenden and Platts" advertising simply "House, Sign, and Ship Painting." Meanwhile, Solomon Jones reopened the original store on Main and Washington Streets. His 1826 advertisement suggests that he had been the more skilled as well as the senior partner and the one who was an engraver on wood and metal. Jones seems to have left Middletown sometime before February 1829, when his brother Augustus P. Jones advertised "For Sale or Rent./ THE Shop formerly owned and occupied by JONES & BUSH, Painters, situated on the west side of Main Street, above Washington Street." By 1844 Solomon Jones had moved back to Marlborough, and in 1850 he was working there as a painter, residing with his sister's family. The inventory of his estate three years later included books, an assortment of carpentry tools, a "Paint Kitt," a glazier's diamond, engraving tools, graining tools, and various related materials. Jones may also have been an inventor; in his inventory is a "Patent Right for Chirns & a lott of Churns." He was quite well off financially, with $515 in cash and savings, $800 in real estate, and several small notes to relatives and others.

No signed works by Solomon Jones have been uncovered, but he can be linked at least circumstantially to a number of tavern signs in or near the lower Connecticut River Valley, including those of Jared Carter and Humphrey Williams (cat. 33, 36). More compellingly, one of the debtors listed in his probate papers was innkeeper William G. Buell, of Chatham, whose sign is in the collection of Old Sturbridge Village.

References: *Middlesex Gazette*, 22 May 1823, 7 April 1824, 28 July 1824, 5 Jan. 1825, 12 Jan. 1825, 7 April 1825, 22 June 1825, 2 Nov. 1825, 28 Dec. 1825, 4 Jan. 1826, 8 March 1826, 12 April 1826, 17 May 1826, 18 March 1829; *American Sentinel*, 2 April 1823, 16 April 1823; E. G. Storer, *The Records of Freemasonry in the State of Connecticut, with a brief account of its origin in New England* . . . (New Haven: E. G. Storer, 1859), p. 359; John D. Hamilton, *Material Culture of the American Freemasons* (Lexington, Mass.: Museum of Our National Heritage, 1994), p. 39

Stephanus Knight (1772–1810)
(active in Enfield 1796–1808)

A versatile handyman and painter, Knight's account book records mending and painting furniture, sleighs, and houses for his Enfield neighbors. The book documents that Knight painted (or repainted) at least three tavern signs in Enfield—for tavernkeepers Samuel Bestor (1802 and 1808), Amos Alden (1806), and Daniel Abbe, Jr. (1807). Knight also executed signs for Joseph Olmsted, hatter; Sylvester Lusk, saddler; and Jonathan Button, shoemaker, among others. The Selectmen's records for Enfield show that in 1796 he was paid "for 15 boards painted & lettered for post guides." He painted additional post guides in 1804 and 1808.

References: Stephanus Knight, mss. account book, 1795–1809 (CHS Library); Francis O. Allen, *The History of Enfield . . .*, (Lancaster, Pa.: Wickersham Prtg., 1900) pp.1251, 1291, 1320.

William Laughton (possibly 1794–1870)
(active in Hartford 1819–23, 1838)

In 1820, Laughton thanked "his friends and the public for the encouragement they have given him in his profession for a year past." Like Hiram Cauldwell, Laughton drew patent application illustrations as well as painting Masonic regalia and signs. He was still in Hartford in 1823, when he announced "a handsome assortment of Masonic Aprons, plain and gilt, Cheap, Masonic Carpets." His whereabouts for the next several years are unknown, and he may have worked as an itinerant painter. However, he returned to Hartford by 1838, as he is listed in the City Directory of that year as a "fancy painter." A William Laughton who died in Hartford in 1870 at age 76 may have been the artist.

References: *Courant*, 20 June 1820, 17 June 1823; *Hartford City Directory*.

E. McNeil (dates unknown)
(active in Litchfield 1830)

McNeil was a jack-of-all-trades, specializing in metal work of all varieties. He advertised that he could repair old tin, cast brass, copper, and steel; work sheet iron and lead; and repair watches and brass and wooden clocks. The fact that he also painted and gilded signs suggests the versatility needed by a craftsman living in rural Litchfield County. Nor could he be choosy concerning payment, promising that any "articles necessary for the use of my family will be received for work if paid down." In ill health by 1830, he relied on the Messrs. Sanford, Litchfield chairmakers, to collect work and return it to his customers.

References: *Litchfield Enquirer*, 22 April 1830.

Samuel B. Middlebrooks (1794–1838)
(active in Bridgeport 1821–38)

see Matthew Curtis

Miller & Fitch
(active in Hartford 1831)

Miller and Fitch's earliest known advertisement appeared in 1831, describing the pair as "House, Ship, and Sign Painters; Glaziers and Paper Hangers," and offering to imitate wood and marble, manufacture fan lights, and supply mixed paints. The firm later advertised their "Fanlight Manufactory," adding as an aside, "Also, All kinds of House, Sign and Transparent Painting, done to order at short notice."

References: *Courant*, 29 March 1831, 20 Sept. 1831.

J. C. Nichols (dates unknown)
(active in Bridgeport 1827–42)

In 1827 Nichols offered house and ship painting, glazing, and paper hangings, and stocked "a general assortment of Paints, Oil, and Naval stores." He is probably the same man who in 1842 advertised similar goods and services as the firm "Nichols & Gridley."

References: *Republican Farmer* (Bridgeport), 22 Aug. 1827, 29 March 1842.

Norman Ormsby (1798–1842)
(active in Hartford 1823)

see Hugh Gourley

Samuel Stillman Osgood (1808–85)
(active in Hartford 1827, Charleston, South Carolina 1829–30, London, New York 1836–37, Boston 1840, California

Osgood's birth date has been listed as 1798 (in New Haven) or 1808 (in Boston). According to French, he came to Hartford from Boston in 1825 and opened a studio in the Eagle Hotel. An 1827 advertisement offered "Fancy, Sign, Military, Standard, Masonic and Ornamental Painting" in the same location William Rice and other sign painters had occupied previously. The 1828 Hartford City Directory listed him as a "Portrait Painter." After several years elsewhere, he returned to Connecticut in 1842 and resumed painting portraits before departing for California, where he died.

Over three dozen works, mostly portraits, are signed by or attributed to Osgood, including a self-portrait owned by the National Academy of Design.

References: *Courant*, 9 April 1827; Bénézit, 6:450; Groce and Wallace, p. 480; *Index of Am. Ptgs.*; French, p. 60.

Harlan Page (1791–1834)
(active in Coventry 1813)

Page apprenticed as a joiner but his "delicate" health caused him to turn instead to art. Page painted the inn sign for the establishment inherited by Horace Rose in Coventry in 1813 (cat. 23). This may have been his only sign, for in the same year twenty-two year old Page married and became active in religious matters. In 1814 he "publicly professed his faith in Christ, and spent the rest of his life travelling about preaching." Shortly thereafter he developed a close association with the American Tract Society, working first for the Boston branch, then, in 1825 for the New York office, drawing and engraving illustrations for their many publications. The small engravings in these books show the same type of illustration as the bird-in-hand on the Rose sign—moral scenes with well-known phrases. The Tract Society published a memoir of Page following his untimely death in 1834. The volume includes a portrait of Page and many of his own writings, showing the depth of his religious conviction.

References: Mary Kingsbury Talcott, ed., *The Genealogy of the Descendants of Henry Kingsbury of Ipswich and Haverhill, Mass.* (Hartford: Case, Lockwood & Brainard Co., 1905), pp. 299–300; Mrs. William Minor, *Coventry in Retrospect: 250 Years* [1962?], p. 46; William A. Hallock, *Memoir of Harlan Page: or the Power of Prayer and Personal Effort for the Souls of Individuals.* (New York: American Tract Society [1835]).

Abner Reed (1771–1866)
(active in East Windsor 1798–1801, Hartford 1803–1808)

Much has been written about Reed's engraving career, and many extant works are known, including Masonic aprons, bank notes, trade labels, landscapes, maps, portraits, and book illustrations. His painted works are less familiar, though he is known to have painted and gilded carriages, sleighs, signs, military regalia, and furniture. Sign painting references appear in Reed's newspaper advertisements as early as 1798, when he was working in his native East Windsor. According to Reed's account book, in 1801–02, he or his employees painted signs for four clients: L. Terry, J. Watson Jr., A. Allen, and J. Phelps, probably East Windsor innkeeper Joseph Phelps, who began operation in 1801. Now in the collection of the Wadsworth Atheneum, the Phelps sign shows a clear connection with Reed's work as an engraver for banks and the government: both sides use images based on U.S. coinage of the mid-1790s (see fig. 63).

Reed continued to offer sign painting as one of his services after moving to Hartford in 1803. In addition to engraving, his 1805 advertisement lists "Painting in general, especially Signs, on wood, canvass, tin, or glass, in any manner or form" as well as military regalia. Still in Hartford in 1808, he maintained a supply of tavern signs "ready painted of various divices [sic], the name only wanting to complete them for hanging." Reed returned to East Windsor in 1811, and though he produced many engravings in subsequent years, no more painting activity is recorded.

References: *Courant*, 23 July 1798, 20 Oct. 1800, 23 Nov. 1803, 9 Jan. 1805, 18 Dec. 1805, 30 March 1808, 14 Aug. 1811, 28 Aug. 1811; Groce and Wallace, p. 528; Harlow, p. 111; Donald C. O'Brien, "Abner Reed: A Connecticut Engraver," *CHSB* 44, no. 1 (1979): 1–16.

Frederick F. Rice (1814–77)
(active in Hartford 1840–77)

see William Rice

William Rice (1777–1847)
(active in Massachusetts 1800–15, Hartford 1816–47)

William Rice was born in Petersham, Massachusetts, and moved to Worcester with his family sometime in the 1790s. Except for a brief period following his 1799 marriage to Martha (Patty) Goulding, he seems to have remained in Worcester until about 1815. Rice claimed to have begun painting in 1800. In 1806, just after the death of his father, Luke, William Rice opened a shop in a newly-built section of Worcester, where he offered gilding, varnishing, sign painting and house painting. He experimented with merchandising later that year, purchasing thirty dozen bamboo

and dining chairs, and in 1808 took as his partner his brother-in-law, Palmer Goulding. The pair offered "Sign Painting, Military Caps, Stands of Colors, Knapsacks, &c. Likewise, Burnish, Guilding, do. on Glass, &c. Correct Profile Likenesses taken." In production were "fifteen hundred Tin Frontices for Soldiers' Caps, done with real hard Japan, ornamented with gold and silver leaf."

By 1816 Rice had moved his family to Hartford, opening a shop over tailors Dimock and Marsh in State House Square. There he engaged in "all sorts of Painting, such as/ SIGNS, Of all descriptions in the newest style./ CARRIAGES, Coaches, chaises, sulkeys, stages, 1 horse waggons, &c./ LETTERING, Fire-buckets, window shutters, guide boards vessels, &c./ MILITARY. Standards for cavalry, artillery and militia, drums, knapsacks caps, canteens, &c./ DOORS. Inside and out painted in imitation of satin, wood, mahogany, and curled maple, nearly as handsome as the real wood./ FURNITURE Painted and varnished to imitate satinwood and curled maple./ GUILDING AND VARNISHING. Furniture, chairs, apothecaries' draws and bottles, picture-frames, &c./ FAN-LIGHTS Made in the newest style and handsomely gilt./ House-Painting & Glazing done in the best manner, and with pure stock./ Floors painted in imitation of Italian marble, &c."

By 1818, Rice's shop featured a sign with a lion, and he boasted that "he executes SIGN PAINTING in a superior style, on an entire new plan, with mineral smalt, which will never tarnish but grow brighter with age." He moved a few times, tried selling paints, shared space with house painter William Thompson, and finally, in 1820, took over the shop previously occupied by sign painters C. and W. Andross (q.v.). A particularly large and ornate 1823 ad described Rice's firm as a "Fan-light Manufactory," with "Sign Painting, Plain and Ornamental also carried on at the same place, and as the style of his painting is so generally known," Rice claimed, "he need only to inform those in want of Signs, that no endeavors shall be wanting on his part to accommodate and please them."

In the 1828 Hartford City Directory, Rice listed himself as an "ornamental Painter." The 1838–42 directories continued to list "Rice W. sign painter," but in 1843, the firm was renamed "Wm. Rice & Co., Sign Painters." Rice's partner was his son Frederick F. (1814–77), who had been painting for at least three years. Rice may also have employed his son, painter George W. Rice (1803–87), and his son-in-law, joiner Erastus Robbins (1799–42). In 1845 Rice's firm moved to the newly expanded American Hotel Building. After William died in 1847, son Frederick continued the firm until his own death in 1877.

William Rice is one of the few sign painters who regularly signed his work, and a large body of signed works exists. The eighteen Rice signboards thus far located suggest a preliminary chronology to his work. The earliest sign, created for Thomas Tarbox about 1807, has a shield shape (cat. 19). This is followed in the 1820s by several horizontal rectangles that feature a large lion or eagle, or sometimes one of each (cat. 28, 37). Signs with a central oval generally date to the 1830s (cat. 50). The latest signs have an elaborate signature, enclosed in a scroll, and may indicate the work of son, Frederick F. Rice (cat. 55). Geographically, Rice's work appeared mostly in Hartford and Litchfield counties, plus a few towns to the north or east of this area. Most of the inns that displayed his signs were second-generation establishments on well-traveled turnpikes.

References: *Massachusetts Spy, or Worcester Gazette,* 13 Aug. 1806, 31 Dec. 1806, 9 March 1808; *Courant,* 16 April 1816, 27 Aug. 1816, 28 March 1820, 23 July 1822; *Mercury* 12 May 1818, 3 Nov. 1818; *The Times and Hartford Advertiser,* 6 Nov. 1822, 14 Oct. 1823.

Isaac Sanford (d. 1842)
(active in Hartford 1785, 1791–97, 1819–23, Litchfield 1785–88)

An accomplished silversmith, engraver, and painter, Sanford partnered with Miles Beach of Goshen and Litchfield (1785–88), with a Mr. Walsh of Hartford (1789), and with William Johonnot of Hartford (1789–90). Sanford's sign painting is known from his year with Mr. Walsh. The partnership of Sanford and Walsh offered a wide range of gilding and painting, including portraiture, miniatures, coats of arms, signs, and chaises, plus indoor and outdoor house painting. They painted frescoes showing landscapes, and hunting and maritime scenes. Sanford was still offering to paint signs in 1791, after he began working independently, but though his silversmith and engraving business continued for several years, subsequent advertisements make only occasional reference to sign painting. In addition to living in Hartford, he also traveled to England and resided in both Providence, Rhode Island (1824), and Philadelphia, where he died in 1842.

No signs by Sanford have been identified. His engraved trade card of 1820 and a miniature portrait of East Windsor merchant Solomon Porter, ca. 1795–1800, survive at The Connecticut Historical Society.

References: *Mercury,* 22 Nov. 1789; *Courant* 31 Jan. 1791, 13 Feb. 1792, 4 Nov. 1793, 2 June 1794, 16 July 1794, 15 Sept. 1794, 8 Dec. 1794, 2 Feb. 1795, 17 April 1797; Newton C. Brainard, "Isaac Sanford," *CHSB* 19 (Oct. 1954): 122; *CHSB* 33 (Oct. 1968): 106; Peter Bohan and Philip Hammerslough, *Early Connecticut Silver, 1700–1840* (Middletown, Conn.: Wesleyan University Press, 1970), p.251.

Isaac Sheffield Sizer (b. 1801)
(active in New London 1822–23)

Isaac S. Sizer was predominantly a fancy and Windsor chair maker, documented in New London in 1822 and 1823. In addition to finished chairs, he advertised painting supplies, chair bottom wood, and "Sign Painting, Gilding, and various kinds of ornamental painting, executed with neatness and dispatch." According to Evans, Sizer worked briefly in the Groton woodworking shop of James Gere in 1822 and 1827.

References: *Conn. Gazette,* 14 May 1823; Evans, pp. 430, 710.

Samuel Sizer (possibly 1779–1810)
(active in Middletown 1806)

Samuel Sizer is known as a house, ship, coach and sign painter and gilder. He also offered "pieces in Heraldry and Masonry." Genealogical searches, though not conclusive, suggest that this Samuel may have been the father of Isaac S. Sizer, and if so was born 1779 and died 1810, living most of his life in New London.

References: *Middlesex Gazette,* 21 Feb. 1806; Lillian Hubbard Holch, comp. and ed., *Sizer Genealogy* (Brooklyn: Bowles, 1941), pp. 211–13.

George W. Smith (dates unknown)
(active in Hartford 1841–66)

see Chauncey Case

Timothy Swain (1788–1838)
(active in New London 1812, 1837, New York City 1816, 1826–31, Franklin, Tennessee 1822)

Swain took over the New London fancy and Windsor chair shop of Thomas West in 1812. According to Evans, he worked in New York City ca. 1816 and may have worked at several western locations between 1817 and 1825. An 1822 Franklin, Tennessee, advertisement offered sign painting, glazing, and paperhanging as well as chairmaking. Swain was back in New London by 1837, when he once again advertised "HOUSE AND SIGN PAINTING, Glazing & Paperhanging."

References: *Conn. Gazette,* 1 April 1812, 29 March 1837; Evans, pp. 429, 640–41.

Lemuel Swift (dates unknown)
(active in Hartford 1805–07)

see Chester Andross

Zenas Swift (dates unknown)
(active in Hartford 1807–11)

see Chester Andross

Isaac Van Cott (dates unknown)
(active in Norwich 1849+)

see Philemon Van Cott

Philemon Van Cott (1797–1843)
(active in Norwich 1836)

Philemon Van Cott was born in New York State and was still in New York as late as 1833. He had moved to Norwich by 1836, according to the Norwich *Courier,* which noted that "P. VAN COTT,/ House painter & Glazier" had "engaged a first rate Sign and Ornamental Painter." We do not yet know who this sign painter was. Philemon's son, John D. Van Cott (1823–54), was listed as a "painter" in the 1850 census. Another painter, Isaac H. Van Cott (b. 1821), was living nearby. Possibly a son of Philemon,

Isaac was listed as a painter in an 1849 Norwich directory and advertised a full rage of ornamental painting in the 1857 Norwich directory.

References: *Norwich Courier*, 30 March 1836; Norwich City Directory, 1849, 1857.

Nathaniel Wales (dates unknown)
(active in Hartford 1803–15, Litchfield 1806)

Nathaniel Wales was probably born in Windham, Connecticut, where several individuals by that name lived. He was working in Hartford as a sign painter and fan light maker as early as 1803. Three years later he advertised in Litchfield, offering, in addition to sign painting, "LIKENESSES painted on Canvas or Glass, for Eight Dollars each." In that same year Wales painted the portraits of Capt. and Mrs. Nathan Sage of Oswego, New York, though it is unclear if Wales traveled there or if he painted the couple on a trip to their native Connecticut. A Nathaniel Wales shows up on the Hartford census in both 1810 and 1820. If this is the same Nathaniel Wales, he did not live in Hartford continuously, for in 1815 he was in Charleston, South Carolina, advertising as a portrait painter.

Four additional portraits are credited to Wales—Mr. and Mrs. Hezekiah Parmelee, Jr., of New Haven, and Dr. and Mrs. Joseph Silliman. His experience in portraiture and his location in Hartford suggest Wales as a likely painter of the Henry Sill / Ebenezer F. Bissell sign in the collection of the Windsor Historical Society (see fig. 5).

References: *Courant*, 8 June 1803; *The [Litchfield] Witness*, 5 Feb. 1806; *Litchfield Monitor*, 5 March 1806; Charleston *Courier*, 4 May 1815; *Index Am. Ptgs*; Nina Fletcher Little, "Little-Known Connecticut Artists, 1790–1810," *CHSB* 22 (Oct. 1957): 98–99, 111–12; Little, *Paintings*, pp. 170–73;

[?] Walsh
(active in Hartford 1789)

see Isaac Sanford

Josiah Winslow Wentworth (1755–1841)
(active in Norwalk ca. 1776–82, Norwich 1783–84)

Carriage maker Josiah Winslow Wentworth was born in Boston. In 1776 he moved to Norwalk, where he built a house and carriage-maker's shop opposite the house of his brother Edmund. His marriage to Mary Hanford of Norwalk is well-documented; during the revolution Josiah was clearly a patriot, but his wife's family were Tories. Eventually Mary moved to Canada with her brother, Thomas, and her son, Thomas Hanford Wentworth. By 1783 Josiah W. Wentworth relocated to Norwich, where he advertised as a coach and chaise maker; he also painted chaises, signs, and heraldry. Sometime before 1800 Wentworth moved to Sag Harbour, Long Island, where he remarried. He remained in Sag Harbour until 1824, moving then to New York City where he died.

References: *Conn. Gazette*, 16 Jan. 1784; John Wentworth, *The Wentworth Genealogy: English and American* (Boston: Little, Brown, and Company, 1878), 571–72.

Thomas West (1786–1828)
(active in New London 1807–28)

Evans documents West as a Fancy and Windsor Chair maker in New London, 1807–28. That he also painted signs is known from a single 1823 advertisement, which included among his services, "Sign Painting, Guilding,/ &c./ done with neatness, and on short notice."

References: *Conn. Gazette*, 22 April 1807, 26 April 1815, 26 March 1823; Evans, p. 715.

TABLE 1
Chronology of Sign Painters in Connecticut

Earliest documented working date in Connecticut	Name	Location(s) in Connecticut

PAINTERS ACTIVE BEFORE 1790

1766	Abraham Delanoy	New Haven
1776	Josiah W. Wentworth	Norwalk, Norwich
1782	Webster James	Norwich, Hartford
1785	Isaac Sanford	Hartford, Litchfield
1789	[?] Walsh	Hartford

PAINTERS ACTIVE 1790–1815

1793	John S. Barrow	Hartford, Middletown
1793	Beatty & Co.	Norwich
1794	Samuel Blydenburg	Hartford
1794	John Grimes	Hartford
1796	Youngs Hosmer	Hartford
1796	Stephanus Knight	Enfield
1797	Caleb Galpin	Berlin
1798	Abner Reed	East Windsor, Hartford
1798	John Graham	Hartford
1798	John C. Bull	Hartford
1801	Luther Allen	Enfield
1803	Nathaniel Wales	Hartford, Litchfield
1805	Alfred Janes	Hartford
1805	Almarin Janes	Hartford
1805	Lemuel Swift	Hartford
1806	Samuel Sizer	Middletown
1807	Thomas West	New London
1807	Zenas Swift	Hartford
1807	Chester Andross	Hartford
1809	Isaac Allyn	New London
1810	Phipps Deming	Farmington, Hartford
1811	Henry Bodge	Hartford
1811	Jonathan Hartshorn	Hartford
1812	Timothy Swain	New London
1813	Harlan Page	Coventry

PAINTERS ACTIVE 1815-1850

Earliest documented working date in Connecticut	Name	Location(s) in Connecticut
1816	Abial A. Cooley	New London
1816	William Rice	Hartford
1818	William F. Andross	Hartford
1819	William Laughton	Hartford
1821	Samuel B. Middlebrooks	Bridgeport
1821	Matthew Curtis	Bridgeport
1822	Isaac S. Sizer	New London
1823	Hugh Gourley	Hartford
1823	Solomon Jones	Middletown, Marlborough
1823	Thomas K. Bush	Middletown
1823	Norman Ormsby	Hartford
1823	Abial Canfield	Bridgeport
1823	William Curtis	Bridgeport
1824	David T. Johnson	Norwich, Middletown, New Haven
1824	Jason Griffin	Middletown
1824	Samuel Holt	Hartford, Windsor
1826	Hiram Cauldwell	New Haven
1826	David Finch	Bridgeport
1827	Samuel S. Osgood	Hartford
1827	J. C. Nichols	Bridgeport
1828	George Burnham	Hartford
1829	William Goodrich	Middletown
1829	Lucius Bidwell	Middletown
1830	E. McNeil	Litchfield
1831	Miller & Fitch	Hartford
1831	William Griffin	Brooklyn
1833	Isaac G. Farden	Litchfield, Hartford
1834	Joseph J. Grant	Hartford
1836	Philemon Van Cott	Norwich
1838	Chauncey Case	Hartford
1838	Osmyn Case	Hartford
1838	Erastus Granger	Hartford
1840	Frederick F. Rice	Hartford
1841	George W. Smith	Hartford
1842	Theodore Drake	Bridgeport
1849	Isaac Van Cott	Norwich

TABLE 2
Known Working Locations of Sign Painters in Connecticut, 1760–1850

(Connecticut location with dates of documented activity at specified location)

BERLIN

Caleb Galpin, 1797–1803

BRIDGEPORT

Matthew Curtis, 1821–64
Samuel B. Middlebrooks, 1821–38
Abial Canfield, 1823
William Curtis, 1823
David Finch, 1826–29
J. C. Nichols, 1827–42
Theodore Drake, 1842

BROOKLYN

William Griffin, 1831

COVENTRY

Harlan Page, 1813

EAST WINDSOR

Abner Reed, 1798–1801
    (also Hartford)

ENFIELD

Stephanus Knight, 1796–1808
Luther Allen, 1801–11

FARMINGTON

Phipps Deming, 1810
    (also Hartford)

HARTFORD

Isaac Sanford, 1785, 1791–97, 1819–23
    (also Litchfield)
Webster James, 1788
    (also Norwich)
[?]Walsh, 1789
John S. Barrow, 1793
    (also Middletown)
John Grimes, 1794–98
Samuel Blydenburg, 1794–1803
Youngs Hosmer, 1796
Abner Reed, 1803–08
    (also East Windsor)
John C. Bull, 1798–1805
John Graham, 1798–1800
Nathaniel Wales, 1803–15
    (also Litchfield)

Alfred Janes, 1805
Almarin Janes, 1805
Lemuel Swift, 1805–07
Chester Andross, 1807–22
Zenas Swift, 1807–11
Phipps Deming, 1811–15
    (also Farmington)
Henry Bodge, 1811
Jonathan Hartshorn, 1811–12
William Rice, 1816–47
William F. Andross, 1818–19
William Laughton, 1819–23, 1838
Hugh Gourley, 1823–50
Norman Ormsby, 1823
Samuel Holt, 1824–25, 1841–45,
    1853–57, 1864–84
    (also Windsor)
Samuel S. Osgood, 1827
George Burnham, 1828
Miller & Fitch, 1831
Isaac G. Farden, 1833
    (also Litchfield)
Joseph J. Grant, 1834–37
Erastus Granger, 1838–55
Chauncey Case, 1838–63
Osmyn Case, 1838–60
Frederick F. Rice, 1840–1876
George W. Smith, 1841–66

LITCHFIELD

Isaac Sanford, 1785–88
    (also Hartford)
Nathaniel Wales, 1806
    (also Hartford)
E. McNeil, 1830
Isaac G. Farden, 1833
    (also Hartford)

MARLBOROUGH

Solomon Jones, 1850
    (also Middletown)

MIDDLETOWN

John S. Barrow, 1804
Samuel Sizer, 1806
Solomon Jones, 1823–26
    (also Marlborough)
Thomas K. Bush, 1823–25

Jason Griffin, 1824
David T. Johnson, 1830–35
    (also Norwich, New Haven)
Lucius Bidwell, 1829–32
William Goodrich, 1829–31

NEW HAVEN

Abraham Delanoy, 1784–87
David T. Johnson, 1843–76
    (also Norwich, Middletown)
Hiram Cauldwell, 1826–27

NEW LONDON

Thomas West, 1807–28
Isaac Allyn, 1809–12
Timothy Swain, 1812, 1837
Abial A. Cooley, 1816
Isaac S. Sizer, 1822–23

NORWALK

Josiah W. Wentworth, 1776–82
    (also Norwich)

NORWICH

Josiah W. Wentworth, 1783–84
    (also Norwalk)
Webster James, 1782–84, 1803–04
    (also Hartford)
Beatty & Co., 1793
David T. Johnson, 1824
    (also Middletown, New Haven)
Philemon Van Cott, 1836
Isaac Van Cott, 1849

WINDSOR

Samuel Holt, 1860

Checklist of Connecticut Tavern and Inn Signs by Current Location

Compiled by Philip D. Zimmerman and Margaret C. Vincent

(Not including signs at The Connecticut Historical Society. Includes all known signs by William Rice)

* An asterisk beside the catalog number indicates that the sign was included in the exhibition *Lions & Eagles & Bulls: Early American Tavern & Inn Signs from The Connecticut Historical Society.*

Abby Aldrich Rockefeller Folk Art Center, Colonial Williamsburg Foundation, Williamsburg, Virginia

1. Sign for Hawley's Inn, by William Rice, ca. 1820s
Probably Sandisfield, Massachusetts
Innholder: A. Hawley
Signed: On eagle side in lower right, "Rice."
Description: Horizontal rectangular sign, encased in moldings, with oval field containing text and image, 37-7/8" x 56-1/8".
Images: Lion tethered to a chain on one side, eagle with federal shield on the other.
Text: "A.HAWLEY'S / INN."
References: Smith, *Tavern Signs*, listed p. 32.

Colebrook Historical Society, Colebrook, Connecticut

2. Sign for Seymour's Inn (fragment), ca. 1836
Colebrook, Connecticut
Innholder: Rufus Seymour (licensed 1836–44)
Attributed to William Rice, on the basis of similarity of stylistic details.
Description: Now a circular fragment used as table top, with one surface painted white, approx. 24" in diameter. Probably was a horizontal rectangular sign with oval panel with date cartouche in center against a brickwork background (similar to that documented on sign for Pinney's inn, 1836, presently unlocated).

Fairfield Historical Society, Fairfield, Connecticut

3. Sign for Hull's Tavern, dated 1785
Fairfield, Connecticut
Innholders: Hull family, possibly Stephen Hull (b. 1724)
Description: Vertical panel with pediment and applied moldings, 32-1/2" x 23-3/4".
Images: On both sides, profile view of riderless black horse, centered on panel.
Text: On pediment, "1785"; above image, "HULL"; below image, "ENTERTAINMET" with "N" above the "ET".
References: Robert E. Hull, *The Ancestors and Descendents of George Hull and Thamzen Michell* [sic] (Baltimore: Gateway Press, 1994), illus. p. 132.

H.F. du Pont Winterthur Museum, Winterthur, Delaware

4. Sign for Archer's Inn, dated 1815
Suffield, Connecticut
Innholder: Thomas Archer (active 1814–29)
Description: Octagonal signboard with shaped, attached pediment, 21" x 54".
Images: An eagle with federal shield on one side, and a rising sun on the other, each painted over Connecticut state vine cluster symbols.
Text: "1815 / T.ARCHER'S".

Hinman Tavern, Burlington, Connecticut

5. Sign for Hinman's Tavern, date unknown
Burlington, Connecticut
Description: Dimensions unknown.
References: Smith, *Tavern Signs*, listed p. 41.

Historical Society of Glastonbury, Glastonbury, Connecticut

6. Sign for Treat's Inn, dated 1818
Glastonbury, Connecticut
Innholder: David Treat (active 1818–21)
Possibly by William Rice, based on similarity to the sign for Tarbox's inn, CHS, cat. 19.
Description: Oval signboard, suspended from a joined frame, 38-3/4" x 21".
Images: Eagle with federal shield on one side, eagle with Connecticut state shield on the other.
Text: "D.TREAT. / 1818."
References: Benes, *Two Towns*, illus. no. 236, p. 120.

Keeler Tavern Museum, Ridgefield, Connecticut

7. Sign for Timothy Keeler's Inn, dated 1788 over 1804 [?]
Ridgefield, Connecticut
Innholder: Timothy Keeler, Jr. (active 1772–1815)
Description: Vertical panel with pediment and applied moldings, 36" x 23-1/2".

Images: On one side, profile view of leaping black horse with male rider in eighteenth-century attire; on the other side, profile view of two running black horses with Native American riders.

Text: Dates on pediment; below image, "T.KEELERs *INN*" over earlier name(s).

References: Smith, *Tavern Signs*, illus. p. 20.

8. Sign for William Keeler's Inn, probably 1820s

Ridgefield, Connecticut

Innholder: William Keeler (active 1815–27)

Description: Horizontal oval sign, with name band border enclosing image, 34-1/2" x 49".

Images: Four horses pulling a closed stagecoach.

Text: "W.KEELER'S / HOTEL."

References: Smith, *Tavern Signs*, illus. p. 21.

Middlesex County Historical Society, Middletown, Connecticut

9. Sign for Cheny's Inn, ca. 1813

Portland, Connecticut (then called Chatham)

Innholder: Daniel Cheny (active 1813–18)

Description: Vertical oval signboard, 41-1/2" x 30-1/2".

Images: Masonic symbols on one side, and a three-masted merchant ship on the other.

Text: "D. CHENY" in curving black banner above Masonic symbols and below ship.

References: *Great River*, illus. no. 61, p. 176.

The New-York Historical Society, New York City

10. Sign for Fitch's Inn, ca. 1810

Bolton, Connecticut

Innholder: Elijah Fitch (active 1810–42)

Description: Vertical rectangle with double-lobed pediment, encased in moldings, 43-1/2" x 23".

Images: Crescent moon.

Text: "E,Fitchs / iNN".

References: Illus. fig. 19.

11. Sign for Taylor's Tavern, dated 1785 and 1800

Possibly Norwalk, Connecticut

Possibly Levi Taylor (active 1798 and possibly earlier)

Description: Vertical panel with pediment and applied moldings, 41" x 23".

Images: On one side, profile view of head, centered in circular medallion, with 13 stars and the text, "LIBERTY", over an earlier image of eagle with outswept wings. On other side, eagle with federal insignia, centered in circular medallion, with 13 stars and the text, "UNITED STATES OF AMERICA".

Text: On pediment, "1800" over 1785; under present image, "L.TAYLOR / TAVERN" with another name (indecipherable) below that.

References: Smith, *Tavern Signs*, illus. p. 28.

No longer extant

12. Sign for Viets's Inn, by William Rice, ca. 1820s

East Granby, Connecticut

Innholder: Luke Viets (active 1797–1834)

Signed: "Rice" in lower right above name band.

Description: Horizontal rectangular sign, encased in moldings; dimensions unknown.

Images: On one side, pair of large crossed keys, above a black name band; other side unknown.

Text: "1790. / L. VIETS."

References: *MBTS*, illus. p. 83. Sign burned prior to 1958.

Norfolk Historical Society, Norfolk, Connecticut

13. Sign for Pettibone's Inn, by William Rice, dated 1819

Norfolk, Connecticut

Innholder: Jonathan Humphrey Pettibone (active 1815–32)

Signed: On both sides in lower right, "Rice".

Description: Horizontal rectangular sign, with large oval field around smaller, central oval bordered by rays. Similar on both sides, 40" x 50".

Images: None.

Text: "J.H.PETTIBONE's / INN." with "1819." in center, in gold letters.

Old Sturbridge Village, Sturbridge, Massachusetts

14. Sign for Buell's Inn, ca. 1820s–40s

East Hampton, Connecticut

Innholder: David Buell (active 1826–29); William G. Buell (active 1849–56)

Description: Horizontal rectangular sign, 50-1/4" x 59-1/2".

Images: On one side, a dog holding a pheasant in its mouth, in a forest setting; on the other side, a man fishing.

Text: In name band below image, "WM.G.BUELL."

15. Sign for Carpenter's Inn, date unknown

East Windsor, Connecticut

Innholder: S. V. Carpenter

Description: Vertical rectangular sign with double-lobed pediment and applied moldings, 37" x 21".

Images: Floral festoon under text.

Text: "S;V / CARPEN / TERS / INN".

References: Smith, *Tavern Signs*, listed p. 37.

16. Sign for Mallory's Inn, ca. 1810–47

Barkhamsted, Connecticut

Innholder: Amasa Mallory, active 1810–51

Description: Horizontal rectangle with large oval panel, gold lettering, 25" x 57".

References: Smith, *Tavern Signs*, listed p. 37.

Present location unknown

17. Sign for Adams's Inn (fragment), ca. 1800–05

North Canton, Connecticut

Innholder: Ezra Adams (active 1802–30)

Possibly by Richard Brunton (d. 1832)

Description: Vertical oval panel, 40-3/4" x 15-3/4".

Images: On one side, a sailing ship; on the other, an eagle with shield.

Text: On ship side, over image, "ENTERTAI[NMENT]", below image, "BY / E. ADA[MS.]"; on eagle side, over image, "[ENTERT]AINMENT", below image, "BY / [E. A]DAMS."

References: Watercolor rendering, by John Matulis, ca. 1940, *Index of American Design*, National Gallery of Art, Washington, D.C., 1943.8.14990. Attribution to Richard Brunton made by William Lamson Warren.

18. Sign for Bates's Inn, dated 1794

Haddam, Connecticut

Innholder: Eleazer Bates (active 1794-98 and possibly later)

Description: Vertical signboard with a shaped pediment and skirt, held within joined frame having turned columns, dimensions unknown.

Images: One side displays a bull's head, the other shows an American flag.

Text: On bull's head side, below image, "HADDAM"; on flag side, on pediment, "AP • 23 • 1794", below image "ELEAZER • / BATES •".

References: Correspondence, CHS museum research files.

19. Sign for Clark's Inn, date unknown

Seymour, Connecticut

Innholder: David B. Clark (active ca. 1846 and earlier)

Description: Horizontal rectangular sign, dimensions unknown.

Images: On one side, a boy holding a white horse hitched to a carriage; other side unknown.

Text: In black name band below image, "D. B. CLARK".

References: Rev. Hollis A. Campbell, *Seymour, Past and Present* (Seymour: Sharpe, 1902), illus. p. 43.

20. Sign for Collins's Inn, dated 1820?

Falley's Crossroads, near Pittsfield, Massachusetts (now Huntington)

Possibly by William Rice

Description: Reported to be similar to the Daniel Loomis inn sign, CHS, cat 28.

Reference: Correspondence, CHS museum research files.

21. Sign for Mineral Springs Hotel, dated 1824

Woodstock, Connecticut

Innholder: Hezekiah Bugbee (active 1824–31)

Description: Horizontal oval signboard, dimensions unknown.

Images: None.

Text: "MINERAL SPRINGS. / H. Bugbee / 1824." on one side; other side unknown.

References: Clarence Winthrop Bowen, *The History of Woodstock Connecticut*, 8 vols. (Norwood, Mass.: Plimpton Press, 1926), illus. vol. 1, p. 465.

22. Sign for Pinney's Hotel, by William Rice, dated 1836

Riverton, Connecticut (Barkhamsted Township)

Innholder: Reuben Pinney (licensed 1836–53)

Signed: in scrolled banner in lower right, "RICE".

Description: Horizontal rectangular sign with oval field enclosing image and text, dimensions unknown.

Images: On one side, an eagle with federal shield, brickwork background surrounding oval; other side unknown.

References: Richard G. Wheeler and George Hilton, ed., *Barkhamsted Heritage: Culture and Industry in a Rural Connecticut Town* (Barkhamsted: Barkhamsted Historical Society, 1975), illus. p. 154 (drawing by Douglas E. Roberts).

23. Sign for Robertson's Tavern and Village Hotel, by William Rice, dated 1831

Windsorville, Connecticut (East Windsor Township)

Innholder: William Robertson (active 1818–32)

Signed: In lower right, "[RI]CE".

Description: Horizontal rectangular sign with large oval name panel enclosing image and text, 37-7/8" x 56-1/8".

Images: On one side, an eagle with the federal shield; on the other, a single, central star.

Text: On the eagle side, "ROBERTSONS / TAVERN"; on the star side, "VILLAGE / HOTEL".

References: Correspondence, CHS museum research files.

24. Sign for the Shipman Hotel, ca. 1841

Rocky Hill, Connecticut

Innholder: Samuel Shipman (active 1841–56)

Description: Horizontal rectangular sign, with oval field enclosing text, dimensions unknown.

Images: Central floral device.

Text: "S.SHIPMAN'S / HOTEL."

References: Terry, *Old Inns*, illus. p. 135.

Private collection

25. Sign for Stoughton's Hotel, by William Rice, dated 1816

Wapping, Connecticut (South Windsor Township)

Innholder: Harden Stoughton (active 1815–ca. 1860s)

Signed: On one side, in lower right, "RICE."; dated in lower left, "1816".

Description: Horizontal rectangular sign, encased in moldings; red spandrels and black oval field enclosing name and design in gold, 48" x 72".

Images: Signature side has a central, eight-petaled floret surrounded by an elaborate filigree lozenge terminating in arrow points. Other side has a larger, central eight-petaled floret.

Text: On both sides, "STOUGHTON'S/HOTEL." framing the design.

St. Mark's Lodge No. 36, A.F. & A.M., Simsbury, Connecticut

26. * Sign for Holcomb's Inn, dated 1802

Granby, Connecticut

Innholder: Luther Holcomb (active 1802–08)

Description: Vertical oval sign panel with scalloped edge, suspended from a joined frame with shaped pediment and skirt and turned columns, 59-1/4" x 28-3/8".

Images: Masonic symbols on one side, and an eagle with federal shield on the other.

Text: On both sides, "1802 / L. HOLCOMB / ENTERTAINMENT."

References: Illus. fig. 34.

Shelburne Museum, Shelburne, Vermont

27. Sign for Bradley's Hotel, dated 1817
Guilford, Connecticut
Innholder: Minor Bradley (active ca. 1822–56)
Description: Horizontal rectangular sign, 43-1/4" x 30-1/4".
Images: Two horses pulling closed stagecoach on one side, other side similar.
Text: "THE STRANGER'S HOME / M. BRADLEY / 1817".
References: Smith, *Tavern Signs*, listed p. 33.

Silvermine Tavern Restaurant, Norwalk, Connecticut

28. Sign for Jacobs's Inn, ca. 1820s
Thompson, Connecticut
Innholder: Abel Jacobs (active 1814–32)
Description: Horizontal oval sign, repainted, with name band border enclosing image, 27" x 41".
Images: On each side, four horses pulling a closed stagecoach.
Text: "THE TRAVELLER'S REST. / ABEL JACOBS."
References: Smith, *Tavern Signs*, illus. p. 46.

29. Sign for Lewis's Inn, dated 1812 over 1800
Bristol, Connecticut
Innholder: Abel Lewis (active 1800–19)
Description: Oval sign panel fixed within a joined, turned frame, 48" x 26-1/2".
Images: Masonic arch and symbols on one side, and tree on the other.
Text: "1812 [over '1800'] / A: LEWIS'S / INN".
References: Smith, *Tavern Signs*, illus. p. 46.

Simsbury Historical Society, Simsbury, Connecticut

30. Sign for Jeffrey Phelps's Inn, by William Rice, ca. 1829
Simsbury, Connecticut
Innholder: Jeffrey O. Phelps (licensed 1820–32)
Signature: On both sides in lower right, "Rice".
Description: Horizontal rectangle, 43" x 49-3/4".
Image: Eagle with federal shield and plough, similar on both sides.
Text: In black name band below image, "Jeffery O. PHelps".
References: Terry, *Old Inns*, illus. p. 47.

Torrington Historical Society, Torrington, Connecticut

31. Sign for Griswold's Inn, by William Rice, ca. late 1830s
Torringford, Connecticut (section of Torrington)
Innholder: Thaddeus Griswold (licensed 1804–40)
Signed: On both sides in lower right, "Rice".
Description: Horizontal rectangular sign, with oval field with flocked background enclosing name, 26" x 55".
Images: One side has a central, eight-petaled floret.
Text: On both sides, "GRISWOLD." in gold letters.

Wadsworth Atheneum, Hartford, Connecticut

32. Sign for Goodwin's Inn, by William Rice, ca. 1820s
Hartford, Connecticut
Innholder: James Goodwin (active 1811–41)
Signed: At lower center on both sides, "RICE."
Description: Horizontal rectangle, encased in moldings, 49-1/2" x 74-3/4".
Images: Lion tethered to a chain, similar on both sides except for position of tail.
References: *Great River*, illus. no. 59, pp. 173–74.

33. * Sign for David Bissell's Inn and Joseph Phelps's Inn, dated 1777 and 1801
East Windsor, Connecticut (now East Windsor Hill, in South Windsor)
Innholders: David Bissell (active 1777–87); Erastus Wolcott (active 1787–1801); Joseph Phelps (active 1801–02); John Pelton (licensed 1816–17)
Repainting in 1801 attributed to Abner Reed, on basis of documentation in Reed's day book for work done on "J Phelps" sign, February 1801; painter of earlier imagery unidentified.
Description: Vertical panel with pediment and skirt, applied moldings, and attached columnar frame, 50-1/2" x 31-1/2".
Images: On side 1, a profile view of a head with Liberty cap, centered in a circular medallion with sixteen stars and the word, "LIBERTY." On side 2, an eagle perched on a branch, no shield. Earlier paint layer features circle of interlacing rings with text, "The 13 United States".
Text: On both sides, in black name band below image, "J. P" over earlier names; on skirt, "1801." over earlier date(s).
References: Illus. fig. 63; Earle, *Tavern Days*, illus. pp. 150–51, 153. Watercolor rendering, by Alfred Parys, ca. 1940, *Index of American Design*, National Gallery of Art, 1943.8.20; published Hornung, no. 235, p. 76. Abner Reed's account book, 1800–01, CHS Library, cited *MBTS*, p. 11.

Westmoreland Museum of Art, Greensburg, Pennsylvania

34. Lion and eagle sign, late 1810s
Probably New England
Attributed to William Rice on the basis of similarity to known Rice lions
Description: Vertical rectangular sign, 27-3/8" x 22-1/2".
Images: On one side, front section of a lion; on the other, an eagle with federal shield.
References: Smith, *Tavern Signs*, illus. p. 39.

Wethersfield Historical Society, Wethersfield, Connecticut

35. Sign for Wethersfield Village Hotel, ca. 1840–60
Wethersfield, Connecticut
Innholder: James Standish (1827–1902)
Description: Horizontal rectangular sign with dark oval field enclosing name, 51-5/8" x 61-3/4".
Images: None.
Text: "WETHERSFIELD / VILLAGE / HOTEL."
References: Benes, *Two Towns*, illus. no. 241, p. 122.

Windsor Historical Society, Windsor, Connecticut

36. * Sign for Sill's Inn and Bissell's Inn, ca. 1814

Windsor, Connecticut

Innholders: Henry Sill (active 1816–19); Augustin Drake (active 1820); Ebenezer Fitch Bissell, Jr. (active 1821–23)

Possibly painted by Nathaniel Wales (active in Hartford 1803–15)

Description: Shaped sign board, 47-1/2" x 23".

Images: Oval portraits of War of 1812 naval heroes: on side 1, Capt. James Lawrence, and on side 2, Com. Oliver Hazard Perry, taken from contemporary engravings.

Text: "BISSELL." over earlier name.

References: Illus. fig. 5.

Conservation Treatment Protocol

Williamstown Art Conservation Center: Early American Tavern and Inn Signs
from The Connecticut Historical Society Collection 1998–2000

Initial treatment protocol discussions were held between the conservation team and the staff of The Connecticut Historical Society at the time of the initial collection survey, April-June 1998, and during the proposal stage for the first signs. Discussions concerning amendments, refinements, and exceptions continued almost weekly throughout the project.

General Philosophical Approach:

Due to the historic nature and exterior function of these painted objects, conservation treatment was limited primarily to study and preservation, with limited cleaning and consolidation. Structural stabilization, including decisions about hardware, were undertaken for the purposes of safe exhibition and travel. Surface treatments, such as paint consolidation and grime removal, were executed with materials that would not alter the appearance of the original surfaces. The removal of restoration coatings and later overpaint was considered on a case by case basis, as was inpainting, which was only rarely performed. Generally, early twentieth-century "restorations" were left in place, as reminders of the earlier aesthetic of repainting such signs for exhibition. However, our working premise was to leave the signs looking as if they had not been "restored."

Decorative Surfaces:

A. CLEANING: The extent of paint surface cleaning included loose surface dust and grime, and extraneous deposits, especially if these appeared to be related to pre-collection storage locations (e.g., barns, sheds, attics, etc.) rather than original use(s). Embedded grime from exterior use was not removed and only the gentlest surface cleaning solutions and methods were employed. Mild, neutral water-based solutions were used for the most part. The desire was to prevent instances needing corrections in saturation, such as temporary blanching, as we wanted to avoid varnishing and inpainting for the most part.

Exceptions included:
1. Later oil, varnish, or shellac coatings, often sloppily applied, which were uneven, discolored, or glossy. These were usually discernable as "restoration" additions, probably applied in the twentieth century to saturate the colors. In most cases, these

later coatings were completely removed and the surfaces left unvarnished.
2. Signs, which had original or very old coatings, and were of the type described as having been varnished originally. A few of these had their coatings thinned, if they were excessively discolored and grimy. Others had only surface grime removed, with the coatings left untouched. Most of these signs were probably not varnished originally, so except as noted for consolidation purposes, signs did not receive resinous coatings.
3. Salt deposits, which were adversely affecting the paint-to-wood bond, were reduced using poultices or wicking papers and de-ionized water.

B. CONSOLIDATION: Many signs had either powdery or flaking surface paint, so consolidation was accepted as necessary for the long term stability of the remaining decorative schemes. The fact that a significant portion of the collection would be in a traveling exhibition reinforced the need for consolidation. In general flaking or powdering paint was treated with as little intervention as possible, using low concentration, water-based consolidants, which did not need solvents either for delivery or cleanup. Many surfaces were treated either locally or overall using warm gelatin or isinglass. No applied heat or metal tools were used to lay down loose paint, in order to avoid altering the surface sheen.

Exceptions included:
1. Occasionally the severe condition of the paint demanded a stronger adhesive. This was associated with the need to relax and secure very thick, stiff, curled paint layers, such as the heat damaged paint on the Stiles inn and Thompson Hotel sign (cat. 41), where dilute Beva D8 was used in conjunction with ethanol. A small Teflon tool was used to coax the paint back into position.
2. In several cases of loose, strewn smalt or sand, dilute (4%) Acryloid B-72 in xylene was applied, as this resin formed a better adhesion between the upper particles and the lower paint or mordant layer. This clear varnish also did not detract from the sparkly effects intended by the use of such paint inclusions.

C. "RESTORATION" REMOVAL: A handful of signs, dating primarily from the eighteenth century, had been repainted during the late decades of the nineteenth century or early decades of the twentieth century. The removal of such repaint was decided on a case by case basis, but was rarely undertaken, as the restoration was generally considered a significant element of the object's history. Several of these "restorations" were signed and dated and appear to have been executed in overly thick, somewhat intractable oil paint.

Exceptions included:

1. Major removal of overpaint was undertaken only in three cases, for varying reasons. In each case, the decision to attempt removal was made only after testing indicated that the overpainting could be safely removed without injury to the remaining original paint:

a. On the sign for the Blatchly inn (cat. 10) garish twentieth-century colors were removed from the one side that had been overpainted, revealing two early images; an early twentieth-century photograph documented the pre-overpaint appearance.

b. On the sign for the Field inn and Abbe Inn and Tea Room (cat. 24), both sides displayed identical overpainting, documented ca. 1914-17, with outlines of an earlier image and lettering clearly visible in raking light; overpaint was removed from one side only, leaving the other intact as an example of Colonial Revival aesthetics.

c. On the sign for Ely's inn and Village Hotel (cat. 19), both sides displayed identical repainting dating to the 1830s; substantial portions had already been removed on one side, revealing portions of an eagle underneath and effectively destroying the 1830s surface. Remnants of the 1830s surface were removed, fully uncovering the earlier image and signature.

2. Minor removals were undertaken when small additions were clearly post-use, discolored, and soluble.

D. NEW VARNISHES OR INPAINTING: In general these techniques were not considered appropriate for the signs, except in rare individual cases, with the concurrence of curatorial staff. If a coating was suggested, it was employed as a consolidant where no surface change was anticipated (see section B). In general no attempt was made to mitigate the effects of weathering inherent to these objects, except at the specific request of curatorial staff, and after discussion with the conservators.

Exceptions included:

1. If upon removal, garish modern paint colors had permanently stained the porous wood, this damage was disguised by repainting in a color more typical of the period. This typically involved only small local areas, except for the frame posts on the Blatchly inn sign (cat. 10).

2. If the image was particularly detailed and painterly, with only a few distracting losses, these were occasionally inpainted in reversible media (e.g., the sign for Porter's inn, cat. 27).

3. If coatings were thinned on signs believed to have been originally varnished, occasionally a thin matte Soluvar layer was applied to even out the gloss (e.g., the signs for Carter's and Mason's inns, cat. 33, 51). All cleaned, gilded lettering was left uncoated, as is common practice for preserving the metallic lustre.

4. Earlier wood repairs and new structural replacements were toned and painted to blend with the surrounding paint. (e.g., old bare wood inserts on the Temperance Hotel sign and new sections on the David Loomis and Wedgwood inn signs, cat 22, 38, 54).

Wood Supports and Construction:

A. OLD REPAIRS: In general old repairs were left in place as evidence of the history of the sign. This included wood or metal patches, inserts, or fabricated portions of frames. Where there was some question about the period of all or parts of the sign, the issue was resolved at the curatorial level, with technical support from the conservators. Particular cases are discussed in the entries.

Exceptions included:

1. Old repairs were removed or adjusted if they were causing ongoing stress or damage to the sign. In general all old wood and metal repairs and fasteners were reinserted in their original locations, following any dismantling.

2. Repairs that were recent and not appropriate to the period were removed with curatorial approval (for example, an incorrect and awkward molding design on one edge of the Field inn and Abbe Inn and Tea Room sign was replaced with one matching the rest, cat. 24).

B. NEW REPAIRS OR STABILIZATION: In general repairs were limited only to those which were necessary for the long-term survival of the sign. The fact that these signs would be traveling occasionally influenced the recommendations for stabilization, for example if the joinery was extremely weak, causing the sign to flex when handled, or if the support posts were broken. All joinery stabilization was implemented with reversible techniques (e.g., sliding steel pins for the David Loomis and Porter inn signs, cat. 22, 27). In general the condition of the wood was accepted as part of the history of the use and the measure of exposure to New England weather. In a few cases the wood support was considered too weathered or punky to travel. (e.g., the Bement inn sign, cat. 9).

Exceptions included:

1. Occasionally cosmetic replacements or repairs were executed in response to curatorial request or at the suggestion of the conservation team (e.g., the replacement of a spline between two main boards in order to visually close a light gap, on the Daniel Loomis inn sign, cat. 28). In a few cases wood sections were rotted sufficiently to warrant major consolidation and partial rebuilding. Reconstruction was attempted rarely and only when surviving evidence of the original form(s) existed, as on the posts of the Wedgwood inn sign (cat. 38).

2. If there was no way to safely display a sign in its proper

double-sided orientation: e.g., the General Wolfe sign no longer had a frame or a proper place to attach hanging hardware (cat. 4). At curatorial request, in order to be able to safely suspend the signboard in a manner consistent with the rest of the collection, a new, simple, wooden frame was constructed and painted to blend with the original board.

Metal Hardware Hanging Systems:

A. USE OF ORIGINAL HARDWARE: The use of the original hardware was the method of first choice for suspension of the signs, for both in-house use and for the traveling exhibition. Most signs had enough of their original hardware remaining for the proper swinging suspension from two points of attachment. Radiography was used to check corrosion levels on those iron hangers suspected of weakness due to corrosion or fabrication flaws.

Exceptions included:
1. If the original hardware was deemed too weak for the weight of the sign, another system of display was designed (e.g., a strong, lightweight steel cable was attached as an auxiliary support for the Bissell inn sign, cat. 7).

B. REPLACEMENT HARDWARE: Nails or bolts, where needed, were fabricated to blend with existing ones. If they were not necessary to support the weight of the sign or their loss did not affect the proper attachment of the hardware to the wood, no replacements were added. Several signs were missing their hanging hardware, and after much discussion, it was decided to employ a master blacksmith to fabricate these replacements on a case by case basis. Each sign was studied for clues relating to the shape and placement of the original hardware. A generic iron rod profile with loop termination was selected, with designs varying only in the strap attachment and clearance length needed. New hardware on two signs was also bent to swing past existing finials, a technique used on several original installations. All new hardware was signed and date-stamped to distinguish it from original hardware, and painted with flat, vinyl-based paint.

C. CLEANING AND PROTECTIVE COATINGS: Most of the hardware was cleaned of previous coatings, such as wax or oil, and recoated with Acryloid B-48n. Corroded metal was gently mechanically cleaned prior to the application of an oxidation inhibitor and a coating. The method of installation attachment should be designed to protect the original metal from further abrasion (e.g., plastic- sheathed hooks). Many pieces of hardware have old paint layers, some needing consolidation. Some ironwork had been painted the same color as the body of the sign. In general no inpainting of the hardware was suggested.

Exceptions included:
1. At the discretion of curatorial staff, some corrosion effects (rust stains coming through the sign's paint) were lightly inpainted, if they affected the legibility of the sign (e.g., the David Loomis inn sign, where the rusted straps extended onto the painted face of the sign, interfering with the lettering, cat. 22).

Further Readings

GENERAL HISTORICAL AND ART HISTORICAL WORKS:

Ames, Kenneth L. *Beyond Necessity: Art in the Folk Tradition*. Winterthur, Del.: The Winterthur Museum, distributed by Norton, New York, 1977.

Ayres, James. *Two Hundred Years of English Naive Art, 1700–1900*. Alexandria, Va.: Art Services International, 1996.

Baker, L.H. *The Favorite Motor Ways of New England*. New York: MacNair, 1915.

Barber, John Warner. *Connecticut Historical Collections*. New Haven: By the author, 1836.

Bickford, Christopher P., and J. Bard McNulty, eds. *John Warner Barber's Views of Connecticut Towns, 1834–36*. Hartford: The Acorn Club and The Connecticut Historical Society, 1990.

Bogart, Michele H. *Artists, Advertising, and the Borders of Art*. Chicago and London: University of Chicago Press, 1995.

Brandimarte, Cynthia A. " 'To Make the Whole World Homelike': Gender, Space, and America's Tea Room Movement." *Winterthur Portfolio* 30 (Spring 1995): 1–19.

Brown, Dona. *Inventing New England*. Washington, D.C.: Smithsonian Institution Press, 1996.

Buel, Richard, Jr., and J. Bard McNulty, eds. *Connecticut Observed: Three Centuries of Visitors' Impressions, 1670–1940*. Hartford: The Acorn Club, 1999.

Chapin, Howard Miller. "Rhode Island Signboards." *Rhode Island Historical Society Collections* 19 (1926): 20–32, 53–64.

Chew, James Lawrence. "Famous Old Taverns of New London." *Records and Papers of the New London County Historical Society*. New London, Conn.: New London County Historical Society, 1895. Vol. 2, pt. 1, pp. 69–85.

Christensen, Erwin O. *The Index of American Design*. New York: Macmillan and The National Gallery of Art, Smithsonian Institution, Washington, D.C., 1950.

Christy, Miller. *The Trade Signs of Essex, a Popular Account of the Origin and Meanings of the Public House & Other Signs Now or Formerly Found in the County of Essex*. London: Griffith, Farran, Okeden, and Welsh, 1887.

Colles, Christopher. *A Survey of the Roads of the United States of America*. New York, 1789. Facsimile ed. Walter W. Ristow, ed. Cambridge, Mass.: Belknap Press of Harvard University Press, 1961.

Connecticut: A Guide to its Roads, Lore, and People. Workers of the Federal Writers' Project of the Works Progress Administration for the State of Connecticut. American Guide Series. Boston: Houghton Mifflin, 1938.

The Connecticut Historical Society. *Morgan B. Brainard's Tavern Signs*. Hartford: The Connecticut Historical Society, 1958.

Conroy, David W. *In Public Houses: Drink and the Revolution of Authority in Colonial Massachusetts*. Chapel Hill and London: University of North Carolina Press, for the Institute of Early American History and Culture, Williamsburg, Va., 1995.

Corn, Wanda M. *The Great American Thing. Modern Art and National Identity, 1915–1935*. Berkeley, Los Angeles, and London: University of California Press, 1999.

Crawford, Mary Caroline. *Little Pilgrimages among Old New England Inns*. Boston: Page, 1907.

Crofut, Florence S. M. *Guide to the History & Historic Sites of Connecticut*. New Haven: Yale University Press, 1937.

Daniels, Bruce Colin. *The Connecticut Town: Growth and Development, 1635–1790*. Middletown, Conn: Wesleyan University Press, 1979.

Delderfield, Eric P. *Introduction to Inn Signs*. New York: Arco, 1969.

———. *Stories of Inns and Their Signs*. North Pomfret, Vermont: David & Charles, 1974.

———. *British Inn Signs and Their Stories*. North Pomfret, Vermont: David & Charles, 1965.

Drake, Samuel Adams. *Old Boston Taverns and Tavern Clubs*. Boston: Butterfield, 1917.

Dupont, Jean-Claude, and Luc Dupont. *Les enseignes d'hier a aujourd'hui*. Quebec: Musée de la Civilisation, 1998.

Earle, Alice Morse. *Stage-Coach and Tavern Days*. New York: MacMillan, 1900.

Endell, Fritz. *Old Tavern Signs—An Excursion in the History of Hospitality*. Cambridge, Mass.: Houghton Mifflin, 1916.

Evans, Nancy Goyne. *American Windsor Chairs*. New York: Hudson Hills Press, in association with The Winterthur Museum, 1996.

Field, Edward. *The Colonial Tavern: A Glimpse of New England Life in the 17th and 18th Centuries*. Providence: Preston & Rounds, 1897.

Forbes, Allen, and Ralph M. Eastman. *Taverns and Stagecoaches of New England*. Boston: Printed for the State Street Trust Company, 1954. Vol. 2.

Fowble, E. McSherry. *Two Centuries of Prints in America, 1680–1880; A Selective Catalogue of the Winterthur Museum Collection*. Charlottesville: University Press of Virginia for The Winterthur Museum, 1987.

Garvin, Donna-Belle and James L. Garvin. *On the Road North of Boston: New Hampshire Taverns and Turnpikes, 1700–1900*. Concord, N.H.: New Hampshire Historical Society, 1988.

Gildrie, Richard P. "Taverns and Popular Culture; Essex County, Massachusetts, 1678–1686." *Essex Institute Historical Collections* 124 (July 1988): 158–85.

The Great River: Art & Society of the Connecticut Valley, 1635–1820. Hartford: Wadsworth Atheneum, 1985.

Hamilton, John D. *Material Culture of the American Freemasons*. Lexington, Mass.: Museum of Our National Heritage, distributed by University Press of New England, Hanover, N.H., and London, 1994.

Heal, Sir Ambrose. *The Signboards of Old London Shops: A Review of the Shop Signs Employed by the London Tradesmen during the XVIIth and XVIIIth Centuries*. London: Batsford, 1947.

Hornung, Clarence P. *Treasury of American Design: A Pictorial Survey of Popular Folk Arts Based upon Watercolor Renderings in the Index of American Design, at the National Gallery of Art.* 2 vols. in 1. New York: Abrams, [1976].

Horowitz, Elinor Lander. *The Bird, the Banner, and Uncle Sam: Images of America in Folk and Popular Art.* Philadelphia and New York: Lippincott, 1976.

Hughes, Arthur H., and Morse S. Allen, *Connecticut Place Names.* Hartford: The Connecticut Historical Society, 1976.

Isaacson, Philip M. *The American Eagle.* Boston: New York Graphic Society, 1975.

Inn Signs: Their History and Their Meaning. London: The Brewers' Society, 1969.

Jenkins, Stephen. *The Old Boston Post Road.* New York: G. P. Putnam's Sons, 1913.

Johnson, Clifton. *Highways and Byways of New England.* New York: Macmillan, 1915.

Kent, Louise Andrews. *Village Greens of New England.* New York: Barrows, 1948.

Kern, Arthur, and Sybil Kern. "Alcoholism and the Temperance Movement in Early American Folk Art." *The Magazine Antiques,* February 1998, pp. 292–99.

Kettell, Russell. *Pine Furniture of Early New England.* New York: Dover, 1929.

Knight, Sarah Kemble. *The Private Journal of A Journey from Boston to New York in the Year 1704.* 1st ed. Albany: F.H. Little,1865. Reprint ed. Boston: Small, Maynard, 1920.

Knittle, Rhea Mansfield. *Early Ohio Taverns: Tavern-sign, Barge, Banner, Chair and Settee Painters.* The Ohio Frontier Series, No. 1. Ashland, Ohio: By the author, 1937.

[Larwood, Jacob] see Schevichaven, Herman Diedrik Johan van.

Lathrop, Elise L. *Early American Inns and Taverns.* New York: McBride, 1926.

Lipman, Jean, and Alice Winchester. *The Flowering of American Folk Art: 1776–1876.* New York: Viking, in cooperation with the Whitney Museum of American Art, 1974.

Lipman, Jean, et al. *Five Star Folk Art: One Hundred American Masterpieces.* New York: Abrams, in association with The Museum of American Folk Art, New York, 1990.

Lipson, Dorothy Ann. *Freemasonry in Federalist Connecticut, 1789–1835.* Princeton: Princeton University Press, 1977.

Little, Nina Fletcher. *American Decorative Wall Painting, 1700–1850.* New York: Dutton, 1989.
———. *Little by Little: Six Decades of Collecting American Decorative Art.* Boston: Society for the Preservation of New England Antiquities, distributed by University Press of New England, Hanover, N.H., and London, 1998.
———. *Paintings by New England Provincial Artists, 1775–1800.* Boston: Museum of Fine Arts, 1976.

Lord, Priscilla, and Daniel J. Foley. *The Folk Arts and Crafts of New England.* Rev. ed. Radnor, Pa.: Chilton, 1975.

Malcolm, Andrew H. *U.S. 1, America's Original Main Street.* New York: St. Martin's, 1991.

Marlowe, George Francis. *Coaching Roads of Old New England.* New York: Macmillan, 1945.

Mason, H. F. Randolph. *Historic Houses of Connecticut Open to the Public.* Connecticut Booklet No. 5. Stonington, Conn.: The Pequot Press, 1966.

McClinton, Katherine Morrison. *Antique Collecting for Everyone.* New York: Bonanza Books, 1951.

Meadows, Cecil A. *Trade Signs and Their Origin.* London: Routledge & Paul, 1957.

Miller, David, ed. *American Iconology: New Approaches to Nineteenth-Century Art and Literature.* New Haven and London: Yale University Press, 1993.

Mirzoeff, Nicholas. *Introduction to Visual Culture.* Routledge, 1999.
———. *The Visual Culture Reader.* Routledge, 1998.

Moore, William D. "American Masonic Ritual Paintings," *Folk Art. Magazine of the Museum of American Folk Art*, Winter 1999/2000, pp. 58–65.

Museum of Our National Heritage. *Masonic Symbols in American Decorative Arts.* Lexington, Mass.: Museum of Our National Heritage, 1976.

Nolley, Scott W., and Carolyn J. Weekley, "The Nature of Edward Hicks's Painting," *The Magazine Antiques,* February 1999, pp. 282–89.

Norman, Philip. *London Signs and Inscriptions.* London,1893. Reprint ed. Detroit: Singing Tree Press, 1968.

Northend, Mary Harrod. *We Visit Old Inns.* Boston: Small, Maynard, 1925.

Nutting, Wallace. *Connecticut Beautiful.* Garden City: Garden City Publishing, 1923.

Oliver, Celia, and Robert Shaw. *An American Sampler: Folk Art from the Shelburne Museum.* Washington, D. C.: National Gallery of Art, 1987.

Parker, Wyman W. *Connecticut's Colonial and Continental Money.* Connecticut Biecentennial Series 18. Hartford: The American Revolution Bicentennial Commission of Connecticut, 1975.

Pease, John C., and John M. Niles. *A Gazetteer of the States of Connecticut and Rhode-Island.* Hartford: William S. Marsh, 1819.

Prentice, Thomas. "Historic Taverns in New England." *The Connecticut Magazine* 7 (1902–03): 459–72.

[Prince, Thomas.] *The Vade Mecum for America.* Boston, 1731.

Quimby, Ian M.G., and Scott T. Swank, eds. *Perspectives on American Folk Art.* New York: Norton for The Winterthur Museum, 1980.

Raitz, Karl, ed. *A Guide to the National Road.* Baltimore and London: Johns Hopkins University Press, 1996.
———. *The National Road.* Baltimore and London: Johns Hopkins University Press, 1996.

Reese, Robert E. "The Stage Tavern: Product and Victim of Progressive Transportation." *Journal of the Lancaster County Historical Society* 71 (1967): 198–208.

Rice, Kym S. *Early American Taverns.* Chicago: Regnery Gateway, in association with Fraunces Tavern Museum, New York, 1983.

Rhoads, William B. "Roadside Colonial: Early American Design for the Automobile Age." *Winterthur Portfolio* 21 (Summer/Autumn 1986): 133–52.

Schaffer, Marguerite S. "Negotiating National Identity," in Hall K. Roghman, ed. *Reopening the American West.* Tempe: University of Arizona Press, 1998.

Schevichaven, Herman Diedrik Johan van [Jacob Larwood] and Hotten, John Camden. *The History of Signboards, From the Earliest Times to the Present Day.* London: John Camden Hotten [1866].

Schlereth, Thomas J. *Reading the Road: U.S. 40 and the American Landscape.* Knoxville: University of Tennessee Press, 1997.

Sears, John. *Sacred Spaces.* New York: Oxford University Press, 1989.

Serwer, Jacquelyn. "Heroic Relics: The Art of Robert Cottingham." *American Art* 12 (Summer 1998): pp. 7–25.

Shackleton, Robert and Elizabeth. *The Quest of the Colonial.* New York: Century, 1907.

Smith, Helene. *Tavern Signs of America: Catalog.* Greensburg, Pa.: McDonald/Swärd, 1988.

———. *Tavern Signs of America: History.* Greensburg, Pa.: McDonald/Swärd, 1989.

Some Olde London Shope-signes and Streete Tablets. (many of which no longer exist) of the XVII–XVIII and XIXth Centuries. London: Privately printed for F. Cornman, 1907.

Spitulnik, Karen. "The Inn Crowd: The American Inn, 1730–1830." *Pennsylvania Folklife* 37 (1972–73): 25–41.

Stauffer, David McNeely. *American Engravers upon Copper and Steel.* New York: The Grolier Club, 1907.

Stebbins, William. *The Journal of William Stebbins: Stratford to Washington in 1810.* Introduction by Leonard W. Labaree. Hartford: The Acorn Club, 1968.

Storer, R. W. E. G., comp. *The Records of Freemasonry in the State of Connecticut, compiled from the Journals of the Proceedings of the Grand Lodge.* New Haven: Storer, 1861.

Swan, Mabel M. "Early Sign Painters." *The Magazine Antiques,* May 1928, pp. 402–5.

Taverns of Yesteryear. Philadelphia: C. Schmidt & Sons, 1960.

Terry, Marian Dickinson, ed. *Old Inns of Connecticut.* Hartford: Prospect Press, 1937.

Thompson, Peter. *Rum Punch & Revolution: Taverngoing & Public Life in Eighteenth-Century Philadelphia.* Philadelphia: University of Pennsylvania Press, 1999.

Trowbridge, Mrs. Elford Parry, comp. "Connecticut Houses: A List of Manuscript Histories of Early Connecticut Homes Presented to the Connecticut State Library by the Connecticut Society Colonial Dames of America." *Bulletins of the Connecticut State Library, Hartford* 7 (1916).

Venturi and Raush. *Signs of Life: Symbols in the American City.* Washington, D.C.: Renwick Gallery, Smithsonian Institution, and Aperture, 1976.

Venturi, Robert, Denise Scott Brown, and Seven Izenour. *Learning from Las Vegas.* Rev. ed. Cambridge: MIT Press, 1977.

Wagner, Charles Louis Henry. *The Story of Signs: and Outline History of the Sign Arts from the Earliest Recorded Times to the Present "Atomic Age."* Boston: MacGibbon, 1954.

Weekley, Carolyn J., with the assistance of Laura Pass Barry. *The Kingdoms of Edward Hicks.* Williamsburg, Va.: Abby Aldrich Rockefeller Folk Art Center, in association with Abrams, New York, 1999.

Welsh, Peter C. *The Art of Enterprise: A Pennsylvania Tradition.* Harrisburg: Pennsylvania Historical and Museum Commission, 1983.

Whiteside, Clara Walker. *Touring New England.* Philadelphia: Penn Publishing, 1926.

Witzel, Michael Karl. *The American Gas Station: History and Folklore of the Gas Station in American Car Culture.* New York: Barnes & Noble, 1999.

Wolf, Bryan Jay. "All the World's a Code: Art and Ideology in Nineteenth-Century American Painting." *Art Journal* 44 (Winter 1984): 328–37.

———. *Romantic Re-Vision: Culture and Consciousness in Nineteenth-Century American Painting and Literature.* Chicago and London: University of Chicago Press, 1982.

Wood, Frederic J. *The Turnpikes of New England, and Evolution of the Same through England, Virginia, and Maryland.* Boston, 1919. Abridged ed. Pepperell, Mass.: Branch Line Press. 1997.

Yeoman, R.S. *A Guide Book of United States Coins.* Edited by Kenneth Bressett. Golden Books, 1999.

Yoder, Paton. *Taverns and Travelers.* Bloomington: Indiana University Press, 1968.

PAINTERS' MANUALS

An Account of a New Process in Painting. London, 1820.

Baird, Henry Carey. *The Painter, Gilder and Varnisher's Companion.* Philadelphia, 1869.

Bentley, Thomas. *Prospectus of the Various Paints for the Preservation of all Work Exposed to the Weather and the Interior of Houses, Manufactured Exclusively by Thos. Bentley.* London, 1817.

Berkeley, Dr. H. R., and W. M. Walker. *Practical Receipts for the Manufacturer, the Mechanic & for Home Use.* London, 1902.

Cadet-de-Vaux, Antoine Alexis. "Memoir on a Method of Painting with Milk." *The Repertory of Arts & Manufactures* 15 (1801): 411–21.

Callingham, James. *Sign Writing and Glass Embossing—A Complete Practical Illustrated Manual of the Art.* Philadelphia, 1871.

Campbell, Orson. *Treatise on Carriage, Sign and Ornamental Painting.* DeRuyter, N.Y., 1841.

Dossie, Robert. *The Handmaid to the Arts.* London, 1764.

Elliott, T. *The Modern Painter.* London, 1842.

Field, George. *A Treatise on Colours and Pigments.* London, 1841.

Field, George. *Rudiments of the Painter's Art or A Grammar of Colouring.* London, 1850.

Haney, Jesse & Co., *Haney's Manual of Sign, Carriage and Decorative Painting.* New York, 1870.

Higgens, W. Mallingan. *The House Painter's or Decorator's Companion.* London, 1847.

Lyford and Boyce, *The Art of Lettering and Sign Painter's Manual.* 2nd ed. Boston, 1871.

Masury, John W. *How Shall We Paint Our House: Popular Treatises in the Art of House Painting.* New York, 1868.

Moss, Roger W., ed. *Paint in America: The Colors of Historic Buildings.* Washington, D.C.: National Trust for Historic Preservation, 1994.

"Paint and Recipes for Wooden Work—ca. 1801." *Connecticut Historical Society Bulletin* 9 (1943): 9–16.

Painter's Gilder's and Varnisher's Manual. London and New York, 1838.

Reynolds, Hezekiah. *Directions for Ship or House Painting.* New Haven, 1812. Facsimile ed., with introduction by Richard M. Candee. Worcester, Mass.: American Antiquarian Society, 1978.

SELECTED MANUSCRIPT AND ARCHIVAL SOURCES

The Connecticut Historical Society

Adams, William. Account book. Simsbury, Conn., 1802–16. Innkeeper.

Barker, Joshua. Account book. Norwich, Conn., 1761–80. Innkeeper.

Brainard, Morgan Bulkeley. Correspondence and miscellaneous papers.

———. Correspondence, notes, and photographs of Morgan B. Brainard tavern signs.

Caulkins, Daniel Huxham. Diary. East Lyme, Conn., 1799–1800.

Chauncey, Elnathan. Account book. Durham, Conn., 1767–76. Innkeeper.

Cheney, Daniel. Account book. Chatham (Portland), Conn., 1838–44.

Geere, James. "Brief remarks on a journey from Groton [Conn.] to Susquehannah, Pennsylvania," 1804.

Grant, Ellsworth S. "The Tavern Signs of Morgan B. Brainard," 1997.

Hammer, Mrs. Alfred. Notes about taverns, prepared for the Connecticut Society, Colonial Dames of America.

Harlow, Thompson R. Papers, 1939–94.

Hayden, Kate L. "Moses Butler's Tavern: An Illustration of Hartford in the Eighteenth Century," ca. 1894.

———. "The Red Tavern, Windsor Locks, Conn., as It Looks in 1894," ca. 1894.

———. "The History of the Yellow Tavern at Windsor Locks, Conn.," 1896.

Knight, Stephanus. Account book, Enfield, Conn., 1795–1809. Painter.

Pendleton, Cyrus E. "Colchester Taverns of Other Days," 1938. On deposit from the Colchester Historical Society.

Reed, Abner. Account book, East Windsor, Conn., 1800–01. Painter.

Root, Timothy, Jr. Account book. Farmington, Conn., 1768–89. Photocopy. Innkeeper.

Root, Timothy, Sr. Account book. Farmington, Conn., 1740–49. Photocopy. Innkeeper.

Smith, Elizabeth Goodwin. "A Short Account of the Flagg Tavern, Hartford," 1920.

Vincent, Margaret C. "Connecticut Inns and Hotels and Their Signboards, 1750–1850," 1999.

———. "Connecticut Sign Painters, 1780–1850," 1999.

Warren, William Lansom. Tax lists of 1796–1798.

Wheeler, Hosea. Account book. Norwich, Conn., 1758–1811. Innkeeper.

The Connecticut State Library

Accounts due the Inn Keeper by the Lodge, Barkhamsted. 1823–24.

Loomis, Israel. Account book. Lebanon, Conn., 1783–1849. Innkeeper.

Owen, John. Account book (day book). Simsbury, Conn., 1769 and 1775. Innkeeper.

Phelps, Arah. Account book. North Colebrook, Conn., 1790–1832. Innkeeper.

Witter, Jacob. Account book. Norwich, Conn., 1758–1811. Innkeeper.

Wooster, Ephraim. Account book. Derby, Conn., 1804. Innkeeper.

Index

Signs in the Collection of The Connecticut Historical Society are indicated in **Boldface**.

Page numbers in *Italics* refer to illustrations or captions.

Regular Roman page numbers indicate text references.

Place names are in Connecticut, unless otherwise stated.

Mallory's (Amasa) Inn sign, 257
Manchester hotels, 227–28
Maniere, John, 246
Mansion House, *47*
maps, 56
Marlborough, 255
Marsh, Deborah, 197
Marsh, Ebenezer, Jr., 197
Marsh, Ebenezer, Sr., 197
Marsh, Elihu, Jr., 197
Marsh, Reginald, 108
Marsh's Inn sign, 24, 30, 61, *124*, 197–98
Marvin, Ozias, 43
Marvin's Inn, *42, 43*
Mason, Andrew N., 230, 231
Mason, Janet Burdick, 231
Masonic imagery, 20–21, 31
    Cady's Hotel sign, 212
    Cheny's Inn sign, 257
    Dyer's Inn sign, 217
    eighteenth century, 24, 40, 42
    Holcomb's Inn sign, 44, 258
    as individualized messages, 91
    Lawrence's (Ariel) Inn sign, 196, 197
    Lewis's (Abel) Inn sign, 259
    nineteenth century, 43–44
    Rice and, 48
    Rose's Inn sign, 206
    Tarbox's Inn and Village Hotel sign, 203,
        212n3
Masons, 185, 186, 186n3, 189, 219
    Order of Freemasonry, 196, 203
Mason's Inn sign, *110, 163,* 230–31, 262
    imagery on, 31, 211n8
Massachusetts currency, 56, *58,* 210n3
Matheson, Joseph, 189
Mathewson, Rufus S., 189, 190n15
Matulis (John) watercolors, 191, 193, 200, 204,
        216, 233, 235
Maxwell, J. Alice, 228
May, Sibyl Huntington, 190n11
McKinney, Burt, 227
McNeil, E., 250, 254, 255
Mechanics Bank of New Haven, 209–10
Mechanic's Hotel sign, 71, *156,* 225–26
meeting house imagery, 220–21
Memorial Hall Museum, Pocumtuck Valley
    Memorial Association, 198n1
Meriden inns, 36, 51, *52*
Merriam, Nelson, 51
Middlebrooks, Charles, 246
Middlebrooks, Samuel B., 246, 254, 255
Middlebrooks, Spencer Curtis, 246
Middlesex Gazette, 28, 41, *42,* 249
Middletown
    inns, 41, 42, 236–37
    sign painters, 255
Middletown Gazette, 216n1
Milford inns, 36
military heroes imagery, 40, 59, *59,* 188–90, 211.
    See also Cumberland, Duke of; Washington,
    George; Wolfe, James

Miller, David, 11
Miller & Fitch, 250, 254, 255
Mills, Samuel, 220
Mineral Springs Hotel sign, 258
miniature painting, 25
Modern Alphabets (Delamotte), 75, *76*
modernist aesthetics, 108–9
moldings, sign, 26, 28
Montcalm, Marquis de, 188
Montville inns, 217–18
moon image, 257
Moore, Elisha, 199
Moore, Frederick J.
    Hartford photograph circa 1885–87, *88*
Moore, Nelson A.
    Hartford photograph, circa 1850, *88*
    West Springfield, Mass. painting, 106, *107*
Morgan, Shapley, 199, 200
Morgan B. Brainard's Tavern Signs, 4
Morningstar Lodge No. 28, Enfield, 203
Morris, John Emery, 237
Mortlake House (or Manor), 189
Mount, William Sydney, 9
mounting signs, 102
Mowry's Inn sign, 242n1
Munson's (Levi) hotel, 52
Mygatt, Joseph, 36

Narragansett pacers (horse), 184
Nathan Liverant & Son, Colchester, 99
National Museum of American History, 12n2
nationalization, 16–17
Natural History of Foreign Quadrupeds (Bewick),
    63
Neagle, John, 9, 20–21
needlework pictures, tavern sign, *24*
New Hartford inns, 46
New Haven
    inns/hotels, 36, 38, 40, 62
    Mechanics Bank, 209–10
    sign imagery references in, 54n29
    sign painters, 255
    stage schedule from, 46
New Haven Colony inns, 36
New London
    inns, 38, 39, 42, 225–26
    sign imagery references in, 54n29
    sign painters, 255
    transitional sign types, 50
New-London Coffee-house, 225, 226
New London Gazette, 199n2
New Milford inns, 197–98
A New Universal Atlas (Tanner), *46*
New York State Historical Association, 12n2
New-York State Historical Society, 257
New York State inns, 200–201
Newburyport, Mass. inns, 59, 188
newspaper advertising, inn and tavern, 88, 89
Nichols, Frances (Boston antique store), 98
Nichols, J. C., 250, 254, 255
Norfolk Historical Society, 257
Norfolk inns, 42, 196–97, 257

North, Enos, 219
North Canton inns, 258
North Colebrook inns, 219–20
North Haven inns, *39, 40*
Norwalk, *42,* 259
    inns, 36
    sign painters, 255
Norwich
    hotels, 49
    sign painters, 255
numbering styles, 28–29
Nutting, Wallace, 96, 235

object history, 22–35
    fabrication, 25–28
    form and decoration considerations, 22
    place, 29–30
    shapes and images, 30–31
    sign decorating, 28–29
    time of manufacture, 24–25
    weathering, 32–33
Odessa, Del., sign painters, 26
oils, paint, 72
"Old Ship" tavern sign. *See* Hayden's Inn sign
The Old Stage Coach (Johnson), 101n18
Old Sturbridge Village, 12n2, 257
Oliver Cromwell (warship), 186
Olmsted, Joseph, 249
Order of Freemasonry, 196, 203. *See also* Masonic
    imagery
ordinary, 30, 36, 39
Ormsby, Norman, 247, 254, 255
ornamental ironwork, 25
Osgood, Samuel Stillman, 250, 254, 255
outdoor advertising, 88, *92, 93*
    early twentieth century, 91–92
    horizontal, 89, *89*
    "Sign-ic or Scenic?" Contests, 1929, *91*
oval signboards, 26, 28, 198, 201, 206, 209–11,
        212, 221, 226, 258
overgilding, 72
Oxford inns, 237
oysters image, 220–21

Page, Harlan, 8, 205–6, 250–51, 254, 255
paint analysis/conservation, 68, 83n5, 261–62
    of grounds, 71–72
    of oils, 72
    preferential weathering and, 80, 82–83
    previous layers removal, 78, 238
paint brushes, 72
The Painter's, Gilder's and Varnisher's Manual, 68,
    72
Palmer, W., 242
Palmer's Inn sign, *177,* 242
pantagraph, *73, 74*
Parmelee, Mr. and Mrs. Hezekiah, Jr., 253
Partyka (Martin) watercolors, 220
Parys (Alfred) watercolors, *58,* 191, 206, 210
Passell's Inn. *See* Pearsall's (Samuel) Inn
Pat Lyon at the Forge (Neagle), *20,* 20–21
Patapaug (Pautapaug). *See* Centerbrook

Tarbox, Thomas, 202, 203
Tarbox's Inn and Village Hotel sign, *103,* 105,
    131, 202–3
    Masonic imagery on, 212n3
    multiple images on, 33
    Rice as painter for, 44, *45,* 251
    smalting on, 76
Tattoo, Shave, Haircut (Marsh), 108
taverns, demise of, 48
Taylor, Levi, 257
Taylor's Tavern, *42,* 43
Taylor's Tavern sign, 257
The Teakettle and Tabby Cat (tearoom), 99
tearooms, 98, 99
Temperance Hotel sign, 11, *15, 166,* 232–33
    Collins's Hotel sign and, 224
    conservation of, 262
    free-hand drawing on, 72, *73*
    painting of, 28
    tin leaf on, 77
Temperance Movement, 20, 48–49, 205, 233
Terry (L.) sign, 25
The Death of Wolfe (West), 188
Thomas, J., 220
Thompson, Orrin, 50
Thompson, William, 251
Thompson Hotel. *See* Stiles's Inn and Thompson
    Hotel
Thompson Hotel sign. *See* Stiles's Inn and
    Thompson Hotel sign
Thompson inns, 48, 55n47, 222–23
Thompson Lee's Genuine Bilious Pills or Family
    Physic, 60
Thompsonville, 50, 51
Thompsonville Hotel, 51, *51*
Three Crowns Tavern sign, 241n2
Tilden, Austin, 227
tin leaf, 77
tongue-and-groove joints, 26
Torrington Historical Society, 259
Total Abstinence Society, 233, 233n2
Townshend Acts, 190
transfer techniques, 72–74
The Traveller's Rest. *See* Jacobs's Inn sign
Treasure Island (Stevenson), 94, *96*
Treat, David, 256
*Treatise on Carriage, Sign and Ornamental Paint-
    ing* (Campbell), 68, 74
Treat's Inn sign, 256
tree images, 199, 210, 220–21, 230–31. *See also*
    Charter Oak image
Trumbull, John, 190n11
turning profiles, 28
Two Women (Pinney), 216n3
Tyler, Daniel, 189
Tyler, Mehitable Putnam, 189

Underground Railroad, 241
Union Hotel, Farmington, 210
Union Hotel sign. *See* Mallett's Hotel sign
urban signs, 30

Vade Mecum, 38
Van Cott, Isaac H., 252–53, 254, 255
Van Cott, John D., 252
Van Cott, Philemon, 252–53, 254, 255
Van der Hayden, Annatje Perrie, 239
Van der Hayden, John, 239
Van der Hayden, John, Jr., 239
Van der Hayden's Inn sign, 74, *173,* 239
varnish, 76, 216, 261–62
Venturi, Robert, 6, 86
Verdict of the People (Bingham), 105
Vernon Hotel sign, 77, *158,* 214n1, 227–28
    carving, 79n30, 80, 83
    flocking, 217n2, 230n1
Viets, Luke, 257
Viets's Inn sign, 55n46, 211n2, 257
Village Hotel sign (Enfield), 33, 76. *See also*
    Tarbox's Inn and Village Hotel sign
Village Hotel sign (Windsorville). *See* Robert-
    son's Tavern and Village Hotel sign
Village Inn, Enfield Conn. *See* Tarbox's Inn and
    Village Hotel sign
Vincent, Margaret C., 2, 4–5
    on Connecticut sign painters, 7, 8, 9, 104
    on militia captains, 211
    on traveling public, 86
vine leaves, 28, 209, 210n1. *See also*
    grapes/grapevines imagery
The Voice of the City of New York Interpreted
    (Stella), 108

Wadsworth, Daniel, 179–80
Wadsworth, Daniel Sydney, 234
Wadsworth, Elisha, 233, 234
Wadsworth, Eliza A. Sisson, 234
Wadsworth, Jeremiah, 244
Wadsworth, Lucy (daughter), 234
Wadsworth, Lucy Woodford, 234
Wadsworth, Seth, 234
Wadsworth, Sidney, 233, 234
Wadsworth Atheneum, 192, 259
Wadsworth's Inn sign, 52, *167,* 233–34
    copper-colored leaf, 77, *77*
    eagle imagery, 60, *63*
    flocking, 230n1
    lion imagery, *57, 63, 64*
    photograph, *35*
    Rice signature, 230
Wales, Nathaniel, 9, 253, 254, 255
Wallingford inns, 194–95, 201
Walsh (Hartford sign painter), 252, 254, 255
Walter's (Joel) inn, 42
Wapping hotels, 258
War News from Mexico (Woodville), 18–19, *19,*
    104
Warhol, Andy, 108
Warner's Hotel sign, *67, 162,* 230
Warren Lodge No. 50, Andover, 206
Washington, George, 59, 188
    Bissell's (David) and Phelps's Inn sign, 192
    Grosvenor Inn sign, *95,* 237–39
    as sign image, 98, 105

Van der Hayden's Inn sign, 239
"Washington pieces," 210n3
Waterford inns, 208–9
Waterloo Tavern sign, 240n2
Watervliet, N.Y., inns, 239
Way, Daniel and Ruth, 199n1
weathering, 22, 32–33
    laboratory analysis and, 68
    paint oils and, 72
    preferential, 79n30, 80, 82–83, 187
    repainting and, 77–78
    sign style and design and, 71
Webber, Sandra L., 5, 6, 11, *68*
    Hayden's "Old Ship" rendering, *71,* 187
Wedgwood, J., 220
Wedgwood's Inn sign, *150,* 210–11n6, 220–21,
    262
Weekley, Carolyn, 10
Welch's (Benjamin) Inn, 42
Wentworth, Edmund, 253
Wentworth, Josiah Winslow, 254, 255
Wentworth, Mary Hanford, 253
Wentworth, Thomas Hanford, 253
West, Benjamin, 9, 63, 188
West, Thomas, 252, 253, 254, 255
West Greenwich, R.I., inns, 199–200
West Rock, New Haven (Church), 18, *18*
West Springfield, Mass. (Moore), 106, *107*
Westchester inns, 7, 205
Western Star Lodge No. 37, Norfolk, 219
Westmoreland Museum of Art, Greensburg, Pa.,
    259
Weston, in Colle's *Survey, 42*
Wethersfield Historical Society, 259
Wethersfield inns, 36
Wethersfield Village Hotel sign, 259
Wheeler's (Stiles D.) Litchfield House, *47*
Whitney Studio Club, 108
Whittlesey, John, 36
Wightman, Asa, 208–9
Wightman, Mercy Smith, 208, 209
Wightman, Timothy, 208
Wightman's Inn sign, *138,* 198, 201n1, 208–9
Wilbur, B. S., 240
Wilcoxson, Maria Louisa McEwen, 237
Wilkins tavern sign, 198n1
Wilkinson, Almedus, 207, 208
Wilkinson, Brownell, 208
Wilkinson, Joseph, 208
Willard, Mrs. S. P., 233
Willard's (Samuel) Inn, 48
William Augustus, Duke of Cumberland, 40, 185
*William Rush Carving His Allegorical Figure of
    the Schuykill River* (Eakins), 11
Williams, Benjamin, Jr., 40, 184, 218, 219
Williams, Benjamin, Sr., 219
Williams, Humphrey, 218, 219
Williams, J., 215
Williams, Libbie Dickinson, 219
Williams, Patience Pratt, 219
Williams, Roxanna Bushnell, 219
Williams, Stephen, 244